## NOTES FOR PROFESSIONAL LIBRARIANS AND LIBRARY USERS

This is an original book title published by International Business Press®, an imprint of The Haworth Press, Inc. Unless otherwise noted in specific chapters with attribution, materials in this book have not been previously published elsewhere in any format or language.

## CONSERVATION AND PRESERVATION NOTES

All books published by The Haworth Press, Inc., and its imprints are printed on certified pH neutral, acid-free book grade paper. This paper meets the minimum requirements of American National Standard for Information Sciences-Permanence of Paper for Printed Material, ANSI Z39.48-1984.

## DIGITAL OBJECT IDENTIFIER (DOI) LINKING

The Haworth Press is participating in reference linking for elements of our original books. (For more information on reference linking initiatives, please consult the CrossRef Web site at www.crossref.org.) When citing an element of this book such as a chapter, include the element's Digital Object Identifier (DOI) as the last item of the reference. A Digital Object Identifier is a persistent, authoritative, and unique identifier that a publisher assigns to each element of a book. Because of its persistence, DOIs will enable The Haworth Press and other publishers to link to the element referenced, and the link will not break over time. This will be a great resource in scholarly research.

# Handbook of Family Business and Family Business Consultation
## *A Global Perspective*

# International Business Press®

## Books of Related Interest

*The Integration of Employee Assistance, Work/Life, and Wellness Services*
by Mark Attridge and Patricia A. Herlihy

*Your Family, Inc.: Practical Tips for Building a Healthy Family Business*
by Ellen Frankenberg

*Handbook of Family Business and Family Business Consultation:*
*A Global Perspective* by Florence W. Kaslow

*Reconciling Relationships and Preserving the Family Business: Tools*
*for Success* by Ruth McClendon and Leslie B. Kadis

## Family Therapy Books of Related Interest

*Clinical Epiphanies in Marital and Family Therapy: A Practitioner's*
*Casebook of Therapeutic Insights, Perceptions, and Breakthroughs*
by David A. Baptiste

*The Therapist's Notebook for Families: Solution-Oriented Exercises*
*for Working with Parents, Children, and Adolescents* by Bob Bertolino
and Gary Schultheis

*Family Therapy and Mental Health: Innovations in Theory and Practice*
by Malcolm M. MacFarlane

*Family Behavioral Issues in Health and Illness* by J. LeBron McBride

*Creating Family Solutions for Drug and Alcohol Abuse* by Eric E.
McCollum and Terry S. Trepper

*Emotional Cutoff: Bowen Family Systems Theory Perspectives* edited
by Peter Titelman

# Handbook of Family Business and Family Business Consultation
## *A Global Perspective*

Florence W. Kaslow, PhD, ABPP
Editor

International Business Press®
An Imprint of The Haworth Press, Inc.
New York • London • Oxford

For more information on this book or to order, visit
http://www.haworthpress.com/store/product.asp?sku=5491

or call 1-800-HAWORTH (800-429-6784) in the United States and Canada
or (607) 722-5857 outside the United States and Canada

or contact orders@HaworthPress.com

Published by

International Business Press®, an imprint of The Haworth Press, Inc., 10 Alice Street, Binghamton, NY 13904-1580.

PUBLISHER'S NOTE
The development, preparation, and publication of this work has been undertaken with great care. However, the Publisher, employees, editors, and agents of The Haworth Press are not responsible for any errors contained herein or for consequences that may ensue from use of materials or information contained in this work. The Haworth Press is committed to the dissemination of ideas and information according to the highest standards of intellectual freedom and the free exchange of ideas. Statements made and opinions expressed in this publication do not necessarily reflect the views of the Publisher, Directors, management, or staff of The Haworth Press, Inc., or an endorsement by them.

Most identities and circumstances of individuals discussed in this book have been changed to protect confidentiality. In a few cases, individuals have given permission to use their name and circumstances.

Cover design by Lora Wiggins.

**Library of Congress Cataloging-in-Publication Data**

Handbook of family business and family business consultation : a global perspective / Florence W. Kaslow, editor.
    p. cm.
    Includes bibliographical references and index.
    ISBN-13: 978-0-7890-2776-4 (alk. paper)
    ISBN-10: 0-7890-2776-3 (alk. paper)
    ISBN-13: 978-0-7890-2777-1 (soft : alk. paper)
    ISBN-10: 0-7890-2777-1 (soft : alk. paper)
    1. Family-owned business enterprises—Handbooks, manuals, etc. I. Kaslow, Florence Whiteman.

HD62.25.H35 2006
658'.045—dc22

                         2006006666

# CONTENTS

## PART III: FAMILY BUSINESSES AND CONSULTATION TO THEM IN VARIOUS COUNTRIES

# ABOUT THE EDITOR

**Florence W. Kaslow, PhD, ABPP,** is President of Kaslow Associates, a family business and team development consultation firm located in Palm Beach Gardens, Florida. She is board certified in family, clinical, and forensic psychology by the American Board of Professional Psychology; is the past and founding president of the International Family Therapy Association; and is a past president of the International Academy of Family Psychology.

Dr. Kaslow has guest lectured and conducted workshops throughout the United States and in several dozen other countries on family business and other family related topics, and consulted with family firms in numerous countries. She is a Fellow of the American Psychological Association and of the Family Firm Institute (FFI), and mentor for the latter, and holds a certificate in Family Business Advising from FFI. She serves on the Editorial Board of the *Family Business Review* and numerous other journals. Dr. Kaslow is a prolific book author and editor (28 books), as well as a contributor to the literature through journal articles (over 170) and numerous book chapters. She has received many national and international awards in recognition of her various outstanding contributions.

*Handbook of Family Business and Family Business Consultation*
Published by The Haworth Press, Inc., 2006. All rights reserved.
doi:10.1300/5491_a

# CONTRIBUTORS

**Haluk Alacaklioglu, MBA,** graduated from Harvard Business School with honors. He has been consulting with multinational corporations and family businesses throughout Europe, the Middle East, and Asia since 1989 on corporate and family business governance, building high-performance boards, and family-business management. He led the commission to devise a Corporate Governance Code of Best Practices in Turkey (2002) and contributed to the revised Code for OECD (2004).

**Zaher Al Munajjed, MBA,** is a graduate of Harvard Business School with a master's degree in international law. He has been working for and advising major family business groups in Saudi Arabia for more than twenty-five years. He has been an international associate of the Aspen Family partners since 2002.

**Joseph H. Astrachan, PhD,** is Wachovia Eminent Scholar Chair of Family Business, a professor of management and entrepreneurship, and the director of the Cox Family Enterprise Center at the Coles College of Business, Kennesaw State University, in Kennesaw, Georgia. He is also Distinguished Research Chair of Family Business at Loyola University's Chicago Business School and the editor of *Family Business Review,* a scholarly publication of the Family Firm Institute.

**Naomi Birdthistle, PhD,** is a lecturer in entrepreneurship at the University of Limerick, Ireland. She received her PhD from UL in 2004, where she examined small family businesses as learning organizations. She is a prominent researcher on family business issues; her areas of expertise are succession and taxation planning, family business management, learning and training for family businesses, and the role of women within the family business.

**David Bork** has been one of the world's leaders in the field of counseling family businesses since 1970. He is the founder of the Aspen Family Business Group. A proponent of the family systems approach to family business, he pioneered the integration of family systems theory with sound

*Handbook of Family Business and Family Business Consultation*
Published by The Haworth Press, Inc., 2006. All rights reserved.
doi:10.1300/5491_b

business practice. Bork is the author of *Family Business, Risky Business: How to Make It Work,* and co-author of *Working with Family Business: A Guide for Professionals.* In 1998 the Family Firm Institute awarded Bork the coveted Richard Beckhard Award.

**Leslie Dashew, MSW,** is the president of Human Side of Enterprise, LLC, and a partner in the Aspen Family Business Group. She has been an advisor to families in business and families of wealth for more than thirty years and has been honored for her contributions to the field by being named a Fellow of the Family Firm Institute. She has authored three books and many articles and chapters related to this field.

**François M. de Visscher, MBA,** is founder and president of de Visscher & Co., an international financial consulting and investment banking firm for family-owned businesses based in Greenwich, Connecticut. He is a member of the board of his own family business, N.V. Bekaert, a multibillion dollar steel wire manufacturer headquartered in Belgium. A CPA, he was previously a partner at the investment bank of Smith Barney in New York.

**W. Gibb Dyer Jr., PhD, MBA,** is the O. Leslie Stone Professor of Entrepreneurship and the academic director of the Center for Economic Self-Reliance in the Marriott School of Management at Brigham Young University. He received his MBA from Brigham Young University, and his PhD in management philosophy from the Massachusetts Institute of Technology. Before coming to BYU, he was on the faculty at the University of New Hampshire, and he has served as a visiting professor at IESE (Instituto de Estudios Superiores de la Empresa) in Barcelona, Spain. He publishes widely on the topics of family business, entrepreneurship, organizational culture, and managing change in organizations.

**Josiane Fahed-Sreih, PhD** from the Sorbonne University, is currently the director of the Institute of Family and Entrepreneurial Business at the Lebanese American University and an assistant professor there, teaching topics in management such as management theory, project planning and management, and corporate governance. She is the Middle East coordinator for the Family Firm Institute. She has participated in and organized major conferences, workshops, and seminars, both locally and internationally. She has presented and consulted on management issues in many Arab countries, including Saudi Arabia, Dubai, Jordan, Kuwait, and Bahrain, as well as in France. She recently published a book titled *Facts and Figures Concerning Family Business in Lebanon.* The Institute of Family and Entrepreneurial Business is a research center, holding a data bank on family businesses in Lebanon and the region.

**Bill Gordon, MBA,** joined Family Business Solutions in 2004 after the merger of his own consultancy, Family Council Works and FBS. His primary expertise lies in helping family business owners professionalize their relationships with the business, whether actively working in the business or pursuing alternative careers elsewhere. As a shareholder in a fifth-generation family business, he has direct experience with the complex mix of family, business and ownership issues. Bill led the process of creating and chairing a family council as a key part of the overall governance structure in his own family business. He is a regular speaker at family business conferences in Europe, and between 2002 and 2004 served on the board of directors of the Family Business Network (FBN).

**Salo Grabinsky, MBA,** has been a Mexican writer and speaker since 1986. Grabinsky is a consultant to family businesses throughout Latin America and the Hispanic communities in the United States. He has written seventeen books and a weekly syndicated newspaper column. He holds a certificate as a Fellow of the Family Firm Institute (FFI) as well as other international awards for his passionate work helping entrepreneurs and family enterprises grow and survive.

**Jane Hilburt-Davis, MSW,** is the founder and president of Key Resources, an international consulting firm. She is a nationally recognized expert in the field of consulting to family businesses and co-author of the book *Consulting to Family Businesses.* Currently she is president elect of the board of directors of the Family Firm Institute.

**Dennis T. Jaffe** has an MA in management and a PhD in sociology from Yale University. He is a professor of organizational systems at Saybrook Graduate School in California, a founding member of Aspen Family Business Group, and the executive director of the Family Business Center, San Francisco State University. He is author of *Working with the Ones You Love,* and a co-author of *Working with Family Businesses.*

**Juliette Johnson, ACA,** is senior manager of the BDO Centre for Family Business. She has extensive experience advising some of the most successful family businesses in the United Kingdom and internationally. She is one of the U.K.'s leading advisers in dealing with the younger generations in family businesses, and she has written numerous articles on this subject. She is a visiting lecturer at the European Business School, London.

**Mark Jones, FCA,** is the regional chair of the BDO Centre for Family Business in the Midlands, United Kingdom. He has extensive experience in dealing with the balancing of board and family aspirations in a family company. He has qualified and trained in the area of organizational management, strategy, and corporate governance, which provides parity in dealing with the role of the board and of family members in a business.

**Dirk Jungé, CFA,** is chairman of the Pitcairn Financial Group. He holds a BS in economics and finance from Lehigh University in Pennsylvania and graduated with honors. A fourth-generation member of the Pitcairn family, he has been involved in the family office for more than twenty years, serving in numerous capacities, including handling investments, marketing, and client services. Dirk is involved on numerous corporate and philanthropic boards. He is also a consultant and frequent speaker at conferences and seminars on the financial services industry, investment management, and family governance issues.

**Leslie B. Kadis, MD,** is a consultant, author, and psychiatrist, honored as a Fellow by the American Psychiatric Association for his professional and community work. He is a cofounder of the Carmel Institute for Family Business, an organization offering professional expertise to family firms around the world, and a past member of the editorial board of the *Family Business Review.* Les co-authored, along with his wife Ruth, *Reconciling Relationships and Preserving the Family Business: Tools for Success* (The Haworth Press, 2004).

**Ji-Hee Kim, PhD,** is an assistant professor of entrepreneurship in the Business Administration Department at Minot State University, Minot, North Dakota. Dr. Kim earned a doctorate in family business management with an entrepreneurial and international perspective from Ewha Womans University, Seoul, Korea. She is the author of a successful textbook, *Family Business: How to Start and Manage,* the first textbook in family business in Korea. She is also the author and co-author of more than forty research papers on various aspects of family business and entrepreneurship.

**Sam H. Lane, PhD,** is a corporate psychologist who has worked with a broad range of family businesses over the past twenty-six years. Dr. Lane received his PhD from Texas Christian University. He is a member of the Aspen Family Business Group, the Family Firm Institute, and many other professional organizations.

**Peter C. Leach, FCA,** a partner with BDO Stoy Hayward, has more than twenty-five years of experience advising some of the largest, most successful family-owned businesses in the United Kingdom and internationally. He pioneered research into family businesses in the United Kingdom and, from its inception in 1992, was founder and is now chair of the BDO Centre for Family Business and co-author of the definitive U.K. text, *The Guide to Family Business.* He is a visiting Fellow at Cranfield School of Management, and a regular lecturer at Henley Management College and The London Business School.

**Francis Martin, FCA, MBA,** is one of Northern Ireland's leading advisers to family business. He led the development, management, and delivery of a Family Business Program on behalf of Invest NI, Northern Ireland's Business Support Agency. The program has provided assistance to family-owned businesses in identifying and understanding the family issues that impact upon the success and continuity of their businesses.

**Ruth McClendon, MSW,** is a consultant, psychotherapist, and author. Her expertise is in reconciling relationships and creating family firms that survive for generations. She is cofounder of the Carmel Institute for Family Business, a global consulting organization, and a founding board member and Fellow of the Family Firm Institute, a national forum for family business practitioners. Her latest book, along with her husband, Leslie B. Kadis, MD, is *Reconciling Relationships and Preserving the Family Business: Tools for Success* (The Haworth Press, 2004).

**Kenneth McCracken, LLB,** is a founding director and consultant of Family Business Solutions, Ltd. He has specialized in advising and consulting with family businesses since 1995 and has played a leading role in the development of the family business field in the United Kingdom. He was president of the founding board of Family Firm Institute (United Kingdom), the world association for family business professionals. In 2001 he was awarded the FFI international award for interdisciplinary achievement. He was a founding editor of *The Family Business Client* and is a regular speaker and writer on family business issues.

**Kristi S. McMillan, MS,** is the associate director of the Cox Family Enterprise Center at Kennesaw State University, where she earned her master of science in conflict management. Since 1994 she has been working with family-owned companies in numerous capacities. She is also a founding member of the Georgia chapter of the Association for Conflict Resolution.

**Barbara Murray, PhD,** is a prominent consultant, teacher, and writer on family business matters. She is a founding director of Family Business Solutions Ltd., based in the United Kingdom, and an affiliate of Lansberg-Gersick Associates, based in the United States. She specializes in working with family businesses during succession transitions and in the implementation of systems of governance for the family enterprise. Barbara was the executive director of the Family Business Network (FBN, the world association for family businesses) between 2002 and 2004; the founding editor-in-chief of *Families in Business* magazine, and member of the editorial review board of *Family Business Review;* and a founding Fellow of IFERA, the International Family Enterprise Research Academy.

**Dorothy Nebel de Mello, PhD** (University of Chicago), is a fellow and past board member of the Family Firm Institute. She is president and cofounder of the Instituto da Empresa Familiar and partner of Nebel & Mello Consultores Associados, her consulting firm, in Sao Paulo, Brazil.

**Bill O'Gorman, MSc,** is the director of the Centre for Entrepreneurship Research at Waterford Institute of Technology, Ireland. An entrepreneur, he also has extensive experience working as a senior manager in multinational organizations and as an academic. His main areas of research are new enterprise creation, entrepreneurship, and SME growth and development. He was responsible for setting up the John C. Kelleher Family Business Centre at University College Cork.

**Denise Paré-Julien, BSc, DSA,** is a graduate of Université du Québec a Montréal and HEC, Montréal. She was a manager for many years. Denise serves as a facilitator, speaker, and advisor to business families; her main interest is implementing governance structures in family-owned firms. She has been working with Business Families Foundation since 1998, is a member of CAFÉ (Canadian Association for Entrepreneurial Families), and of the Family Firm Institute (FFI). She is also a faculty member for the FFI Launching Pad program.

**Joseph Paul, MS,** has worked with families since 1978, specializing in the development, application, and transfer of leadership and the resolution of family issues that interfere with the development of assets. He is the co-author of several assessment devices, including the Aspen Family Business Inventory, the Wealth Management Inventory, and the Aspen Family Foundation Inventory. He is a director emeritus and fellow of the Family Firm Institute and a partner in two consulting firms: the Aspen Family Business Group (North America) and Global Family Business Advisors (Europe and the Middle East).

**Annette Rahael, MBA,** is a family business advisor and runs her own company, Annette Rahael Consulting Ltd., in Trinidad, West Indies. She worked for eighteen years in her family business before establishing her consulting practice. She holds bachelor's degrees from the American University of Beirut and from Florida Atlantic University, and obtained an executive master's of business administration from the Institute of Business at the University of the West Indies. Currently she is the only person in the Caribbean who holds a certificate in family business advising from the Family Firm Institute.

**Marcus Spillane, ACA,** is founder and managing director of Mercier Private Equity Ltd., an Irish private equity fund specializing in investments in owner-managed and family-owned businesses. He is a chartered accountant and previously worked in the merger and acquisitions group of an international professional services firm. He grew up within a family business and has first-hand experience of many of the issues facing Irish family businesses today.

**Marta Vago, MSW,** is a coach and advisor to entrepreneurs, professionals, and business-owning families in the United States and abroad. She brings degrees in human behavior, plus hands-on business knowledge and over twenty-five years of consulting experience to working with clients from diverse cultural, ethnic, and religious backgrounds. She received the Family Firm Institute's 2004 International Award for furthering the understanding of family business issues between countries.

**Jorge J. Yunis** graduated from the School of Business at Pontifical Catholic University of Chile. He has completed postgraduate programs in Europe and the United States and has served as a finance lecturer, academic director, and professor of the Strengthening of Family Business Programme at Gabriela Mistral University. He has held management positions at Ernst & Young, Citibank, and founded EQUITY in Chile and EQUITY SBC–USA. He is a member of FFI and director of Risk Programmes of UK-Based Euromoney Institute of Finance.

# Foreword

I very much welcome the opportunity to write the Foreword to this book. It is very closely related to the work I hold to be so important.

I have lived in, worked in, and traveled to more than fifty countries. As an internationally recognized family business consultant, I have been privileged to hold leadership positions in professional organizations that serve family business educators and consultants. I have had the opportunity to serve as the vice president of international development of the Family Firm Institute (FFI), and later serve as its president. FFI is an international organization whose members serve as consultants and advisors to family businesses around the world. I have also been vice president of the United States Association for Small Business and Entrepreneurship (USASBE) with responsibilities for the family business division. USASBE is the U.S. affiliate of the International Council for Small Business.

I believe that people, regardless of culture, are more alike than they are different; however, the differences are critically important and must be understood and respected. Empathy, the capacity to understand and respond to the unique experiences of another, is the bridge spanning the chasm that separates people from one another. With empathy as our guide we can expand our boundaries, reaching into unexplored territory to create deep understanding and heartfelt relationships. These relationships serve as the foundation upon which the family business consultant can provide the technical expertise and consulting skills that the leadership of various family businesses request and seek.

Dr. Florence Kaslow has invited an impressive array of family business consultants, representing diverse cultures, to write chapters describing their unique perspectives about family businesses and family business consultation, in their respective countries. Other leaders in the field of family business have contributed chapters describing various consulting models and trends which impact businesses and family business consultation from a global perspective.

This is the first book written in the field of family business that exclusively addresses the complex issues inherent in transcultural and multicultural family business consultation. It is an essential book given that the field

*Handbook of Family Business and Family Business Consultation*
Published by The Haworth Press, Inc., 2006. All rights reserved.
doi:10.1300/5491_c

of family business consultation continues to expand across all geographic borders. Family business consultants understand the need to be culturally knowledgeable and sensitive. Those consultants who have become leaders in the field not only have factual knowledge and expertise; they have a passion to be learners and students of culture. Culture affects all functional areas of business and family life. This book is intended not only for those who consult transculturally with family businesses in countries other than their own, or aspire to do so, but also for those professionals who consult cross-culturally, that is, with family businesses that are located in the same geographic area as they are, but do not share the same ethnic and cultural background. It is also an important reference and resource for CEOs and other leaders of family businesses, as well as for instructors and graduate students in university-based business programs and family business and entrepreneurship centers.

The authors share their valuable wisdom regarding the art and science of family business consultation. Their in-depth knowledge, extensive experience, unique insights, and global perspectives in the field of family business consultation will serve as a valuable resource for family business CEOs, other leaders, and managers, professional advisors such as lawyers, accountants, estate planners, and psychologists, as well as educators, researchers, media professionals writing and speaking about family businesses, government officials and policymakers, and others who share an interest in families and the environments in which they interact.

I would like to thank Dr. Kaslow, who is a highly esteemed Fellow of FFI and a mentor for aspiring family business consultants, on behalf of this field for her vision, tenacity, and courage to spearhead the writing of this book. Also, thanks are extended to the many authors who participated in the authoring of the chapters. You have made a major contribution to the field of family business consultation. Thank you, also, to the publishers, The Haworth Press, Inc., for their foresight and trust in assisting us in filling an important void in the family business literature.

I wish you, the reader, every success in applying the information that you gain from this book.

*Joyce Brockhaus, PhD*
*President*
*The Brockhaus Group*
*St. Louis, Missouri*

# Preface

Family businesses have existed for centuries. They are an almost natural creation of families who live and work together over time, and need and want to take care of and provide for one another in the present as well as in the future. Whether the activity is farming, some kind of craft making, cooking or serving food, or more sophisticated enterprises such as manufacturing, these endeavors exhibit mutual and reciprocal concerns for one another, family connectedness, and loyalty. No doubt when they needed it families throughout the ages sought advice from trusted elders in their community, be they tribal or clan leaders, religious leaders, those thought to be sages, or a special person deemed to be able to be helpful.

Over the years, more formal structures have been created and people learned how to start and run businesses in many ways, varying from apprenticing in them from childhood to learning about them in high-powered MBA programs.

In the past several decades family businesses have increasingly been recognized as having some dynamics, functions, missions, and objectives that differentiate them in some significant ways from nonfamily businesses. As their uniquenesses and idiosyncrasies as a separate genre became more apparent, a new specialty began to emerge through the ingenious efforts of creative, energetic, intelligent, well-educated, independent, and innovative individuals who called themselves family business consultants or advisors; they have replaced the trusted elders of long ago.

In the mid-1980s several groups of these pioneers met separately and then coalesced in the United States and formed the Family Firm Institute. Concurrently, a similar development was occurring in Europe and led to the formation of the Family Business Network in Scotland. Both exciting developments have continued unabated for two decades and have been replicated, emulated, and created anew in many other countries throughout the world. This book attempts to capture and distill the essence of these phenomena.

*Handbook of Family Business and Family Business Consultation*
Published by The Haworth Press, Inc., 2006. All rights reserved.
doi:10.1300/5491_d

And so it came to pass at an FFI conference in 2003 when I presented a workshop, "How to Write for Publication," that several participants wanted to know "Where is your book on family business?" given that I was alluding to my books on other topics but only to pertinent articles on family business. My response was something along the lines of "There have been so many excellent books published recently on a whole host of family business subjects and I have not identified any serious gap which needs filling." After the workshop, I toured the book exhibit to see if this was an accurate observation.

Generally, it was. But I found no book that approached family business and family business consultation from an international perspective. And I knew immediately that this would be the landscape of "my book." I quickly discussed the idea with a few respected colleagues who were consulting in various countries, and they concurred that this could, indeed, be an area in which I could bring together a group of experienced consultants who could make a substantial contribution to the field and provide a broad overview of what is transpiring. Several issues of the *Family Business Review* have done this on a smaller scale but without the space to present it in the historical and financial context that we are able to provide here.

One objective was to assemble the best group of contributing authors that I could from representative countries. Unfortunately, not everyone invited was available to accept, particularly from Israel, Spain, South Africa, Switzerland, and Venezuela, and we regret their lack of a presence here, but it is more important to focus on what came to fruition and appreciate that. We believe this volume encompasses a wealth of historical data about the field; of family business struggles and successful experiences; of family business consulting and advising activities; of setting up and orchestrating all kinds of structures, including Boards of Directors, Family Offices, Family Philanthropies, Family Councils, and helping firms globalize and deal with globalization of their wealth. All authors have great organizational savvy and are acknowledged leaders in their realm of operations.

My sincerest appreciation is expressed to all of the authors who worked so diligently to write their chapters, sometimes in a language that is not their first language, and to adhere to the rigorous time schedule and writing guidelines. They have all been extraordinary, and it is easy to understand why they have all become leaders in the field. Many others who have provided information to the authors and to me are acknowledged for their generous assistance in the chapters.

I have worked with the staff at The Haworth Press on numerous books, and once again I want to convey my deepest gratitude to them all for their continuing confidence in the value of my work, for their encouragement, for their willingness to take risks when I go in new directions, and for their very personal and immediate attention to my requests. To the publisher, William Cohen, who has been so accessible, and all of the staff with whom I work so closely, particularly Bill Palmer, Robert Owen, Sandy Jones Sickels, Margaret Tatich, Jennifer Durgan, Anissa Harper, and Peg Marr—many, many thanks.

And as always, to my husband and financial consultant, Solis Kaslow, thanks for your patience while I have been immersed in editing and writing. And to my loyal secretary and assistant, Gladys Adams, as usual, without your assistance and calm perseverance this project would not have been completed. Thank you one and all.

# PART I:
# ESTABLISHING THE CONTEXT

Chapter 1

# Brief History of the Family Firm Institute

Florence W. Kaslow

Trying to put together the history of an organization, and even more so of a field, is a precarious venture. It is no doubt both a foolhardy endeavor and one that takes spunk and courage. With trepidation we have undertaken this task, as it seems essential that such a history be included in this book and help to set the context for what appears in the following chapters. Every effort has been made to encompass an accurate, albeit incomplete, factual history, as well as to capture some of the enthusiasm and intellectual fervor of the visionaries, practitioners, academics, and researchers who created and helped legitimize the field.

Sincere thanks go to many individuals, including Rod Correll, whose photocopied paper on the beginnings of FFI (Correll, 2002) was provided to me by Dennis Jaffe; to Leslie Dashew, who shared her "raw notes" from the FFI Fellows Meeting of 2002 (L. Dashew, personal communication, 2002); to Judy Green, for sending one of her articles (Green, 2003); to Joyce Brockhaus who provided an outlined chronological history she had prepared (J. Brockhaus, personal communication, 2002); to Barbara Murray for sending me an article on the background of FBN; to Joseph Astrachan for factual data on the journal's history; and to Nancy Drozdow and Ruth McClendon—both of whom were at the early formative meeting at Wharton School in 1986 and who, like several of the others already mentioned, read and commented on earlier drafts of this chapter. (In the various reports, the chronology of events was found to vary, and so some statements may not be totally accurate in their time frame.) The *Yellow Pages,* FFI's inclusive resource guide (FFI, 2004), proved an excellent and accurate resource, particularly regarding chronology of presidential leadership and the Body of Knowledge documents.

From this vantage point an attempt has been made to provide the best succinct synopsis of the emergence of the Family Firm Institute, predominantly in North America, that we can. Any such account reflects the in-

*Handbook of Family Business and Family Business Consultation*
Published by The Haworth Press, Inc., 2006. All rights reserved.
doi:10.1300/5491_01

volvement of the persons who wrote the earlier materials on which this summation partially is predicated, the particular lens through which they viewed the developments, and the specific network of people with whom they and I are associated. Apologies to those whose contributions have inadvertently not been included; it has not been possible to mention everyone involved in the launching and development of a complex, multifaceted field. (The current author takes responsibility for the interpretations and commentary offered.)

## IN THE BEGINNING

In 1968, the first known book in the field was published. Written by Leon Danco, it was a significant book, and he has remained a highly esteemed person in the field (see Danco 1982a, 1982b). Other books began to appear in the early 1980s, but it was not until late 1982 that a meeting was convened at Richard Beckhard's New York apartment by Beckhard and Ivan Lansberg (Beckhard & Dyer, 1983) to gather together those who they knew were interested in family business consultation.

In his paper on the history of FFI, Correll indicated that he graduated from SOM (The Yale School of Management) in 1985. While at Yale, he studied with and worked for Lansberg, then an associate professor. Lansberg was teaching individual and group behavior, the experientially taught core organization behavior (OB) course for first-year students, and was about to inaugurate a course on family business. Correll, who came out of a family business background, took Lansberg's course, and found the experience eye-opening and fun (2002, p.1). He went on to become Lansberg's teaching assistant and opted to stay on for another postgraduate year to do research with him on family business succession.

During 1985 Correll heard Lansberg's vision for a Family Firm Institute, and was introduced to its eventual cofounders: Beckhard, a faculty member at MIT Sloan School of Business, Barbara Hollander, Elaine Kepner, Aaron Levinson, and George Raymond. This group, including Lansberg, plus Robin Raymond, went on to become the founding board of FFI. Allegedly, each contributed $2,000 to help defray the organization's start-up expenses (J. Brockhaus, personal communication, 2002). From all reports, Beckhard's enthusiasm permeated the meeting and helped motivate the group. Following that, some additional friends of Lansberg—including John Davis, Kelin Gersick, Ernesto Poza, and John Ward—began to work with Lansberg and Joe Astrachan, then an OB doctoral student at SOM, in developing a strategy for transforming FFI from a dream, shared by some of those involved in consulting who were networking with one another, into a reality, that is, an organization of those working in, teaching about, and researching family business.

During this formative period, two critical meetings were held that culminated in the creation of the Institute. A meeting of the seven founders alluded to previously was held in Safety Harbor, Florida, in 1985. At this gathering, tentative agreement was reached about the FFI's mission; the form it should take (membership organization); services it should provide (networking); and what its products would be (annual conference, academic journal, newsletter, directory). From all accounts, a charter was drafted at this meeting. Like many organizations in their start-up stages, there were obstacles to overcome, such as getting the schedules of busy people coordinated so that they could agree on the next meeting date to hammer out the main issues, and keeping the level of interest high between contacts of the potential founding members so headway could continue to be made. Correll's role (self-described) was acting as "the glue," recording what was going on, helping people focus on what needed to be done, and spurring further action.

The results of this strategic planning meeting led to a subsequent meeting at the University of Southern California in November 1985. This meeting was attended by the founders mentioned earlier, plus others from various professional backgrounds, including Craig Aronoff, Jeff Barach, John Davis, Nancy Drozdow, Kelin Gersick, Fredda Herz Brown, Tom Hubler, Amy Lyman, Ruth McClendon, Stephen Swartz, Karen Vinton, Ed Wachtler, and Mary Whiteside. Many of these individuals also became founding members several months later, at which time the details about mission, form, services, and products were elaborated further and Ed Wachtler was appointed legal counsel. A charter was drawn up and filed (some time between 1984 and 1986), and a board was elected. Hollander, an energetic and respected leader, was chosen as the first president. Thus, the Founding Board was composed of the seven original pioneers and an additional fifteen people who also became founding members (FFI, 2004).

The USC meeting was organized by John Davis. In addition to discussing organizational matters, the assembled group focused on gender issues, first within the family business, then about each person's own gender and self. From the beginning, both women and men have played a major role in FFI.

The next step was to solicit additional members for this fledging organization. Hollander enthusiastically took the lead, and other founding members also went through their lists of friends and associates to see who else would be appropriate to invite to join. Correll created a database to record the information on these individuals, and FFI was launched officially in 1986.

Initially, Hollander, who Drozdow and others considered the soul of FFI, operated the organization out of her home, assisted by a friend. She was perceived as providing vision and fine leadership. The amount of paperwork soon overwhelmed them, and Correll volunteered to take on the day-to-day responsibility of keeping FFI operational (Correll, 2002, p. 4). At first the position was nonpaying, but as the core group of leaders signed up other members and it became clear that FFI could afford to pay a salary to an executive director, Correll was hired for the position, (probably) in spring 1987. He served from then until the annual conference at Beaver Creek, Colorado, in 1991 (FFI, 2004, pp. 1-2). While he held this position, FFI was housed in his consulting offices in Johnstown, New York. The first employee was his wife, who helped welcome potential members and orient them to FFI. The second person hired worked on conference details, helped with the newsletter and the *Family Business Review (FBR)*. When the membership grew to over 400 (some time around 1990), an office manager was added.

Other major players in the early days were Alan Kepner (Elaine Kepner and Beckhard's son), who attended some of FFI's earliest meetings; Ben Benson and Ron Drucker (able accountants who were among the first of their profession to join FFI); Jerry Le Van (a lawyer and early practitioner of family business consulting); Peter Beaudoin (also an accountant and a strategic thinker); Marta Vago (a mental health professional with a great understanding of the multicultural issues within family business); Paul Karofsky (one of the earliest directors of a significant university-based family business center and study group); and Dirk Dreuz (a banker from U.S. Trust, who was a special help to Correll as he sought to develop income streams for FFI). Another person who played a key role in FFI from its beginning was Kathy Wiseman. Kathy has been described as "an excellent process consultant" at FFI Board meetings, highlighting the Board's process, defining its vision, and keeping it vibrant (Correll, 2002). Many have commented on the high level of commitment and selfless dedication to FFI of many members in the early years.

## THE EXCITING SECOND PHASE

After the reputedly exciting meeting at USC, subsequent Board meetings were held for several years in Beckhard's New York City apartment. Much vigorous discussion on the evolution of the field permeated the meetings. Beckhard is remembered as having served as the Board's conscience and is considered by many to have been the wise elder statesman of FFI.

Board meetings combined business with social interaction. They have been described as stimulating, productive, and exhausting.

Allegedly, there were conflicting perspectives among the founders about FFI's mission and objectives, and among individuals from the different disciplines, which made it difficult to create a truly integrated, interdisciplinary culture at the outset. FFI stood out as having the potential to provide "a chance for interdisciplinary collaboration designed to help family businesses that risked coming apart at the seams to operate more effectively, because the 'guys and gals on the hard side of the equation' (lawyers, accountants, bankers, insurance providers) could not get along with those on the soft side (psychologists, psychiatrists, anthropologists, educators)." Correll (2002, p. 7) indicated that he often felt like he spent most of his time trying to heal the breach and make peace rather than helping to build a new interdisciplinary profession that could potentially help those who had been through "the family business wars."

Some allege that another serious challenge for the new Institute was the attitude of "the old guard," respected practitioners who had already established successful practices as consultants to family business and who thought of FFI and its members as "upstarts." Eventually this rift between old and new was healed. This type of situation is not atypical in the history and sociology of new organizations.

Numerous individuals reported that an important conference was held at Wharton School, the Graduate Business School at the University of Pennsylvania, in 1986. Some of those present were David Bork, Leslie Dashell, John Davis, Nancy Drozdow, Dennis Jaffe, Les Kadis, Elaine Kepner, Joe Paul, Norman Paul, and Michael Shulman. It was the first time Dashell was exposed to the concept of advisor to family business as a profession, and she, like other newcomers, was intrigued by it. Those present came by virtue of an invitation from Peter Davis, based on who he thought should be at the meeting. The vast majority of attendees had mental health backgrounds. Those present formed a study group known as the Wharton Forum. At one meeting of the forum group, members discussed whether they should become involved in FFI, which was already in its formative phase. The two groups ultimately joined together. A book by David Bork, a participant in the Wharton Forum, was first published during this time (Bork, 1986; 1993).

A brief history on the Wharton Center seems appropriate here as it predates the formation of FFI (L. Drozdow, personal communication, 2004). The Center for Applied Research (CFAR) was Wharton's largest research center which had been focusing on systematically studying family business beginning in 1981. The center's director, Peter Davis, had been working with a number of family firms, including Anheuser Busch. By 1982 the center had planned a series of workshops for members of family firms: next generation, CEOs, and women. The first workshop took place at Wharton in 1982 or 1983, and these continued to be developed and presented through most of the 1980s. It is believed this center may have been the first to offer programs for family businesses at an academic institution. In 1983, Wharton offered its first "Women in Family Business" program, which was led by Barbara Hollander and Matilde Salganicoff, affiliates of the Wharton Center. Drozdow worked with Davis, Hollander, and Salgonicoff to design these workshops and deliver them. Drozdow states (personal communication, 2004), "That is when I began to hear about the idea of creating an institution to move the field along. From my view, Barbara was tenacious in her wish to create FFI."

Drozdow organized the next family business conference—still pre-FFI, at Wharton—probably in 1986. Since the prior meeting at USC had only twenty-four people in attendance, it was assumed a similar number would come. Instead, after seventy-five had registered, they had to turn people away because they were beyond standing-room capacity in the classroom space arranged. In one year the field had already exploded. Among those attending this conference were David Bork, Pat Frishkoff, Kathy Wiseman, Gibb Dyer, John Davis, Rick Aberman, and Ivan Lansberg.

At this conference hints of the divisions that might occur surfaced; there were some who were less interested in collaboration and sharing information, and some who were more interested. At around the same time Wharton Center split off their workshops and moved them into Wharton's executive education center. Peter Davis left the Wharton Center and became opposed "to the formation of FFI" (L. Drozdow, personal communication, 2004). At the end of the Wharton Conference, a group met to listen to Barbara Hollander talk about the idea of FFI. Shortly after that, FFI was officially formed as described earlier. During the 1980s, Lansburg and Beckhard were both including family business material in courses at their respective institutions, Yale and MIT. Harvard had an owner-president program in the mid-1980s, which continues today. Ron Taguiri, John Davis, and By Barnes were involved in the Harvard program. The CFAR spun off from Wharton Center in 1987 but maintained an amicable relationship. Today the CFAR is a large firm with offices in Philadelphia, Pennsylvania, and Cambridge, Massachusetts, which continues to offer a variety of services to family businesses.

Sibling competition was evident early on. Fortunately, over the past decade, some of the strained relationships have become collaborative rather than competitive. One of the issues that rumbled underneath the surface and remained unspoken was the competition among members to be the acknowledged leaders and consultants rather than focusing on the sharing of intellectual capital, and whether FFI should be a closed versus an open organization.

Jossey-Bass, Inc., became the initial publisher of the *Family Business Review*. This relationship lasted from 1988 until 1996. Ivan Lansberg was the first editor (1988-1990). Kelin Gersick joined him as coeditor for a short while and then became sole editor from 1990 to 1993. Max Wortman Jr. held the post from 1993 to 1995, and Joseph Astrachan has been the editor since 1995. The journal was published by FFI from 1996 until 2004, when Blackwell took over as the publisher.

## EARLY NATIONAL CONFERENCES
## AND OTHER SIGNIFICANT OCCURRENCES

The next conference was held in 1987 at Provo, Utah, during Hollander's presidency (1986-1990). Gibb Dyer served as convener, and David Bork was a featured presenter. Several hundred people were in attendance, indicating the continued mushrooming of interest in the field. It was the first time members of a family business made a presentation at an FFI meeting, and established what has become an often repeated and valuable tradition. Such presentations help broaden consultants' understanding of families' perspectives.

At this juncture, a controversy surfaced over whether FFI should be for family business advisors or for leaders of family businesses. By this time, other relevant developments were under way. For example, Pat Frishkoff had founded the Austin Family Business Program at Oregon State University in 1985, probably the first such program in the United States, and Craig Aronoff of Kennesaw State University had begun establishing study groups.

The 1988 conference, listed as the first (official) conference in the FFI *Yellow Pages* (FFI, 2004), was held in Boston with Mary McCollom-Hampton as convener. Ed Friedman presented his work on "Generation to Generation," based on the multigenerational family systems theory generated by Murray Bowen (Bowen, 1978/1988). At this meeting, the Board started talking about a certification process; discussions continued for three years, and subsequently led to setting up the interdisciplinary Body of Knowledge (BOK) task force. The then extant knowledge base was put together for an issue of the *Family Business Review*. The atmosphere was heady; many new members were present, attesting to the growing significance and credibility of the fledgling profession.

Davis, California, was the site of the 1989 conference; Amy Lyman was the convener. Multidisciplinary consulting teams were in evidence. Jim Farrah of Farrah Pants spoke from the vantage point of a family business owner. The first Research Day was held. Various awards had been created and were conferred. More awards were established during the ensuing decade to recognize various types of outstanding contributions to the field, and all are conferred at the annual conference.

At the 1990 conference in Atlanta, Steve Swartz succeeded Hollander as president. Featured events were a presentation by the Huntsmen Chemical family and an important panel on ethics in family business. A mission statement was developed indicating FFI had decided to focus on advisors to business organizations. The first "affinity" group was launched.

The theme of the 1991 conference in Beaver Creek, Colorado, was "How can family businesses best be served?" Attention was paid at the board meeting to such issues as bankruptcy and the need to raise money for the organization. A planning meeting was held at Dashew's house, near the conference site, to discuss how to develop a collaborative professional model of practice.

## FFI EXPANSION

By 1992, with more than 770 active members, including consultants, educators, and family business owners, and the demand growing for increased professionalism in the delivery of its products and services, it appeared that FFI needed both a new office that was closer to the hub of its activities than Johnstown, New York, and a larger, better-trained staff. Correll realized that his personal vision for FFI, which entailed creating a think tank for helping family businesses operate more effectively, was slightly different from the one that had evolved (Correll, 2002), which was to define and shape the field of family business consultation, to determine the core knowledge content that constituted adequate preparation for being a consultant, and ultimately to disseminate this information to those teaching and training others to became family business consultants and advisors. Therefore, he suggested to the Board that it seek a replacement for him, and he participated in the selection of his successor, Judy Green, PhD, in 1992, under whose administration the office was moved to Boston, and the organization has flourished.

At the conference in 1992 in Boston, Craig Aronoff took the reins as president. Frank Pittman, MD, a family psychiatrist, spoke about movies about family business and showed some film clips illustrative of how movies portray business families. The first Educator's Conference was held. Consistent with FFI's goals, this conference focused on emerging opportunities, university-based research, teaching, and outreach programs that work. Each subsequent year, an Education and Research Conference has been held—not always in conjunction with the FFI conference. A decline in membership occurred around this time, but the trend was quickly reversed and has continued upward since 1995.

By the conference in New York in 1993, an investment banker orientation had come to the fore. This meeting was apparently the first that was more like a convention. The first advanced practitioners meeting was held there. There was continued discussion about the issue of certification; however, it was deemed still to be cost prohibitive. Reportedly John Ward expressed the belief that financial firms would dominate the field. Attorney members decided to create their own organization. Regional chapters and study groups had been formed in some areas and were meeting formally. An increasing number of these continue to be established each year.

At the 1994 conference in Scottsdale, Arizona, there was a theatrical production of the "box company" with multidisciplinary dialogues about assumptions about family businesses; an ad hoc consulting group interfaced with an improvisational theatre group. It was a revealing presentation. A lovely and memorable black tie event was held at the Desert Botanical Gardens. A special social event, usually of this kind, has since become an annual gala tradition.

At the 1995 conference in St. Louis, the theme was "Family Business: Gateway to the Future." Different professional tracks were established in the program. A major effort was being made to expand membership, and the field was beginning to be recognized more broadly. Cochairs Joyce and Bob Brockhaus had their son, Robert Jr., open the conference, holding to the theme of young people being the key to ensuring the future of the field.

## THE FAMILY BUSINESS NETWORK
## ENTERS THE SCENE

### Creation of IMD

According to Murray, Schwass, & Ward (2003), Lausanne, Switzerland, is "widely acknowledged to be the family business capital of the world" (p. 41). Lausanne has long had a tradition for being a major center of various diverse educational endeavors, including in the field of business. They indicate that what is thought to be the world's first *international* family business program began in 1988, which is the same year FFI held its first official national convention. As often happens, when it is time for a new idea or field to be launched, recognition of the need for this to occur erupts simultaneously in several places—sometimes in tandem and sometimes quite separately. The origins of IMD have been attributed to a Canadian family business entrepreneur who spent a sabbatical year at IMI (the predecessor institution to IMD) in Lausanne. He sought information or courses on family business, and finding virtually nothing, he wanted to fill the market gap by seeing if a seminar on family business could be organized. He thought Lausanne would be a good locale in which to do this since Europe is at the center of multigenerational, dynastically oriented businesses.

Upon learning of three professors in the United States who already had an active interest in family business—namely, John Davis, Ivan Lansberg, and John Ward—they were contacted and a seminar titled "Leading the Family Business" was instituted. In 2003, Murray, Schwass, & Ward reported that since the inception of this seminar, 750 participants from about 400 families and 40 countries have attended it. This multiday seminar, sponsored by a well-respected international business school, draws participants from some of the oldest and largest business families that have international interests.

Activities and offerings at the IMD have expanded in the ensuing seventeen years. Alden Lank now holds one of the first named family business professorships there. The center has staff who engage in family business research concerned with deepening the understanding of what factors contribute to making family businesses more effective. Case study research is also carried on at this center in Switzerland. Among primary foci are ownership forms and adaptive strategies.

## THE FAMILY BUSINESS NETWORK IS BORN

Paralleling the development of educational offerings at IMD, the idea of establishing an association of family business leaders emerged as a "small group of visionaries created the Family Business Network (FBN) in Lausanne" in 1990. The objective was to have a worldwide association devoted exclusively to increasing the quality of leadership and management of family-owned firms.

The original benefits were a newsletter and an annual conference; the latter has grown from an attendance of 40 at the 1990 conference in Lausanne to approximately 500 by 2002. The current membership numbers around 1,600 from 50 different countries.

FBN strives to enable international networking, international learning, and international community building. There are local chapters and peer groups for networking. There is also a Building the Future program for next-generation leaders, and initiatives to "support entrepreneurship in underdeveloped countries" (Murray, Schwass, & Ward, 2003).

Whereas FFI has evolved primarily as an organization of family business advisers, FBN is geared predominantly to family business owners. They share in common the goal of educating potential successors and improving the practices and effectiveness of family businesses. There is some overlap in membership. It appears that the organizations have complementary and supplementary agendas with different target membership populations and some differing goals.

With this succinct mention of FBN included to illuminate another aspect of and parallel trend in the family business world which was happening concurrently, we return to focus on FFI in the more recent past.

## BODY OF KNOWLEDGE

Work on the core document that embodies the essentials of what family business professionals should and need to know began in the early 1990s. Fredda Herz Brown became first chair (1995-1998) of the Body of Knowledge committee. She was succeeded by Karen Vinton (1998-2001), and the current chair is Mark Voeller (2001- ). The BOK book has been published and distributed by FFI since 1999 (see FFI, 2005, for most current version).

This book contains a "comprehensive set of the FFI resources" and includes "a history of the BOK committee, a compilation of the products of the Body of Knowledge Committee," some family business cases, and information on the Certificate Program and on the *Family Business Review.* It is updated annually and many parts are to be perceived as works in progress, such as the Resource Guides (FFI, 2004, p. ii). Much of this material is used in the "Essentials Course" for those aspiring to become family business advisors. The resource guides contain salient information from the five core disciplines which are considered to constitute the foundation to be mastered for proficient and skilled family business advising:

- Behavioral science
- Financial aspects
- Insurance
- Legal issues
- Management science

The BOK mission statement and the FFI Code of Ethics, adopted by the FFI Board in April 2001, are also included. [The Code of Ethics is also included in the *Yellow Pages* (FFI, 2005)].

The progenitors of this comprehensive BOK document have labored long and hard to put together an interdisciplinary handbook that recognizes and respects what is drawn from each of the contributing core disciplines. The sometimes rocky quest for a truly collaborative approach is reflected in the materials proffered. Each area can be addressed separately, when indicated, or dealt with from an integrated perspective, when this would be the more beneficial approach. In this author's opinion, the BOK is a marvelously rich resource for family business advisors, long-term and just beginning, and should be reviewed periodically as a refresher course.

## THE SECOND DECADE

An important development in 1998 was the formation by the Board of Directors of an International Committee. By then Joyce Brockhaus and others, including David Bork, Bob Brockhaus, Francois de Visscher, Florence Kaslow, Ivan Lansburg, and Marta Vago, were all teaching and consulting abroad. Joyce Brockhaus was appointed Vice President of International Initiatives (1999-2001), an annual International Award was inaugurated (2000), and seven County Coordinators were appointed, representing Sweden (1998), Israel (1998), Finland (1999), the Netherlands and Belgium (1999), South Africa (1999), Korea (2001), and Lebanon (2001). International members currently provide leadership roles on the FFI Board of Directors and committees; actively participate in program development and presentations at annual conferences and other educational forums; conduct research; and contribute articles to the *Family Business Review.*

The realization that the field of family business advising was one of international importance also led to the decision to hold two conferences in countries other than the United States in the early years of the twenty-first century, as is shown in the following listing.

| | |
|---|---|
| 1988 | Managing Succession in Family Firms—Boston, Massachusetts |
| 1989 | Ownership, Control, and Family Dynamics—Davis, California |
| 1990 | Celebrating Family Business—Atlanta, Georgia |
| 1991 | How Can Family Business Best Be Served?—Beaver Creek, Colorado |
| 1992 | Family Business at the Crossroads—Boston, Massachusetts |
| 1993 | Family Business: A Generation Comes of Age—New York, New York |
| 1994 | Challenging Assumptions—Scottsdale, Arizona |
| 1995 | Family Business: Gateway to the Future—St. Louis, Missouri |
| 1996 | Power Up the Family Business—Philadelphia, Pennsylvania |
| 1997 | Family Business: Progress and Prophecy—New Orleans, Louisiana |

| 1998 | Continuity and Change: Expanding the Possibilities—Portland, Oregon |
|---|---|
| 1999 | Strategies for the New Millennium—Chicago, Illinois |
| 2000 | Family Business 2000—Washington, DC |
| 2001 | 2001: A Family Business Odyssey—London, England |
| 2002 | Building Communities of Practice in the Family Business Field—Dallas, Texas |
| 2003 | Benchmarks for the Family Business Professional—Toronto, Ontario, Canada |
| 2004 | Revolutionary Ideas for the Family Business Field—Boston, Massachusetts |
| 2005 | Varied Architectures: The Art and Science of Designing Family Enterprises—Chicago, Illinois |

Another noteworthy development included the formalization of the requirements for the certificate in family business advising and the awarding of this coveted credential to those who qualify. In addition, in 2001 FFI began recognizing as Fellows those who had been members of FFI for ten or more years and had made a significant contribution to the field and the organization by holding leadership roles in FFI, making presentations at conferences, and being published in *FBR*. In 2004, the criteria were expanded to include having completed the certificate in family business advising program. The list of those who are Fellows reflects an impressive array of talent in the field and includes some of the founders, plus many others who became involved in the late 1980s and early 1990s. (See FFI, 2005, pp. 1-6, 1-7.)

This article would be incomplete without mention of those who have served so ably as FFI presidents during the past decade and guided its expansion in depth and breadth; with marvelous backup support from Judy Green of Management Associates, and her staff. (Previous presidents were mentioned earlier.)

| 1994-1996 | Kathleen K. Wiseman |
|---|---|
| 1996-1998 | Mike Cohn |
| 1998-2001 | Francois M. de Visscher |
| 2001-2002 | Joyce Brockhaus |
| 2002-2005 | Glenn R. Ayres |

## Themes That Pervade Fellows Meetings and FFI Activities

Dashell, in her notes based on the FFI Fellows meeting held in 2002, and Jaffe, in his thoughts noted subsequent to the meeting (D. Jaffe, personal

communication, 2002), drew together various themes that have been prominent in the organization over time and highlighted questions that were
raised. (Revised and reordered by chapter author):

1. Increasing membership
2. Professional rivalry and competition
3. Certification—To do or not to do, and if so, how?
4. Assuring financial stability of FFI
5. Proprietary vs. shared knowledge
6. Senior members welcoming new ones; openness
7. International focus
8. How much can a volunteer organization take on?
9. Are we a professional or a trade organization?
10. How are the professional issues in this organization parallel to those
    of our clients?
11. Is FFI a viable research organization?
12. Recognition of senior contributing members as Fellows, which be-
    gan in 2001

Other themes have emerged since the Fellows group began.

13. How can we add value as a group of Fellows, and what are our
    needs?
14. What is the legacy of the founders of this field, and how can it be
    preserved?

At the meeting in Dallas in 2002, Dirk Junge asked, "Where is FFI now?"
Updated information indicates that FFI then had the following:

- 1,025 members (educators, professionals, researchers).
- An $850,000 annual budget; trying to break even this year.
- A membership goal set at 2,004 members by 2004.
- Conferences: There is a dependence on these for income, as well as
  for sponsors, so we might consider additional conferences throughout
  the year.
- The elected Board of Directors serves as the governance body. How
  large should it be?
- FFI has invested in a Web site, in *FBR,* and in launching of a certificate program—all of which depleted FFI reserves. The certificate program, launched in 2001, is making money. (Publication of *FBR* has
  recently been taken over by Blackwell Publishing, thus freeing FFI of
  an enormous portion of this expense.)

Some of the other salient questions raised and points made at the 2002 Fellows meeting (L. Dashew, personal communication, 2002) included the following:

1. Can we make this a fellowship?
2. What do we need as individuals (elders) and as a collective group from FFI? (Facility and opportunity to meet at FFI, and administrative coordination?)
3. What can we contribute to one another and to FFI?
4. How do we admit new Fellows?
5. Can we offer assistance to *FBR*?
6. How can we be of service to our profession?
   a. Could there be strategic dialogues periodically with the Editorial Board?
   b. We (the Fellows group) are a network, to be utilized on an ad hoc basis, rather than a structured organization, connected vis-à-vis the Web.
7. What does FFI need, and can the Fellows group provide a forum to discuss this? (This was done at the 2004 Fellows meeting.)
8. Is it too soon to formalize our informal network?
9. FFI conferences are a place to reconnect.
10. It would be a problem for the Fellows group to take a formal role in the organization; this group should not be confused with the existing governance.

Some other ideas expressed at this meeting follow (L. Dashew, personal communication, 2002; D. Jaffee, personal communication, 2002):

1. We do not (or should not?) come to FFI conferences "to hang out with other Fellows."
2. We should have a "master's course" of some kind, or a separate track for Fellows of at least a few sessions at the annual meetings.
3. Rather than being either/or, FFI conferences should be a place that allows taking care of our own needs *and* giving back, and being a model of a multidisciplinary group.
4. We could meet in small groups of six to eight people to discuss issues and share ideas about mutual concerns.
5. Our existence gives credibility to the certificate program.
6. Perhaps we could get together the day before the FFI meeting begins for informal contact.

7. We might use open space processes to foster personal connecting and encourage Fellows' participation in the activities of boards/committees.
8. Fellows should sometimes have dinner with new conference participants; this would help encourage their joining FFI.
9. Many Fellows would welcome senior case consultations from one another based on a presentation to enhance their learning.
10. Being engaged in addressing leading-edge questions is important to building a community of mutual support in our ongoing learning that is reciprocal. It serves to bring a good deal of knowledge to the fore and allows us to learn what one another are doing, and it allows us to keep growing.
11. We need time to develop a repertoire of cases and experiences, and time to evolve how we want to be and what we want to do—organic growth (internally structured).
12. As "elders," we need to see what engages others, and out of that serve the rest of the organization. We have to recognize the need for intimacy in the dialogue as well.

The first retreat for Fellows only was held in Palm Beach, Florida, in February 2005, with twenty-six Fellows in attendance. Many of the themes enumerated were addressed, and several of the central ones were the building of a community of trusted colleagues among the Fellows; greater collaboration across specialties; contributing books and articles we have written and videotapes we have made on our own work as family business consultants to a central archive as part of our legacy; increasing the amount of research being done in the field; and doing our own succession plans. All agreed this inaugural meeting had been an excellent next step on the journey of Fellows seeking to (1) improve service to family businesses; (2) continue making a contribution to FFI and its members; and (3) gain enrichment and replenish ourselves so that we are sometimes in the receiving rather than the giving role.

## THE EMERGENCE OF THE FAMILY BUSINESS ADVISOR

### Summation

Families in business are hardly a new phenomenon—they have existed in all cultures, all eras of history, in literature and drama, and more recently in the analysis of businesses around the world. One can assume that many such businesses have always relied on some kind of advisors. Yet it was only near the close of the twentieth century that a distinctly new profession emerged—that of the "family business advisor," or consultant. This development was followed by the emergence of family business researchers and educators. Taken together, they now constitute a cadre of family business professionals (Green, 2003).

In 1985, a group of professionals and family business executives in the United States recognized the need for interdisciplinary collaboration in the advising of family-owned businesses and, as a result, went on to found the Family Firm Institute, Inc., in 1986. As indicated earlier, the founding Board of Directors included several pioneers in the field of family business, among them Richard Beckhard, Barbara S. Hollander, Elaine Kepner, and Ivan S. Lansberg. Several others who joined them hailed from their own family businesses, notably Aaron Levinson of Levinson Steel Company, and both George and Robin Raymond of the Raymond Corporation (Green, 2003, p. 280).

These founders envisioned the Family Firm Institute as a "three-legged stool" focused on serving a membership encompassing consultants, educators, and family business owners (J. Brockhaus, personal communication, 2002). They planned that FFI would carry out its mission in three ways:

1. Host an annual conference to bring together members from across the nation—now from around the world—to share knowledge and research in the field of family enterprise. (This has been done successfully since 1988).
2. Organize regional study groups and workshops so that members could be involved in "grassroots networking" with peers and discuss common problems and challenges in the family business arena. (This, too, has occurred, with various groups and chapters now existing in Brazil, England and Scotland, and throughout the United States; there is also an online study group in Portuguese.)
3. Publish a journal, *The Family Business Review (FBR)*—a publication that would combine research findings and their implications, conceptual ideas, contributions on practice and theory, and actual case studies on family-owned businesses. (An outstanding journal has eventuated.)

These three objectives have remained the core of FFI's activities and have contributed to the educational development of family business advisors both inside and outside of the FFI membership. Annual conferences have remained the focal point; they feature a multiplicity of varied presentations and social, networking events. Attendees include experienced professionals as well as individuals entering the field from what are now called the "core disciplines" (behavioral science, finance, law, and management science) who exchange information, expertise, experience, and research results (Green, 2003).

## Conferences

Conferences have grown in attendance from twenty (the number attending the first FFI conference in Boston, 1988, hosted by Boston University School of Management), to more than 500 people. Conferences have been held at venues all over the United States, as well as in London, England, and Toronto, Canada.

## Publications

*FBR* remains the only scholarly journal in the world dedicated exclusively to family business research. In 1996, FFI published a special issue, *The Best of FBR: A Celebration,* edited by Beckhard—a 268-page commemorative edition containing the decade's most vital research and analyses on family-owned business. Recently *FBR* has focused on various international themes, specifically *Family Business in Eastern Europe,* autumn 1997; *Family Business in the New Entrepreneurial Economy: A Global Perspective,* December 2001; and *The Role of Family in Business: International Perspectives,* September 2002.

In addition, numerous books have appeared in the past decade heralding a growing body of literature on different family business topics (see, for example, Gersick, Davis, McCollum-Hampton, & Lansberg, 1997, and McClendon & Kadis, 2004), which expand the dissemination of the latest research and thinking in the field.

## Other Important Developments

In the early 1990s, university-based forums and family business centers began to emerge. These forums are designed specifically for business-owning families to come together to learn how to strengthen their overall communications, both in the family and in the business; to learn more about the key components for keeping the family business healthy; and to expose them to the most cutting-edge thinking in the field. Some businesses use the centers for direct consultation to their own family enterprise. Concurrent with the advent of the forums and centers, the appearance of another kind of family-business professional has evolved, the family business educator.

There are now more than 100 such programs around the world. FFI provides information and links to this part of the field through the publication of its annual *Yellow Pages* (a directory) and as an important component of the FFI website at www.ffi.org. In addition, FFI has cohosted conferences for educators, researchers, and advisors in collaboration with such institutions as UCLA's Anderson School, the University of San Diego, McGill University in Montreal, Northeastern University Center for Family Business in Boston, and the University of Wisconsin-Madison Family Business Center (Green, 2003).

## EIGHTEEN YEARS LATER

Currently, there are members of the FFI who were originally educated in all of the core disciplines in nearly every country in the world. Since 2001, when FFI established the Certificate Program in Family Business Advising, the certificate has been conferred on thirty-seven people (as of October 2004). Some of the forty-eight certified members and the now ninety Fellows have been serving as mentors to those trying to attain a certificate. Although the majority are from the United States, certified advisors also come from Canada, Europe, Mexico, South America, and elsewhere. In addition, the topic of family business education for those individuals remaining in their own core professions is on the agenda of numerous professional associations, such as AFFHE (Attorneys for Family Held Enterprise); ABA Section of Real Property, Probate and Trust Law; The American College (insurance) Certificate in Business Succession Planning; and AAMFT (American Association for Marriage and Family Therapy).

Research is entering into a second generation. Although *FBR* remains the only scholarly journal devoted exclusively to issues and opportunities related to family-owned enterprise, other high-quality journals have featured articles on this topic, including *Journal of Business Venturing: Special Issue on Family Business* (2003); *Journal of Small Business and Enterprise Development* (2002); *The Journal of Corporate Renewal* (2002); *Journal of Entrepreneurship* (2001); *Journal of Family and Economic Issues* (2001); *Harvard Business Review* (Green, 2003); *The American Journal of Family Therapy* (Kaslow, 1993); and *Contemporary Family Therapy* (Kaslow, 2004).

In the early 1980s one had to persuade the press (and educate it) about the economic impact of family-owned business. Today one can hardly pick up a major newspaper without seeing an article on family-owned business; unfortunately, these are often about the more dramatic and atypical businesses (such as *The New York Times* article of December 10, 2002, "Knives

Drawn for a $15 Billion Pritzker Family Pie") than the ones family business advisors consult daily.

Some university MBA programs have added courses on family business ownership and management in the past decade—signaling greater recognition of the importance of academic preparation for this responsibility.

### Implications for the Management of Family-Owned Businesses

It is premature to claim that this emerging field is solely responsible for the ongoing viability of family businesses that are creating and sustaining economic growth worldwide. However, some claims can be made (Green, 2003, p. 281) that family business owners (or business-owning families) can expect the following:

- Solid and specific responses when inquiring about the family-business education of their advisors; i.e., there are associations, certificate programs, and numerous conference opportunities for beginning or continuing education in the field.
- An expanding pool of advisors who have been trained in both the "hard" and the "soft" side of the field, hopefully leading to a decrease in the number of the proverbial "elegantly drafted estate plans" not implemented because of conflicts within the family.
- Their "most trusted advisor" to have a cadre of professional colleagues in related fields to call upon should they be needed; no single profession can respond to the complexity of the issues surrounding a family-owned business. An advisor without interdisciplinary colleagues can be a liability.
- Increasingly sophisticated research about the key issues facing them; they can also drive this research by suggesting research topics and participating in and funding this research.
- Leveraging the consistent interest of the press to further establish the critical role of family enterprises in the world economy.

## CONCLUSION

Family business consultation has emerged as a specialization; however, consultants'/advisors' roles and functions are still being developed and explored; only now is their history beginning to be written. Their influence will need to be tracked and documented longitudinally, across industries, cultures, and professions. The integration of the thoughts and needs of practitioners with those of visionaries and academics is an ongoing process of juggling, balancing, and listening to one another that will continue to evolve. Nonetheless, clearly unique and sophisticated resources are available to family enterprises today that did not exist as recently as a quarter-century ago. How family business advisors, educators, researchers, and business-owning families work together in the coming decades to continue to extend the economic reach of family enterprise globally will be critical to the health and well-being of citizens and countries worldwide.

It is difficult to encompass the excitement and ingenuity that permeate the intellectual and philosophic history of the launching of a new field. The factual history is easier to document. We have attempted to capture and convey both.

## NOTE

Various efforts were made to get someone knowledgeable to write a chapter on the Family Business Network and IMD. These efforts led to naught, yet it seemed important to provide at least some mention and a brief synopsis of those two organizations. Gratitude is expressed to Barbara Murray for sharing the article she had written (Murray et al., 2003).

## REFERENCES

Beckhard, R. & Dyer, W.G., Jr. (1983). Managing continuity in the family owned business. *Organizational Dynamics,* pp. 5-12.

Bork, D. (1986; 1993). *Family business, risky business: How to make it work.* New York: AMACOM; republished by Aspen, CO: Bork Institute for Family Business.

Bowen, M. (1978; 1988). *Family therapy in clinical practice.* Northvale, NJ: Jason Aronson.

Brockhaus, J. (2002). FFI time line. Xeroxed paper.

Correll, R. (2002, January). Recollections of the beginnings of the Family Firm Institute. Paper written in preparation for the FFI Annual Meeting in Dallas, Texas.

Danco, L.A. (1982a). *Beyond survival: A business owner's guide for success.* Cleveland, OH: University Press.

Danco, L.A. (1982b). *Inside the family business.* Englewood Cliffs, NJ: Prentice Hall.

Family Business Review (1988-2004). Various relevant articles.

FFI (2004). *The body of knowledge (BOK) book.* Boston: Family Firm Institute.

FFI (2005). *Yellow pages: A resource guide for family business professionals.* Boston: Family Firm Institute.

Gersick, K., Davis, J., McCollum-Hampton, M., & Lansberg, I. (1997). *Generation to generation: Life cycles of the family business.* Boston, MA: Harvard Business School Press.

Green, J. (2003, March). The emergence of the family business advisor. *International Investor,* pp. 280-281.

Kaslow, F.W. (1993). The lore and lure of family business. *American Journal of Family Therapy, 21*(1), 3-16.

Kaslow, F.W. (2004, September). Consultation with the Z family's technology business: A weekend retreat. *Contemporary Family Therapy, 26*(3), 231-240.

Kepner, E. (1983). The family and the firm: A co-evolutionary perspective. *Organizational Dynamics,* pp. 57-70.

McClendon, R. & Kadis, L.R. (2004). *Reconciling relationships and preserving the family business: Tools for success.* Binghamton, NY: The Haworth Press.

Murray, B., Schwass, J., & Ward, J.L. (2003, September/October). Lausanne: Where it's at. *Families in Business,* pp. 41-43.

Chapter 2

# International Expansion
# of Family Business Consultation:
# Consulting in Different Countries

Marta Vago

In this chapter, family business consulting in the international arena is explored from both historical and cross-cultural perspectives. Common patterns and enduring challenges family business consultants encounter in working with transnational clients and in managing international practices are identified. Options for contributing to the international family business arena are offered, and mechanisms for clarifying consultants' personal motivations and professional goals are suggested.

In today's global economy, every business must "internationalize" its perspective, whether it does business in other countries or not. Similarly, family business consultants must "internationalize" their perspectives in working with business families both in their own countries and in others. Most family businesses today can succeed only to the extent that they have factored global issues into their thinking. The same applies to family business consultants. This chapter focuses on some of the special concerns and unique challenges of family business consultants who work in the international arena.

Key terms used throughout the chapter have been defined as follows: "international" means two or more nations; "transnational" refers to the crossing of national boundaries; and "cross-cultural" connotes the convergence of divergent religious, ethnic, and/or social influences on human and institutional behaviors.

Some cross-cultural consulting dynamics are universal. They apply whether family business consultants drive across town or fly across oceans to meet with clients. Other cross-cultural issues are more relevant to consulting situations in which business families engage consultants from abroad. These issues can pose specific challenges between transnational consul-

*Handbook of Family Business and Family Business Consultation*
Published by The Haworth Press, Inc., 2006. All rights reserved.
doi:10.1300/5491_02

tants and individual international clients. This chapter is written from the viewpoint of transnational consulting, with special emphasis on U.S.-based family business consultants who are active in the international arena.

The rationale for focusing primarily on cross-cultural dynamics between American consultants and international clients is simple: Most transnational consultants are U.S. based and this is likely to be true for some years to come. This is primarily due to the fact that the field of family business-consulting came into being on U.S. soil. Its pioneering professionals were U.S. based. The majority of the Family Firm Institute's (FFI) founders were American, and 70 percent of its members still are American. How the growing number of family business professionals residing around the world will influence transnational family business consulting remains to be seen.

## *"INTERNATIONALIZATION" OF FAMILY BUSINESS*

For more than a decade, the visibility of the family business field worldwide has risen steadily. The recognition of family business consulting as a professional specialty is beginning to mirror the trend. The launching of the Family Firm Institute in 1986 set the stage and made it possible for both developments to occur. Once the conversation regarding the unique nature of family businesses began, it was only a matter of time before it became a rallying point for professionals from law, accounting, financial planning, banking, psychology, and family therapy, as well as for educators, researchers, and management consultants.

"Succession" was the universal language that helped spread the word about family business in professional communities and business communities alike. Academics lent credibility to the field, and "soft side" professionals put a human face on it. Researchers provided empirical data to practitioners, and consultants shared practical communication and problem-solving skills with family business clients. The vocabulary of succession both captured the minds and connected with the hearts of business families everywhere. Succession became the arena in which business families in all parts of the world could initiate important, and often difficult, conversations. As consciousness around succession concerns grew, so did the recognition by business families in different parts of the world that, with appropriate professional help, they could communicate better, plan more effectively for the future, manage smoother transitions from one leader to another, and enhance the longevity of the family legacy.

The universal challenges of succession and the promise of family business consulting catapulted family business consultants into the international arena. Collaboration between the Family Firm Institute and the Family Business Network, the international organization for business families, helped accelerate the pace at which family businesses worldwide began to seek assistance from family business consultants (see Chapter 1). Given the scarcity—or absence—of experienced family business professionals in most countries, family businesses turned to experts from abroad, primarily the United States, and to a large extent still do.

### Importance of Privacy and Secrecy

Scarcity of homegrown talent is not the only reason family businesses retained—and continue to retain—consultants from outside their own countries. Wealthy business families guard their privacy with great care and want as few people as possible to know anything about their affairs. High-profile families must maintain a certain public image, and, consequently, they trust few people with the truth behind that image. Some of these families go so far as to meet with family business consultants on secluded islands or chartered boats to ensure total privacy and anonymity. Clearly, few business families have the means to afford such privacy. However, business families at all economic levels tend to want the same thing: to hire the best consultant their money can buy and share the consultant's time with as few people as possible.

Business families' openness to work with consultants from abroad varies greatly around the world. It is safe to say the more insular a culture or country is, the more resistant to hiring "outside" consultants its business families are likely to be. Similarly, the less international in perspective a family business is, the less likely its owners are to avail themselves of consulting expertise outside their own country.

That said, family business consultants are ill-advised to equate the feelings of individual business families regarding "outside" family business consultants with the prevailing attitudes of their home culture. It is important to remember that the spirit of innovation that allows some family businesses to thrive while others falter may make them more amenable to seeking the counsel of family business consultants in general and from abroad in particular.

## THE INTERNATIONAL CONSULTING ARENA

The context in which international family business consultants do their work is complex and constantly changing. Economic cycles, political shifts, demographic changes, and social trends impact family businesses as much as do cultural norms, religious beliefs, and ethnic traditions. Our world is becoming increasingly seamless, as wireless technology, the Internet, global media, migration, and travel connect more and more people in different countries, living in different time zones, and speaking different languages. The new global marketplace demands both speed and accuracy in communication, including cross-cultural communication. In this high-stakes business environment, family business consultants must master the same challenges as their clients. Cultural literacy may be the primary competitive advantage some transnational family business consultants enjoy over others.

Family business consultants in the international arena are called upon to make ever-finer discernments regarding what is and what is not different about the issues family businesses face in various parts of the world. Similarly, they must become increasingly skilled in determining what interventions will achieve the proper balance between what is specific to a particular family in a specific culture and what are universal principles that have stood the test of time.

Family business consultants' own cultural biases inevitably influence what they perceive, think, and do when they work with family businesses in other countries. These biases include not only what they assume about their clients but also what they might assume about the consulting process itself. Some interesting books have been written regarding the impact of culture on corporate environments and doing business around the world. Among them, two stand out. *Tribes* (Kotkin, 1992) offers valuable insights into ethnically based business networks and how they further their members' collective business advantage. *Riding the Waves of Culture* (Trompenaars, 1994) is an indispensable guide to managing cultural complexities in the global marketplace. It is worth noting that Trompenaars's reference materials are predominantly from the fields of psychology, sociology, human behavior, and organization dynamics, the same professions that figured prominently in initially defining the family business field.

Since its launch in 1988, *Family Business Review,* the official publication of the Family Firm Institute, has given increasing attention to family business–related issues in different countries and cultures. In 1992, 1995, 1997, and 2000 *Family Business Review* devoted special issues to international perspectives on family enterprise, including ethnic, religious, and cultural dynamics.

Cross-cultural content in *Family Business Review* has primarily addressed family business issues that are specific to certain countries or regions, including Australia (Moores & Mula, 2000), Brazil (Curimbaba, 2002), Canada (Rothstein, 1992), China (Gatfield & Youseff, 2001), Finland (Koiranen, 2002), Germany (Klein, 2000), the Gulf Region (Davis, Pitts, & Cormier, 2000), Hong Kong (Yeung, 2000), Hungary (Hisrich &

Fulop, 1997), India (Manikutty, 2000), Italy (Corbetta, 1995), Latin America (Poza, 1995), the Netherlands (Floren, 1998), New Zealand (Keating & Little, 1997), the Philippines (Santiago, 2000), Poland (Welsch, Hills, & Hoy, 1995), Portugal (Howorth & Ali, 2001), Romania (Pistrui, Welsch, & Roberts, 1997), Scotland (Dunn, 1995), Singapore (Lee & Tan, 2001), Spain (Gallo, 1995), and the United Kingdom (Dunn, 1996; Dunn & Hughes, 1995). These articles address common family-business issues, such as succession or governance, focus on family-business challenges specific to a country, religion, or ethnic group, or explore both topics in tandem.

Some articles in *Family Business Review* have taken a comparative approach to cross-cultural dynamics in families and family enterprise. See for example articles on family businesses in Asia (Gersick, 1992); Australia, Canada, and Sweden (Andersson, Carlsen, & Getz, 2002); Central Europe, Western Europe, and the United States (Donckels & Lambrecht, 1999); Bulgaria and Romania (Poutziouris, O'Sullivan, & Nicolescu, 1997); East Asia (Chau, 1991); East and West Germany (Pistrui, Welsch, Wintermantel, Liao, & Pohl, 2000); India and Canada (Sharma & Rao, 2000); India and the United States (Salyards, 2000); Italy and the United States (Corbetta & Montemerlo, 1999); Romania and Italy (McKibbin & Pistrui, 1997); Romania, Poland, and the United States (Gundry & Ben-Yoseph, 1998); the United Kingdom, Germany, and Spain (Welsch, 1997); the United States and Australia (Smyrnios et al., 2003); and the United States, Finland, Chile, and Taiwan (Davis et al., 1996).

A handful of *Family Business Review* articles have addressed issues of transnational family business consulting and how family business consultants can meet the challenges of working with business families of different cultures in different countries (Donckels & Lambrecht, 1999; Lansberg & Perrow, 1991; Vago, 1995; Ward, 2000). Although "Ethnicity, Family and Family Business: Implications for Practitioners" (McGoldrick & Troast, 1993) does not address transnational consulting per se, its value to family business consultants should not be underestimated. As the Family Firm Institute's membership becomes more international, it is inevitable that *Family Business Review* will become increasingly responsive to transnational issues.

To date, research studies represent the preponderance of *Family Business Review* articles on international and cross-cultural issues. *Family Business Review*'s emphasis on research is understandable to the extent that it aims to be an academic journal. However, the utility of the research to transnational family business consultants varies greatly and tends to be somewhat limited. By contrast, this chapter is written from the cross-cultural perspective of a transnational family business consultant. While its content is supported by research both in and outside the family business field, the author's observations are gleamed predominantly from more than twenty-five years of consulting across cultures and continents, as well as from her own personal experiences.

## CONSULTING IN THE INTERNATIONAL ARENA

### Perceptions of Consultants and Consulting

The notion of business consulting is so recent in some parts of the world that some languages, such as Hungarian, have no word for it and have had to incorporate the English term into their vocabulary. The concept of family business consulting is even so new to the extent that most people in most parts of the world—including the United States—have never heard of it. Insufficient contextual meaning for family business consultation inevitably leads some business families to have unfounded, unrealistic, and/or inappropriate expectations of family business consultants from abroad.

In some cultures, consultants are looked upon as teachers and sages, not as skilled technicians in a particular field of endeavor. In these cultures, family business clients expect consultants to tell them what to do, whether they choose to follow the advice or not. A patriarch may engage a family business consultant from abroad to help manage succession but refuse to accept a female successor, no matter how qualified she may be. Similarly, a family business consultant may be called upon to mediate conflicts among family members, only to have his or her input ignored for fear of upsetting certain family members or violating long-standing family traditions.

Transnational family business consultants who insist clients come up with their own answers and solutions to problems may do little more than frustrate them. Frequently, business families outside the United States are astonished that they should be expected to have any answers or solutions. Their position is: "If we knew what to do, we wouldn't need you." Consequently, many transnational consultants may not be around long enough to witness the results of their efforts.

Most family businesses require consultants from abroad to submit proposals replete with detailed agendas, precise time frames, and specific approaches that, together, will lead to perfect results. Many business families are loath to accept that consultants have little, if any, control over family members' or anyone else's behavior. Such clients cannot understand why consultants, if they are any good, cannot predict what will happen and within what period of time. In contrast, some business families are satisfied with a basic proposal that describes what process might prove useful to produce certain results and how long it is reasonable to expect the process to take. These clients recognize the unpredictable nature of consulting engagements, especially when family relationships are involved.

It is safe to say, the less business families know about the family business field, the more likely they are to seek reassurance from structure and detail. Managing the proposal process without frightening or alienating potential clients can be a tough challenge for transnational family business consultants. As always, cultural literacy is a great asset in dealing with the wide range of concerns persons from different racial, religious, and ethnic backgrounds are bound to have regarding consultation in general and working with an "outside" family business consultant in particular.

## Dynamics of Power, Authority, and Control

Issues of power, authority, and control are embedded in every consulting relationship, but family business consultants in the international arena face a dizzying array of permissions, limitations, and injunctions that vary from culture to culture and from client to client. The degree to which consultants have the power to influence change, the authority to challenge and keep people accountable, and the control over various aspects of the consulting process are determined by many factors.

The amount of power, authority, and control a family business yields to a consultant from abroad is rooted in cultural precepts, religious principles, social customs, family traditions, individual personalities, attitudes toward gender and age, and any combination of these. Without exception, at least two of these factors are at play. Family business consultants in the international arena can be sure of one fact: No matter how much power, authority, and control they think they have, they will be proven wrong with time.

## Professional and Personal Boundaries

Family business clients almost always extend social invitations to their consultants from abroad. It is the polite thing to do, as they are far away from home, staying in a hotel in a foreign country whose language they may not understand. However, business families may invite outside consultants to social occasions for other reasons, as well. Personal settings give business families the opportunity to check out foreign consultants more thoroughly. How consultants conduct themselves at dinners, sporting events, receptions, and fund-raisers gives business families insight into the consultant they would not obtain otherwise. Lest one assume snobbery is at the root of this "testing" process, it is prudent to recognize that some business families outside the United States may consider poise, gracious manners, and ease in handling unfamiliar circumstances indications that the consultant is mature and sensitive enough to warrant the family's trust and confidence.

The more influential and wealthy the business family, the more likely it is to put consultants under such scrutiny. Family business consultants can gain or lose currency with transnational clients based on considerations they know nothing about or might not understand even if they were aware of them. Cultural literacy allows consultants to anticipate what personal traits and behavioral characteristics may matter more or less to certain business families in different parts of the world. Family business consultants who can act naturally under unnatural circumstances are at an advantage in the international arena.

In sum, transnational family business consultants are wise to remember that personal qualities may carry as much, if not more, weight as professional matters and that invitations from family business clients almost always serve more than social purposes. U.S.-based family business consultants whose discipline of origin frowns on "dual relationships," such as in psychology, must use great care and caution when they join clients in social activities. That said, trying to avoid dual relationships puts many transnational family business consultants in a bind. If they decline social invitations from their clients in other countries, the clients may feel insulted. If they accept such invitations, they may run afoul of their professions' codes of ethics.

When transnational family business consultants adhere to the professional codes of their home countries, their efficacy in working with international clients might suffer. For example, they may forfeit opportunities to gain their clients' trust and confidence more quickly. Speed in establishing rapport and working alliances with family business clients is especially important in the international arena. Geographic distances and other travel-related considerations translate into short time frames to accomplish ambitious agendas, tight scheduling with little room for spontaneous interaction, and weeks, if not months, between face-to-face meetings.

Both stateside and abroad, many family business consultants are challenged in reconciling some basic principles of family business consulting with certain ethical guidelines of their professions of origin. There are no easy answers to the dilemmas transnational family business consultants face in trying to optimize their own and their clients' resources, including time, money, knowledge, and personal experience. As the family business profession grows, so should family business consultants' options in serving their clients within acceptable legal and ethical bounds.

Apart from navigating professional and legal issues in the international arena, family business consultants' greatest challenge is how to honor their clients' most cherished values and principles, without compromising either the psychological distance necessary to assist clients or the ability to emotionally connect with business families in different parts of the world.

### Endings and Follow-Up

U.S.-based consultants value process issues more than their colleagues in other countries do. As such, they place great emphasis on follow-up and the importance of the consulting relationship itself. Consequently, they are regularly disappointed when their transnational family business clients consider the consulting engagement over once the stated goals are achieved. The clients perceive no valid reason to reconvene with the consultant, until or unless new issues come up. Nor do they understand the purpose of "keeping in touch" with the consultant. Although many U.S.-based family business consultants are accustomed to stateside clients' resistance to follow up, they tend to be puzzled when transnational clients show little or no interest in maintaining contact, no matter how successful the consulting engagement might have been.

Many transnational family business consultants find it disconcerting that it is harder for them to disengage from clients at the conclusion of the consulting assignment than it is for their clients to disengage from them. U.S.-based, "soft side" family business consultants are especially challenged in this regard. This is not surprising. The combination of relationship orientation and process orientation sets them up for disappointment in consulting to family enterprise in the international arena.

Regardless of professional origins, allowances, or constraints, few family business consultants are prepared for the emotional experience of working with clients in other parts of the world. They expect the professional challenges to be high, but they do not expect the level of attachment they may come to feel toward clients halfway around the world. Among the contributing factors is the "pressure cooker" effect of spending many hours in a few days with a client family. During this time, family business consultants tend to have little outside contact or stimulation, due to limitations ranging from time zones and Internet capabilities to fatigue and security concerns. All increase the emotional intensity of consulting to family businesses in the international arena and foster transnational consultants' emotional attachment to their clients.

### Emotions

Few qualities define a nation's character so much as how its people deal with emotions, both in feeling them and in expressing them. "Warm," "cold," "open," and "reserved" are words people everywhere use to describe how persons, groups, and nations deal with the emotional aspects of their circumstances and relationships. Like everyone else, family business consultants are products of their own culture, religion, and ethnicity. Therefore, they are just as likely as their clients to either emphasize or de-emphasize emotions in dealing with issues, including those that are unique to family enterprise. Family businesses usually have highly charged emotional environments. Therefore, trying to keep emotions out of the family business consulting process will yield no better results than trying to keep them out of family relationships. Transnational family business consultants walk an even more challenging tightrope in this regard than do their colleagues who consult to stateside clients, most of whom are less than seventy-five miles away.

It is difficult to strike the right balance between rationality and emotionality when consulting to business families, no matter who or where they are. Achieving that balance in the international arena is even more challenging. Different cultures place varying emphases on emotions and their expression. People from southern countries (e.g., southern Europe, Latin America) tend to be more emotion driven than are persons from northern regions (e.g., northern Europe, Canada). In highly structured societies, rationality is likely to take precedence over emotions. In repressive regimes, emotions may be luxuries few people can afford. Because business families are embedded in their local culture, it is safe to assume they are in concert with prevailing attitudes and customs regarding emotions and their expression. Therefore, transnational family business consultants should be prepared to adapt to their clients' frame of reference regarding emotions more than vice versa.

A perfect match between a client's and a consultant's emotional landscape is a rarity. The question is how far apart they can be and still work well together. It is a commonplace that U.S.-based consultants tend to have an emotional bias, whether they think they do or not. When "pursuit of happiness" is a constitutional right and "openness" defines American society, how could an American, including a family business consultant, not be biased toward expressing emotions? In the international arena, even the most cool-headed, rational and objective American may be perceived as too emotional.

It is also helpful to remember that Americans were among the first to embrace psychotherapy as a legitimate pursuit. As mentioned earlier, many of the founders, directors, and charter members of the Family Firm Institute were trained in the behavioral sciences. Even today, a large percentage of the Family Firm Institute's members are mental health professionals, and many continue to practice as psychotherapists, marriage and family counselors, industrial psychologists, and organization development consultants outside the family business field. "Soft side" professionals drove the development of the family business field, including defining its body of knowledge.

Willy-nilly, how transnational family business consultants factor emotions into working with family business clients is what differentiates them from all other advisors to family enterprises around the world. Proper attunement to a business family's ability to deal with challenging emotional issues, together with their willingness and desire to do so, constitute the unshakable foundation on which family business consulting engagements stand or fall. It takes a combination of empirical data, self-knowledge, psychological insight, intellectual rigor, empathy, daring, and discipline for transnational family business consultants to help clients of different nations, cultures, religions, and ethnicities to realize their goals and aspirations. Interest in transnational family business consulting is not enough.

## CRITICAL SUCCESS FACTORS IN CONSULTING TO FAMILY BUSINESSES INTERNATIONALLY

In addition to mastering the many challenges already mentioned, U.S.-based family business consultants are prudent to pay attention to the following considerations.

### Academic Achievement

Although some Americans may eschew the value of higher education in becoming successful in business and life, few people around the world share their sentiments. On the contrary, higher education is the sine qua non of respectability in most parts of the world. In many countries, including Mexico and India, only persons with engineering degrees are taken seriously in business. A degree in free-market economics, in combination with fluency in English, is now a basic requirement for conducting business successfully in formerly communist Central and Eastern European countries.

With the growing influence of global alliances, such as the European Union, transnational family business consultants with postgraduate degrees are likely to fare better in the international arena than are their less-pedigreed competitors. The more prestigious transnational family business consultants' degree-granting institutions are, the more favorably their potential family business clients will look upon them. Academic affiliations with marquee institutions such as Harvard University and The Wharton School of the University of Pennsylvania are bound to bolster the credibility of a family business consultant in the international arena. This is true even when their expertise is limited to teaching and research and, consequently, is devoid of hands-on business and/or business-consulting experience.

Interestingly, in some cases, academic degrees and university affiliations help to level the playing field for female transnational consultants in some parts of the world. Even in traditional, male-dominated cultures, business families may be amenable to hiring outside female consultants, as long as they are properly pedigreed academically. If they can get along with male decision makers and gain the trust of key female family members, female family business consultants in the international arena are likely to be perceived as "neuters" and may well enjoy a competitive edge over female consultants who practice in their own countries. How well female transnational family business consultants will fare in the international arena long term remains to be seen. Based on the history of the general marketplace, the author expects the percentage of female family business consultants in the international sphere to fall as the number of male family business consultants around the world rises.

### Life Experience

After education, perhaps nothing carries more weight in the international arena than the maturity of the family business consultant. Chronological age helps, but it is not enough. Business families want to work with consultants who have far more than intellectual understanding of what it takes to achieve both business success and family harmony. They want to feel assured the consultants they have hired have been through enough in life to bring wisdom, not just information, to what they do. Family business consultants must pass the "age test" in most parts of the world, but U.S.-based consultants bear a greater burden in this regard than do their colleagues from most other countries.

America's youth culture, together with the perceived ease with which Americans can gain affluence, suggests to many potential clients that U.S.-based family business consultants are out of touch with the real world. Right or wrong, pedigreed American academics and U.S.-based consultants with university affiliations are perceived as more attuned to the challenges of family enterprise, as well as more mature and experienced than their non-academic colleagues to offer useful advice to family businesses and business families.

## Cultural Sophistication

Many well-to-do business families around the world are deeply involved in the cultural life of their countries. Some are philanthropists of renown. It is safe to assume that a significant number of business families who engage outside family business consultants are major sponsors of cultural events in their communities. Some well-to-do business families are passionate about the arts and are serious collectors of art and antiques. Family business consultants with a working knowledge of art and other collectibles of worth may gain currency with transnational clients who place great value on such things. Again, this is not a matter of snobbism, but a search for common ground that allows some family business clients to connect with transnational consultants in ways that would be impossible otherwise.

In the cultural arena, U.S.-based consultants again carry a higher burden of proof. The United States continues to be perceived as a cultural wasteland, despite ample evidence to the contrary. This misperception is fed by Hollywood blockbusters that parade across movie and television screens in many parts of the world. Like other people around the globe, business families have a love-hate relationship with American popular culture. Therefore, transnational family business consultants who are culturally sophisticated and hip at the same time enjoy an advantage in establishing rapport with both current generations and successor generations in family enterprise.

Being well traveled is usually a plus for family business consultants in the international arena. This is not necessarily a matter of elitism on the part of the clients, although it can be, especially among families of great wealth. Conversations between transnational family business consultants and their clients regarding art, music, and travel can and do serve many purposes. They may be litmus tests for determining transnational consultants' maturity, life experience, and knowledge beyond what they learned in school. They may provide common ground to help establish rapport between consultants and clients. They may allow clients and consultants to talk meaningfully about matters of mutual interest, beyond the business at hand. Ultimately, the universal language of arts and travel may well be the best means to establish emotional connections between people of different cultures, races, and religions, including between family business consultants and their clients.

## Adaptability

Consultants in the international arena need to adapt to the customs and rituals of their clients, without undermining their efficacy in working with them. Maintaining proper balance between flexibility and adhering to structure is no easy task. Casual attire, approximate meeting times, leisurely lunches, and late dinners may rule in some parts of the world, while strict dress codes, punctuality, working lunches, and formal dining in the evening prevail in others. Transnational family business consultants must discern what is essential to serving their clients' needs and what is not. They need to determine when it is prudent to adapt to local customs and at what point they lose credibility and control, along with their authenticity and self-regard, by doing so.

Both family business consultants and family business clients can hide behind local customs, mores, and traditions to avoid dealing with thorny issues. Transnational family business consultants who are knowledgeable about cross-cultural issues are able to take local habits, customs, and practices into account without losing leverage in working with their clients.

### *Personality*

Family business consultants must be able to intuit clients' different comfort levels with people of varying personalities and to calibrate their own conduct accordingly. Transnational family business consultants are more challenged in interpreting the behavioral cues of their clients than are their homegrown counterparts. This is especially true for U.S.-based family business consultants. As mentioned earlier, the relative openness of American consultants may put them at a disadvantage in the international arena. Americans' basically optimistic outlook and "can do" attitude may ring hollow outside the United States. Their friendly demeanor and ready smile may engender more distrust than comfort in some parts of the world. As a Central European client put it: "Americans smile too much. It makes you wonder what they're hiding."

Be they Americans or citizens of other countries, many transnational family business consultants tend to underestimate the impact their voice volume, social demeanor, communication style, self-presentation, dress, use of humor, body language, and other "soft" considerations have on their clients. Even the most cross-culturally attuned outside consultants are likely to either underplay or overplay certain aspects of their personalities in dealing with clients. In general, transnational family business consultants are wise to assume that most business families throughout the world prefer professionals who are more reserved than outgoing in their comportment and interactions.

It is important to note that while American culture values and promotes extraversion in conduct, the opposite is true just about everywhere else in the world. That said, U.S.-based family business consultants with introverted personalities are likely to enjoy an advantage in the international arena that they may lack at home.

### Abiding Interest in Cross-Cultural Issues

A driving curiosity about different nations, cultures, religions, and ethnic groups distinguishes a small group of transnational family business consultants from others who are satisfied with doing just enough cultural "homework" to serve a specific client engagement. Both groups of consultants have much to offer to family businesses worldwide. However, only consultants in the first group bring cross-cultural wisdom—and not just facts and information—to working in the international arena.

Family businesses that want cross-cultural wisdom from consultants may be willing to pay a premium for it. However, they also expect a great deal from such consultants in return, as they should. Fortunately, it does not take long for a business family to find out how cross-culturally savvy a particular family business consultant is. Transnational consultants who are passionate about understanding cross-cultural dynamics can rest assured that their passion, knowledge, and wisdom do not go unnoticed by their clients.

## CRITICAL FAILURE FACTORS IN CONSULTING TO FAMILY BUSINESSES INTERNATIONALLY

In addition to identifying critical success factors in transnational family business consulting, it is prudent to consider critical failure factors (CFF), as well. Clearly, CFF are likely to be flip sides of the CSF discussed earlier. However, there is one that is not, namely, lack of staying power in the international consulting arena. Without extensive professional contacts, business connections, and personal networks in other countries, few transnational family business consultants can become—and remain—actively engaged and successful.

Family business consulting is a business like any other business. Consultants must invest time and money to establish viable practices, whether stateside or abroad. Those who compete in the international arena carry a double burden: They must devote resources to both building a transnational practice and keeping their domestic practice alive.

Strategic alliances between family business consultants have helped many to establish a sustainable presence in the international consulting arena. While some of these alliances are informal, opportunistic, and short term, others are formal, well planned, and long term by design. With few exceptions, family business consultants with significant transnational practices are parties to one or more strategic alliances comprised of educators, consultants, advisors, and researchers in the family business field.

## OPPORTUNITIES FOR FAMILY BUSINESS CONSULTANTS IN THE INTERNATIONAL ARENA

As the family business field expands its international presence, family business consultants will have more opportunities to contribute to the success of more businesses in more countries around the world. They can assist family businesses and business families by working with them directly. They can offer consulting services at different levels of profit or for no profit at all. They can work with one family business at a time or with groups of family businesses simultaneously. Group seminars and workshops allow business families of modest means to gain access to family business consultants whose professional fees exceed the financial capabilities of individual families. Pro bono workshops for family business groups in underdeveloped countries deliver incalculable benefits to business families who would never be able to enjoy them otherwise.

Family business consultants who desire a presence in the international arena can also help family businesses indirectly. They can leverage their knowledge through various university-based or private educational programs by helping to develop curricula and/or delivering course content. They can serve a wide swath of family businesses through their own publications or by contributing to others in the field. They can also train and coach new-generation family business consultants both stateside and abroad for a fee or on a pro bono basis.

The options for family business consultants to make a difference in the international arena are many. The opportunities to generate significant income from doing it are limited, except for a handful of consultants who entered the field early and/or have formed joint ventures or strategic alliances with other family business consultants. No doubt, it is prestigious to consult in the international arena, which is why so many family business consultants want to do so. However, it can be years before family business consultants have enough information and experience to decide if consulting in the international arena is right for them.

## THE TRANSNATIONAL FAMILY BUSINESS CONSULTING EQUATION

The international family business consulting field offers unparalleled opportunities for professional growth and personal satisfaction. However, it is also fraught with frustrations and disappointments. Ultimately, every family business consultant must decide what combination of professional satisfaction, personal fulfillment, and financial reward makes transnational consulting an attractive value proposition.

The joys of transnational consulting are in the hearts of family business consultants. The advantages are in their minds. The benefits are in their pocketbooks. One fact is certain: It behooves family business consultants to make clear what they hope to gain by working in the international arena. It may be helpful to ask themselves: "If I had to pay to work with family businesses in other countries and had the money to do it, would I? If yes, why; if no, why not? In order to decide what is an acceptable return on investment for working in the international arena, family business consultants are encouraged to determine what premium they are willing to pay for experiences they would not have otherwise.

Clearly, the answers to these questions are highly personal, as well as revealing. For better or worse, they surface family business consultants' motivations for seeking transnational consulting engagements. Motivations run the gamut from making money, empowering family businesses in emerging economies, and professional development, to research opportunities, travel, and cultivating a global network of business and personal relationships.

Family business consultants may seek transnational consulting assignments for one reason and later pursue them for another. No matter what their original reasons may be, once they begin working in the international arena, they soon realize that many of their experiences are foreclosed to others. With every transnational engagement, family business consultants' perspectives of family enterprise widen and their appreciation of different peoples and cultures deepen. Transnational consulting can be fulfilling and exciting, even life changing. However, it can also be seductive. It is easy to lose sight of the purpose for doing it.

All consultants in the international arena must eventually decide what balance between remuneration, intellectual stimulation, dedication to service, lifestyle considerations, and other factors will work for them. There is no one formula for all, nor will any formula work at every stage of a specific consultant's life and/or career. Every formula is destined to outlive its usefulness, and family business consultants are advised to keep this in mind when they calculate the anticipated costs and benefits of working in the international arena.

The international family business consulting field is a work in progress, as is every transnational family business consultant, every family enterprise, and every business family around the world.

## REFERENCES

Andersson, T., Carlsen, J., & Getz, D. (2002). Family business goals in the tourism and hospitality sector: Case studies and cross-case analysis from Australia, Canada and Sweden. *Family Business Review, 15*(2), 89-106.

Chau, T.T. (1991). Approaches to succession in East Asian business organizations. *Family Business Review, 4*(2), 161-179.

Corbetta, G. (1995). Patterns of development of family businesses in Italy. *Family Business Review, 8*(4), 255-265.

Corbetta, G. & Montemerlo, D. (1999). Ownership, governance and management issues in small and medium-size family businesses: A comparison of Italy and the United States. *Family Business Review, 7*(4), 361-374.

Curimbaba, F. (2002). The dynamics of women's roles as family business managers. *Family Business Review, 15*(3), 239-252.

Davis, J.A., Pitts, E., & Cormier, K. (2000). Challenges facing family companies in the Gulf Region. *Family Business Review, 13*(3), 217-237.

Davis, J.A., Swartz, J., Blakely, E.B., Chang, C., Eyzaguirre, J.G., Mattson, R., & Petker, J.D. (1996). A comparison of four countries' estate laws and their influence of family companies. *Family Business Review, 9*(3), 285-294.

Donckels, R. & Lambrecht, J. (1999). Are family businesses different? What we know from Western European business research that could be applied to the reemergence of family-based enterprises in East Central Europe. *Family Business Review, 12*(2), 171-188.

Dunn, B. (1995). Success themes in Scottish family enterprises: Philosophies and practices through the generations. *Family Business Review, 8*(1), 17-28.

Dunn, B. (1996). Family enterprises in the U.K.—A special factor? *Family Business Review, 9*(2), 139-155.

Dunn, B. & Hughes, M. (1995). Themes and issues in the recognition family businesses in the United Kingdom. *Family Business Review, 8*(4), 267-291.

Floren, R.H. (1998). The significance of family business in the Netherlands. *Family Business Review, 11*(2), 121-134.

Gallo, M.A. (1995). Family businesses in Spain: Tracks followed and outcomes reached by those among the largest thousand. *Family Business Review, 8*(4), 245-254.

Gatfield, T. & Youseff, M. (2001). A critical examination of and reflection on the Chinese family business unit and the Chinese family business clan. *Family Business Review, 14*(2), 153-158.

Gersick, K.E. (1992). Ethnicity and organizational forms: An interview with William Ouchi. *Family Business Review, 5*(4), 417-436.

Gundry, L.K. & Ben-Yoseph, M. (1998). Women entrepreneurs in Romania, Poland and the United States: Cultural and family influences on strategy and growth. *Family Business Review, 9*(1), 61-73.

Hisrich, R.D. & Fulop, G. (1997). Women entrepreneurs in family business: The Hungarian case. *Family Business Review, 10*(3), 281-302.

Howorth, C. & Ali, Z.A. (2001). Family business succession in Portugal: An examination of case studies in the furniture industry. *Family Business Review, 14*(3), 231-244.

Keating, N.C. & Little, H.M. (1997). Choosing the successor in New Zealand family firms. *Family Business Review, 10*(2), 157-171.

Klein, S.B. (2000). Family businesses in Germany. *Family Business Review, 13*(3), 157-181.

Koiranen, M. (2002). Over 100 years of age but still entrepreneurially active in business: Exploring the values and characteristics of old Finnish family firms. *Family Business Review, 15*(3), 175-187.

Kotkin, J. (1992). *Tribes: How race, religion and identity determine success in the new global economy.* New York: Random House.

Lansberg, I. & Perrow, E. (1991). Understanding and working with leading family businesses in Latin America. *Family Business Review, 4*(2), 127-147.

Lee, J.S.K. & Tan, F. (2001). Growth of Chinese family enterprise in Singapore. *Family Business Review, 14*(1), 49-74.

Manikutty, S. (2000). Family business groups in India. *Family Business Review, 13* (4), 279-292.

McGoldrick, M. & Troast, J.G., Jr. (1993). Ethnicity, families and family business: Implications for practitioners. *Family Business Review, 6*(3), 283-299.

McKibbin, P. & Pistrui, D. (1997). East meets West: Innovative forms of foreign trade finance between Italian family enterprises and emerging SMEs in Romania. *Family Business Review, 10*(3), 263-280.

Moores, K. & Mula, J. (2000). The salience of market, bureaucratic and clan controls in the management of family firm transitions: Some tentative Australian evidence. *Family Business Review, 13*(2), 91-106.

Pistrui, D., Welsch, H.P., & Roberts, J.S. (1997). The [re]-emergence of family businesses in the transforming former Soviet Bloc: Family contributions to entrepreneurship development in Romania. *Family Business Review, 10*(3), 221-237.

Pistrui, D., Welsch, H.P., Wintermantel, O., Liao, J., & Pohl, H.J. (2000). Entrepreneurial orientation and family forces in the new Germany: Similarities and differences between East and West German entrepreneurs. *Family Business Review, 13*(3), 251-263.

Poutziouris, P., O'Sullivan, K., & Nicolescu, L. (1997). The [re]-generation of family-business entrepreneurship in the Balkans. *Family Business Review, 10*(3), 239-261.

Poza, E. (1995). Global competition and the family-owned business in Latin America. *Family Business Review, 8*(4), 301-311.

Rothstein, J. (1992). Don't judge a book by its cover: A reconsideration of eight assumptions about Jewish family businesses. *Family Business Review, 5*(4), 397-411.

Salyards, D.M. (2000). Doing business in India: A Minnesota entrepreneur's experience. *Family Business Review, 13*(4), 331-338.

Santiago, A.L. (2000). Succession experience in Philippine family businesses. *Family Business Review, 13*(1), 15-40.

Sharma, P. & Rao, A.S. (2000). Successor attributes in Indian and Canadian family firms: A comparative study. *Family Business Review, 13*(4), 313-330.

Smyrnios, K.X., Romano, C.A., Tanewski, G.A., Karofsky, P.I., Millen, R., & Yilmaz, M.R. (2003). Work-family conflict: A study of American and Australian family businesses. *Family Business Review, 16*(1), 35-51.

Tan, W. & Fock, S.T. (2001). Coping with growth transitions: The case of Chinese family businesses in Singapore. *Family Business Review, 16*(2), 123-139.

Trompenaars, F. (1994). *Riding the waves of culture.* Chicago: Irwin Professional Publishing.

Vago, M. (1995). Why fish must learn to see the water they swim in. *Family Business Review, 8*(4), 313-325.

Ward, J.L. (2000). Reflections on Indian family groups. *Family Business Review, 13*(4), 271-278.

Welsch, H., Hills, G., & Hoy, F. (1995). Family impacts on emerging ventures in Poland. *Family Business Review, 8*(4), 293-300.

Welsch, J. (1997). East meets a West-German-multinational family firm during reunification and transition: A personal voice. *Family Business Review, 10*(3), 303-308.

Yeung, H.W. (2000). Limits to the growth of family-owned business? The case of Chinese transnational corporations from Hong Kong. *Family Business Review, 13*(1), 55-70.

# PART II:
# VARIOUS MODELS OF FAMILY
# BUSINESS CONSULTING/ADVISING

Chapter 3

# The Aspen Family Business Group Consulting Process: A Model for Deep Structural Change and Relationship Shift in Complex Multigenerational Enterprising Family Systems

Dennis T. Jaffe
Leslie Dashew
Sam Lane
Joseph Paul
David Bork

This chapter presents the model developed over the past seventeen years by the Aspen Family Business Group. It presents pathways for working with complex families regarding issues of family and business/wealth management, drawing on the perspectives of family therapy and process consulting primarily, but informed by the perspectives of law, estate planning, and business management. It approaches the family as a whole system, and through using it we build capability in the family for making choices and taking aligned action. It engages the family in a dialogue and problem solving process that moves through both the family and business domains of the family. It helps family members create structures, agreements, and relationship skills not just to resolve a single crisis but to develop the capacity to respond to increasing numbers of people and increasing complexity as they move through the generations. Through a case example, we show how a family can gather and create a "constitutional convention" to develop effective governance, alignment, and communication. Case vignettes are interspersed throughout the chapter to demonstrate the points being made.

*Handbook of Family Business and Family Business Consultation*
Published by The Haworth Press, Inc., 2006. All rights reserved.
doi:10.1300/5491_03

## THE CHALLENGES OF TRANSFORMATION
## IN ENTERPRISING FAMILIES

It is quite a task for a wealthy family to effectively own and manage a business and other substantial ventures, sustain connection in their family, and successfully pass their assets, capabilities, and values across generations. They need a lot of help. The helpers include, at various times, estate planners, lawyers, tax and insurance specialists, accountants, investment advisors, management consultants, and family therapists. They all have their own skills, perspectives, and models of the family and what it needs. However, a family does not see its needs divided into these disciplinary packages. They want help with challenges, but increasingly they want integrated, holistic, long-term resolutions. The advisor cannot work as a lone wolf, but must become part of a team whose members integrate and align their interventions to meet the needs of the family.

Our approach to family business consulting aims to create a metastructure that can accomplish this task, and work with families to manage transitions and develop their own capabilities to meet the complex challenges they face. People come into this type of work from various "professions of origin" and then proceed to learn techniques, models, and approaches that span all the disciplines. Each advisor may apply his or her own disciplinary solutions to tax, financial, or estate problems, but within a container of helping the family manage its transition.

Family business consultants or advisors have begun to create a set of models, tools, and approaches to help families. They begin with a view of the family and its various enterprises (often much more than a single operating company) as a whole system. Their desire is not to deliver a solution to the family but to do this with the family in such a way that the overall capability of the whole family/business/wealth system is increased. They are therefore not doing transactions with the family, but helping the family in a process which not only responds to the challenge but also offers the family added capability to face the next crisis on its own. They therefore help the family develop and learn how to use tools, structures, agreements, and enhanced relationship skills to manage their complex affairs. This has been called *process consulting* and is an alternative to the traditional expert consulting role.

The work of advising a family is a process of learning and capacity building. The client cannot be a single individual, such as the family leader or patriarch, but must be the whole family system. It also follows that there will be a high degree of involvement from all members of the family, not just those involved in the business and financial entities. Another aspect of consulting is that the solutions to problems do not lie in the business area alone, but must also focus back on the family relationships—the deep emotional connections, rivalries, hurts, and shared experiences that make up the fabric of a family. A consultant must be able to respond to the business and financial issues and must also be prepared to delve into the emotional dimensions that may block the formulating of reasonable business agreements and prevent family growth and development.

## HISTORY AND DEVELOPMENT OF THE ASPEN MODEL

The members of the Aspen Family Business Group came together in 1987 in the formative years of the Family Firm Institute (FFI). Each of us had a foot in two worlds—the world of organization development and process consulting, and the world of family systems. We were just becoming aware of the financial and business dimensions of family business and estate planning. We profited from the framework that was developing at FFI through the work of numerous early members, many of whom are contributing authors to this book.

At the FFI conferences we came together around our passion for working with families, our desire to create a learning community to process the challenges we were facing, and the many ways that we were learning in this emerging field. We decided not to work together as a consulting firm per se, but as an association that would create joint research, projects, and learning activities for families and their advisors. We have presented at each of the FFI conferences and at many other gatherings for families and advisors as we were developing our ideas. We have written a book for advisors (Bork, Jaffe, Dashew, Lane, & Heisler, 2004) and several books for families (Dashew, 1997; Bork, 1986; Jaffe, 2004), and have created the Aspen Family Business Inventory (Jaffe & Paul, 1998), an assessment tool for families in business (visit our Web site, aspenfamilybusiness.com for additional descriptions of our work).

At the root of our approach are two foundations—family systems theory and organizational development. We all feel that the family system is the substratum of family business, and we have drawn deeply, as others have, from the intergenerational perspective of Murray Bowen (Bowen, 1978; Kerr & Bowen, 1988) and other structural intergenerational family therapy models. We draw on Bowen's genogram to frame the family relationships (McGoldrick & Gerson, 1985), and on his concepts of intergenerational transmission, individuation as a core task in the family, unraveling of communication triangles and emotional short circuits, and looking at effects of birth order, gender, and family legacy as core for understanding the family's "stuck points" in their business and development.

While our conceptual models come from family systems, our interventions derive more from the tradition of organizational process consulting, as taught by Douglas McGregor, Edgar Schein, Ron Lippitt, Chris Argyris, Dick Beckhard, Rosabeth Kanter, Warren Bennis, Herb Shepard, and Peter Senge (all cited in Weisbord's 1978 history of the field). They taught us to attend to the role of our self as we entered the family system (which we also learned from family therapy) and to look at what we were doing—the behavior we were modeling—as well as what we were saying. They taught us that our goal was to develop the family, not tell them what to do. They taught us techniques for convening large family groups as learning communities and for helping them develop their own structures for governance and leadership. The legacy of both of these traditions will be seen in our model.

As we grew more mature in our work, we found ourselves working with larger and more complex families. Our model initially focused on generational transitions within one family business and family succession. Over time, we have begun to work also with families who span many generations and who have multiple financial and business enterprises. We are now working with large communities that began as families but are now networks of families. Some of them have sustained a common heritage and identity and governing structure over several generations, and we have learned from them. The center of our own personal growth, and our most important learning laboratory, has been our annual Aspen Family Business Gathering, held the first week of August in Aspen, Colorado, for the past fifteen years. The gathering is attended by members of business families—not just the people in the business, but all members of the family who care to attend. Generally, each family brings people from two or more generations (once we had fourteen members of four generations of a family from Colombia), often including teenagers and young adults. The format is not for the "experts" to lecture or present to families (although we do present a conceptual framework and some tools to help families understand their experience and develop a common language). Rather, it is an opportunity for families to dialogue and learn from one another across families and across generations. At the gathering each family introduces themselves and shares their genogram (a family diagram of their members in several generations and their relationships to one another). We have workshops on challenges each family faces, and small group dialogues for business leaders, spouses, next generation, in-laws, family members not involved in the business, women, and other "interest" groups. We have meals together and lots of afternoon time for fun and informal contact. We transcribe some of what the different groups report, and we learn from their experience.

The families tell us that they benefit immensely as well. For some of them, it is the first time they get to meet other families with similar dilemmas. Although people have come to the gathering from all over the world, they find that every family is unique, but the challenges they face of combining family and business are also shared and common. Many of the families attending also work individually with a consultant, but we find that the dimension of shared learning and the community that is formed provides another kind of learning that cannot be found in individual consultation. They have also helped us develop our ideas about consulting, and by keeping in touch and checking in periodically, we have been able to develop a perspective of the effects of our work over many years. In fact, we have worked with a few of our family clients for more than two generations!

## PRINCIPLES OF OUR PRACTICE

Eight core principles form the foundation of our practice:

### Engage the Entire System

Our client is the family and its business(es). Thus, we engage the entire system in the process and all constituents: family members, owners, key nonfamily employees, and other advisors. Our involvement with all stakeholders is based on a respect for all and recognition that any part of the system can lead or hold back the rest. The theory of cognitive dissonance is relevant here: the more one is engaged in analyzing a problem and coming up with a solution, the more committed he or she is to seeing it implemented. This is generally true, even if the particular solution is not the one a given individual prefers.

For example, when we are exploring the vision for the future of a family and its business, it is important that we gain the perspective of all generations to include the family members who are actively engaged in the business as well as those who are not. This gives us the opportunity to explore what is important to all groups, as well as their hopes and dreams. Then we can help them develop a shared understanding of what is possible and what is not.

> Mrs. T became the chairperson of the family's large road construction company upon the death of her husband. Although she had been her husband's "sounding board" during their life together, she had no business background. Her two offspring were involved in the business, but not in leadership positions. She was concerned that the (nonfamily) president was not competent or trustworthy. The president, on the other hand, felt the family did not appreciate him, his hard work, or the results he had achieved in the five years since the founder had died (even though he tripled the volume and profits). The gulf between

family and nonfamily constituents increased over the years, creating more distrust and frustration all the way around.

Our work with them included educating the family about how to measure the effectiveness of the president and creating the setting for a shared look at the future. Together, we developed the strategic direction for the company and a "dashboard" of measures that were agreed upon by all groups to assure that the company was progressing as planned. The involvement of both generations of family members, key executives, and members of the board helped everyone feel valued and increased the trust and openness in the system.

### *Complex Systems Require Interventions Based on a Wide Range of Behavioral Science Interventions and Knowledge*

As complex human systems, family businesses have subsystems that are not normally together (family and business) and often overlapping roles (family membership, ownership, employment). We use a combination of process consultation and structural interventions based on a foundation of organizational development, human systems theory, and individual and family psychology to address this complexity. We often work on different levels of intervention concurrently (e.g., establishing infrastructure, helping to work through conflict, and/or clarifying roles and accountabilities at the same time).

We define "structural interventions" to mean establishing legitimizing structures for communication (family councils, boards of directors, management teams) and governance (via boards of directors, constitutions, shareholder agreements).

> For example, in the previous case, the daughter-in-law did not feel she had a right to participate in discussions relating to the family and its businesses because she did not work in the family business. However, she was the mother of the heirs to the business and was concerned about decisions being made which would affect her children. By establishing a family council in which all family members sixteen years of age and older could participate, the daughter-in-law lent her considerable intelligence and objectivity to the family and its deliberations. She helped the family to look objectively at the work of the president and, because of her own experience in business, realized the importance of acknowledging his contributions.

However, commitments to rational agreements and contracts typically will not control family dynamics. Family issues must be dealt with directly. Our process interventions include skill building (especially interpersonal skills) as well as team building, process design, and sharing of knowledge. We help families learn how to listen effectively to one another to appreciate the contributions of differing perspectives, often through the use of personality inventories such as the Myers-Briggs Type Indicator (Myers, Kirby, &

Myers, 2003), and how to share their perspective in an assertive, rather than an aggressive, manner.

### Attend to the Family's Advisory System

Many consultants neglect the advisory system that is attached to every client-family. We believe it is important to attend to the status of the client's advisors and the advisors' relationships with one another as we become part of that advisory system. Our attention to this dimension of our client's situation has led us to a typology of advisory systems that helps us make better initial assessments and plan our entry. This typology is as follows:

- Disjointed—The advisors are unknown to one another.
- Autonomous—The advisors are known to one another only through the client.
- Partially aligned—Some advisors are connected through client, and others work cooperatively.
- Collaborative—Advisors are known to one another and led by one. Needs of client are superordinate to any advisory competition.
- Advisory team—An interactive team led by client focuses on interdisciplinary collaboration to meet the needs of the client.
- Strategic alliance—Advisors from two or more disciplines work in an ongoing collaborative relationship.
- Consulting firm—A preexisting interdisciplinary team is hired by client.

Our entry into the client and advisory systems will be influenced by which type we seem to be joining. A situation in which the client is clearly leading an integrated advisory system will be very different from one in which the advisors are engaging in what we call "the dance of most trusted advisor status." In the latter case, the client leadership is often immobilized by ongoing competition among two or three advisors. Although the best work usually takes place when we enter and work conjointly as part of a team, it is not always possible to configure such a team. At the very least, it is the consultant's responsibility to honor the realities of the existing advisory system, be a good collaborator, and make skillful referrals when necessary.

Because we are working at the interface of the family and business and engaging the entire system, we recognize that we must work as part of an interdisciplinary team and thus collaborate with professionals from other disciplines. We utilize the expertise of our colleagues from various technical specialties. For example, most families struggle with how to treat offspring "fairly." Many think that "fair" means "equal." We suggest that there may be other ways to cut the pie such that everyone feels treated fairly. We may suggest that the offspring working in the family business receive ownership of the stock in the company while those not active in the business receive cash distributions from insurance proceeds which equal the value of the business share they might have received. This is a strategy in which the expertise of our colleagues from the financial planning field can lend great assistance as part of the team. Accounting, legal, banking, executive compensation, and career planning specialists are among those whose talents are often part of such an interdisciplinary team.

### Our Work Is About Helping Both Individuals and Systems Move in a Positive Direction

Our initial assessment process helps us understand the starting point for our work with the family and then creates the foundation to identify or establish a shared vision for the future. The interventions must be based on an assessment process that includes both family and business dynamics. We utilize a combination of group meetings, individual interviews, tools (such as the Aspen Family Business Inventory [Jaffe & Paul, 1998]), and review of family and business documents as part of our assessment.

We believe in the positive potential of a client system, assuming that it is at least a somewhat an "open" system and allows input from outside of its boundaries. This openness may be described as a "willingness to learn and grow," to listen openly, and/or to be a learning environment. David Bork's analysis of 250 family interventions led him to generate the "Ten Qualities of Successful Families in Business" (Nelton, 1991), which outlines qualities that we help families to learn (see Chapter 16 for discussion of these Ten Qualities).

On occasion we find that key people in the system are not truly open at a point in time to change. In this case we may determine that this is not a "doable deal" and decline the opportunity to work with the client at this time, or we may find a way to move despite the impediment. For example, several times we have advised second-generation sibling groups that they can meet even without the participation or active involvement of their patriarch, to begin to explore how to work as a family team when the time comes to take up their responsibility. This involves the generation discovering their own responsibility and acting on their own, without necessarily generating a confrontation with the patriarch.

The parents invited us in to meet with the family because they were struggling with identifying a successor. The father and the employees felt that the son who had worked there for many years had the skills and disposition to be a successor. The younger son, on the other hand, had left the business some years ago and had been in conflict with many employees. The mother was unwilling to consider any succession option that did not include the younger son as leader, no matter what anyone said. Her rigidity and unwillingness to consider what others thought was a workable solution made the engagement impossible at that time.

## Change Involves Helping Clients Reframe Their Experience in a Constructive Light

The way that clients perceive their situation, what is possible, and why things are being done is the foundation for how they act. Much of our consulting involves showing clients that there are other ways to see their situation and what is possible. This "reframing" provides an alternative meaning to a situation that makes sense to the client. For example, a fear of bringing the family together is often expressed as "I don't want my family to make the choices about what I do with my company." Reframing would suggest that the family meeting is not an attempt to institute a family democracy, but rather is about listening to other people's ideas and sharing one's own hopes and desires.

The way a topic is framed sets the boundaries and direction of the dialogue—many times the conclusion follows from the premise. Often families will have conflicts because of the way they are framing a situation. They do not stop to consider alternatives because they are so emotionally involved, they want to be right, and they cannot see the big picture. They tend to see alternatives as black and white, either/or options, rather than exploring middle grounds or other alternatives. Then they react to how they see the events, rather than the way they are. By reframing we provide a different interpretation that leads to a conclusion that is easier to deal with— we get them to see it differently.

One of the effects of reframing is a shift in the emotional state of individuals as a result of a different meaning being given to something, such as an incident in the past or the reason a relative is doing what she is doing. When we change the emotional mind-set or the interpretation of an event or situation, we open up possibilities. For example, a family was frustrated by the trouble and conflict that arose in the transition to the next generation. The consultant reframed their struggle by saying, "Most families have trouble with succession—it is normal—it may take three to five years," which made them more patient. Or a son feeling that "Dad doesn't ever want me to run things—he is holding me back" was reframed and softened by noting that "Some fathers have trouble letting go."

### Change Requires Trust, Integrity, and Communication

The initial responsibility of the consultant is to create a context that is safe enough for the family to have conversations they have been avoiding. To do this the advisor must be seen as trustworthy in the eyes of a critical mass of the client/family. This requires a high level of integrity on the part of the consultant in maintaining neutrality and connection to all parts of the system. This also requires that we use our "selves" effectively, maintaining appropriate boundaries, avoiding dual relationships, and using self-disclosure in a manner that aids the growth of the client.

For example, most of us conduct an initial educational program for the client system as a beginning point in our work together. During this time, we present the family with an understanding of the typical dynamics, pitfalls, and developmental stages of families in business. We usually involve the family in dialogue and exercises in which they participate actively. During this meeting, we carefully listen to each member of the family, demonstrating that we are interested in each person's perspective and that we are not coming into this work with a bias toward one member or another. We work for the whole family, not the family leader, which means that we must make our initial contract with the family.

Maintaining a calm, nonreactive demeanor assuring that each person's point of view is honored (even if we might disagree with it) is essential to creating a safe harbor. Many family members have great trepidation about talking openly, and they need a great deal of help to feel safe and comfortable. Establishing ground rules for the meetings of the family (e.g., respectful listening, showing up on time, being open to exploring a range of alternatives) is another tool that encourages a sense of security and safety.

### Focus on Differentiation and Individuation of People and Subsystems

Ultimately, regardless of professional background, successful family business consultation can be measured in the degree of differentiation and clarity of boundaries it has stimulated in individuals and in the client system. The concept of differentiation (Bowen, 1978; Kerr & Bowen, 1988) addresses the development of individual maturity within the context of family relationships. We have expanded the use of this concept from the individual psychological level to those of the individual fiduciary and governance subsystems.

In the family business context, individual differentiation is more than just about becoming a mature adult. It is also relevant in the context of growing into new fiduciary roles, for example, becoming a CEO, a director, or a trustee. Friedman (1988) outlines the traits of the "differentiated leader." In coaching successors into taking on these fiduciary roles we often describe the process as "finding one's voice," as a director or family council member. In many ways this aspect of differentiation is about becoming a peer to one's parents professionally and responsibly exercising authority with siblings and parents.

We have expanded the concept of individual differentiation into our work with subsystems of the larger family/business system. At the subsystemic level we are stimulating underdeveloped (and nonexistent) subsystems into well-differentiated ones (e.g., board of directors meetings that are not sidetracked by family dynamics). Whether through the creation of a "real" board of directors, family council, shareholders group, or management team, we are in each case helping family business subsystems become more differentiated. This means they become less emotionally reactive, become more rational and factual in their deliberations, have clearer boundaries, and have a clear vision about their collective responsibilities. It is obvious to us that we cannot create well-differentiated subsystems from poorly differentiated individuals.

## *Follow the Time Frame of the System, Not of the Advisor*

Because of the complexity of a family business system, we believe that the timing of interventions and change may not fit nicely into our schedules or time frames. Rather, they are organic and reflect the nature of each client system. We often have a long-term relationship with our clients, wherein they access us at different points in their individual, family, or organizational life cycles to be of assistance in handling the challenges that face them at different times. We may see what needs to be done and who needs to do what in the family to bring the family to the outcomes they desire. However, the rate of absorption of change for the family as a whole may not follow a plan we desire, or even the desired pace of individual members.

> The father called us to assist with the transition to the next generation of family leadership. His brothers had resented his selection as president, and he did not want his six offspring to have the same problem. He felt he knew which of his children would be the best choice but was concerned that if he made the selection, the young man would be doomed to be resented by his siblings. We

developed a process of education of the six siblings about leadership, the needs of the business, and the roles they could each play as board members and employees. We engaged different siblings in educational experiences that helped them gain insight into themselves as well as one another. The process took two years, but at the end the sibling group selected the young man whom the father thought would be best. He could have made the announcement two years before, but would not have engendered the support of all siblings for the successor president.

## MOVING FROM PERSONALITY-CENTERED TO PRINCIPLE-CENTERED FAMILIES

A major premise underlying our work is that in order for a family-owning business to be successful it needs to be organized and live according to a set of agreed-upon principles, rather than that their processes being dominated by the personality of an individual. When the process is dominated by people with strong personalities, then the decision-making, problem-solving and interpersonal relationships are subject to all the risks associated with ill-defined interpersonal interactions: conflict, poor communication, greed, a sense of entitlement, personal agendas, egotism, sibling rivalry, or just "having a bad day." Although these factors may still exist in a principle-centered family, their negative impact is greatly minimized. These principles transcend any one person's power and level the playing field. Effective families prenegotiate areas of potential conflict, and this helps the family better weather times of crisis.

A parallel situation on a much broader scale exists in the United States where we operate according to rules of law instead of as a monarchy or dictatorship. The difference is that in a democracy the power is vested in the rules, not in a person. These rules of law are institutionalized in our Constitution, Bill of Rights, and other governance documents. We advocate that the family develop similar understandings, agreements, and expectations as a way of managing and organizing themselves. These agreed-to principles are put into a family constitution. A constitution is an instrument of governance that establishes a framework and a forum for a group of equals to deliberate issues, create policies and procedures, clearly define rights and obligations of participants, and make decisions about important issues that they share.

As a family goes through generations and its branches have more people who are less connected, they need a governance apparatus that sets up structures to regulate the family members' shared financial and business dealings and ensure that each member receives predictable and fair treatment. A constitution expresses the will of the family for future generations. Most important, it creates a foundation for maintaining trust within the family and for guiding the distribution of resources. It helps clarify everyone's expectations so family members do not have to "read the tea leaves" to understand what Mom or Dad or Uncle Donald have in mind for them. It gives family members the basic security of knowing what they can expect from the business, as well as how they can participate in it.

The constitution also institutionalizes the idea that each individual has consciously made a decision to join with the others. Tantamount to this decision is the commitment to live by these principles. It is somewhat similar to when the thirteen sovereign states wanted to institutionalize their relationships to reduce conflict and create a single more powerful entity. In this case the constitution emerged as a masterfully constructed document that balanced the competing interests of the individual states as a whole and defined the common values that would guide the new country's stance in the world.

Like the U.S. Constitution, a family constitution sets high standards that may not always be followed and practiced. Sometimes behavior falls short of expectations and a sense of entitlement overwhelms an obligation to duty and to the stewardship of the family and the business. What happens then? Unlike state governments, most families do not have good judicial systems to mediate disputes. A constitution can help by defining mechanisms for resolving disputes.

We suggest that a strong commitment to and emphasis on the use of well-constructed business plans with regular monitoring contributes greatly to the success of the interaction of the three major elements of the governance structure. The family constitution can be conceptualized as the integrated statement that brings together several types of agreement that regulate the family, its various enterprises, and the relations of family members as owners and managers to each of the businesses and the family as a whole (see Jaffe, Bork, Lane, Dashew, & Paul, 1998, for some examples of constitutions).

Though every family constitution is unique, we have come to see that certain common features must be in place for families to evolve and achieve their goals. Some constitutions are quite detailed when created, and others add new areas and greater specificity as the family grows. Some families initially choose to create a brief, less comprehensive document, which is amended later. We do not advocate each family's constitution contain all of the same elements. It should cover the issues most relevant for a particular family's situation. However, some areas are commonly found in each enterprise.

We typically begin with components such as a Governance Structure, a Family Mission Statement, a Statement of Values, a Vision Statement, a Description of the Governance Structure, a Family Employment Policy, a Shareholder's Buy/Sell Agreement, a Description of the Estate Plan, a Compensation, Dividend, and Distribution Policy, a Shareholder Position Paper (for large family enterprises), and an Investment Policy. Space does not allow us to go into great detail on all of these, but we thought it would be helpful to explain several that seem to be important and appropriate in most situations.

### Governance Structures and Agreements

Governance represents a structural component that balances personal, family, business, and financial issues and concerns. It provides a thoughtful, inclusive, informed, sensitive, and effective management of the family's involvement and anticipates and resolves conflicts and challenges that might arise. It creates the capacity for the family to "pass the baton" and defines the terms of their legacy and stewardship to future generations. Good governance creates an organization for representative groups to oversee investments and provides a voice to disparate members of the family. Structures offer vehicles to address group problems, provide focus and cohesion, and make it easier for managers to be with owners and vice versa.

Governance Structures help families to do the following:

- Optimize their jointly owned assets
- Integrate a broad financial portfolio
- Find a voice for all family shareholders
- Stay together and connected across generations
- Facilitate succession
- Minimize conflict
- Respond fairly to individual's values, perspectives, and interests
- Develop productive, effective, and fulfilled adults

Governance helps a family regulate the relationships among three key constituent subgroups: the family owners, the whole family, and the business managers.

Some family owners may not participate in managing the day-to-day operation of their business. However, all owners have responsibility for enterprise oversight to make sure the management team to which they delegate operations is accountable for carrying out their mandates. Ownership oversight in a business entity is accomplished by an ownership group, which may take different forms depending on the nature of the legal entity. For example, it may be general partners in a family limited partnership, a Board of

Directors in a corporation, or managers in a limited liability corporation. Depending on the situation, the ownership group will probably need to be representative of a larger group.

A second major component of the Governance Structure is the Family Council. The purpose of the council is to educate, make agreements, ensure understandings about the role of the family in the business, and promote the harmony, growth, development, and welfare of its members. It is typically composed of all adult members of the family, including spouses, and has regularly scheduled meetings. Many councils meet at least once a year, but most meet twice, in a retreat setting for a few days. They schedule time for family relaxation and fun. These retreats (or work sessions, as we call them) can provide a deep, meaningful vehicle for family members to share what they are up to and to talk about issues such as the future and purpose of the business. In these meetings issues can be presented, information can be shared, misunderstandings can be cleared up, and private matters can be resolved without escalating to involve the whole business.

The third major component is the Management Team. The Board manages relations in two directions, with the family owners and with the CEO and the Management Team of the business, family office, or investment group. The Management Team is usually composed of family and nonfamily top managers who lead and run the business. It is answerable to the Board and ultimately to the family. This can present a difficult relationship because nonfamily members may never feel they have full power or legitimacy. It may put family members in dual roles as Board members, ownership group members, as well as family managers. In these cases, each person with multiple roles must work to clarify in what role he or she is acting.

### Family Mission and Values

Although it can take many different forms, the Family Mission and Values Statement captures the essence and energy of the group. It is critically important that it be developed collaboratively among family members. The process of creating the statement is probably more important than the end product. The Mission Statement explains why the family is in the business, the relationship of the family to the business, and what they want the business and the family to stand for. Most contain a statement about the philosophy of management the family wants the business to have as well as some ideas about the relationship of the family and the business to the community and society. A Family Values Statement lays out the core foundation for the family's approach to one another and the world in general. It is "what we stand for." Some families incorporate the Statement of Values in the Mission Statement, while most find it easier to separate the two. These values describe how family members should treat one another and act in the world, and what values they would like to see reflected in the business.

The Statement of Standards (or Code of Conduct) sets expectation for "family citizenship." It lays out guidelines for what is expected in return for enjoying the resources and support of the family. Some of these expectations might have to do with business activities, but most have to do with responsible ownership, stewardship, and leading personally constructive lives. This Statement of Standards can be extremely helpful in communicating to the next generation the wisdom gained by the senior generation through "life's hard lessons."

Together all of these "statements" help establish the legacy of the family and the current generation's commitment to stewardship; they are the bedrock upon which the family operates.

### Family Employment Policy

Every family-owning business needs to address the question of the employment opportunities for family members. A Family Employment Policy sets down the understandings, policies, processes, and procedures to ensure orderly and effective entry into the operation of the family business. Some of the specific questions it addresses are as follows: Who is eligible to join the family-owned enterprise or investment entity? What preparation is required? At what point are they eligible to join? How do they make their wishes known? What are the criteria for joining the firm? Who oversees the application process? How will accountability be addressed? What happens if there are problems?

The Family Employment Policy is extremely important in guiding the career development of the next generation as they contemplate their personal and career futures. It is important to communicate it as early as possible so those who are entering college will have some sense of what is possible. Some families insert a requirement that an individual must work in another business for five years prior to entering the family business, and some state explicitly that a family member must be applying for a "real job," not one made up for his or her benefit. The policy also should address family members who are adults, have a midlife transition, and want to enter the business.

The Family Employment Policy ensures that family members will have the proper preparation, commitment, and attitude for working in the business. Hopefully this will help prevent the oft-found pitfall of a person's later trials and tribulations being the result of a foggy, ill-defined, and confusing entry process. It also addresses the issue of ensuring that family members who percolate up the management chain into senior positions are well prepared for their responsibilities and can fulfill the commitment of increasing shareholder value.

## Family Compensation, Dividend, and Distribution Policy

Who gets how much money and why is always a lightning rod issue in a family business because it becomes a litmus test of fairness and tends to tap "old tapes" from the history of the family. The most important feature of this component of the constitution is the clear definition of boundaries of how individuals receive money.

The following rough guidelines help define these boundaries.

- Family members should receive compensation and benefits from the company based on being an employee and separate from their ownership position.
- Family member employees should be paid a fair market value salary for their position in the company.
- Other monies and benefits to come out of the company should be based on ownership and distributed on a pro rata basis.
- The compensation scheme should be based on performance, not longevity.
- Large amounts of money should only be taken out of the company in good years, and only out of profits, after the other cash needs have been satisfied.
- Family members should adopt lifestyles commensurate with their level of income and not depend upon great amounts of extra money coming out of the company to make ends meet.

All money coming out of the company should be in the most tax-advantaged way. Parents should not use money from the company as a source of their gifting. We suggest these policies be supplemented by a comprehensive five-year cash flow projection that serves as a tool for family members to communicate and agree upon balancing the priorities of capital needs of the business with the interests of the shareholders. It also helps balance and create agreement and understanding among diverse ownership groups, some of whom may work in the business and some of whom do not.

### Buy/Sell Shareholder Agreements

A Buy/Sell Shareholder Agreement is extremely important, as it specifies the parameters of any transfer of ownership. In the absence of a Buy/Sell Agreement, ownership transfer occurs based upon the whim and emotion of the moment rather than agreed-to principles, and prevents dissolution of a business relationship because conditions are not specified by which someone can dispose of his or her ownership, thus resulting in a stalemate. Agreeing to principles ahead of time regarding the transfer of ownership is one more tool to promote harmony and ensure the ultimate success of the enterprise. The process of working out the terms of the Buy/Sell Agreement frequently triggers productive and useful conversations among family members and forces a focus on a multigenerational perspective. Because the needs or status of family members may change, this agreement should be revisited at regular intervals.

Although many issues need to be addressed in a Buy/Sell Agreement, several of the most important ones follow:

- Who can be an owner?
- What are the trigger events for ownership transfer, such as death, disability, or someone deciding to sell his or her stock?
- How shall an ownership position be valued and what are the terms of the purchase?

All three of these areas are important to get nailed down so that everyone can understand exactly what the arrangement is.

The question "who can be an owner of the company?" typically triggers a discussion of the degree to which the ownership should proliferate through future generations or will be more concentrated as time goes by. This question has ramifications for the family as well as the business. If the family chooses the proliferation path, then it must come to grips with issues of an ever-increasing number and diversity of the ownership base as well as questions as to how to address the ever-decreasing "financial pie." The valuation area can be challenging because many times families crank down the value for estate-planning purposes which makes other ownership transfer transactions difficult.

In sum, developing a constitution is no guarantee of success. The constitution will be worthless if the signers do not take it seriously as the centerpiece of family governance. They have to come to meetings, honor the rules, and work with one another in the spirit embodied in the document. Families who devote the time and effort to developing such a document have taken a major step forward toward achieving their success.

## PUTTING IT ALL TOGETHER:
## *A MULTIGENERATIONAL GOVERNANCE CASE STUDY*

This case study is created from a composite of many family business situations to illustrate typical consulting protocols and typical family business issues. Any similarities between the family business in this case study and any of our client families is coincidental.

The story of the Janus family begins as many family businesses stories do. The first chapter is about a powerful founder, Drake Janus, who had that combination of limitless energy, charisma, uncanny judgment, and a vision of the future that made things happen around him. Most people spend their lives reacting to the twists and turns of life. Drake was one of those men that creates twists and turns because he built the road. And just as other heroic figures throughout history have done, he raised a family that knew him in a very different light than the public did. The force of his personality profoundly shaped the lives of his children, grandchildren, and great-grandchildren. One of his grandchildren, Marcie, is fond of paraphrasing Exodus when it speaks about the sins of the father being visited upon the children unto the third and fourth generations. One gets the feeling that she is only partially joking.

But Drake passed away twenty-two years ago at the age of eighty. His wife and the mother of their two children preceded him in death by several years. He was survived by his son, David, and daughter, Laura, and five grandchildren, and two of his eventual eight great-grandchildren.

Drake's parents and grandparents had been farmers in the Midwest who migrated to the foothills of the Rockies where they became cattle ranchers. Over the years they acquired more farmland until Drake, an only child and only grandchild inherited 3,000 acres of land, which was eventually developed into commercial properties. He became an entrepreneur who bought businesses with a sixth sense of discerning their potential for growth and an intuition for when to sell. He liked to say he was in the business of doing business and never allowed himself to become emotionally attached to any business that was not providing him with a return on investment. By some he was seen to be ruthless, to others he was a visionary. Some say he was both. Either way one viewed him, he was widely known to have used his considerable wealth to build the careers of more than a few politicians.

His only son, David, was expected to follow in his shoes and assure that Drake would be remembered as the patriarch of the Janus dynasty. His only daughter, Laura, was expected to and did marry someone who would help perpetuate the family dynasty. She was sent to school in the East primarily to find a "suitable husband." But she always knew that to her father "suitable" meant someone who would help her brother protect and grow the kingdom her father had created, and she accomplished her task well. Her husband, Eric, became a business partner with her brother, and together (mostly by way of Eric's financial background) the two expanded the Janus family empire.

The Aspen Family Business Group (AFBG) was engaged to work with the family after the majority ownership had been passed on to Drake's five grandchildren. Laura died from cancer eight years prior to our work with the family. Through a combination of gifting and inheritance, Laura's two children, Marcie, age fifty-nine, and Charlie, age forty-nine own 25 percent each of Janus Operations (see Figure 3.1).

At age eighty, David had divided his 50 percent ownership equally among his three children: Sam, age fifty-six; Joyce, age fifty-three; and Hank, age fifty-one. All the members of the fourth generation (we label them G-4) collectively owned all of the companies in the family's portfolio; however, all five members of the Board of Directors were members of Generation 3 (G-3). This was indicative of the passive role the shareholders were playing. Although there were annual meetings of the shareholders, the fourth generation were mainly an obedient audience and deferred to their elders. Chairmanship of the Board rotated every other year between Sam Sr. and Marcie (see Figure 3.2).

The first cousins, Hank and Marcie, were also in executive positions in different companies owned by the holding company. David's son, Sam Sr., was the CEO of the holding company Janus Operations when we began our work. The G-4 first cousins, Sam Jr. and Dave, and their second cousin, Jane, all worked in midlevel management positions in separate Janus Operations companies.

Through a complicated course of events, misunderstandings, and miscommunications, the family had divided into two camps over allegations that

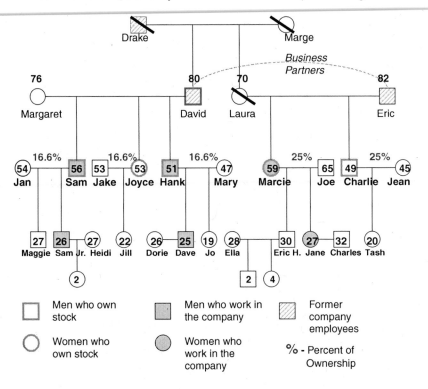

FIGURE 3.1. The Janus family genogram.

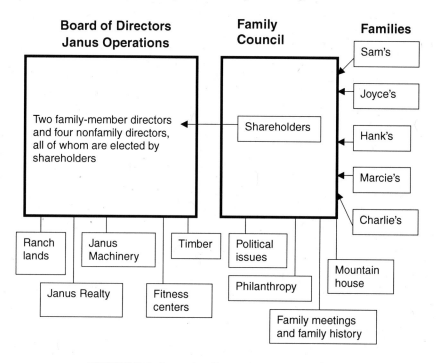

**Board of Directors Janus Operations**

**Family Council**

**Families**

Two family-member directors and four nonfamily directors, all of whom are elected by shareholders

Shareholders

Sam's

Joyce's

Hank's

Marcie's

Charlie's

Ranch lands

Janus Machinery

Timber

Political issues

Mountain house

Janus Realty

Fitness centers

Philanthropy

Family meetings and family history

FIGURE 3.2. Janus family governance structures.

Sam was mismanaging the holding company to the benefit of himself and his children. Sam's brother and sister supported Sam, while their cousins, Marcie and Charlie, were on the verge of suing Sam for mismanagement. To complicate the situation further, there were also separate (but less severe) conflicts or misunderstandings within the two sibling groups.

At the time our engagement began, the directors (G-3 plus Janus Operations external accountant) were meeting every two months as a Board, but the atmosphere was always full of and conflict and rarely productive. The Board discussions had deteriorated to micromanagement of companies driven by mistrust among the owners.

The family's search for a consulting firm began when their accounting firm sent out a request for proposal and selected the Aspen Family Business Group from the responders. In their letter of understanding to us they said we were chosen because of our strong focus on the family and because our assessment process analyzed the functioning of the whole system including family, owners, and managers. Although the language of the RFP defined the family's goals in terms such as "a refinement of long-term direction," "facilitating a strategic planning process," and "developing a succession plan," between the lines we read mistrust, unfairness, questions of competence, and fear of consequences of dealing directly with issues. All of these "between the lines issues" are familiar to our practice group and are the kind of issues that families often worry about but are loath to discuss. Our proposal described the seven steps of our assessment process and explained how we integrate the findings of the assessment process into our interventions.

## Family Assessment and Initial Work Session

Soon after being awarded the contract to work with the Janus family, the two Aspen consultants set up a schedule for individual interviews in the days prior to the two-day family work session. We met with each member of the family in confidence, to get their perspectives on each area, but also to create a relationship with each one and make it clear that their voice would be heard. Each family member also took the 100-question Aspen Family Business Inventory (Paul & Jaffe, 1998) and their responses were recorded for presentation to the family at the work session.

The following concerns and attitudes were identified via the Assessment Protocol:

1. People in the family do not trust one another's motives.
2. Past conflicts have not been settled and there is a buildup of ongoing resentment and negative feelings.
3. There is not a free and open flow of communication.
4. When a family member has a problem with another family member, he or she often does not deal with that person directly.
5. They find it difficult to communicate openly about sensitive or uncomfortable issues.
6. They do not have a strong and clear vision or plans for the future of the business.
7. Roles and responsibilities of family and nonfamily managers are not clear, and people are not accountable for results.
8. Some family members in the business would not be successful in comparable jobs with other companies.
9. Family conflicts are not resolved within the family, and they then influence business operation decisions too much.

The work session was held for two days to review the assessment and discuss the pathway forward. Afterward, the consultants offered recommendations for the next steps:

- Hold a one-day work session for Generation 3 (without spouses) to discuss "unfinished business" among the five siblings and cousins.
- Convene a Constitutional Convention, consisting of two family members from each family branch with one representative from Generation 3 and one from Generation 4, to develop recommendations about family governance agreements.

The extended family agreed to these recommendations and scheduled the next meeting. Most family members left the first work session with hope for the future.

## Second Work Session: Constitutional Convention

The G-3 work session and the Constitutional Convention were demanding both emotionally and intellectually. The five members of Generation 3 spent the first day together taking stock of the past, the present, and the future. It was clear to everyone that the trust issues among the members of Generation 3 were easily the biggest liability for the future of the family and its businesses. The conclusion of the group was that the best way to rebuild trust was to commit themselves to their children's desire to hold together and grow the legacy that had been given them. It was assumed that the restraining influence of the troubled past would diminish as the family had successes in sharing authority and responsibilities. Generally, Generation 3 finished the day feeling like their hearts and minds had shifted from a sense of caution created by the past to a sense of hope for how the future might be different for them and their children.

The next two days were devoted to the Constitutional Convention. The ten family representatives organized task forces for working on strategic planning, governance structure, mission statement, employment policy, code of conduct, mountain house (the family vacation compound), philanthropy, and family history and meetings. Some of these task forces had time to meet during the two days and others were deferred until later.

## Third Work Session: Crisis of Trust

Between the Constitutional Convention and the third family work session online discussion groups were created and a series of conference calls (monitored by one of the consultants) were held. Much progress was made by the various task forces; however, during this time tensions in G-3 also began to erupt and the consultants had numerous telephone contacts with a number of family members. Some family members were threatening to drop out of the process, and others were afraid that Marcie, Charlie, and their spouses might take legal action against other family members. It seemed that the only factor restraining this legal action was the fear of upsetting the members of G-2 (Margaret, David, and Eric). This prompted the consultants to draft a letter to the entire family. A portion of that letter read as follows:

*We are at a stage now where all of the task forces are at work creating recommendations regarding the structures and processes that will become the new organizational infrastructure for the Janus Operations. These task forces will report on their progress at the next family meeting in May. It may well be that enough progress will be made before that meeting so that changes in the by-laws can be voted on at the annual shareholders meeting.*

*It must also be recognized that when our clients are in the midst of these changes it often seems that they are not as aware of the progress as we, the outside consultants, are. It is also the case that the process is more anxiety producing for some family members than for others.*

*We have had numerous individual discussions and exchanges of e-mails as your family searches for the new organizational structures to govern your fiduciary activities. Some of you have been truly afraid that the relationships in the family were more at risk now than they have ever been, and the old adage that "sometimes things feel worse before they get better" has been very vivid for some of you. But your consultants have a great deal of faith in the capacity of families to "self-correct" and for people to weather stressful times full of change.*

*Our job is to keep you all talking to one another in spite of what you are feeling about each other or about your consultants. One of our biggest challenges is helping the family decide whether they will organize everything around the family politics or around the goal to maximize return on investments. The first approach would be built on a perception that mistrust between the branches will continue to exist and everyone needs to do whatever they need to do to protect their personal interests. The latter approach (maximizing returns on investments) assumes that everyone has the entire family's best interests at heart and trust will be rebuilt. This quandary in the family regarding which factors to organize around has created numerous side conversations. As would be expected, this quandary has been most visible in the governance task force discussions. Because mistrust is a concern, significant energy has been expended in the family over sorting through which branches would have "control" under what circumstances.*

*In family business situations that are strongly influenced by mistrust we consultants have a dilemma. If we help the family organize their structures and processes around mistrust, we run the risk of institutionalizing the mistrust and making it stronger. If, on the other hand, we push for organizing everyone's efforts around creating wealth and assuming trust will build, we run the risk of ignoring the harm that one branch of the family might bring to others.*

*In the goals you defined in your RFP you asked for help in creating a shared vision, a strategic plan, and a reorganized governance structure. In just two sessions you have created a great deal of momentum (as seen in your task forces) in realizing each of these goals, plus taken on a few others.*

*We believe that if we can help you all talk about these important issues and take advantage of your best thinking then we can create a win for everyone. If we can keep you all talking in a skillful way then we have a good chance to hold the branches together long enough to pass the torch to G-4. The level of trust among G-4 family members is much higher than among G-3, and this will make it easier for them to organize their activities and systems around presumptions of trust. If these assumptions about the differences in the level of trust within each generation are generally accurate, then it is in everyone's best interest to focus on succession of the Board positions to the next generation in a prudent period of time. To do this we have the following suggestions for our next steps.*

*In order to accomplish this we suggest the following series of meetings to be held in preparation for the next annual meeting of the shareholders. They would propose changes to bylaws that would reconfigure the operations to be more representative of the family.*

The family's response to this proposal led to two meetings prior to the board meeting, one for the family members in David and Margaret's branch, and one for Laura and Eric's branch. These meetings were crucial in keeping everyone at the table, and in the end both branches of the family agreed not to initiate any lawsuits until the family had had an adequate opportunity to reorganize itself.

Both branch meetings had "straw votes" from the shareholders (G-4) who voted in favor of the supporting the reconfiguration of the Board. These straw votes were discussed by each branch, and G-3 family members were reminded of their resolution in their daylong meeting prior to the Constitutional

Convention. In that meeting G-3 had committed themselves to organize their thoughts and actions around the desire to create opportunities for G-4 to carry the family legacy forward. Our theory was that the more we could position G-4 to act as the fiduciaries they were supposed to be, the more stability we would bring to the system.

The special Board meeting followed, and the Board voted to submit an amendment to the bylaws to the shareholders to reconfigure the Board. The Board also voted on several of the task force–recommended bylaw changes and referred these recommendations to the shareholders for approval.

In a conference call with all shareholders, Sam Jr. and Marcie's daughter, Jane, were asked by the other shareholders to be cochairs of the shareholders' meeting and create the agenda, which they did. Sam Jr. and Jane ran the first meeting at which the shareholders were actually in charge and participating.

## Follow-Up

Eighteen months later, the new Board has been in place for nine months. The shareholders drafted a shareholders' position paper one year ago, and this led the Board to require that Sam Sr. present a revised Compensation and Performance Review Plan for Janus Operations and its subsidiary companies. This has created some tensions, since family members in the Janus companies have never had performance reviews. But the Board has been firm with Sam Sr. and it appears that Performance Review standards for family employees will be in place soon.

The second shareholders' meeting was held six months ago, and the new nonfamily Board members attended. The chairman of the Board (a nonfamily member) reported on the influence the Shareholders' Agreement had had on the planning the Board was doing.

Some of the task forces that had been created were disbanded after accomplishing their mission (i.e., Mission Statement, Codes of Conduct, and Family Employment Policy Task Forces). The Strategic Planning Task Force stayed in place but will become a committee of the Board.

The Philanthropy Task Force recommended that collective charitable activities of the family come within the purview of the newly created Janus Family Council instead of being a function of Janus Operations. They also recommended that the Family Council create a family-controlled charitable foundation to manage their various philanthropic activities. Likewise, the Mountain House Task Force and the Family History and Meetings Task Force have become permanent committees and will report to the Family Council when it is created in the next six months.

## CONCLUDING THOUGHTS

As we and the family business consulting field move into our third decade, several new dimensions are emerging. The clearest direction we see is a move from a multidisciplinary mode of consulting—in which several professional advisors each contributed their expertise—to what we would call a transdisciplinary view. In this model, senior advisors from a variety of disciplines are evolving a practice that works with complex families on issues of governance, agreements, succession, and wealth management that integrates several disciplines and creates a learning community for the family. Many family members, as advisors and new leaders in their family, are mastering the skills of family advising and becoming family business consultants as well. More and more, we see multiple family offices, family wealth advisors, and various advising firms offering not the wisdom of their discipline alone but integrating the various disciplines to offer something closer to the model that we have outlined here. We feel that this development will create a whole new generation of advisors who have grown up in professional service firms and who develop as they grow and mature into transdisciplinary family business and family wealth advisors.

## REFERENCES

Bork, D., Jaffe, D., Dashew, L., Lane, S., & Heisler, G. (2004). *Working with family businesses.* Ft. Worth, TX: Aspen Family Business Group.

Bowen, M. (1978). *Family therapy in clinical practice.* New York: Jason Aronson.

Dashew, L. (1997). *The best of the human side.* Tucson, AZ: Beowelf Publications.

Friedman, E.H. (1988). *From generation to generation.* New York: Guilford Press.

Jaffe, D. (2004). *Working with the ones you love.* Ft. Worth, TX: Aspen Family Business Group.

Jaffe, D., Bork, D., Lane, S., Dashew, L., & Paul, J. (1998, Summer). "We the people . . . to form a more perfect union . . ." *Family Business, 11,* pp. 43-51.

Jaffe, D. & Paul, J. (1998). *Aspen Family Business Inventory.* Ft. Worth, TX: Aspen Family Business Group.

Kerr, M. & Bowen, M. (1988). *Family evaluation: An approach based on Bowen theory.* New York: W.W. Norton & Company, Inc.

McGoldrick, M. & Gerson, R. (1985). *Genograms in family assessment.* New York: W.W. Norton.

Myers, I.B, Kirby, L. (rev.), & Myers, K. (rev.) (2003). *Introduction to type* (6th ed.). Palo Alto, CA: Consulting Psychologists Press.

Nelton, S. (1991, April). Ten keys to success in family business. *Nation's Business, 7,* pp. 43-45.

Weisbord, M. (1978). *Productive workplaces.* San Francisco, CA: Jossey-Bass.

Chapter 4

# Hilburt-Davis/Dyer Consulting Model

Jane Hilburt-Davis
W. Gibb Dyer Jr.

In this chapter we discuss our family business consulting model originally described in our book *Consulting to Family Businesses* (Hilburt-Davis
& Dyer, 2003). Until a few years prior to the book's publication, only a
handful of books had been written about family businesses, and of those,
only a few had been written for the family business consultant. They typically concentrated on only one aspect of the process, that is, strategic planning, process consulting, or relationship issues in the family business. Missing was a systematic approach to the skills and competencies needed in
working with these unique systems. This chapter summarizes our ideas and
offers a model for working with family businesses which first appeared in
*Consulting to Family Businesses.*

First, it is necessary to define a *family business.* There are various definitions of family businesses that we might use; however, for our purposes, we
use the definition from Dyer (1986) in *Cultural Change in Family Firms*
and from Hilburt-Davis and Dyer (2003, p. 5) in *Consulting to Family Businesses.* It is an organization in which family members influence the ownership and management decisions.

We have made the following assumptions in our model:

1. Family businesses require a unique consulting approach.
2. Family business consultants require special skills and competencies.
3. Family business consulting calls for a systematic approach which
   combines the action research method of assessment and change (commonly used in organization development) with a systems approach.

The following case illustrates the challenges faced by family business
consultants. It is evident that the Thomas family is struggling with the man-

*Handbook of Family Business and Family Business Consultation*
Published by The Haworth Press, Inc., 2006. All rights reserved.
doi:10.1300/5491_04

agement of the family, agreement on business goals, and transition of both the leadership and ownership of the company.

## THE CASE OF THOMAS GEMS

At age seventy-five, Mort Thomas has worked in the jewelry business for almost fifty years. He first worked with his uncle, and then opened his own store forty-five years earlier. Over the years, the business has grown and Mort now owns a total of eight stores with total annual sales of approximately $12 million. Mort's wife, Shirley, died six years earlier, after battling cancer for two years. Mort was considering cutting back when Shirley became ill. He was devastated by her death and changed his mind about retiring. He was left wondering, "What should I do with all this time on my hands?" He and Shirley had planned to move to the Southwest, where they owned a condominium and where their oldest daughter, Harriet, age fifty, lives with her husband and three children.

The two younger children, Mark, age forty-eight, and Steve, age forty-four, are in the business. Mark is the general manager, and Steve is in charge of marketing and sales. Mort is president and owns all the equity in the company. Although Mort has told everyone that Mark will succeed him as president, he has not completed any formal succession or estate planning. The brothers argue constantly in the office. They each report every argument to Mort, who tries to resolve their disagreements, usually without success. Mort says that the current conflicts are "killing him" and he can't even think about succession planning until his sons begin to act more "like adults" and get along better. The nonfamily employees are often dragged into the siblings' battles and report that morale is at an all-time low.

Mort comes to the office every day, even though he no longer has any formal duties. Mark notes that Mort is "driving him nuts" because he still wants to be involved in day-to-day operations. In spite of all this, the business continues to expand and be profitable, providing a good living for Mort and his two sons. But the family issues are beginning to spill over into the business. The manager of one of the stores, Tom, who has been with the company for fifteen years, is now threatening to leave. The HR director has tried to get the brothers to hold executive management meetings, but each one ends in an argument. Mort has little in savings or retirement; his assets are all in the business. His attorney, David, has worked with him for thirty years and has given up trying to get him to create an estate plan. Over the years, Mort has made secret deals with his kids, loaning them money as they ask. He says he just "can't say no." One of Mort's friends, also in the jewelry business, had heard Jane Hilburt-Davis speak at an estate-planning meeting. He knew about Mort's problems and had given Mort Jane's number. The request for consultation came from Mort, just after Mark asked for a $21,000 loan. (Hilburt-Davis & Dyer, 2003, pp. 31-32)

This case is typical of a family business referral. The issues presented are complicated and raise the following questions for the consultant: Where do I start? Who is the client? Do I begin with the family? Do I begin with the business? How do I help them work through these conflicts? Can I handle this alone? If not, who else needs to be on the team? What do I do about employee morale?

As we look at the Thomas Gem case, we can explore what makes consulting to family businesses unique and significantly different from working with nonfamily enterprises. We have found differences in four areas:

1. Systems perspective
2. Process/content
3. Multidisciplinary teamwork
4. Emotions

### Systems Perspective

Traditional advisors and consultants work in the three systems of a family firm (see Figure 4.1), often as if the systems were separate and distinct from one another.

For example, organization consultants work largely within the business systems. Family therapists, on the other hand, usually deal only with the family; accountants work with the business or ownership systems. What distinguishes family business consultants is that they work in the interface

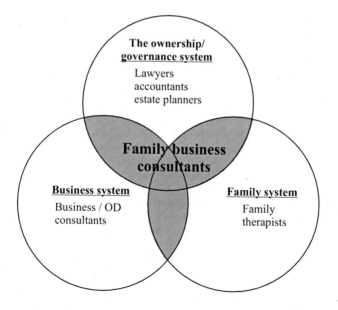

FIGURE 4.1. Hilburt-Davis/Dyer model.

of the three systems (circles), within the shaded area. Family business consultants may help a family in conflict decide who does what in the business, define job descriptions, and determine compensation and benefit packages. This work would include not only improving the relationships (family system) of Mort and his adult children but also would involve succession planning of both the ownership and management, and improving employee morale (business system). Without the skills, training, and experience to maintain a systems perspective and work with all three systems, the consultant will not be able to create lasting changes. A family business consultant has no choice but to work in the interface of the three interacting circles and must be prepared to deal with issues in each.

Improving employee morale by team building would be a short-term solution that would not last without reducing the tension among the family members. The family tension was related not only to the succession and estate planning issues but also to Mort's unresolved grief. Basic understanding of the concepts of systems is crucial for this work. An organization consultant might do a terrific job with the communications in the stores as well as working with the management team. An attorney could develop succession plans with the documents required in the transition of ownership. A therapist could help resolve the family conflicts. But unless the interacting systems of ownership, family, and business are integrated, the benefits will be short-lived.

Systems thinking is also about creating structures to manage the interactions among the systems. It involves working with multiple levels of the client system and the complex web of relationships. (See Levels of Intervention.) The family's reality has been constructed over time by their interplay and interactions. As we help them build new ways of dealing with one another, they develop more effective methods of solving problems. Much of our work is building structures, processes, and procedures, such as family employment policies, shareholder agreements, and codes of conduct to manage and monitor the interaction among the systems. It involves creating healthy boundaries, not barriers, between the family and the business.

These structures can provide the safety and predictability to rebuild trust, necessary for agreements and consensus. An agreed-to process for managing the conflicts between Mark and Steven can be the foundation for solving the larger issues of management transition and company ownership. The ongoing dialogue, negotiations, compromises, exchanges of ideas, and collaboration between the families and the business should sustain both the firm and the family over the long run. Clearly the boundaries between the Thomas family and the business have broken down.

## Process/Content

Traditionally, the OD consultant has focused on the *process* of change and the attorney on the *technical aspects* of change. In working with family businesses, the consultant must be able to provide information as well as manage the change process. Content and technical expertise as well as knowledge of change management are needed to work with family businesses. The advisor must know the difference between process and content, understand the importance of each, and use not one but both as the situation indicates (Hilburt-Davis & Senturia, 1995). For example, the family business consultant working with the Thomas family must be able to answer specific questions about the estate plan, transfer of ownership, and management issues in the succession process, as well as manage and guide the change process in the organization.

We have also found that most change efforts in family businesses are not likely to succeed unless there is the right combination of both content and process on the part of the consultant, creating outcomes as well as process improvement. Figure 4.2 indicates that the information/content and emotional input exist in a reinforcing loop (Hilburt-Davis & Dyer, 2003).

Improvements on the technical side, such as defining a sound estate plan or clear roles and responsibilities, promote healthier relationships that in turn support good business practices. This is why multidisciplinary consulting teams are essential when working with family businesses, since no single professional has all the content information and process skills needed. It is unrealistic, for example, for any one professional to be expected to understand the complexities of estate planning, but it is critical that, if they work with family businesses, they understand the tax consequences of not having an estate plan. "Process" consultants, such as organization development

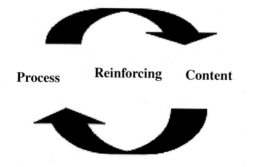

**Process**     **Reinforcing**     **Content**

FIGURE 4.2. The reinforcing loop of process content.

consultants and family therapists, should have familiarity with corporate and governance structures, and financial terminology. "Technical" consultants, such as accountants and lawyers, should be familiar with key psychological issues, such as family developmental life cycles and the impact of crises on family dynamics. As we do our work with family firms, we often need to "hand off" critical aspects of the change process to an accountant or an attorney or, even better, to work as part of a multidisciplinary team.

### Multidisciplinary Teamwork

Family business consultants come to the field from a variety of different professional backgrounds, such as accounting, law, family therapy, and organization development. Each of these professions has a body of knowledge and provides its practitioners with technical expertise that is critical to helping family businesses. Multidisciplinary work is not unique to family business advising and is not new. OD consultants, in particular, appreciate the benefits and advantages of teamwork, yet too often they attempt to tackle the complexities of family businesses alone. These complexities can overwhelm those who have worked independently, and clients are increasingly expecting their advisors to work as a team. In order to attain the potential benefits of a team approach, the professionals must understand what each has to offer and how they can work together. Several team models can be employed depending on how often they work together, the level of coordination, the members' commitment to the team, and how often *and* how they work together:

1. *Consulting (interdisciplinary) teams*—This is a preexisting team hired by the client.
2. *Collaborative (multidisciplinary) team*—These advisors from different disciplines meet in a study group forum, get to know each other's work, and bring one another into client situations on an as-needed basis or in a "shadow" consulting function.
3. *Accidental*—These advisors meet and connect only through the client and coordinate their efforts only in their work with that particular client.
4. *Dysfunctional*—These advisors are unknown to one another, even if working with the same client, with no coordination.

Despite the recognition that consulting teams offer more comprehensive advice, they also pose challenges. (It is accepted conventional wisdom among therapists that the client will not improve if served by a therapy team that has problems of coordination, competition, or conflict [Framo, 1981]). Team members must deal with the following questions before beginning their work together:

- Who will be the quarterback?
- Who will see that the work is coordinated?
- How will the billing be handled?
- How will differences of opinion be managed?
- Who will be the liaison to the client?
- How will the client be sold on the multidisciplinary team?
- How will competition for the best idea or the best recommendation be dealt with?
- How will everyone find the time necessary to plan for the tasks of team maintenance as well as meeting the client's needs?

The ethical issues of each profession will also need to be addressed; here are a few examples of questions that might be raised by each advisor on the team:

- *Lawyers* will ask: Who is my client?
- *Therapists* will ask: What are the issues of confidentiality? What are the boundaries; for example, can I have lunch with my clients?
- *Advisors from financial fields* will ask: What are the financial priorities and how do they fit into the family priorities and values? How are the intangible assets of the family included in the valuation?
- *Organization development and management consultants* will struggle with the depth of the level of intervention: What do I do with the conflict in the family that is causing low morale among the nonfamily employees?

This leads to the fourth significant difference between traditional consulting and family business consulting.

### Emotions

Another unique feature of consulting to family businesses is the issue of emotion. Emotions influence individuals in all workplaces, but family businesses are particularly emotionally charged. Clients may become angry, bear long-standing grudges, scream, and cry in both the family and work settings. Entrepreneurs, who often lead family businesses, are noted for being rather volatile and difficult to work with. Changes during the consultation may upset previously established patterns of behavior and communications causing intense emotions to rise to the surface as power, rewards, and benefits and ownership, family, and work role definitions are altered. Thus, consultants must be prepared to help their clients work through the emotions they experience as changes are made to improve the health and longevity of the family and the business.

Critical to any discussion of emotions in family firms is the question of the depth of intervention needed to achieve lasting and positive changes. Roger Harrison (1970), in "Choosing the Depth of Organizational Interventions," describes a useful framework for thinking about interventions in family firms. He suggests that consultants to nonfamily firms must also consider the depth of intervention, but are not usually dealing with the depth and intensity of such long-standing emotions that can simmer in families in business. We have adapted Harrison's framework to our work as described in the next section, followed by examples of interventions and assessment questions used in the Thomas Gems case.

## LEVELS OF INTERVENTION

### Level 1: Analysis and Development of Operations

- Who does what job; what is the governance structure; how is the company doing?
- What are the job descriptions of everyone, family and nonfamily, and how are they determined?
- Who makes ownership and management decisions?
- What is Mort's plan for succession?
- Is there a board of directors with some independent, nonfamily members, and how does it function?

### Level 2: Individual Performances and Structures for Implementation

- Who are the best people for which jobs? Who trains the employees?
- Is there an employee handbook?
- What are the hiring/firing policies?
- What are policies for the next generation entering the business?

### Level 3: Analysis of Working Relationships

- Does the family have a mentoring program for incoming family members?
- Are there Family Council meetings and how do they work?

- What is the reward system?
- How does the family make decisions or plan strategically?

## Level 4: Interpersonal Relationships

- How does the family communicate or solve problems?
- How do Mark and Steve make decisions for the business?
- What are the family values and do they steer the business?
- What are the family dynamics?

## Level 5: Intrapersonal Analyses

- What are the issues for Mort in his inability to let go?
- What, if any, is the unresolved history of the sons' conflicts?
- Is therapy needed?
- How long term and deep are these unresolved issues of grief, miscommunication, and inappropriate behavior?

Choice of an appropriate intervention should be determined by the following:

- Each level requires specific skills and competencies.
- The technical and emotional issues exist in a reinforcing loop.
- The lower the level, the more hidden and private are the issues and the more difficult and sometimes more risky it is to access and change.
- The benefits at the lower level (Levels 4 and 5) are less transferable in nonfamily businesses and more transferable in family businesses. The emotional impact is greater, especially when dealing with owners and upper-level management.
- If focusing on the technical issues does not get a response, then it may be appropriate and necessary to move to the emotional levels.
- Do not start with the emotional levels, but be ready for them.

Integrally related to the intense emotionality of families in business together is the ability of consultants to identify and resolve their own emotional struggles. If we have not worked through our own experiences, whether negative or positive, our own agendas may take over or, worse yet, we may become ineffectual. We think that this risk is considerably higher when working with family businesses than in traditional firms. If we acknowledge our own "triggers" we are less susceptible to the family's pull on us, which is very strong in a family in crisis. The end result of doing our own emotional work is that we don't confuse out own reactions with those of our client; we can stay mentally alert; we can jump into tough situations with courage and wisdom; and we can use our feelings as data and keys to solutions, rather than acting them out. Therapists and other "change agents" refer to this dynamic as countertransference (Shapiro & Carr, 1991).

We would add the following guidelines:

- Intervene at a level no deeper than your skills and training allow. For example, at the deeper levels, a qualified, licensed therapist may be required to manage the intensity of emotional reactions or to treat an individual with serious mental health issues.
- Intervene at a level no deeper than that described in the initial contract without getting permission from the client system.
- Communicate regularly with your consulting team or other advisors involved with the family business to make certain that you are working together toward the same goals.

This does not mean putting our own feelings aside, but we should examine them and use them strategically. For example, working with the Thomas family business, the consultant who has trouble dealing with conflict might have been the "peacemaker" in his or her own conflict-ridden family and may have a very difficult time dealing directly with the yelling and intensity of Mort and his sons. The old adage that we cannot take our clients farther than we have gone ourselves and what we know about our clients and ourselves can make the difference between success and failure in the engagement (Duhl, 1983).

## THE CONSULTING MODEL

Our model provides a systematic approach. It describes a modification of the action research method of assessment and change commonly used in organization development. It also takes into account human systems dynamics (HSD) which have "emerged at the intersection of the non-linear sciences and the traditional social sciences" (Quade, Perme, Eoyang, Barton, & Holladay, 2004). Because the steps are iterative, interactional, and include repeated cycles of data collection, feedback, and intervention, we have outlined them in a circular fashion in Figure 4.3.

The stages of the consulting model are outlined in Table 4.1.

The *first contact* for help usually comes to us over a phone call, or more recently through an e-mail and is followed-up with a phone call. In this initial conversation with a prospective client, several questions need to be

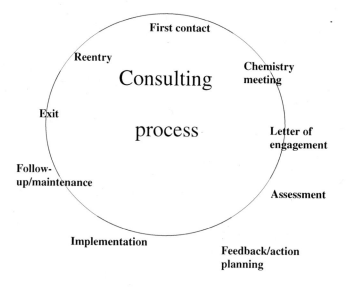

FIGURE 4.3. The consulting process.

asked: Who is calling? Who/what is the source of the referral? Does the referral source affect how you will work with the client? What skills will be needed in this engagement? It's also important to remember the following adage: "Clients call not to change, but as a result of change." Potential clients call because they have experienced some change in their lives that has motivated them to call for help. It is important in that first contact to determine the source of that distress. In our case, the first contact with Mort was a phone call just after Mark's request for a $21,000 loan (Table 4.1).

After the initial contact with the client, a *chemistry meeting,* during which both client and consultant can test the "chemistry" between them, is set up to discuss the issues facing the client in more detail. One of the goals of this meeting is to see if this is a good fit between the client and consultant and, importantly, to define the client (Table 4.1). Family businesses are best served by the consultant who defines the family business system (see Figure 4.1, which presents the three-circle model) as the client. It is also important to establish an atmosphere of trust and safety to lower the defensiveness that is often present. The unconscious processes and issues—the topics that remain "under the table"—will surface only in an atmosphere of trust. In the case of the Thomas family, these issues were Mark's gambling, revealed during this meeting, with Mort's support through other loans; growing anger among senior management in the business who felt the family was creating a "hostile environment" at work; and Harriett's (the daughter/

TABLE 4.1. The phases of the consulting process.

| Phase | Goal | Questions | Desired Outcomes | Risks |
|---|---|---|---|---|
| First contact | To assess the motivation for change and to understand the major players | Who owns the problem? Who has leverage? What is the referral source? How have you been introduced? What has just happened to prompt this call? | Appointment for chemistry meeting | Underestimating the complexity; overestimating your abilities |
| Chemistry meeting | To assess if the issues and personalities are a good match. Construct a rough genogram with the family | What is the problem? How do they describe it? How do others see it? What are the goals/desired outcomes? What resources is the family business willing to invest in the change process? What expectations do they have about you and your work? Where is the energy for change? | Agreement to work together; transition from referral to engagement; beginning to build trust | Rushing to judgment; not getting enough information needed to contract; not stating your own biases (e.g., democratic participation, fairness, open communication, importance of conflict) |
| Contract/letter of engagement | To write a contract that defines the scope, time frame, products of the work, and expectations of client and consultant | What is the mutually agreed upon work? How will fees be charged? What is the scope of the work? | Signed contract; commitment of resources to the work | Underestimating the work, time, and fees; too narrow a focus. Focuses on what you will do to the exclusion of what they want. |
| Assessment | Complete picture of business and family; understanding of the presenting and real problem; broaden the perspective; provide map for change process | What is the family's vision? What are the presenting themes? Where's the energy (positive and negative)? What is the real problem? How well can they manage/handle/use the data (meta-assessment)? What is the work to be done and what will get in the way? | Understanding of the problem and suggestions for interventions | Having preconceived ideas about the problem; not getting information about the whole system. not seeing technical solutions; not appreciating multiple realities; inability to take systems perspective; having too narrow a focus. |

| | | | |
|---|---|---|---|
| Feedback/action planning | To organize the data collected in the previous phases. To provide a forum for discussion, consensus, prioritizing, and planning. | What environment is best for this feedback? Who should be present? What is the best format for the data to be given? How does the family react to the report? How does the consultant react to their reactions? How does the action move from passive listening to active planning? | To reach a consensus for action steps to be taken | Over- or undersimplifying the report. Not being prepared for family's response. Not being able to reach a consensus on the goals. Not introducing the information in a manner that the family can handle and move to an action plan. Not to act effectively to the family's reaction of acceptance, denial, resistance, rejection, or a combination thereof. |
| Implementation phase | To help the client-system manage the change process effectively. | What are the most effective interventions, based on the data gathered and the reciprocal feedback between the consultant and client? What are the most likely reactions to the change process? What level of intervention is needed? What should be the focus of the change process? What type of change is needed to achieve the mutually agreed upon goals? What is the most appropriate use of the multi-disciplinary team with this particular family business? What will the resistance look like? What should be the consultant's response to the resistance? (Ongoing questioning of the interventions will give us answers about the next steps to take). | To achieve the mutually agreed on goals defined in the feedback meeting. | The outcome is always unpredictable. Being inflexible and approaching with a 'cook book' for the family to follow. Not finding the balance between structures and allowing things to unfold creatively. The same information, process and actions bring different results to different clients. Having a limited repertoire. Over or under simplifying the family's ability to achieve its goals. Not being prepared for the family's response. Not being able to achieve the goals. Not introducing the interventions in a manner that the family can accomplish. Not to respond effectively to the family's acceptance, denial, resistance, or rejection or a combination. Not being prepared for the 'ripple effect' or social multiplier of the changes occurring. |

sister) anger and fear that her father and brothers would destroy the business. The consultant created an environment of trust and safety by (1) establishing ground rules of confidentiality; (2) defining rules of behavior, a code of conduct ("Everyone gets a chance to speak"); (3) building a collaborative process ("We'll work on this together"); and (4) directing energies at the problem, not one another ("I need to know about the problems and then we will begin to focus on solutions").

The two-hour chemistry meeting with the Thomases included Mort, Mark, Steve, and Harriet (see Table 4.1). The agenda was as follows:

- Introductions and ground rules
- Three-systems model
- Description of the problem
- Description of the consultation process
- Setting goals
- Determining the next steps

The *proposal/engagement letter* is designed to clarify the relationship and nature of the contract between the consultant and the client. This letter forces the consultant to identify the client, which is often difficult for attorneys and therapists who are accustomed to identifying a single individual as the client, even though they are working for the benefit of the entire family system. The letter should outline the work to be performed and the expectations that the consultant has of the client. The time, money, and effort to be expended are described, along with the method of payment. Finally, the letter should describe who will serve as the liaison (administrative, scheduling, meeting, preparations, and so forth) between the client and the consultant (Table 4.1).

Once the client has agreed to engage you as a consultant, the real work begins. An *assessment* of the family business system is the first step in diagnosing the client's problems effectively (Table 4.1).

The assessment has several objectives:

1. To provide a roadmap
2. To complete a realistic picture of the situation
3. To give the members of the family and business an opportunity to tell their stories
4. To prepare feedback that will enable the family to prioritize the problems to solve
5. To evaluate any discrepancies between the *presenting* problem and what your understanding is of the *real* problem
6. To understand what it is like to work within the boundaries

7. To assess the impact of the consultant's presence on the system
8. To determine how effectively the family can use the feedback
9. To identify special problems, such as addictions, personality problems, or ethical, legal, or financial issues that require referral to a specialist

A valuable tool developed and used by intergenerational family therapist, the genogram, as described by McGoldrick, Gerson, & Shellenberger (1999), in *Genograms: Assessment and Intervention,* organizes large amounts of information in a concise and efficient manner. It resembles a family tree, with additional symbols to depict interactional dynamics (also see Kaslow, 1995).

Interviews are invaluable for understanding the three systems of a family firm and to help answer questions raised. The following are several tips that we have found useful when conducting interviews:

- Interview data should be anonymous when possible, but not confidential. Themes/issues/problems should be organized and presented at a family meeting only in summary form.
- Consultants should encourage interviewees to own and share information. It is important to discuss the issue of *secrets* before the interviewing process begins. We make it clear that it is usually not useful for consultants to hold secrets. If family members have something they want to tell us, they need to understand that we will decide whether it needs to be discussed openly. The decision to share the information is theirs. However, helping members of the client systems to "own" their feelings, ideas, and beliefs is often essential if one is to create a more open, problem-solving atmosphere.
- Develop a picture of the whole system, from multiple realities.
- Understand the difference between the presenting problem ("Mark and Steve fight all the time") and the real problem (no plan for succession; sons being given mixed messages; Mark's gambling; no code of conduct in the business; weak governance).

During the interviews, the consultant should attempt to gather information about the three systems of the family business. The areas of assessment include the following:

1. Family
   a. Roles and relationships
   b. Cultural patterns and values

     c. Decision-making procedures
     d. Communications
     e. Conflict management
   2. Business/Management
     a. Mission
     b. Strategy
     c. Structure
     d. Technology
     e. Culture
     f. Systems (such as reward, incentives, and information)
     g. Processes (such as communication and decision making)
     h. Leadership (selection, development, and criteria)
     i. Finances
   3. Ownership/Governance
     a. Mission and goals
     b. Legal form
     c. Distribution of ownership
     d. Documentation (shareholder agreements)
     e. Board of Directors or Advisors
     f. Leadership (selection, development, and criteria)

There are three interconnected steps in what we call *feedback and action planning* (Table 4.1).

First, the consultant must organize and feed back the data in a meaningful way to the client. The basis for this step is the belief that acquiring information can promote change (Poza, Johnson, & Alfred, 1998). Second, the consultant may make some suggestions to resolve the problems facing the client, but the client must own any solutions; therefore, the consultant and client must jointly problem solve to come up with solutions that can be implemented, with commitment. Finally, the consultant works out a detailed action plan with the client in order to implement the solutions that have been agreed on.

Giving feedback based on the assessment consists of both organizing and presenting the report. If done correctly, it can simultaneously (1) teach; (2) establish new norms; and (3) challenge old ways of defining and trying to solve the problems. Whether this succeeds depends on several variables: chemistry between the family and the consultant; competencies of the consultant; the quality of the report and the ability of the family to process and use the information.

While simultaneously respecting what the client describes and what the consultant uncovers, the consultant must present the data in a way that the family can hear and accept. The saying that it is the "difference that makes the difference" applies here (Watzlawick, Weakland, & Fisch, 1974). If the information is too different from the family's views, they will not believe it. If the data is too similar to the family's views, they will be unimpressed and wonder what they needed a consultant for! One suggested format for organizing the feedback is the SWOT analysis: strengths, weaknesses, opportunities, and threats. We have found that a PowerPoint bullet-type presentation is more effective than merely presenting the data orally. The consultant can use the bullets as starters for discussion.

Another approach to organizing data is to do a Force Field Analysis, a method developed by Kurt Lewin (1951). This approach requires the consultant to establish the base line for the performance of the firm and family. In other words, they must address how they are functioning now in relationship to how they ideally should be functioning. The consultant outlines the forces that are driving the performance of the firm and family to a certain level and then describes those forces that are restraining or undermining effective performance. The family can then begin to discover ways to eliminate restraining forces or add driving forces to improve performance. Listed here are some sure ways to become bogged down in the feedback meeting:

- Focus on the negatives, rather than the positives.
- Impose your values and goals on the process.
- Ignore the process; focus only on the content and the technical.
- Avoid those issues that the family has not faced.
- Allow yourself to be sidetracked from the real work that has to be faced.
- Focus on the past.
- Miss the patterns of behavior and communications.
- Impose a solution rather than creating an environment that encourages safety, creativity, and risk taking so they can formulate solutions.
- Confusing neutrality with objectivity.

Literally, intervention means "to come between." This is what happens in the *implementation phase* (Table 4.1).

This is the "moving, changing" stage in Kurt Lewin's three phases of the "unfreeze, move/change, refreeze" model. We also want to emphasize the iterative process of our change efforts. In our interaction with our clients, patterns emerge as we learn and teach new solutions. For more on the lessons we can learn from the life sciences and organization change, see *Facilitating Organization Change,* by Olson and Eoyang, (2001) No matter what we as consultants do or how effective or ineffective we are, the family business will not be the same after our entry into the system. Our presence changes the context. In the same way, we will not be the same after an engagement. Ask yourself, "What have I learned from each engagement? How am I different after each engagement? If I haven't changed in my thinking or working, why not? How has the client changed?"

Once we understand, through the assessment and feedback, the nature of the client's problems and are equipped with good theory, we can begin to take steps to choose the appropriate interventions to help the client. Table 4.2 outlines the goals, questions, desired outcomes, risks, and potential problems associated with the implementation phase of the consulting process. In our experience, success in the implementation phase is related to (1) what the client brings; (2) what the consultant brings; and (3) the agreement that the client and the consultant have on the goals of the consulting engagement.

## TYPES OF INTERVENTION

Many of the interventions listed here have been described in the family business literature. Rather than describing all of them in detail, we will briefly mention those we commonly use that focus on individuals, relationships, or systems and how the dynamics of these individuals, relationships, and systems play out in the family, business, or ownership/governance systems. (For a more detailed description of these types of interventions, see Hilburt-Davis & Dyer, 2003). Of course, as we have said before, any intervention will affect other systems, but the initial focus of these interventions is described in the following table (Adapted from Dyer, 1994).

### Exit Strategy

How and when we leave a client engagement depends on whether the work has been accomplished and the goals achieved. These will often evolve and change as the consulting engagement develops. What may start out, as in the Thomas Gems case, as resolving the initial conflict and boosting employee morale, evolved into a succession planning process and leadership training of the two brothers, Mark and Steve, as they began to work together more cooperatively. The consultant should regularly evaluate if the work is on track and if the client thinks that the consultant is facilitating a process in a useful way. The change process does not usually happen in a linear manner. It is necessary, however, to understand the fundamentals to be prepared for surprises, emerging events, and, seemingly random occurrences.

TABLE 4.2. Types of Interventions.

| Type | Family | Business | Ownership |
|---|---|---|---|
| Individual | Goal setting<br>Career planning<br>Counseling/coaching | Coaching<br>Skill sets/goals<br>Mentoring<br>Executive coaching<br>Performance reviews | Decisions to stay or leave<br>Inactive shareholders<br>Stock ownership for nonfamily and in-laws |
| Interactional, the in between | Conflict<br>Family roles<br>Family dynamics<br>Boundaries<br>Retirement<br>Sibling and cousin teams<br>Copreneurs<br>Relationship issues<br>Interactional dialogue | Role clarification and negotiation<br>360° feedback<br>Educational<br>Organizational structure<br>Team building<br>Employment policies for family members | Boards of Directors<br>Board of Advisors<br>Ownership council<br>Shareholder agreements |
| Systemic | Family councils<br>Family retreats | Strategic planning<br>Leadership<br>Nonfamily managers<br>Entry/exit policies<br>Comp/benefits for family and nonfamily<br>Professionalization of the business<br>Culture<br>Structural changes<br>Professionalization of the firm | Valuations<br>Leadership<br>Governance structures<br>Boards of drectors |

The Hilburt-Davis/Dyer model is an iterative model that recommends a step-by-step process, with evaluations at the end of each step. At any point, the client and/or the consultant may suggest a return to an earlier stage in the process. For example, if the implementation phase is not achieving the goals, it may indicate a need to return to the assessment phase to gather more data, interview more people, or get a deeper understanding of the family/business dynamics. Decisions regarding the direction, pace, and steps of

the consultation should be made collaboratively; and mid-course correc-
tions taken if necessary. If the process is not collaborative, or the consultant
ignores the signs of a failing process, the relationship will end before the
work is done. If steps of the process are carefully followed, and client and
consultant work together, the consultant and client work as a team to accomplish the goals. The door will remain open for further work together in
the future.

## CONCLUSION

Consulting to family businesses is the most difficult, and potentially the
most rewarding, of all consulting work. Our approach to working with family firms is significantly different from working with nonfamily businesses.
Systems thinking is crucial to helping family firms, as is having both content knowledge of specific solutions as well as process skills to help family
firms move through the change process. We have found that successfully
managing each stage of the consultation process from first contact to exit
offers the family business consultant the best chance for success. A "cookie
cutter" approach is a recipe for failure. In this chapter, we have discussed
each stage and encourage family firm consultants to be aware of a variety of
situations that they may encounter so they will be able to help tailor their
advice and interventions.

As we consider the challenges and special skills required by family businesses, we want to emphasize the rewards that are inherent in this work. Not
only do we see businesses succeed, but we also experience improved family
relationships. We suggest that, although all have certain common patterns
and issues, each one is different, with its own unique history, dynamics, and
themes. We want to encourage consultants to learn more about these complex systems and caution those who have not yet appreciated the unique
challenges to proceed with caution.

## REFERENCES

Duhl, B.S. (1983). *From the inside out: Creative and integrative approaches to
training in systems thinking.* New York: Brunner/Mazel.
Dyer, W.G., Jr. (1986). *Cultural change in family firms: Anticipating and managing
business and family transitions.* San Francisco, CA: Jossey-Bass.
Dyer, W.G., Jr., (1994). Potential contributions of organizational behavior to the
study of family-owned businesses. *Family Business Review, 7*(2), 109-131.

Framo, J.L. (1981) The integration of marital therapy with sessions with family of origin. In A.S. Gurman & D.P. Kniskern (Eds.), *Handbook of family therapy* (pp. 133-158). New York: Brunner/Mazel.

Harrison, R. (1970). Choosing the depth of organizational intervention. *Journal of Applied Behavioral Science, 6*(2), 182-202. [Reprinted in W. French, C. Bell, & R. Zawacki (Eds.) 1994, *Organization development and transformation: Managing effective change* (pp. 413-424).]

Hilburt-Davis, J. & Dyer, W.G., Jr. (2003). *Consulting to family businesses: A practical guide to contracting, assessment, and implementation.* San Francisco, CA: Jossey-Bass/Wiley.

Hilburt-Davis, J. & Senturia, P. (1995, Fall). Using the process/content framework: Guidelines for the content expert. *Family Business Review, 8*(3), 189-199.

Kaslow, F.W. (1995). *Projective genograming.* Sarasota, FL: Professional Resource Press.

Lewin, K. (1951). *Field theory in social science.* New York: Dell Paperback.

McGoldrick, M., Gerson, R., & Shellenberger, S. (1999). *Genograms: Assessment and intervention.* New York: W.W. Norton.

Olson, E. & Eoyang, G. (2001). *Facilitating organization change: Lessons from complexity science.* San Francisco, CA: Jossey Bass/Pfeiffer.

Poza, E., Johnson, S., & Alfred, T. (1998). Changing the family business through action research. *Family Business Review, 12*(4), 311-323.

Quade, K., Perme, C., Eoyang, G., Barton, K., & Holladay, R. (2004). Tried and true: How the emergent theory of human systems dynamics informs the long-term success of large group events. *OD Practitioner, 36*(3), 14-18.

Shapiro, E.R. & Carr, A.W. (1991). *Lost in familiar places: Creating new connections between the individual and society.* New Haven, CT: Yale University Press.

Watzlawick, P., Weakland, J., & Fisch, R. (1974). *Change: Principles of problem formation and problem resolution.* New York: W.W. Norton & Co.

Chapter 5

# Preserving the Family Business: An Interpersonal Model for Reconciling Relationships

Leslie B. Kadis
Ruth McClendon

Good relationships are the foundation for the survival and ultimate success of all business enterprises undertaken by families. When a family maintains mutual respect and repairs the inevitable rifts among its members, it will flourish—and the family business itself will prosper. When family members are unwilling or unable to reconcile and reestablish trust, their enterprise is highly vulnerable and may even fail—unless or until changes are made to ameliorate relationship ruptures. (McClendon & Kadis, 2004, p. 1)

Consulting to family businesses requires assessing some of the most complex systems we have ever seen. The consultant not only takes into account the three traditional systems, family, management, and ownership, but also the overlap and interaction among them. In addition, when thinking about family businesses, a family business professional considers the context in which the family business operates, the appropriate life cycle concerns of the individuals, the family dynamics, and the legal framework in which the business and the family operate. And, since one of the main purposes of a business is to make money, market and financial considerations come into play as well. It is no wonder that family business advisors need a model to guide them through this maze.

Several different consultation models are available. Each is usually specific to the original discipline of the advisor; attorneys, accountants, organizational development specialists, and behavioral health specialists each approach the family business from their own perspective. Our model of consultation to family business arises from our behavioral health back-

*Handbook of Family Business and Family Business Consultation*
Published by The Haworth Press, Inc., 2006. All rights reserved.
doi:10.1300/5491_05

grounds and is based in an interpersonal perspective. We focus on family relationships and believe that business difficulties occur when relationship problems prevent appropriate problem solving, and, vice versa, when the people cannot solve business problems, the family relationships are impacted. The family feud that resulted in the resignation of the deputy director and five directors of the Molson Brewing Company is a good example.

> As is often the case in family business dynasties, the feud stems from old wounds. According to former and current directors, family members and executives, its origins stretch back two centuries to the tangled alliances of the company's founding family, and a question that has haunted generations: Who are the "real" Molsons . . . only the controlling shareholders or the wider family too? (Frank and Cherney, 2004, p. A1)

This case illustrates the major premise that led us to develop our model: interpersonal wounds, old and current, create ruptures in relationships which affect both family well-being and business operations. Our Reconciliation Model was developed to address this specific and common problem—reconciling relationships that have ruptured in the face of old wounds.

## *EVOLUTION OF THE RECONCILIATION MODEL*

With our background in behavioral health, particularly psychotherapy, we gravitated early on to the work of Eric Berne, who emphasized the importance of human interaction in the development and functioning of all people. Berne taught that (as opposed to the prevailing wisdom of his day) people are not the eternal victims of their early development and that current behaviors and interactions can be changed (Berne, 1964). The Gouldings (Goulding & Goulding, 1995) took Berne's work a step further, focusing on the ways people can change. They emphasized the individual's power to make "early decisions" and developed a strategy for addressing the consequences of early wounds through a process they named Redecision Therapy. With these tools they were able to help people recognize their autonomy in making early decisions and then redecide to think, feel, and function differently in the present.

Building on the work of Berne and the Gouldings, we added a family systems component and, in the late 1970s, developed our three-stage model of relationship therapy with couples and families. This work is presented in a series of journal publications and books (McClendon & Kadis, 1983; Kadis & McClendon, 1998a, 1998b).

Next, in the early 1980s, we became interested in family business and the special dynamics and issues of business-owning families—complex processes, entangled alliances, and multiple demands. Individuation, a core human concern, was made more difficult in business-owning families in which people live, love, and work together, sometimes for all of their lives. Separation from the family and establishing new core relationships also seemed more difficult when financial resources, inheritance, sense of self-worth and importance were on the line. In order to help people who were members of business-owning families accomplish core developmental tasks and survive and thrive within their world, we needed to understand and investigate multiple additional frameworks.

In past years, when considering the psychology of the family and its individual members, the field of family business largely relied on the family-of-origin approach of Murray Bowen (Bowen, 1978; Friedman, 1991). This approach, which focuses on the developmental processes of separation and individuation and the nature of transgenerational patterns and bonds, has proven extremely useful. The theory, essentially a model that focuses on an individual, combines individual and systems notions; if any one member successfully individuates, the pattern of interaction among all individuals will change. The underlying assumption is that if old patterns are interrupted, then new relationships will work better.

The field of consulting to family business had several models that served us well when putting our ideas together. The first of these models appeared in 1982. The authors, Tagiuri and Davis (1982), envisioned three overlapping circles, each one representing a different category of involvement: ownership, management, and family. Others noted that the people in each category had different wants and needs with respect to themselves and the business, and that these wants and needs were, at times, mutually exclusive. For example, family managers are often more interested in reinvesting profits to grow the business, and family members without involvement in the business tend to focus on the relationships and family wholeness. The three-circle model helps consultants focus on the potential sources of conflict that are built into the family business. Because the circles overlap and some family members fill multiple roles, a potential for misunderstanding and conflict stems from the uncertainty about which role a family member is playing at any given time.

Gersick and colleagues (Gersick, Davis, McCollum-Hampton, & Lansberg, 1997) extended the Taguiri and Davis model to include the idea of generational differences that operate within the three circles. In the Gersick model it is also important to take into account the needs of the founding, sibling, and cousin generations. The three-generation subgroup operates as a system that is superimposed on the three circles. Both of these models consider the family business as a system that functions in accordance with its own rules rather than as a group of people rationally trying to achieve a set of goals.

Finally, in developing the Reconciliation Model, we turned to and were aided by the philosophy and work of the South African Truth and Reconciliation Commission (1998). The process developed to restore a country devastated by apartheid was the same process we needed to incorporate to restore relationships in a family business devastated by old wounds.

Models are important—they help order available information, organize one's thinking, and suggest paths to problem resolution. Our model was developed to address the depth of pain that is often experienced by family members who work together in a family business and to help family members and consultants reconcile relationships and preserve the business.

## WHY FAMILY BUSINESS RELATIONSHIPS NEED REPAIR

A family business is a complex web of intertwined relationships especially vulnerable to wounds, violations, and ruptures. This vulnerability comes at least in part from the interpersonal dilemma easily fostered in family business environments and expressed in the ambivalence of the statement "I can't live with you, and I can't live without you."

The literature is replete with examples of family feuds that illustrate this vulnerability and impact the family business. In addition to the aforementioned Molson Brewing Company, numerous other family feuds have influenced the strategic plan, financial health, and well-being of the families involved. And these are just the feuds that were reported in the press. In another specific example, the *New York Observer* reported, "The May family [real estate development] Meltdown showed yet again how personal ambition, designs on power and a lack of a clear succession plan can cause successful family businesses to spiral out of control" (Sherman, 2004, p. 1).

There is an obvious question here: If so much is at stake, why are these conflicts not resolved through standard conflict resolution procedures? The fact is that relationship ruptures are not subject to the logic of the mind, but rather to the logic of emotions. So, what is this process by which relationship ruptures occur and wounds form and fester?

The process is rooted in normal human development in which relationships go through a cycle of rupture and repair that is both normal and healthful. People who are meaningful to us disappoint us in a myriad of small ways every day, ranging from not noticing something important, telling lies that hurt, or failing to keep commitments, all the way to outright betrayal. Ordinarily we recover from these ruptures. In fact, Lewis (2000) has argued that relationship rupture is part of a normal process that builds character. The repair occurs normally because having interpersonal bonds is a primary human need and is central to our physical and emotional development.

Most of us have noticed the momentary disappointment when an old acquaintance does not acknowledge us, when a partner does not notice something we have done, when a boss does not give us the appreciation we think we deserve, or when someone forgets an appointment. If the relationship is strong, if the basic element of trust is present, and if the disappointed person feels good about himself or herself, the relationship repair and the restoration of trust and goodwill occur without incident. If, on the other hand, those disruptions in the bond are repeated, or if they occur in the context of a relationship that is tenuous, repair does not automatically occur and trust and goodwill are not reestablished.

When serious relationship ruptures have occurred and repair is not accomplished, reconciliation becomes necessary. In the context of the family business in which people have to work together as a team to make decisions that affect the business, whether in the day-to-day operations, on the Board, or on the Family Council, reconciliation is essential. Thomas Jefferson described to James Madison his own experience with such a rupture, after he was investigated for leaving Monticello when the British were approaching. He said he had suffered "a wound in my spirit which will only be cured by the all-healing grave" (McCullough, 2001, p. 316).

Reconciliation does not attempt to eliminate conflict, problems, or differences of opinion. Instead the reconciliation process is concerned with reestablishing sundered relationship bonds, which will then allow family members to work together toward a common family goal. In addition, the new accord, bringing with it a structure for addressing future ruptures, can help to avoid future serious alienation, which almost certainly could imperil the family business again.

## *FAMILY BUSINESS SYSTEMS AT RISK*

Because of the intrinsic nature of family business—identity and value, family relationships, power and money all converging—the potential is enormous for individual wounds and relationship ruptures to occur that require active efforts to repair. We have called two of these key systems at risk the *power-over system* and the *disengaged system*.

When thinking about the first of these systems, the oppressive or power-over system, we use a behavioral-exchange model to conceptualize what is happening. This model postulates the existence of a storehouse of items that each of us wants: love, status, supportive relationships, money, and power, for instance. We trade with one another for these commodities, and the nature of the trade defines the relationship. For many business-owning families the store is relatively closed—that is, all the goodies are in, or perceived to be in, the same location, and each exchange affects other exchanges (Jacobson & Margolin, 1979).

Let us explain further. The family is inherently a political system in that some members, because of age, birth order, sex, experience, and access to family resources, are more powerful than others—they have many more goodies in their storehouse to exchange. This effect is magnified in family firms when people are bound not only by family ties and by money but also because the family business is an important arena in which family members can experience their competence. In both the family and the family firm, the exercise of this power can be misused with serious consequences for the business.

Often this misuse of power is simply taking a position or making a decision without consideration of the other person. In one case, the CEO repeatedly bypassed his co-owner sister, acting as if what she thought was not important. At other times the misuse of power is abusive, as in the case of the CEO/president strategizing to eliminate his copresident brother and screaming and cursing at him during family shareholder meetings and at Board meetings. In both of these situations, this misuse of power disrupted the relationships, which in turn impeded the ability of the team to make decisions. In the latter situation, it ultimately led to the abused brother leaving the company at great cost to the business, disrupting the parents' long-held dreams for their family, and fragmenting relationships.

The second family business system at risk is that characterized by emotional disengagement or fragmentation. As we mentioned previously, disengagement can be the result of a power-over relationship in which an abused family member disengages as a way of protecting himself or herself. When this happens in family firms, there are not only emotional wounds for all involved, but also many other possible consequences: The person who disengages may take with him or her important information and skills; buying the disengaged shareholder's stock may have serious financial consequences for the business; and, at the emotional level, a sense of failure and discouragement often can reverberate though the company for years.

In addition to this reactive form of disengagement, some families, in spite of their common ownership interest in the business, have never been emotionally engaged. Without loyalty bonds (Boszormenyi-Nagy & Spark, 1973) family members in the next generation often look for the first opportunity to sell their shares rather than reinvest in the company. When this happens the company loses one of its main assets, what Ward and Aronoff (1991) have called "patient capital."

## A BRIEF OVERVIEW
## OF THE RECONCILIATION MODEL

Our Reconciliation Model for family businesses is an integrative approach presented as a three-stage linear progression, but in actuality the three stages do not follow one another neatly. Each of the stages is distinct in the sense that each has its own associated tasks but, as in any model that focuses on living interacting systems, there is always some overlap and often pieces from the different stages are happening simultaneously rather than sequentially, as we describe them. We present here this brief overview as a prelude to the case study that follows. A more in-depth look at the model is integrated into the case study.

### Stage I: Recognize

Before a problem can be resolved, it must first be recognized—and the people in most families have understandable reservations regarding seeing, hearing, and speaking the truths of the family and its relations through the generations. This first stage of our model therefore seeks to both discover the ongoing and continuous patterns of family interaction that negatively impact the business and the business-owning family, and to devise strategies for changing the relationship system. Our main tasks here are to do the following:

- Discover and identify the truths about current relationship problems.
- Help the family members accept these truths, particularly ones that have been denied and buried.
- Assist the family in reorienting their priorities and creating a common understanding of the problems and the goals.
- Form specific contracts for resolving the key relationship issues and prepare family members for moving ahead.

### Stage II: Reconsider

In the second stage family members reconsider their relationships, through confronting both their present and their past, for the purpose of gaining confidence in mastering the present and participating differently with others in the future. The twin concepts—accept and reconsider—apply to looking honestly and empathetically at the perceptions of both self and others. The main focus of Stage II is to facilitate a safe and structured process through which individual family members can reveal their personal histories and reconsider their relationship past—always with an eye toward achieving a collaborative future.

The tools for Stage II are shown here:

- Establish ground rules for interacting and participating with one another.
- Acknowledge memories.
- Teach people to listen and understand.
- Orchestrate respectful and responsive dialogue.
- Focus on shared interests.

### Stage III: Rebuild

The third stage of our Reconciliation Model focuses on creating an affirming environment, building family cohesion, and developing excellent family teams. This stage extends over time, sometimes even years. In this stage needed changes are worked out in the everyday interactions of running and owning a successful family business. Stage III, then, is the time when family members learn, within the practical arena of being managers and owners of their family business, how to keep the wealth that belongs to their family—its human, intellectual, and financial capital—*in* the family for generations to come.

The goals of Stage III are to do the following:

- Establish trust.
- Foster collaboration.
- Establish restorative policies and governance structures.

### CASE STUDY: C. W. MASON COMPANY

In keeping with our commitment to confidentiality, the names, places, businesses, and other details have been disguised. This in no way affects the sense of the events and the characters. If the reader thinks he or she recognizes either the business or the people, this is most likely a coincidence.

In this example two distantly related and very different families struggle to change the myths and bonds of the past and preserve, for one or both families, the future of an important business.

## Company Information and History

In the mid-1930s a young Yale graduate came to California's Coachella Valley seeking employment. Conrad Mason started his agricultural career trimming fruit and lettuce for forty cents per hour. He loaded grain onto boxcars and through hard work and dedication eventually became foreman of a produce shed. In 1939, when he opened a fresh carrot packing shed operation called C. W. Mason, he found his niche in the fresh vegetable industry.

In 1966 Conrad offered two of his employees the opportunity to become partners in his company. They readily accepted, and Mason Packing quickly became the largest shipper of fresh carrots.

Today, over 400 people work at Mason Packing, which grosses over $180 million per year. The company ships more than thirty different types of fresh vegetables, from asparagus to romaine, 365 days a year. They sell produce to the retail and wholesale marketplace. They are committed to food safety, quality assurance, and employee wellness.

Mason Packing is currently owned by Conrad Mason's partners, with ownership being slowly transferred to their children. Following is a summary business timeline from founding to the present. The vision of Mason Packing remains: To be the world's leading marketer in adding value to produce.

## Timeline

- 1939—Company founded by Conrad Mason.
- 1946—Boyd Reed hired.
- 1949—Daniel Nations hired.
- 1952—Boyd and Daniel borrowed money to buy into business and three-way partnership was formed.
- 1954-1990—Business prospered. As they came of age each of the children from the Reed and Nations families worked in the business, gradually assuming more responsibility.
- 1991-1999—Market changed and business struggled to recover.
- 1996—Conrad Mason died without any insurance and the business assumed a large debt to pay the Mason estate.
- 1998—A payout deal was structured and payout terms established; as a condition of the deal the business had to be restructured. Jackson Nations was made CEO and a representative of the Mason estate was selected to sit on the board until the debt was retired.
- 2001—Company moved to profitability, but mistrust and open conflict were common among next-generation family members.
- 2004—Business continued to be profitable, paying off debt, moving into new markets, and considering changing from a C-Corporation to an S-Corporation.

## Challenges for the Company and the Families

Conrad and his partners ran their company as a casual and mutually respectful alliance of owners. All three participated in management and in deci-

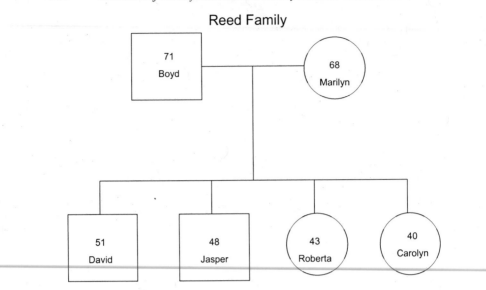

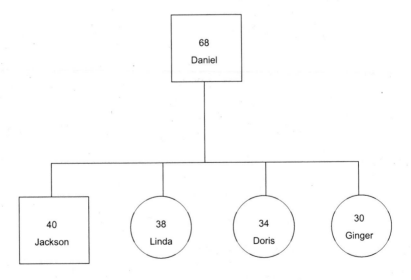

FIGURE 5.1. Genogram of Reed and Nations families.

sion making for their company. Their values were similar; they easily agreed on most issues; and they shared a commitment to equality among themselves. They were very successful as a team.

Unfortunately, tragedy struck in early 1996 when Conrad died suddenly without leaving any insurance to pay off his estate and protect his partners and the business. Daniel Nations and Boyd Reed—the remaining partners and cousins by marriage—were confronted with a large debt owed to the Mason estate. They were also confronted with the need to reform their working alliance, as Conrad's death had been a tremendous loss for both of them. In spite of hard work on both their parts, Daniel and Boyd were soon faced with the difficult decision of selling their company or complying with the demands of the Mason estate to restructure the company and bring in new executive management. They chose to restructure and save Mason Packing for their families.

Daniel and Boyd's decision required many management and operating changes—changes that broke their long-term principle of "everything equal between the families" and created an imbalance of power and position in the next generation. The restructuring and professionalizing of Mason Packing required that many family positions be redefined and that company policies, especially those related to compensation practices, be revised. One Nations family member, Jackson, was elevated to CEO; jobs for other members from both families were reconfigured, involving changes in both status and income for a few, and one family member lost his job. The change resulted in a power imbalance between the families, creating mistrust and triggering long-standing resentments and deep conflicts among the next-generation family members, both between and among the two families.

## Presenting Consultation Problem

In 2002, four years after the reorganization, Jackson Nations, the CEO, contacted us. Financially, Mason Packing was turning the corner, but Jackson had serious concerns about the future direction of the company, his own stress, the next-generation ownership structure, and relationships among family members which were extremely divisive with open conflicts. Following our initial conversations with Jackson, he asked Daniel and Boyd, owners of Mason Packing, to contact us. They did this immediately.

Boyd and Daniel were past retirement age, and both were looking forward to "other things" in their lives. Neither owner had a vision for the company other than their mutual desire to have Mason Packing stay equally in the hands of their two families. Boyd had already established his estate plan and was just waiting until the company debts were paid before transferring ownership to his children. He expressed great concerns about the status of his children within the next-generation group and needed assurance that they would be treated equally within the company. Daniel, divorced and recently remarried, had no estate plan and was just beginning to consider transferring ownership to his biological children.

Following is a relationship timeline summary. See Figure 5.1 for a genogram of the Reed and Nations families.

- 1966-1996—Casual and mutually respectful alliance of owners, with no formal organizational structure.

- 1996—Daniel and Boyd, cousins by marriage, restructured their relationship as two equal partners "until death do us part."
- Boyd's children, being several years older, started working in the business long before Daniel's children were grown and ready. David and Jasper still work in field and plant operations; Roberta worked in the business for a while but moved on to different life plans; Carolyn never worked in the business.
- All four of Daniel's children, before the reorganization, worked in the business in management, sales, and marketing.
- 1998—The major company reorganization mandated by the Mason estate disrupted the family balance: Jackson was promoted to CEO; a manager was placed over David, even though his salary remained the same; Doris quit in anger after her husband was fired. To this day Doris continues to blame Jackson and has remained estranged.
- 1998-2004—The Reed family blamed Jackson for their losses of power and is mistrustful.
- 2004—Daniel and Boyd, beyond retirement age, have agreed to transfer the business to the next generation. They hope that the 50-50 ownership will remain untouched and that salaries, status, and power will remain equal, regardless of management position.
- The Reed and Nations estate plans are different, in part because Daniel had been through a divorce and remarriage, and the relationship between Daniel's new wife and his children, particularly Jackson, is strained. The Reed shares can be transferred in full at any time. The Nations family shares will be transferred slowly over many years.

## Reconciling Relationships—Our Work with the Families

### Stage I: Recognizing the Problems

The first step of our work with the families of Mason Packing involved individual interviews with each family member and their spouses. During these initial contacts we learned of long-held resentments, jealousies, and wounds among siblings. There were also long-term rifts between the Boyd Reed family and the Daniel Nations family. Some family members were not even willing to talk to each other.

These historical family difficulties had been seriously deepened when the company was restructured and Jackson Nations was installed as CEO, so much so that at the beginning of our work, none of the eight second-generation shareholders were interested in working things out. The Reeds perceived Jackson as an oppressor with ultimate power over their jobs and their resources. People were disengaged and, for the most part, talked to each other only when forced to. At the end of our initial interviews, however, six of the eight second-generation members were at least willing to get together one time, because "that's what their dad wanted." No one believed that anything they could do would lead to any positive consequence.

After our initial interviews we met again with "the dads," as they were referred to by the next generation, helping them speak openly with us about the facts and truth of the company changes. They discussed how they were the ones responsible for selecting the new CEO and that it had been their decision to hire Jackson Nations, as he was clearly qualified and the best person for the leadership job. Finally, they admitted that there would not even be a company today if it were not for the demands of the Mason estate and the courageous changes Jackson had made.

With this information clarified, directly from the top, we next conducted a series of meetings with the individual families. The problems presented within each family were very different.

*Boyd and Marilyn Reed family.* Boyd and Marilyn Reed, their four children, and ten grandchildren had cordial relationships but minimal contact. Internal competitiveness that had nothing to do with the company had kept the Reed siblings distant for many years. They had just begun, however, to rally and support one another because of the company problems and the identification of a common outside enemy, the Nations family and especially Jackson.

Our task with the Reed family was to help Boyd take responsibility for his decisions as these contributed to the company changes and to clarify his faith in Jackson. By doing this, he was able to separate himself from his own guilt about his children's redefined jobs and status within the company and, therefore, stop contributing to the alienation between the families. He basically gave his children direction and permission to reconcile their relationships with the Nations family. He furthermore clearly stated that he and Marilyn desired that their children work collaboratively and participate as committed owners, sustaining their investment in Mason Packing.

Three of the Reed family second-generation members chose to go ahead with joint meetings with the Nations. The fourth member, who still holds an important supervisory position at Mason Packing, chose not to participate personally but to trust his siblings in representing him and the family.

*Daniel Nations family.* At the time of our meeting with the Nations family, relationships were seriously strained. Three of Daniel's children and one of his sons-in-law were working in management positions at Mason Packing. Daniel's fourth daughter had left the business when the company was reorganized and her husband lost his job. She had not spoken with her brother since that time and was unwilling to participate in any reconciliation efforts. In addition, since his divorce and new marriage, Daniel had become very distant from his children and everyone was feeling the pain. Finally, as noted earlier, Daniel had not yet begun his estate planning and there was great angst among his children about whether they would ever hold any ownership in Mason Packing.

Our foremost task was to help Daniel clarify his estate plans and then begin to work with his attorney to legalize his wishes. There simply was no reason to go ahead with the next-generation meetings if the Nations children were not secure in the fact of some future ownership. Through the process of helping Daniel define his intentions—to pass his shares of Mason Packing on to his biological children—the Nations siblings learned about supporting one another and their dad. They also were reassured of their dad's interest and support of them. As this occurred, Daniel's children became less threatened by "the other family of owners" and began to open up to the opportunity of getting to know and work with their future partners.

## Stage II: Reconsidering the Past

This stage of the consultation was accomplished in two separate ways. First, we worked separately with each of the two families to address the entrenched conflicts contained within family boundaries. Second, we formed the Mason Packing Family Council, consisting of the six second-generation members who wanted to be involved. The goal of forming the family council was to create a team of collaborating shareholders who would steward the company into a successful and vibrant future.

In the separate family meetings our overall goal was to aid each family of siblings in reconsidering and mending their relationships with one another. Specifically, we aimed to help each person gain confidence in themselves and their own relatives, which, in turn, would allow them to participate differently in their own family and eventually with the other family of owners. In the Reed family, siblings and parents dialogued about personal hurts and struggles— hurts related to sibling rivalries, individual capabilities, and entitlements. In the Nations family there were two important considerations: the jealousies of the "girls" regarding their "favored status" brother and the hurt and abandonment each felt from their father's shift of loyalty and attention to his new wife and her family. At the conclusion of the individual family meetings, members of both families demonstrated an increased understanding and support of one another and a newfound ability to talk about difficult issues, without feeling injured or running away.

The Family Council began with members of both families getting to know one another in the present. We initiated discussions on values and interests and were able to recognize and bring forth long-standing resentments and conflicts between the families. People from both families were feeling used and abused by "the others." Concerns about who received preferential treatment and pay; who did not work hard enough or care passionately about the future of the company; who had more visibility in the community; and who took too much advantage of company perks surfaced quickly. We helped people speak their truths and tell personal stories—we helped them listen, learn, and understand themselves and one another. We utilized the structure of the Family Council to root out and heal old wounds in the service of reconciling ruptured relationships and making way for developing a different future.

## Stage III: Rebuilding for the Future

With the Family Council meetings we also began the work of rebuilding for the future. Second-generation council members had great conversations and made important decisions about where they were going as a company—"to be the world's leading marketer in adding value to produce." They worked diligently to formulate a family employment policy that would prevent recurrence of the previous problems, which had gotten Mason Packing into so much difficulty. They began building a foundation for a different future.

Today the two families still struggle, but they are working together for a prosperous and successful company. They continue their own learning about each other and are slowly building a better working alliance. When "old resentments" pop up people are committed to working through conflicts on behalf of the company and their present alliance. Family Council members have even joined together to "deal with the dads," who are still the decision-making owners, on policies and structures that they believe need changing.

Of particular note is the trust that is slowly beginning to grow. The oldest second-generation Reed family members are almost a generation apart from the Nations second-generation family members. Thus, their personal goals are very different and so are their personal financial positions. This age difference, of course, brings an added level of difficulty to the families' work together and frequently triggers the old mistrust. Today, however, everyone is putting forth an effort to establish agreements that are believed to be in the company's as well as each person's best interest—agreements to prevent history from repeating itself for Mason Packing Company, agreements which provide for a unified, innovative, and successful future. Third-generation Reed family members are now working in the company and benefiting from the commitment of the Family Council and the movement into the future.

## CROSS-CULTURAL APPLICATION OF THE RECONCILIATION MODEL

The word *culture* usually refers to the pattern of doing things, such as making decisions that are common to any particular unit such as the family, the business, or group of families. Ethnic or national background and other important sociocultural elements matter to a great degree because they influence the way individuals develop, family systems operate, and interpersonal behaviors manifest themselves. For example, some cultural groups value overt expression of emotion while others abhor it. Some revere age, whereas others—youth-oriented cultures—do not. Some present themselves much as they conduct their business, through aggression and sharp bargaining; others, appearing "laid back" and almost timid, wait for others' actions. Some focus on the worth of each individual, while others see the group as the important entity. Some regard males as the only gender qualified for leadership roles and others are moving toward full gender equality. These values, which reflect significant differences among people's attitudes and behaviors, certainly affect the way a family organizes its management and conducts its business; however, they affect to a much lesser degree how diverse peoples reconcile their relationship wounds.

Our own experience confirms this; individual value systems are similar throughout the world. This should not be surprising with respect to reconciliation because this model is based on the universal human experience of the formation of interpersonal bonds, their inevitable rupture, and the necessity for reconciliation when repair is not automatic.

## CONCLUSION

Because each and every relationship, family and family business is unique, there can be no single set of answers for healing the inevitable hurts that arise when people live, love, and work together. Our Reconciliation Model is put forth as a guide for family business advisors who daily face the daunting challenges of helping business-owning families stay together, work collaboratively, and create or continue a successful enterprise in an ever-changing world.

Preserving the family business for generations to come takes patience, persistence, commitment, and hard work. Our experience is that when families and family businesses remember that people are more important than things; that the relationship is the problem, not the people; and that everyone has a personal and financial stake in reconciliation, then great things can happen. After all, many families, over the centuries, have not only survived but thrived for the betterment of themselves, their communities, and even the world.

## REFERENCES

Berne, E. (1964). *Games people play.* New York: Grove Press.

Boszormenyi-Nagy, I. & Spark, G. (1973). *Invisible loyalties: Reciprocity in intergenerational family therapy.* New York: Harper & Row.

Bowen, M. (1978). *Family therapy in clinical practice.* Northvale, NJ: Jason Aronson.

de Visscher, F. (2000, Autumn). When shareholders lose their patience. *Family Business Magazine.* Available at http://library.familybusinessmagazine.com.

Frank, R. & Cherney, E. (2004, June 29). Canadian club: A brewing family feud poses risks for Molson beer empire. *The Wall Street Journal,* p. A1.

Friedman, D. (1991). Bowen theory and therapy. In A. Gurman & D. Kniskern (Eds.), *Handbook of family therapy II* (pp. 134-170). New York: Brunner/Mazel.

Gersick, K., Davis, J., McCollum-Hampton, M., & Lansberg, I. (1997). *Generation to generation: Life cycles of the family business.* Boston, MA: Harvard Business School Press.

Goulding, M. & Goulding, R. (1995). *Changing lives through redecision therapy* (3rd ed.). New York: Grove Press.

Jacobson, N. & Margolin, G. (1979). *Marital therapy: Strategies based on social learning and behavior exchange principles.* New York: Brunner/Mazel.

Kadis, L. & McClendon, R. (1998a). *Concise guide to marital and family therapy.* Washington, DC: American Psychiatric Press.

Kadis, L. & McClendon, R. (1998b). Marital and family therapy. In R. Hales & S. Yudofsky (Eds.), *Textbook of psychiatry* (pp. 1313-1330). Washington, DC: American Psychiatric Press.

Lewis, J. (2000). Repairing the bond in important relationships: A dynamic for personality maturation. *American Journal of Psychiatry, 157,* 1375-1378.

McClendon, R. & Kadis, L. (1983). *Chocolate pudding and other approaches to intensive multiple family therapies.* Palo Alto, CA: Science and Behavior Books.

McClendon, R. & Kadis, L. (2004). *Reconciling relationships and preserving the family business: Tools for success.* Binghamton, NY: The Haworth Press.

McCullough, D. (2001). *John Adams.* New York: Simon & Schuster Paperbacks.

Sherman, G. (2004, July 11). Zeckendorf and William B. May lay down arms. *New York Observer*, p. 1.

Tagiuri, R. & Davis, J. (1982). Bivalent attributes of the family firm. Working paper, Harvard Business School, Cambridge, MA. Reprinted 1996, *Family Business Review, 9*, 199-208.

Truth and Reconciliation Commission. (1998). *Report of the Truth and Reconciliation Commission* (vol. 1-5). Capetown, South Africa: Juta.

Ward, J. & Aronoff, C. (1991, September). The power of patient capital—Long-term investment—Family business. *Nation's Business, 79*(9), 48-49.

# PART III:
# FAMILY BUSINESSES
# AND CONSULTATION TO THEM
# IN VARIOUS COUNTRIES

# Chapter 6

# Brazil

## Dorothy Nebel de Mello

Any historical overview of Brazilian family business is intimately related to an overview of the economic evolution of this continent-size country. Although numbers may differ a little according to different data sources such as the Ministry of Labor, the National Bank of Economic Development, or other government agencies, family business is the country's major employer (78 percent of labor) and responsible for its major economic impulse. It is accurate to say that 70 percent of the largest companies and the majority of small and medium-size enterprises are family controlled, representing 10 percent of agribusiness, 30 percent of industry, and 60 percent of services. Most are in the second generation, and out of every 100 companies, thirty survive to the second generation and only five to the third. Around twenty are centennial companies, and less than ten are in the fifth generation.

## HISTORY

### Demographic Trends in Brazil and Family Firms

Brazil, with a territorial extent of 3.27 million square miles, is the fifth largest country in the world, surpassed only by Russia, Canada, China, and the United States.* It covers 47 percent of South America. In 2004 the population of Brazil was estimated at 180 million. This makes Brazil one of the

---

*Data on Brazilian economy, demography and number of family enterprises were gathered at annual reports of BNDES (National Bank of Economic and Social Development), IBGE (Brazilian Institute of Geography and Statistics), SEBRAE (Brazilian Support Service to the Small Business), and the Ministry of Work.

*Handbook of Family Business and Family Business Consultation*
Published by The Haworth Press, Inc., 2006. All rights reserved.
doi:10.1300/5491_06

largest nations in terms of population size (IBGE, Brazilian Institute of Geography and Statistics).

The racial composition of the Brazilian population is quite varied. Until the latter part of the nineteenth century, the population was mainly made up of Portuguese, African, and Amerindian descendants, with a considerate amount of miscegenation. In the latter part of the nineteenth century until the end of World War II, large waves of immigration from Italy, Portugal, Spain, Germany, Japan, Eastern European countries, and the Middle East occurred. These immigrants settled mainly in Sao Paulo, Rio de Janeiro, and southern Brazil. In spite of this diversity of population background and regional differences in culture and values, Brazil has achieved a high degree of unity and a deep feeling that its population forms a people and a nation.

A distinctive feature of Brazil is a high population growth rate. In 1870, the population was 14 million; in 1940, 70 million; and today 180 million. The degree of urbanization is high, with 80 percent of the population living in the cities. The largest metropolitan area in the country is Sao Paulo, with 18 million inhabitants.

According to the World Bank, Brazil is ranked among the middle income countries, in the upper echelon. Measured by the purchasing power parity of money, Brazil's GDP per capita is US 6,500 dollars. However, the income distribution in Brazil is quite concentrated, and 10 percent of the richest residents hold 40 percent of the income (BNDES, National Bank of Economic and Social Development).

Brazil is an industrialized country. In the pre–World War I period, a few attempts were made at promoting manufactured products. In the second part of the nineteenth century, a number of textile firms were founded. In 1885, there were 48 textile firms, with a little over 3,000 employed workers. The industrial structure was followed by other light industries, such as clothing, shoe manufacturing, and food processing. Substantial infrastructure investment was made in railroads, power stations, ports, and others. During World War I, a pronounced growth of both industrial output and production capacity occurred. The 1920s constituted a period of relatively slow growth for the industrial sector. The Great Depression had a severe negative impact on the Brazilian economy, but industrial growth resumed in the 1930s (Baer, 2001). The great spurt of industrial production in the 1930s was accompanied by great structural changes in the economy. Industrialization really started in this decade. The sectoral distribution of Brazilian GDP in 1950 was as follows: agriculture, 24.3 percent; industry, 24.1 percent; and service, 51.6 percent. In 2004, the sectoral distribution is estimated to be the following: agriculture, 10 percent; industry, 30 percent; and service, 60 percent (Carvahlo de Mello, 2004).

The evolution of family firms in Brazil followed these demographic and economic patterns. During the colonial period (1500-1822) and the first decades of the nineteenth century, family firms were practically organized around commerce and agricultural ventures. With the beginning of industrialization the first family firms appeared in the sectors of light industry, commerce, and the import-export businesses. They followed, in general, strong ethnic patterns of formation, due to the important waves of immigration to the country. For instance, Portuguese families would create their own companies or associate with other Portuguese families to form partnerships. The same trends developed with Italian, Spanish, German, Eastern European, Japanese, and Syrian and Lebanese families.

These ethnic patterns of family firm formation began to change in the 1960s, and today they are no longer important. Capital markets in Brazil were never important as a source of capital for companies, and neither were commercial banks. The major funding came from the companies' own retained profits or from official bank loans.

Foreign direct investment was, and still is, very important in the creation of industrial companies in Brazil. Foreign investment brought capital, technical knowledge, management expertise, and marketing approaches to business conducted in Brazil. The country is the preferred recipient of North American, European, and Japanese investments in South America. Of the Fortune 500 companies, 400 have subsidiaries in Brazil.

Around 7 million companies operate in Brazil. About 10,000 of these are large companies, of which 500 are listed in the Stock Exchange. It is accurate to say that practically all small and medium-size enterprises are family firms and that most of the large nonmultinational or state-owned companies are also family owned or controlled (more than 51 percent of voting stock).

### The Beginning of Consultancy in Brazil

Consultancy in family business started in the late 1970s. Before that, however, general purpose consultants had offered their services since the late 1940s. In order to understand the trends in consultancy work, it is important to understand the planning activities in Brazil.

Until the 1930s, the Brazilian government made few attempts to plan the economic development of the country, especially its industrial development. In the 1930s and 1940s systematic analysis and evaluations of Brazilian economic structures for purposes of influencing the country's development became more frequent. Foreigners were very important in the beginning. The first report was published in 1931, titled the Niemeyer Report, after Sir Otto Niemeyer, who worked for the Rothschild Bank (the major creditor institution of Brazil during that time), with the purpose of studying ways for the country to overcome the economic crises created by the Great Depression.

Niemeyer advocated the diversification of the Brazilian economic structure. The next attempt at evaluating the Brazilian economy, recommending changes in its structure and means for achieving them, was made in 1942-1943 by the Cooke Mission, consisting of a group of U.S. technicians sponsored jointly by the Brazilian and U.S. governments. The mission pointed to a number of factors that constituted obstacles to rapid growth, especially to further industrial growth. According to the Cooke Mission, the task of industrialization should be left to the private sector.

In this period gradual decisions of the Brazilian government began to change the structure of the economy through the promotion of import-substitution industrialization. During World War II, the first steel plant in Brazil was constructed with the help of the U.S. government.

After World War II and until the mid-1970s, Brazil had a very important period of development planning and industrial policy implementation. Major companies were founded during these times. The National Bank of Economic Development (BNDES) was founded in 1952, and since then has been the major source of long-term financing in Brazil. In this context of planning, government finance and industrial policy consultants' work became very important.

In the beginning, 1945-1980, this work was directioned toward infrastructure investment projects, mainly transportation and energy. Several consultancy companies were created, such as PLANAVE, HIDROSERVICE, PROMON, and CONSULTEC. Their major focus was in engineering and social costs benefit analysis. Consultancy work for management and marketing was not important during this period.

In the past twenty-five years, Brazil underwent profound changes. First, the rate of growth of GDP changed dramatically. Brazil, which had been a high growth country until the 1970s, became a slow growth country, with some years in which growth was actually negative. Second, instead of preoccupation with economic planning, Brazilian economic policies became oriented toward fighting inflation and controlling foreign and public debts. Industrial plans were abandoned, and Brazil went into a period of "muddling through," with short-run concerns. Third, Brazil became a global competitor in the world market. Questions about management, productivity, quality, education, labor training, and other managerial aspects of business became paramount.

In this new context, the challenges for family-owned companies became more pressing. Family firms became more and more involved with exports and had, at the same time, to be prepared to face competition brought about by the importation of products. This changing context in the 1980s provided the impetus for the development of family business consultancy activities in Brazil.

## Early Leaders: How They Began and Were Trained

The previous section explains when and why the early leaders started doing consultancy for family firms. However, until the 1990s, family business owners would hire professionals who specialized in management, finance, or law, or well-known consultancy firms which would just work with the business aspects of the company, without paying any attention to the role of the family. And they would produce almost no lasting results. But the owners or the companies' CEOs would just keep changing the independent professionals or firms they utilized.

In my view, the "father" of the field in Brazil was the late Professor João Bosco Lodi, who founded his own consultancy in Sao Paulo in the late 1970s, after working for many years as an executive in organization and planning for three major family firms. His background was in philosophy and business administration. He perceived the duality of family/business and started working with the family in business, using a multidisciplinary team when needed. In the late 1990s he cofounded the Instituto Brasileiro da Governança Corporativa (Brazilian Institute of Corporate Governance—IBGC), and in 1997 he and I cofounded the Instituto da Empresa Familiar (Brazilian Family Firm Institute—IEF), as the Brazilian chapter of the Family Firm Institute (which I joined in 1989). In 2000 it became a separate institution, the only Brazilian organization dedicated to family businesses.

Until the late 1990s very few consultants in Brazil specialized in family business and with some kind of training in the field. I started in the 1980s in Rio de Janeiro (and moved my consultancy to Sao Paulo fifteen years ago), following the requests for help and listening to stories about troubled family members' relationships affecting work in their businesses from my family therapy patients. Trained at the University of Chicago, I began working with these families in business, with the clear idea of the intersection between family and business systems and the need to explain their different concerns, as well as the need for strategic planning for the future of the family and the business. I realized the importance of employing a multidisciplinary team to deal with such different issues as family relationships, family and business governance, business continuity, and strategic planning that may arise in working with a family business.

Even today, with the open acknowledgement of the importance of the field, consultancy for family enterprises is provided by lawyers, business management, finance and accounting professionals, general management consultants, former family firm executives, and some psychologists with family therapy background. Formal graduate training is almost nonexistent, with the exception of a few classes given in some business management courses or MBA programs. There are also very few independent programs in family business or series of seminars in different family business issues. And although more and more university students have been writing monographs, dissertations, and final papers on the subject, a great lack of substantial research is still the reality, due to difficulties in funding from the few existing funding agencies, and data gathering is limited, due to the infrequent cooperation of family business owners and executives in accepting interviews and questioning. A consistent bibliography in Portuguese is also scarce and, besides translated work written by foreign authors, the existent books are mostly written by lawyers and general management academics.

## *Collaboration, Competition, and Use of Consultants*

In my personal view, both collaboration across fields and use of multidisciplinary professionals add value to consultancy work. Positive competition can also be of value. However, since the late 1990s, when family business started to be recognized as a separate field, another type of competition appeared among independent consultants and consultancy firms, mostly those without specific trained professionals, trying to show the same or more competency than the trained consultants. This caused unpleasant feelings among professionals and lack of trust among clients-to-be.

Today more family businesses, mostly medium and large sized, are acknowledging the value and need of consultancy work to help them overcome various problems and to plan and prepare for continuity, growth, and change. Small businesses usually cannot afford such assistance and use national agencies such as SEBRAE (Brazilian Support Service to the Small Business).

Most firms have intranet and Internet sites. Use of the Internet has spread throughout the country as an excellent commercial sales and communication vehicle. It is also used by those firms that are exporting for overseas markets. However, the search for and hiring of consultants is not done through the Internet, since a good referral is considered essential.

The consultant may play many roles, depending on the type of work he or she is called on to perform. He or she can be an advisor to the family, the owner, or the business; a coach to the business executives; a mentor to the new generation; or an educator.

Usually the preference is to hire native consultants, not only because of their deep knowledge of Brazilian language, culture, law, and economic policies, but also because of the high rates and devaluation of the Brazilian currency in relation to the euro or the U.S. dollar. There is also the fact that most family business members and family executives do not speak foreign languages.

## CURRENT STATE OF THE ART

Some distinct cultural attributes are related to Brazilian family businesses. The most important is the social and political prestige given to the owning families in Brazilian society. Even with all the recent changes, businesses are still paternalistic and, although more common to smaller firms, they maintain an objective of taking care of the family and their employees.

The patrimonialistic vision of the business is at the core of family business problems for, as clearly stated by a client business owner, "all assets belong to the family and the liabilities belong to the business." I believe protectionism in family business is an attribute of the Brazilian economy.

We could say that in Brazil today, the main concerns of families in business are for survival first, and for continuity, growth, and competition in world markets second. Emphasis is on human capital, knowledge, education, and financial capital to provide for growth. Overcoming obstacles of changing markets and globalization cannot be achieved without the help of expert consultants. Also, separation of ownership and management is an essential step for proactive and modern governance of the family and the business. However, difficulties in finding sources for financing capital due to high interest rates, weak stability of government economic policies, and low return for investment capital make financial stability of the business a primary concern and major challenge. Preservation of family bonds and healthy family relationships is primary to family wealth growth.

Corporate governance, referring to a broad set of social, cultural, legal, and managerial determinant aspects of management, ownership, and control of family enterprises is a complex concept, discussed since the late 1990s. First thought of as a concept applying only to large companies, corporate governance is a broader philosophical view of rethinking for any sized organization, an essential set of tools and rules vital to their survival and growth in this very competitive and changing world market.

The creation of a family council, its rules, and other related issues is as important for a family in business today as creating a board of directors, shareholders agreements, and others for the business. Concern with social and environmental responsibility is viewed as very important, but it depends more on the owner's/CEO's family to set programs to deal with those issues. But a great number of concerned families are part of different nongovernmental organizations' programs and voluntary organizations.

Philanthropic institutions and foundations are not yet a major concern for affluent families but tend to increase as government tax incentives are provided. Family office (see Chapter 19 for a full discussion on this topic) is a brand new concept in Brazil, considered very expensive by Brazilian standards, and only a small percentage of the richest families are interested in starting their own foundations.

Although Brazilian consultants are more concerned about working with both family and business issues, it still is a difficult task. First, most consultants prefer working with issues related to the business, leaving the family issues to psychologists and mediators, most of whom do not have any knowledge of the business issues. Second, the use of multidisciplinary teams or professional pairs with complementary expertise in the family and the business is not yet common to most consulting firms. Third, companies still tend to hire separate professionals, starting with finance and law experts due to their major concern with financial stability. They expect the lawyers to deal with any conflicting issues related to the family. Fourth, because it is always difficult for the family working in the business to deal with their members' diverse interests, feelings, and conflicts, there is deep concern with the fragility of their emotional bonds.

## COMMENTARY

### On Family Councils

First there is a dream. It starts in the entrepreneur's mind to create something, to open a business. He or she has a vision of this business, how it should be, and shares it with his or her family.

This vision changes, in contact with the current reality, with time and the growth of the business. It is embedded with the family's values. And if it survives through generations, although maintaining the core, new values are added and the vision grows. Sharing the vision allows them to write the mission statement of this family and their business, what they stand for, what they want to accomplish, what they value, and the principles of their family governance. With vision and mission at hand for the family and the business, they formalize a set of rules, rights, expectations, and responsibilities of the family for its members and the business. This becomes the family constitution. They create a structure for family governance, where all family matters and those related to their role in the business must be dealt with; this structure in Brazil is the family council.

It will be at the Council's meeting, at least twice a year or when a problem arises, that those issues will be discussed, excluding them from having to be treated during family gatherings, parties, or dinners. This Council will have an elected president, and other elected family members may participate in different Council committees, such as ethics and education.

However safe this structure is, Brazilian families do not create it by themselves, but only when a consultant is called in, for different reasons, and helps them create this structure for family governance. And some families, especially large ones, without knowing it, establish specific meetings that function as informal Councils.

### On Family Philanthropy

It is interesting that social responsibility with the poor, orphans, and other misfortunate members of Brazilian society is in the heart of most families. Good-hearted families donate time, a little money, and work to help underprivileged people. Some start their own philanthropic organizations with the help of family members and neighbors. Through the media, different donation campaigns are organized year-round, and money raised goes to different programs. Besides the government agencies, NGOs, health care organizations, cultural and religious institutions, and large and multinational companies have philanthropic programs and foundations.

Little by little the philanthropic institutions are becoming a booming niche for executives since they are being internally structured and strategically organized. However, very few specialized consultants are called in since these institutions are using their own people for strategic planning.

### On Family Offices

As previously stated, the concept of a family office is new for Brazilian families, and it is considered very expensive to maintain under our standards. Only a very small percentage of the richest families started their own offices with the help of consultants. Therefore, very few are working with this type of structure, and usually Brazilian and foreign private banks and other financial institutions are selected by rich families to manage their fortune. However, I believe the concept does not concern only the management of family assets and property for the sake of future generations to prevent the eventuation of the Brazilian saying "rich grandfather, noble son, poor grandson," but it encompasses planning for the future of the family in business or with businesses.

The preservation of family wealth is a dynamic process involving the maximization of two different types of capital: human capital and financial capital. The first involves family members, their acquisition of knowledge, information, communication skills, and relationship skills. It also involves the creation and practice of a system of representative governance based in a set of shared values, expressing the uniqueness of the family. The second is related to their wealth and how they invest in it. Therefore, the concept of family office involves the utilization of multiple qualitative and quantitative techniques over a long period of time, allowing the family to make the best possible decisions about investments in their human/intellectual and financial capital.

## *On Boards of Directors*

Although corporate governance has been in evidence since the late 1990s and the Brazilian Code of Best Governance Practices (*The Brazilian Institute of Corporate Governance,* 3rd. ed.) is approved by the Brazilian SEC and registered at the Brazilian Stock Exchange, by Brazilian Corporation Law (1997) only publicly held companies must have board of directors. And of these large companies perhaps less than half of them have real boards with outside directors, for outside members and advisors are only now starting to become of concern. Most closely held and limited companies with boards have family members and some advisors related to the family as members.

My recent self-funded research findings (Nebel de Mello, 2002) concerning Brazilian corporate governance indicate the following:

- Owner/manager firms have all-family boards; some have advisory boards or family meetings instead of family councils.
- Sibling partnership firms have family boards, some having family councils, and half have boards with some outside directors and advisors.
- Cousin consortium firms have boards, family councils, and some junior boards.
- Boards of directors are the president/controller's creation, and outsiders are seldom involved in real decisions.
- Strong president/controller firms prefer advisory boards just to uphold family members' decisions.

## *RESEARCH*

As stated earlier, Brazilian research in family business is rare. Published findings are mostly students' dissertations, and even those are more of the survey type. I can talk only about my own findings done on succession/continuity issues and business objectives and family style done between 1997 and 2002 and presented in conferences abroad and FFI annual conferences (Nebel de Mello, 1999, 2000). Those findings were part of an international comparison research study done together with colleagues from South Africa, Italy, Australia, Israel, and the United States. I already mentioned issues related to succession/continuity issues through this chapter. In the following section some findings on business objectives and family lifestyle are reported.

### *Business Objectives*

Although owner objectives may differ according to regional and ethnic differences in culture, values, and business type, size, and developmental stage, right from the start family well-being is always one of their main objectives. Because founders create and embed their objectives into the business, we may say that quality of life (QL) improvement for the family becomes one of their main business objectives. This is most evident in the first generation of controlling owners.

However, in the ongoing survey, the majority of respondents so far, regardless of business type, placed their business survival as the main objective at the present time. This is justified by economic and financial problems due to technological improvement needs and uncertainties caused by competition and globalization, indebtedness, and the instability of the country's economic policies. These respondents were mostly second-generation controlling owners of small and medium-size firms in the expansion/formalization stage.

Therefore, regardless of origin background, these business owners will spend more reinvesting in their business instead of substantially improving the family QL, sometimes sacrificing the family's well-being for a long period. Brazilian family business is full of sad stories of rich owners of large businesses who lost their companies and fortunes because of lack of control over shareholders' excessive spending and ostentatious lifestyle. Real empires (banking, industry, and agribusiness) deteriorated this way.

Survival is also considered the major business challenge, encompassing market entrance and maintenance, and financial and strategic planning. Wealth growth is considered important but a secondary objective at the moment. Therefore, the family quality of life in a larger sense might become of secondary importance because all efforts must be turned to business survival. If QL is influenced by quality of work life, heavy working hours and lots of stress may cause negative effects on QL.

However, it is important to stress that education has become essential for families in business. In order to maintain high education standards for their children, providing good schools and courses, spending to prepare the next generation is the only concession owners are willing to make. For the sake of education, more working hours and less leisure time might affect QL. Until recently, this was true only for Jewish families and those of Japanese, Chinese, and Korean descent.

### Distinct Cultural Attributes

For a long time, Brazil maintained an archaic social structure, the family inclusive. The patriarchal family also persisted for a long time, with all its consequences: the exacerbated paternal power, the paternal authority over the wife and children, and the oldest son as the successor.

Today, even with all the modernization process, many families still revere certain cultural values, such as family prestige. Brazilian society is one in which family prestige is of main importance when compared to other democratic societies where prestige is more of an individual matter. You carry the name you were born with through life and are responsible for its preservation. The first generation, like feudal lords, still sees the company not as an economic entity but as the basis for social and political prestige, which in contrast may lead to its bankruptcy. Paternalistic was and sometimes still is the way these owners manage their employees. Since the business is their family, the employees become part of the family and, in exchange, are expected to be loyal to the family and their business.

There is also a patrimonialistic vision of the family business in which "all assets belong to the family and the liabilities belong to the business." This view is at the core of the family business problems: family social prestige and power, and perpetuation of the family name, all must be kept in and through the family; outsiders will be accepted as managers only in the absence of family candidates. Survey respondents say they will choose only competent successors or professionals but, at the same time, they rate their children as the first choice for their successors, with their male children getting the highest ranking, competent family members next, and outside competent executives third, therefore giving a double-bind message. Along the same lines, family businesses are protectionists, and this is an attribute of the whole Brazilian economy and a serious obstacle for globalization of its market.

Another aspect is that second-generation owners face a serious challenge in the business and the family. If the founder was a charismatic leader and had a strong personality, it will be difficult and will take time for the successor to win respect and acceptance from family members and employees. The new leader will be successful in business only if he or she demonstrates charisma as a complement to high competence.

## EMPLOYMENT PATTERNS

### Spouse/Partner

In small family businesses, mostly in the service and garment industry sectors, the help of spouses/partners is of main importance, even if they lack previous experience or education. There will be no differences in working hours, although family needs, especially in the face of a child's sickness or school meetings, are respected. Depending on size and type of business, they may be in charge of clients, employees, purchases, or payments. Husbands are usually the general managers and in charge of costs, sales, and finance. They will spend long hours in the business and will have little time for the family. In many businesses, wives will be the ones behind the scenes determining salary policies and the spending of money. In many cases, they become their husbands' closest advisors.

In the absence or impairment of their husbands, spouses will take full charge of the business, whether prepared to do so or not. This will continue for a transition period, until a child, other family member, or outside professional will be appointed. This is true for all size businesses. They will seek help from other family members and/or longtime employees, but they may stay in this role for a long time. The number of successful Brazilian businesswomen is growing every day.

### Children/Siblings

Because of the importance given to close family ties, Brazilian family businesses, especially those of Portuguese, Spanish, Italian, Eastern European, Jewish, Chinese, and Korean descent, will try to maintain children and siblings employed in the business. Although there is now a tendency to allow the children the right to decide about their future, family business is still a good possibility. In order to keep the children in the family business, some parents open new enterprises (still part of the family group) trying to satisfy their children's need for developing something on their own.

Early participation is more common in smaller firms, in the agribusiness and service sectors. Outside experience is considered important, but depending on the region and business type this becomes impossible. Despite owners' general agreement on the urgency and importance of establishing standards for entrance in the business, career planning, wages according to performance and position competence, it is a difficult task to be performed here. As stated before, the oldest son is always considered as the successor, and men are preferred. However, more and more daughters are under consideration, especially because of being less competitive with their fathers.

When siblings are employed or at the sibling partnership stage, each will be responsible for an area of the company. At the sibling partnership stage, they will share equal control of the firm.

## Work Dimensions

When business survival becomes of major concern, or when a business is starting or expanding, it requires more working hours, leaving less time for travel, leisure, and free weekends and evenings for the family. When business employees are mostly family members, heavy working hours are seen as necessary regardless of the Brazilian labor law restraints. This happens because family members want their business to develop and grow, becoming a basis for family pride. But it does not always mean job/position satisfaction.

Sometimes nonfamily employees with close ties to the controlling family will work hard expecting future compensation (which does not always happen). This is more common in smaller business organizational structures. Larger organizational structures with many nonfamily employees will not differ much from nonfamily business organizations. They will comply with Brazilian labor law, and heavy and extra working hours will be compensated according to contract policies. However, even in smaller businesses, the younger generation will more and more expect standards and policies equivalent to those in outside businesses. They want to pursue career development and job satisfaction in addition to family and business role differentiation. They also seek more balance between work, personal, and family life.

### Family Dimensions

The respondents to our survey stated that the main challenges families in business confront are to make initial decisions concerning work and family relationships; to do the best for children's education; to encourage the positive management of family conflicts, and to act as facilitators of children's initial decisions on their career planning. Some guilty feelings in Brazilian families are shared by parents who work very long hours away from their children. It seemed difficult for the respondents to initially identify their family conflicts. Frictions and misunderstandings among working family members that arose when they examined, compared, and recognized their differences were recognized as being the more frequent motives underlying family conflict. Usually these frictions are related to everyday matters of the business. Sibling rivalry was rated higher than other conflicts among family members. They mentioned that misunderstandings and differences are discussed until they arrive at a consensus, in frequent family working members' meetings. They also mentioned that these conflicts are part of any staff working together and that they may have productive outcomes. The answers seem to reflect the respondents' concern with the fragility of their businesses; this is especially due to the lack of succession planning, ground rules, separation between family and business, ownership and management, loyalty, and strong family bonds.

Although the gender issue is still present in some companies, it is becoming less and less frequent. There is less friction between brothers/sisters and fathers/daughters working together and more competition/rivalry between brothers and fathers/sons. Because women create better working relationships, sisters and mothers/daughters have less conflicted relationships in business. Mothers act as advisors to their husbands in many instances, especially in conflictive situations, and are able to appoint the most competent among the children, because they know them better and are more rational on what some respondents qualified as family justice matters.

The importance given in Brazilian culture to family prestige, power, and family name is related to the impact of the business on social relationships. However, only in the past few years have foundations and philanthropy became important among successful controlling families. More and more, business social actions are becoming a cultural trend.

### Lifestyle and Retirement Objectives

For all respondents in the survey, retirement is considered a difficult subject to deal with, because it is related to failure, loss of power, and aging. As in our previous survey (Nebel de Mello, 1999), the majority will retire only in old age "when the time will come." The dominant feeling desired is that of being in control, being a successful businessman, and belonging to the business world; although they realize it is needed, planning for retirement is not a common task.

Lifestyle is equal to work, most of the time. Leisure is always mixed with business. Little time is left exclusively for the family. The rule most family business owners follow is: "I worked hard and I am successful. I gave my family and children the best in schooling, social relationships, trips abroad, and the learning of different languages. I am the provider. This is my bond with them." Sometimes discussing soccer games is their closest emotional tie with their children.

What has been happening lately with owners who sell or retire from their businesses is that they either start a second entrepreneurial career, opening another business, they become a board member (when there is a board), or they act as advisors to the next generation. Very few really retire from business life. Today more and more families are engaging in philanthropic work.

## KEY CONFLICTS

As mentioned earlier in my research findings, the major conflicts I encounter when consulting with family members are sibling rivalry and friction, misunderstandings related to the everyday world of the business, and between generations.

However, when working on continuity issues, the major problems are related to lack of written plans. Although most agree on the importance of planning for the future of the family and the business, issues on management transition, ownership, retirement, and governance for the family and the business are the ones to be implemented through my assistance. The following case study is an illustration on some of those points.

## CASE STUDY

The Beldini family (names and type of business were changed to preserve client confidentiality) has been in business for fifty-five years and is still under the first generation, although four members of the second generation have been working in it for the past ten years. The first generation consists of three brothers and two sisters working together, with no in-laws working in the business. They own a large chain of home appliance and furniture stores in fifteen southern countryside cities and are among the top companies in their niche.

I was called in based on the recommendation of a major law firm, whom they had contracted to write shareholders agreements. The lawyers found themselves unable to work on the agreements since the family was organized around the oldest brother, the CEO. He was also president of an all-family board, all members also being the major executives of the business. All would count on the CEO's decisions regarding the family and the business. Family and board meetings were the same, since he would decide everything around the family dinner table.

As an excellent entrepreneur he was able to start and develop the business with fast growth due to the lack of similar companies in those cities. He was able to provide the family with a very good life, houses, cars, and education for the children. He felt the family was happy because of his "equal distribution of assets and property" among them. The family owned everything: what belonged to the business also belonged to the family, but not vice versa.

He had already decided to make his oldest son his successor and his oldest daughter the head of human resources "because she was good with people." All brothers and sisters were supposed do the same with their offspring. This second generation was composed of twelve children, with ages ranging from thirty to sixteen, who would refer to their father and uncle as Don Antonio, an allegory to a Mafia family. Wives and husbands not working in the business were respected but had no voice and had only the task of taking care of their families.

After a first meeting with the whole family where they tried to sound very happy and expressed no problems in the business or among themselves, I asked them permission to interview each group separately: the brothers, the women, and the younger generation. And that is where disagreements, miscommunications, misunderstandings, enmeshment, lack of openness, and lack of appropriate planning surfaced. Using games on power, communication, exclusion, inclusion, and strategies, and getting written answers to structured questions on those aspects, I was able to paint a set of scenarios on what was really happening to the family, what was lacking, and how they could positively use all of their capabilities for the future and continuity of both family and business. I proposed working on the separation of family and business, and the drawing up of the constitution of governance for both family and business: Change and growth for both.

At first Don Antonio hesitated in accepting what was being proposed, worrying whether he would loose power, but the young generation, together and for the first time, had the courage to ask to be listened to and pleaded that they had the right to choose their own future and plan their career in or out of the business.

I started with the family but worked with the business at the same time. It was a difficult task. Every time we would make advances, Don Antonio would feel like he was being threatened and would call in the lawyers. But we were a multidisciplinary team working together, developing family and management strategies and also dealing with legal, financial, and tributary issues.

The work started two years ago, and now the Beldini family has a family council meeting twice a year and a family constitution, the business has a board of directors presided over by Antonio Beldini with three other family members (one brother and the two sisters), the CEO (another brother elected by the board), and four outside directors. There is a finance committee and a legal committee. There is also a junior board. Of the four members of the second generation working in the business, one is already the CFO and the others decided to leave the business and pursue careers on their own.

The company has grown well and is exporting furniture to three other Latin American countries. Don Antonio is now known only as Mr. Antonio Beldini, head of the just-founded Beldini Foundation for Disabled Children.

## CONCLUSION

Family business consulting in Brazil is a growing field. Because most Brazilian businesses are family owned or controlled and there is a high concern with the future, much remains to be done. The preference is for hiring Brazilian consulting firms.

Brazilian family business still needs to develop a set of norms and be more judicious when preparing for the future and the role of the family as investor/shareholder in the business. Brazilian families are confident in their family bonds, loyalty, cooperation, and their part in the family business culture, but there is also concern with the fragility of these emotional bonds.

Brazilian women are arriving to top executive positions in their family businesses for their competence and performance as managers and for their skills in establishing better working relationships and communication. Although there are not yet many women in consulting, family business consulting is a promising field for them.

The emphasis of consulting should be on human capital, providing for survival and growth, and overcoming the obstacles that accompany world changes and globalization.

## REFERENCES

Baer, W. (2001). *The Brazilian economy: Growth and development* (5th ed.). Westport, CT: Praeger Publishers.

Carvalho de Mello, P. (2004). *Economia empresarial.* FGV online, from www.fgv.br/fgvonline.

Nebel de Mello, D. (1999). Brazil, in an international comparison of family business succession issues. Strategies for the New Millennium, Proceedings of the 1999 Family Firm Institute Conference, October 22, Chicago, Illinois.

Nebel de Mello, D. (2000). Brazil, in an international comparison of family business objectives. Proceedings of the 2000 Family Firm Institute Conference, October 26, Washington, D.C.

Nebel de Mello, D. (2002). Brazilian family business, research report. Unpublished paper.

# Chapter 7

# Canada

## Denise Paré-Julien

Canada is a country that spans over 10 million square kilometers; it is made up of very diverse lands from the fertile prairies, to the immense great lakes, through the rugged mountain ranges, to the vast tundra. The country spans from the Atlantic to the Pacific Oceans. Canada is a nation of over 31 million people, the majority of whom live in cities that are within 200 kilometers from its southern neighbor, the United States (Canadian Statistics, 2004). The proximity to the United States and its vast community of family business experts along with the similarity in language and customs of these two neighboring countries has been helpful for sustaining a collaborative practice in the field of family business consulting.

Canada's economy is quickly evolving toward a knowledge-based economy. Statistics show that now three out of four Canadians are employed by a company or an institution connected to the service industry, built on innovation and technology. This industry subsumes prominent sectors such as communications, entertainment, transportation, publishing, and biotechnologies. Most of these sectors are dominated by family-owned firms in Canada; the best example is certainly in the communication industry, where

I would like to thank Barbara Benoliel, Jess Chua, Luanna McGowan, Val Monk, Laura Palmer, Pramodita Sharma, Michael Shulman, and Lloyd Steier for answering my inquiries. Their knowledge about the field and their expertise as educators, researchers, and family business consultants was helpful to me in writing this chapter. I want to extend a special thanks to my friend Michael Galletti, former president of the Montreal chapter of CAFE and family business owner, who proofread these pages for me and gave me his comments and encouragement, and to my friend Walid Chiniara. I would also like to acknowledge Philippe and Nan-b de Gaspé Beaubien from the Business Families Foundation, who were instrumental in my getting involved in this field and also in giving me the opportunity to learn and be in contact with the best minds in the field of family business through the fellows of BFF.

*Handbook of Family Business and Family Business Consultation*
Published by The Haworth Press, Inc., 2006. All rights reserved.
doi:10.1300/5491_07

there are such families as the Shaws and the Rodgers. Another such industry is publishing and printing, with the Péladeau and the Asper families dominating. There are very important business families in the trucking industry and also in pharmacy chains, such as the Jean Coutu Group in Québec (which recently acquired the Eckerd chain based in the United States).

Family businesses in Canada have also dominated the food industry; famous stories such as that of the Steinbergs[1] are still referred to daily in this field, and others such as the McCains[2] are also a major force in this industry. These well-known families have by their stories influenced many other smaller business families and, most of the time, have had a beneficial influence. In our dealings with family business we often hear family owners stating: "We don't want to end up like the Steinbergs." This negative-sounding connotation may mean they want to sell to avoid a fight among the next generation or it can also mean, more often than not: "We'd better plan for succession or else . . ."

## CANADIAN HISTORY WRITTEN
## BY BUSINESS FAMILIES

This vast country was built by business families, some of which existed even before confederation (1867). An example of these would be the Molson and the Eaton families. Many books and articles have been written about these families (Pitts, 2000). To recapitulate briefly, John Molson started brewing beer in Montreal in 1783. This family also became well-known in Québec for being the owners of the famous Montreal Canadians Hockey team. Hockey is a national sport which created its own local heroes, such as Maurice Richard and Jean Béliveau. This hockey team is directly linked with the passionate history of this French Canadian province, where in the past hockey fans rioted in the streets to defend their local hero: Maurice Richard. The Molson family and hockey are synonymous, and their reputation throughout the country is to this day one of a blue-blooded and proud Canadian family. In its sixth generation, the family business is mainly an ownership family, leaving the management of their operating companies to professional managers. This family business is currently undergoing a controversial transition with the merger between Molsons and the U.S. family-controlled Coors.

The Eaton family, on the other hand, has not survived, but it did last for four generations, and its contribution to the development of Canada is important (Pitts, 2000). Founded in the 1850s, Eaton was not only a chain of retail stores spanning from coast to coast but also a catalogue distributing company that enabled people living in rural Canada to order goods and clothing by mail. The Eaton catalogue was a household treasure that remains in the memories of most Canadians born before 1950.

Many more famous business families in Canada that have been part of our history and are now part of our national legacy. For various reasons some of these families have not survived into the twenty-first century and others have broken up and started over again. Nonetheless, they were part of our daily lives and most Canadians followed their demise in the newspapers (Gibbon & Hadekel, 1991). It seems all too often the media pays more attention to the ones in crisis than those that quietly go about conducting their business for generations. There are, however, many other business families that did not make the limelight. These also have contributed greatly to the development of this huge country. What comes to mind are the numerous farm families across this land who have supplied food not only to their countrymen but also to people all around the globe. They still work daily at sustaining this demanding life; their contribution is not always recognized, nor is it as glamorous as that of our more famous business families.

## PIONEERS IN THE FIELD OF FAMILY BUSINESS

### The Canadian Association for Family Enterprise

One can not write about Canada and the field of family business without mentioning the importance of the Canadian Association for Family Enterprise (CAFE). Founded in 1983 by a group of family business owners, CAFE is a not-for-profit association with chapters in thirteen cities across the country. CAFE's mission is to promote the well-being and understanding of the family in business, and its objectives are to educate, inform, and encourage its members in areas of unique interest to family business. CAFE counts over 1,000 family businesses as members who benefit from numerous educational and helpful activities organized by their local chapters and the national office (CAFE, 2004). The most popular activity within CAFE is definitely the PAGs: the Personal Advisory Groups that bring together a dozen or so family business members, each from a different firm and industry, to share their experiences of being part of a family-owned firm. Some of these groups have been meeting monthly for more than fourteen years. Another very popular feature of CAFE is the national symposium it holds every other year, which brings family members of all ages together for an educational and fun activities event. These symposiums have proven to be a great family activity in which each member is able to enrich his or her knowledge about the field and go home with an enhanced feeling of being part of something great: their family business.

CAFE also caters to professionals in the field, through educational programs such as the Family Council program and various seminars for families and professionals. CAFE has been instrumental in networking families with reliable professionals and encouraging their members to seek outside assistance when needed.

### The Business Families Foundation

Another important pioneer in the field of family business, especially on an international level, and known at its inception as the Institute for Family Enterprise, was founded in 1983 by Philippe and Nan-b de Gaspé Beaubien, owners of Télémedia. Now known as Business Families Foundation (BFF), through the years it has been instrumental in the development of the field of family business in Canada, as well as in the United States. The de Gaspé Beaubiens' main contribution was to encourage academics to study and develop educational programs that would answer the specific needs of family-owned firms (Business Families Foundation, 2004). They realized from their own experience that families in business did not take lightly the idea of participating in educational programs and talking about their personal issues. BFF developed, with the help of such people as John Ward, John Davis, Ivan Lansberg, and Harvard Professor Emeritus Louis By Barnes, exclusive programs using the case method and geared to multigenerational family business members. BFF was especially proud of getting spouses involved in these educational sessions and also in gathering many families from different parts of the globe to share and learn from one another. As was often stated by the BFF faculty: "The knowledge is in the room." After experiencing some very successful sessions with prominent families, BFF was persuaded by family participants to offer similar sessions to professionals in order for them to better understand the dynamics of family-owned firms so they could better help families use the tools taught during these sessions. BFF offered a two-day session to seasoned professionals from all walks of life for many years. These sessions, along with the ones offered to families, were influential in developing the field of family business advising, for these families and professionals were exposed to such innovative concepts as the three-circle model and the importance of effective and efficient governance structures (Davis & Taguiri, 1996). The need for specialized outside help was clearly established and a new field of professional advisors was created. A few years ago, the Road Map program, a ten-module multimedia educational program designed by BFF for CAFE families, illustrated this ripple effect between education and the field of family business advising. This program was designed to be given to a group of multiple families and to cater to multigenerations. Team facilitators chosen from CAFE were trained by BFF, with the help of Professor Louis By Barnes, to offer this program in twelve cities across Canada. The training emphasized team facilitating using the case method. One of the outcomes of this program was the training of better-qualified professionals in the field and the increase of awareness within the family business community of the help they could seek and get from these trained facilitators.

At the eve of the twenty-first century, BFF was concerned with the continuity of its work for upcoming generations. BFF decided that to ensure continuity they needed to get Canadian universities involved in the field of family business. The de Gaspé Beaubiens set out to persuade the deans of the most prominent universities in Canada to set up family business centers similar to the ones already established south of the border. A certain number of centers are already operational. The first two were the Business Family Center (BFC, 2004) at University of British Columbia (UBC) in Vancouver, BC, and the other was the Alberta Business Family Institute (ABFI) at University of Alberta (ABFI, 2004). These centers are mainly dedicated to research and education. Providing programs and education are intrinsic components of the field of family business. An enormous amount of information concerning the field is disseminated through seminars and conferences, and it has helped to enlarge the constituency to not only all members of the business family (even those not working in the business) but also to the professionals who serve them. There is a great need to train competent professionals who are aware of the family dynamics and who can, if need be, be called in as a family business consultant to help their clients resolve a particular issue. These centers can also provide an important link between the faculty members and business families. Many of these faculty members are conducting important research and are also writing much-needed case material to be used to help teach professionals and families about the field. Both of these centers now offer the Road Map program, and they maintain close contact with each other, often in partnership with CAFE and their members, for activities and seminars. This new collaborative work between the university centers and the business families will certainly have a positive effect, not only for the growing number of business families but also for the economic health of their communities. BFF is now winding down its separate operations and transferring its knowledge and programs to university centers across the country.

An additional organization set up a few years ago in Canada that has proven to be very helpful to certain larger business families is Private Foundation Canada, which helps business families set up their private foundations. This nonprofit organization is contributing to the growth of the philanthropic sector and getting more and more business families involved in giving back to their community (Private Foundation Canada, 2004). This trend toward establishing foundations and increased philanthropy is popular with business-owning families. It permits family members to play a more active role in their business family, especially those not directly involved in the operations of the business. It also provides an opportunity to initiate younger family members into becoming more knowledgeable and responsible owners and aids in the development of their communities.

## FAMILY BUSINESS CONSULTANT: AN EMERGING PROFESSION

The field of family business consulting is relatively new. We tend to distinguish among three levels of intervention. The first is the professional, such as the lawyer, accountant, estate planner (and many more) that have among their clientele family businesses. The second level is the facilitator, often from a behavioral science background, but not necessarily so, who is called in to facilitate a family meeting or family council or simply to act as a mediator in a dispute. The third level is the family business consultant, who, more often than not, is working with a team of professionals and can address the needs of all three subsystems of the business family: the family, the business, and the ownership.

He or she is the strategic mind behind the process and is capable of working with other professionals who are either already assisting the family or are part of his or her own group of advisors. It is this third level—the family business consultant—who is relatively new to the market. Family businesses know very little about their services. They therefore tend to revert to customary professionals, such as the accountant or lawyer, who are already working with the business to obtain help dealing with some of their family issues.

Some professionals are comfortable dealing with "soft" issues: those issues with a strong emotional component, or simply those dealing with parent/child relationships or sibling rivalries to name a few. Other professionals feel pulled away from their comfort zones when dealing with these issues, and thus try to focus strictly on the business aspects. The latter will usually call in a family business consultant or a facilitator to help the family with the "soft" issues and also to support the professional in whatever he or she is trying to accomplish with the family members, be it a shareholders agreement, an estate freeze, or simply a new will or prenuptial agreement.

Professionals who do feel comfortable dealing with the "soft" issues often are the more experienced and senior partners in firms that are looking for new challenges and enjoy a special relationship with someone important in the firm; for example, they may be acting as the most trusted advisor to the founder for the past several years. Hence, we see more and more professionals of many walks of life taking on a second career in this field of family business consulting. These professionals come in with firsthand knowledge about business and may have personal experience with clients, but they do not deal with the soft issues and the consequences these entail.

In the past few years, there has been extensive media coverage of the enormous transfer of wealth that is about to come about worldwide. Along with this transfer of wealth is the transfer of ownership to a new generation. As a result of this well-documented phenomenon, many of the larger service-providing professions in Canada (such as accountants, lawyers, wealth management, etc.) have realized that if they want to keep their clients, they must learn to attend to the next generation. For this reason, we see emerging new services geared specifically to family businesses with one or two senior members acting as the in-house family business specialist. The profession of family business consultation is slowly taking root in the Canadian landscape.

## COMMON DENOMINATOR

There appears to be an interesting common denominator shared by many of family business consultants. They have firsthand knowledge about family business: they are often "survivors" of their own family firm.

Having surveyed a dozen or so family business consultants in Canada, I was amazed by the presence of this common denominator; many answered that they came from family-owned firms. When writing this chapter I realized that I too could have been part of such a reality. My father decided to sell his firm to his partner when he realized his only son was not interested in taking over his construction firm. He never gave any thought to any of his four daughters becoming his successor, as in those days (mid-1960s) this was unheard of and not an option.

As has been shown in the foregoing, family business consultation is a new and not well-known profession in Canada. How do families reach these consultants and who calls them in? There is no predominant way that these families find their family business advisor or consultant. They might be referred by the professional who is already helping the family, such as their accountant. He or she is often the most trusted advisor to the family firm and can recommend to the founder that he or she seek outside help. The other common route that brings consultant and family together is the call from the most dissatisfied or anxious family member, who, more often than not, is not working in the business. A clear example is when the mother, who is worried about the upcoming succession and who is caught between her husband and children, contacts the consultant.

As mentioned earlier, the role of CAFE and BFF in the field of family business in Canada has been instrumental in linking consultants and families and making business families aware of the services consultants can render. These organizations have offered interesting forums through the years to families who were exposed to family business consultants or facilitators.

What are some of the main issues that these consultants deal with when working with business families? The most common ones are intergenerational communication, succession, and conflict in the ownership realm. One persisting reality is that we are often called when there is a crisis situation; unfortunately, this makes our work with families much more challenging. Sometimes the situation has been going on for decades, but it reaches crisis level when because of ill health or advancing age there needs to be a drastic change in order to ensure the continuity, not only of the business, but even of the family.

Most family business consultants collaborate with other professionals. To be helpful to families, it is important to know where your expertise starts and ends. One needs to know when to bring in specialized technical advisors from other disciplines who can offer the best up-to-date services. A good example of such a collaborative experience is when planning the transfer of ownership. The financial advisor works with the help of the family business consultant, who has dealt with all of the soft issues surrounding the transfer of ownership and what it will mean to various members of the next generation.

In Canada, as in other countries, family business consultants come from various professional backgrounds and each has also developed his or her own area of expertise. Some consultants have become very good at implementing efficient governance structures, such as boards of directors and family councils. Others have been instrumental in coaching both the incoming generation and outgoing generation through the difficult transition period. The family business consultant differs from other professional consultants in the degree of importance and attention he or she gives to the family side of the equation. It is not an easy task to be accepted into the personal sphere of their lives by family members, and the advisor must protect the trust that is instilled in him or her. It is important also to be sensitive to social and cultural differences. In Québec, for instance, a French-speaking province, the consultant needs to be able to offer services in French, as some of the family members might not be comfortable with sharing their feelings in English. In some parts of Québec, people have little need to learn English.

When asked, family business advisors in Canada foresee the future in a very positive light. There is a consensus that the need for their services is great, and many families are starting to ask for this type of outside consultation.

## THE IMPORTANCE OF RESEARCH
## IN THE FIELD OF FAMILY BUSINESS

Researchers in the field of family business are actively working in Canada, and we have some of the top researchers in the field. Their contribution to the understanding of the dynamics of family firms is abundant, and their dedication and insight on the importance of developing research in the field is most impressive. Some of the major people in Canada include Pramodita Sharma, Lloyd Steier, Jess Chua, Danny Miller, Isabelle Le Breton Miller, and Louise St Cyr. Many challenges still face researchers, such as developing family business definitions for all to share and work with. A further challenge is broadening the research to extend beyond issues of succession to more specific needs and questions that face family business members daily. Here is where family business centers in Canada and organizations such as CAFE can create the networking greatly needed between the researchers, the family business members, and the consultants.

The challenge facing the field is to produce research that can generate new theory, as well as research that can produce practical, communicable ideas and concepts that can be put into practice by business families. This in turn will encourage more academics and doctoral students to be drawn to the field of family business. It is our hope that more business families will contribute financially to fund research and share their experiences as well as their needs with teachers/trainers and researchers. The key for the future will be to build on the growing interest about family business as a specific type of organization and to collaborate with other fields of research to acquire a better understanding of the dynamics of business families. Through fundamental research, applied research, and even contracting research which is an important source of funding in Canada, we will create the momentum needed to raise the legitimacy of this field of inquiry.

## A CANADIAN CASE STUDY:
## THE COUSIN CONSORTIUM—THE BORDENS

### Part I: The Borden Family

The Bordens are a second-generation family-owned firm. Despite being only second generation, it is a cousin consortium. The business was created by a sibling partnership, composed of two brothers, who worked together for over forty years. They came from a very large family and needed to earn money to help their parents. Born in the 1930s, the brothers are now in their early seventies. Hugh is the eldest and the brainy one, and Jack is the doer and go-getter. Like most men of their generation, they married early in life and became the breadwinners. Hugh married a teacher, Margaret, and Jack married Evelyn, a young girl from a small farming town whom he met while traveling for the business. Both couples had three children.

The brothers were always very agreeable and were very business oriented. They spent all their waking hours running the business, and when times got rough, they made sure the women never knew, so as not to worry them. After the birth of her first child, Margaret never went back to teaching and Evelyn never worked out of the house. The two families were not very close. The brothers spent many hours together, but the spouses and the children met only on special occasions. Margaret was very demanding of her children, especially concerning their grades. She and Hugh had a son, Mark, and two daughters, Julia and Mariane.

Evelyn, on the other hand was very shy and not very demanding of the two sons and one daughter she and Jack had. The two eldest, Louise and Dave, were very independent of their mother, and the youngest, Richard, born ten years after his brother Dave, was quiet, much like his mother. Both families seem to be leading normal uneventful lives. The brothers often struggled to make sure the business prospered, while their spouses had to raise the children on their own.

Both the fathers were always involved with the business and never spent very much leisure time with their wives and children.

The cousins followed different academic paths. Hugh and Margaret's children all earned university degrees. Mark, a civil engineer, joined the family business when he graduated, and Julia, a human resources major, joined the business after spending ten years in a consulting firm. As for Mariane, she continued her education until she received her master's degree and followed her mother's path and went into teaching at a local college.

As for Jack and Evelyn's children, Louise, the eldest, married her high school sweetheart after graduating. Dave went on to college to get a sales and marketing degree in the hopes of joining the family business as a sales representative. Richard studied social work and went off to Africa to work with AIDS patients (see Figure 7.1).

## Part II: H&J Steel

The core business of H&J Steel is manufacturing steel beams for industrial construction projects. They occasionally also bid on an entire construction project. They have over eighty workers in the mill and thirty people running the office. Half of the workforce has been with H&J for more than twenty years.

Their business is very cyclical and susceptible to the fluctuations of many external variables, such as the price of steel, the exchange rate of the Canadian dollar, and the political environment. The company is located in the province of Ontario, one of the more prosperous provinces in Canada. Despite the fact that the local market was very healthy, they decided to expand south of the border into the U.S. market in the late 1970s.

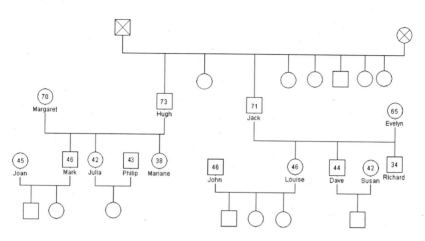

FIGURE 7.1. The Borden family genogram.

In the early 1990s the brothers hired a nonfamily CEO. The business needed more professional management and they both agreed that their children were not CEO material, at that moment. The steel industry was doing well and their business was following the trend, after going through the difficult decade of the 1980s. They were currently experiencing a well-deserved period of relief.

Their first experience with a nonfamily CEO was not very successful. After looking into the reasons why, the brothers realized that they were partly responsible. They seemed to be experiencing some difficulty in turning over control to a stranger.

In 1997 they hired a new nonfamily CEO, Mike Peters, age fifty-eight. Mike was instrumental in attracting Julia (Hugh's second child) into the business. She had the expertise they were looking for. At the time they needed a new HR person and she was perfect for the job. Her brother, Mark, had been with his father and uncle for the better part of twenty years and was now heading the engineering department. He was very much appreciated by his staff and comanagers. Unfortunately, his cousin Dave did not seem to reap the same success as Mark and was constantly at odds with Mark and some of the co-workers in the sales department. He seemed displeased with his progress in the business and felt he should be entitled to a more senior position.

The senior Bordens, Hugh and Jack, were moving further and further away from the daily life of operating a steel company. They remained on the board, but Jack was often in the office only from April to October. Hugh, on the other hand, was seldom in the office and showed up at important meetings when his brother insisted he be there.

Mike Peters was doing a great job trying to manage the business and the family dynamics. He had learned a lot about family businesses through his own experience with a former employer, another family-owned firm, and also by attending seminars on the subject of business families. He was instrumental in persuading the senior Bordens that they needed external help to face the next phase of their family firm's existence: the transition of ownership to the next generation.

## Part III: Enter the Family Business Consultants

When Mike Peters phoned our office, it had been at least three months since Hugh had suffered a mild stroke. Often family-owned firms need a crisis to trigger that ominous call for external help. The senior Bordens had gone through a serious wake-up call, one that Mike Peters also made sure they would listen to. The six cousins were already shareholders, after going through an estate freeze[3] in the 1980s, which seems to be a customary fiscal arrangement in Canada. Apart from this being used as a fiscal solution, no other steps were taken to inform the cousins of their rights and responsibilities and how they would eventually be expected to work together in the next phase of the family business.

Mike Peters succeeded in persuading the senior Bordens that their children were not ready to own the business as a team. He felt, as the current CEO, very strongly, as did some of the influential board members, that they needed external help to deal with some of the family issues that were more and more present and pressing in the business.

### Our Process

As family business consultants we try to work as a male and female team. We realized very quickly that being a team of individuals of different genders helps us to better understand the dynamics that are influencing the family system. We try to interview all family members, even those not working in the business, especially the spouses. They are, after all, the parents of the next generation. Often the family income is dependent on the financial well-being of the family business, so the spouses also have a great deal at stake and are influential members of the family system. After our interviews, we convene a family meeting. We see the family as our client, and this is stated in our initial proposal. We often get some resistance to including spouses in the feedback meeting, but even if they are not included, their input is taken into account in our report.

The first family meeting is crucial. It helps to discuss with the family some of the major issues we have identified and gives us an opportunity to realign our views if the family feels we have misinterpreted their situation. Usually at the end of the feedback meeting, we recommit to working together and prioritize the issues or the topics we want to attend to.

Often one of our major concerns is helping the family to acquire better communication skills and setting up some efficient governance structures. We now relate how this unfolded with the Bordens.

### The First Meeting

We met the senior Bordens over lunch and they told us the story of H&J Steel. They seemed to still enjoy each other's company and Jack seemed very protective of Hugh. Hugh's health was still a concern, but his strength was improving on a daily basis. Neither of them spoke about their wives or their children, but they both seemed to share the same gratitude toward Mike Peters for helping them cope with their transition issues while successfully managing their business.

Once we explained our process, they seemed confident that this might help them deal with the ownership transition issues. They agreed it would be wise to start with separate family meetings and then convene a joint family council. When asked about their board of directors; both men agreed that some of the members had overstayed their usefulness; however, they did not know how to let them go. As consultants, we had in the past assessed a few boards with some interesting results, such as redesigning a board to better suit the needs of the family firm. The senior Bordens agreed this might also be valuable to them.

## The Interviews and Family Meetings

We interviewed twelve family members, Mike Peters, the CEO, and two board members. All agreed on a few points: the senior Bordens got along very well, but neither was very instrumental in helping their children find their places in the business, and if it were not for Mike Peters, the business would not be where it then was.

The board members also seemed to agree that the board functions needed to be reassessed but were concerned about how Mike Peters would react. His position gave him substantial power, and he was not one to be accountable to anybody. When we met with Peters, he was very blunt: "Things need to change." He highly respected the senior Bordens but was not as generous toward the next generation. When asked to explain why he had doubts about them, Peters spoke mostly about David's attitude: "He storms out of meetings when he is not in agreement. He walks around this office as if he owned it! And he challenges my authority in front of other employees!" We then convened two family meetings.

Hugh's family decided they wanted the spouses present at the first meeting; thus seven members of the family were present, since the youngest, Mariane, had no spouse at the time. The meeting went very well. Hugh was very silent but Margaret had much say and so did the two eldest, Mark and Julia, who were working at H&J Steel. Our feedback report was well received, but family members wanted to discuss the issues of shared ownership with the other Borden family. Margaret was concerned about this forced relationship and was quite open in expressing her doubts about the abilities of nephew David. Mark and Julia were less direct, but they too shared the daily difficulties they faced in the business concerning David and his attitude toward Peters's authority. We all agreed to hold another meeting before convening the two families together.

Jack's family meeting was much less informative; only four members showed up, and no spouses were invited, except mother Evelyn. Also absent was Richard, the youngest member of the family, who was working in Africa. Louise, the eldest daughter, did not seem concerned about H&J steel. Her husband was earning a good living and she was raising their three children. David raised the issue of Peters and challenged his father on the need for a nonfamily CEO. Jack responded that he, along with his brother Hugh, trusted Peters's abilities and judgment and that for the moment, neither could identify anyone in the next generation who they thought was CEO material. They agreed on another meeting and when asked if they wanted spouses present, Jack gave a definitive no.

Each family held another family meeting and prepared for the joint family council. Each family identified five values that they would share with the other family and also worked on the profile for the selection process of the next board members. The U.S. market was a concern for both families, so they agreed the next independent board member should have commercial experience in the U.S. market. As consultants, we raised the issue of Peters's employment contract and the importance of meeting his needs in order to ensure his loyalty to the business. Both families agreed that negotiations should be driven by the independent board members, but some benchmarking should be done to make sure the offer took cognizance of industry standards. Another difficult topic was who could attend the Family Council, since both families did not share the same outlook on spouses' participation. It was agreed that for the time being the Family Council would include the senior Bordens and their wives and the six cousins. This was well accepted by the spouses since it was agreed that this should be perceived as a shareholder meeting.

## The Family Council

The first Family Council was set up as a family retreat in a luxurious inn, where family members could relax and enjoy some of the services offered by the in-house spa. The atmosphere was very civil and everybody seemed to enjoy each others' company. They were all surprised to see how alike their five selected values were. The sisters-in-law got along quite well, and Evelyn was more outspoken then she had been in the family meetings. Both Margaret and Evelyn shared with the family members how they had actually spent many years despising the business, since H&J Steel was instrumental in keeping their husbands away from the family. They also shared how resentful they felt about being left out. The next generation had never heard their mothers be so outspoken. They thought this was a great breakthrough.

The family members raised a few more topics that they wanted addressed in the next few months. The shareholder agreement was at the top of the list, and following close behind was the compensation issue. Some family members not working in the business felt that they should be compensated for attending these meetings and their expenses covered, especially if they had to come in from out of town, as was the case for Mariane. Louise also expressed the need for these meetings to be held on weekdays because weekends were family time and she wanted to be with her husband and children. This created an issue for her cousin, Mariane, who was a teacher. They eventually came to an agreement and also appointed family members responsible for getting everyone's opinion about the present shareholders agreement, before the next meeting.

## The Achievements

It took eighteen months, a few family meetings, and three joint family councils for the Borden Family Council to redefine the shareholders agreement, and set compensation policies for family meetings and for Family Councils. They also integrated spouses at a yearly meeting of the Family Council to be held in a vacation setting, with only one item on the agenda: fun. The senior Bordens agreed with the new contract for Peters that was drawn up by a subcommittee of the board. The family was also instrumental in finding two new board members who were more in tune with the needs of the second generation, one of whom had experience setting up a distribution network in the United States. The delicate issue of thanking a few old board members was easily taken care of as soon as the consultants stepped in to assess the existing board members. Two of them instantly handed in their resignations, realizing on their own that their lack of usefulness would soon be an issue.

The family members not working in the business were more and more involved in social activities sponsored by H&J Steel, and their new sense of being part of the family business, despite their nonparticipatory roles, was a welcome change, especially for the mothers.

## The Unsettled Issues

One very important and sticky issue remained: what to do about cousin David. David was strongly encouraged to work with a coach, who had a family business background. One of the main tasks was to help David distinguish his role as owner from his role as employee in H&J Steel. He needed to realize the effect his behavior was having on other workers and on his own reputation. Meanwhile, Julia, still responsible for HR, was having a hard time dealing with employees coming into her office to complain about her cousin. Peters tried to support Julia by raising the issue with David's father, Jack, but Jack was not responsive and felt unable to discuss this with anyone.

Another issue erupted when Jack phoned Peters one day to tell him his son-in-law, John, Louise's husband, had just lost his job. Jack ordered Peters to find John a job starting the next week. When Mark found out, he was about to complain to his father, Hugh, when his mother warned him that his father's health could not deal with all this stress and that it was now time for the next generation to deal with this on their own.

## Still to Come

Mark and Julia are seriously thinking of buying out Jack's family. Jack's children are seriously considering the offer. Louise and her husband are thinking of buying a farm and moving to the country with their children. Richard has decided to remain in Africa for a few more years and needs the income to sustain his living and charity work. And David is considering buying a local hardware store. As for Jack, his hobby is being on his boat in the Florida Keys, and he is also interested in helping David with the hardware store. Evelyn seems to be indifferent, whatever the outcome.

Our role as consultants, in this next phase, will be to assist the families through their buyout and make sure this will be conducted through a fair process, that all stakeholders are taken into account, and that no unsettled issues are left hanging.

## *CONCLUSION*

The conscientious family business consultant has a great future in Canada. I specify conscientious, as I truly think that this is what is going to distinguish the great practitioners from the mediocre ones. The consultants who take great care in giving the right services will be those not pressured by sales of other services, and who will respect their boundaries of expertise while referring families to the right specialist, when needed. These are the ones who will collaborate with the existing professionals already working with these families. They will be the more successful and the most reputable family business consultants. The family business consultants who will remain part of a greater learning community and who will strive to stay up to date with the field of family business will be the ones who will offer their clients learning opportunities, be it in collaboration with the new university-based family business centers in Canada or through such organizations as CAFE. Family business members need to network with other business families and learn from one another. To many consultants this will be perceived as threatening, but to those who are good and conscientious consultants such networking can only be favorable to their reputation and practice. They will hold a long-term perspective and truly have at heart a great interest in actually helping the families with whom they work. They will continuously keep in mind the tremendous responsibility they also carry for the many jobs and families that work for these business families. The price of failure is often quite costly to more than just the family with whom they are consulting.

Family business is a fast-growing field; like most other countries, Canada will witness in the next decade a transfer of wealth much larger than anyone has even imagined. Unfortunately, most of these new owners will need professional help. I say unfortunately because sometimes it will be due to the lack of family preparation (i.e., transmitting the right values or simply grooming the future owners). Other times it will simply be because of lack of preparation for a smooth transfer in ownership and leadership.

On a more positive note, we will be working with a generation of more educated people. Most will have had formal higher education, and in many cases, people will be more in tune with the benefits that change can bring. Examples of this would be learning new methods of communication or any new concept of governance. We will have a greater audience open to new ideas and much more amenable to the concept of continuous learning. I also predict that this new generation will have an intellectual capacity to take in new information at a very fast pace. We will need to be very efficient consultants to keep their attention span and answer their needs in a world of quickly transmitted and instant information. They have been brought up with the Internet and the Web, which provide continuous information and answers at their fingertips. Nowadays if someone sends an e-mail with a request, they expect an answer in the next few minutes or hours. Professionals joining this field have a vast array of state-of-the-art programs and seminars that will guide them through their learning in the field of consultation with family-owned firms. A group of very generous consultants is already working with business families and willing to share their experience with others. I know very few fields of professionals as generous with their time and their acquired knowledge as family business consultants in Canada and across the globe. This collaborative book proves this point.

## NOTES

1. Sam Steinberg, second son of a Hungarian immigrant, took over his mother's tiny food store and built an empire that included real estate, retailing, restaurants, and sugar refining. All of his five brothers worked for him, and Sam had four daughters. After seventy-two years and a terrible family feud triggered by thorny succession issues, the company was sold for $1.3 billion, after being the center of a well-publicized court dispute between Sam's daughters.

2. The McCain brothers, Wallace and Harrison, built McCains Foods company together for over thirty years. They had a serious dispute over succession. The disagreement turned sour and went public. The two brothers parted; Wallace took over Maple Leaf Foods, the giant Toronto meatpacker.

3. Often used as a tax strategy, the principle of the estate freeze is to establish and freeze the value of the business at a given moment in time, in the hands of the older generation. Privileged shares would be issued to the older generation in exchange for the common shares they hold in the company, at a value equal to the frozen market value of the company. In parallel, the younger generation would be issued a new set of common shares, at a token price, thus keeping the control in the hands of the older generation. Usually, such common shares would be held through a family trust. From that day on, any added value to the business will accrue to the benefit of the younger generation. Additional tax structures would be put in place to reduce the tax exposure of the beneficiaries.

## REFERENCES

Alberta Business Family Institute. (2004). "About us." Retrieved September 2004, from http://www.abfi.ca.

Business Families Foundation. (2004). "The Foundation." Retrieved September 2004, from http://businessfamilies.com.

Canadian Association of Family Enterprise. (2004). "About CAFE." Retrieved September 2004, from http://www.cafenational.org.

Canadian Statistics. (2004). "Canada e-book." Retrieved September 2004, from http://statscan.ca/english/pgdb.

Davis, J. & Taguiri, M. (1996). Bivalent attributes of the family firm. *Family Business Review, 9*(2), 199-208.

Family Business Center, University of British Columbia. (2004). "Business Families Center." Retrieved September 2004, from http://www.sauder.ubc.ca/bfc/index.cfm.

Gibbon, A. & Hadekel, P. (1991). *Steinberg: The breakup of a family empire.* Toronto, Canada: Macmillan.

Pitts, G. (2000). *In the blood: Battles to succeed in Canada's family businesses.* Toronto, Canada: Doubleday.

Private Foundation Canada. (2004). "About PFC." Retrieved September 2004, from http://www.pfc.ca.

Chapter 8

# Chile

Jorge J. Yunis

Considering Latin America does not have family-business[1] consultation companies,[2] and that I am the sole leader in this market for the region, the purpose of this chapter is to provide a critical viewpoint for establishing the differences between family-owned businesses and nonfamily businesses. The media in Latin America are extremely critical of family-owned business operations. In addition, few strategic developments have taken place in most family-owned businesses, where they concentrate their business mostly in traditional areas. Notwithstanding these factors, I am able to demonstrate that with robust individual entrepreneurship, the financial and economical standing of family business is above and beyond that of nonfamily businesses. Subsequently, from my perspective as a consultant, the business industry has shown good receptivity to generate the required essential adjustment both from the family management viewpoint as well as the role they occupy in developing their businesses (Medel, 2002). Koljatic (1999) goes so far as to call Chile a "Promised Paradise."

## RESEARCH DATA: THE CONSULTANT'S SOURCE

During eighteen years as a family-business consultant company leader in Latin America, I have serviced 75 families and their over 300 companies. The data provided should illustrate the aspects I consider relevant for this chapter: 93 percent of the market in Chile is made up of family businesses, a figure that represents one of the highest concentrations worldwide. In Latin America, most families are conventional conservative families. Family and traditions are at the forefront of their businesses. Consequently, legacies are thought of as a natural development, as coming from the cradle, implicit in family culture.

*Handbook of Family Business and Family Business Consultation*
Published by The Haworth Press, Inc., 2006. All rights reserved.
doi:10.1300/5491_08

Our families are sustained in a heartwarming relational environment, such that respect toward the figure of the founder is understood; our children remain at home until they complete their university degrees; it is common to share weekly activities and holidays together, etc. In summary, our society is structured around family values, while we halfheartedly observe the generational evolution in other countries and their consequences on the nuclear family.

In fact, family-owned Latin American companies are less competitive than their counterparts in developed countries. Similarly to China and India, Chile is in an accelerated process of transforming their enterprises into world-class competitors. From my personal experience, four countries are leading this change: Chile, since 1984, Brazil, Colombia, and El Salvador. Although 90 percent of all family-owned businesses expect to maintain their enterprises as such, throughout time incubator trends will tend to reduce the percentage of family companies.

Finally, common sense states that we have *"Sabor Latino"* (a Spanish expression suggesting cheerfulness as part of everything done, and how relationships between people are warm and friendly), and this is a robust and extremely unique factor as well as an added value to our professional background. To complement these ideas, and to introduce this chapter, Figure 8.1 illustrates the consultations requested by family-owned businesses between 1998 and 2004.

### PUBLIC FAMILY (FBS) AND NONFAMILY BUSINESSES (NON-FBS): A COMPARATIVE ANALYSIS

I would highlight that no prior assumption was involved for this study (Schwager, 1999); this research was undertaken without any previous hypothesis, with a broad vision in mind. My objective mainly consisted of determining behavioral similarities and differences in both analyzed groups. The reference year is 1999, and this research covers market progression to the current date.

The Chilean stock market is represented by similar quantities of family-owned businesses and nonfamily ventures. Following world trends, this figure is expected to rise, as is the case in developed countries worldwide where between 63 and 70 percent of all stocks belong to family businesses (Yunis, 1998).

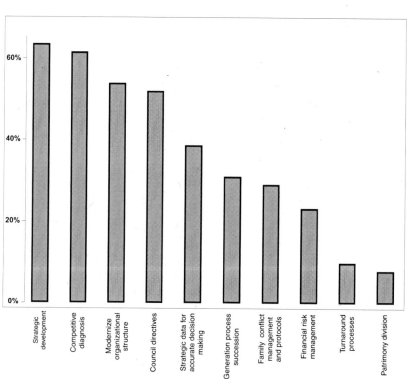

FIGURE 8.1. Family-owned business consultations from 1998 to 2004 (52 companies). *Source:* Equity Strategic Business Consultants, survey 2002-2003.

## *Family-Owned Business Figures in the Chilean Stock Market*

In Chile, a total of forty families are listed on the stock market; in total they hold seventy-seven different companies, but ten families (or 25 percent) have a concentration of forty-seven (or 61 percent) of those businesses. From the forty families, only three have more participation of third parties among their shareholders by retaining less property control, sustaining the management baton, family culture influence, and legacy management. In addition, another twenty-six families act as investors in nonfamily schemes; these act as holding investors and should thus be considered as FBs.

For the period analyzed, non-FBs have executed more transactions than FBs; nevertheless, their reduction is significant, showing a decrease from 47.7 to 41.8 percent. FBs, however, show a constant stock market transaction performance between 33.6 and 35.9 percent.

The IPSA (the Chilean equivalent to Dow Jones 30 average) and its principal stock index is another relevant figure in favor of FBs. To date, the number of FBs included in this index since 1999 increased from eight to fifteen. Noticeably, however, non-FBs experienced a decline from twenty-four to nine.

### Monetary Volumes Transacted

Historically, non-FBs have always surpassed FBs in monetary volumes transacted. In 1999 the rate was 9 times higher, while today this figure is only 2.7. To underline the latter, FB volumes grew 100 percent while non-FBs experienced a dramatic decrease of 38 percent. This represents a fabulous result for our target market.

### Stock Market Capitalization

The proportion of stock market capitalization has been constant during the past several years, where 44 percent corresponds to FBs and 56 percent to non-FBs.

| FBs | Non-FBs |
|---|---|
| Four are valued over US$300 million. | Six are valued over US$400 million. |
| Eighteen are valued over US$150 million. | Twenty-six are valued over US$150 million. |
| Nine are valued at US$100 million. | Five are worth US$100 million. |
| Seventeen are worth between US$50 million and US$100 million. | Twelve are worth between US$50 and US$100 million. |

### Market Price/Book Value Rate

A total of 100 companies have a market price below their book value rate, out of which 50 are FBs and 50 are non-FBs. Price volatility was analyzed by relating the standard deviation and the price average, and weighted with three independent elements: stock market capitalization, transactions conducted, and monetary volume. FBs show a slightly lower percentage variation equal to 8 to 9 percent, and non-FBs fluctuate between 9 and 14 percent.

Conclusively, FBs have a higher correlation between price and net return, whereas non-FBs are volatile, relate to investor behavior, and are involved in a higher speculation market.

## Market Price/Book Net Return Index

In 1999, a huge gap between market price and book net return index existed between non-FBs and FBs; non-FBs were 26.8 times higher than FBs. However, today this situation has been corrected, and FBs show an index of 12.6, and non-FBs, 13.6. Once again, these figures are very positive for FB consultants such as my company. This stronger position reaffirms the conclusion stated in the previous price volatility discussion.

## Concentration of Chilean FBs in Macro Sectors

As illustrated on Figures 8.2 and 8.3, eleven FBs concentrate their business mainly in foods and beverages, nine in animal husbandry and forestry, and six in port and maritime services. On the other hand, non-FBs concen-

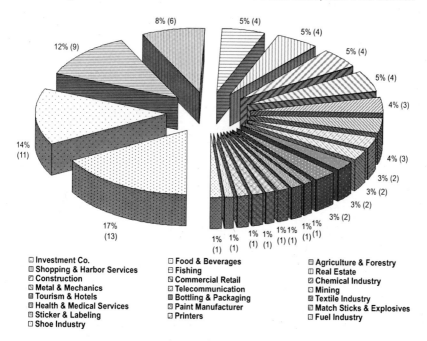

FIGURE 8.2. Public family-owned businesses by economic sector (percent).
*Source:* Equity Strategic Business Consultants, survey 2002-2003.

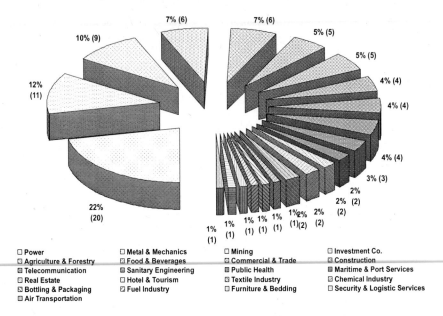

FIGURE 8.3. Nonfamily business distribution by industry (percent). *Source:* Equity Strategic Business Consultants, survey 2002-2003.

trate their business in power distribution, owning twenty companies, and twenty metal mechanical endeavors, as well as nine mining companies. Thirty percent of both FBs and non-FBs analyzed participate in only four macro sectors, an extremely robust and restricted concentration. The remainder are extremely dispersed; more precisely, we found one company per macro sector. To further examine this issue, FBs prefer developing products of natural origin, while non-FBs are attracted to complex industries.

*Investments by Pension Funds*

Relevancy must be given to the fact that pension funds hold stocks in thirty-one FBs and thirty-eight non-FBs. A simple average specifies that pension funds maintain a 7 percent FB patrimony and 10 percent in non-FBs. Consequently, the trend to invest is not radically different considering the pertinent sizes. Pension funds concentrate their investments on non-FBs, mainly in the electrical, public health, and communication industries; however, the same tend to diversify is seen in a wider range of FB-related industries.

*Mutual Funds*

The first empirical observation shows that throughout time, mutual funds have invested in almost the same manner in both categories. However to carry out this analysis from a monetary viewpoint, the comparison represents a volume of investment for non-FBs that is 1.8 times higher than the amount invested in FB-related industries, the former being $107 million and the latter $54 million.

*ADRs: An International Recognition of Strength*

ADR issues in the American stock market were celebrated for eight Chilean FBs and eleven non-FBs, an outstanding performance of our country. This occurrence demonstrates the impressive progress our economy has made and how it has improved on quality management. Chile is achieving worldwide recognition. Both ADR issues represent 8.5 percent FB patrimony and 7 percent non-FB. Consequently, the international market equally values both company groups.

*Longevity: The Business Life Cycle*

An average of fifty-two years of company longevity was the result of the FBs analyzed, surpassing non-FBs that reached forty-five years (see Table 8.1 and Figure 8.4). Only twelve FBs and eight non-FBs exceeded 100 years of business longevity. This analysis indicates that most FBs are already in their fifth family business generation. In addition, in this specific study, we discovered that in Latin America, over 300 hundred FBs have been in existence from 100 and 150 years. I am a board member of the oldest industrial bakery in Chile, operational now for 121 years, and of the oldest reprographic copier company, operational for 82 years.

## FINANCIAL ANALYSIS

### Gross Income

FB gross income improvement is noticeable (Damodaran, 2001; Medel, 1999). In 1999, FBs began with a gross income 82 percent below non-FBs; however, their evolution has since surpassed this by 106 percent, a persistent rate to date. In addition, upon comparing twelve of the highest accumulative rate growth FBs and non-FBs, the former obtained 64 percent versus 18 percent for the latter.

TABLE 8.1. Public family business longevity.

| Company | Year founded |
|---|---|
| Vapores [Compañia Sud Americana De Vapores S.A.] Trasportation | 1872 |
| Carolina [Empresas Santa Carolina S.A.] Vineyard | 1875 |
| Santa Rita [Sociedad Anonima Viña Santa Rita] Vineyard | 1880 |
| Conchatoro [Viña Concha Y Toro S.A.] Vineyard | 1883 |
| Undurraga [Viña Undurraga S.A.] Vineyard | 1885 |
| Falabella [S.A.C.I. Falabella] Departament Store | 1889 |
| D&S [Distribucion Y Servicio D&S S.A.] Merchandise Distribution | 1893 |
| Telsur [Cnt Telefonica Del Sur S.A.] Telephone Company | 1894 |
| Bata [Bata Chile S. A.] Shoes | 1894 |
| Victoria [Fabrica Victoria Puente Alto S.A.] Textile | 1894 |
| Carozzi [Industrias Alimenticias Carozzi S.A.] Food | 1898 |
| Paris [Empresas Almacenes Paris S.A.] Departament Store | 1900 |
| Cristales [Cristalerias De Chile S.A.] Crystal & Glass Products | 1904 |
| Minera [Minera Valparaiso S.A.] Mining | 1906 |
| Fosforos [Compañia Chilena De Fosforos S.A.] Match Sticks | 1913 |
| Tattersall [Sociedad El Tattersall S.A.] Misc. Agricultural Industry | 1913 |
| Volcan [Compañia Industrial El Volcan S.A.] Cement | 1916 |
| Elecmetal [Compañia Electro Metalurgica S.A.] Metallurgy | 1917 |
| CMPC [Empresas CMPC S.A.] Pulp & Paper | 1920 |

*Source:* Chilean Stock Exchange; Equity Strategic Business Consultants, survey 2002-2003.

## Efficiency and Costs

Operations overhead for FBs increased almost equal to the income, which allows us to conclude that FBs tend to be slightly inefficient. However, our analysis shows their gross revenue grew by 45 percent, while their

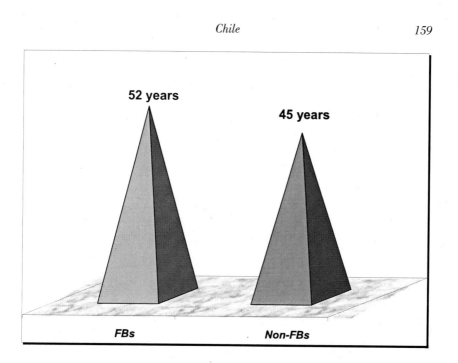

FIGURE 8.4. Average age of FBs and non-FBs. *Source:* Chilean Stock Exchange; Equity Strategic Business Consultants, survey 2002-2003.

operations overhead increased by 46 percent. However, non-FBs had an 18 percent income increase while costs represented 14 percent.

### The Bottom Line

The gradient reference curve for both groups is always positive, and although non-FBs hold a more marked gradient, when performing a year-to-year comparison, FBs largely overcome non-FBs. A comparison of the twelve main collective net earnings in the period analyzed, which shows that FBs surpass non-FBs by 45.5 percent, may help substantiate this conclusion.

### Liquidity Ratio

FBs unquestionably surpass non-FBs in liquidity ratios. For 1999, their liquidity was 1.7, showing an increase to 2.0 to date, while non-FBs dropped from 1.3 in 1999 to .99 in the same period.

## *Net Earnings/Assets Ratio*

On both cases the ratio curve remained at low performances; FBs advanced to 3.7 percent compared to non-FBs reaching 1.3 percent. A possible explanation for the poor performance is the result of investment policies on fixed assets, which determine important charges on result depreciation, particularly for non-FBs, which overcame FBs' fixed assets by 76 percent.

## *Dividend Policies*

Curiously, thirty-two companies (six FBs and twenty-six non-FBs) distributed their dividends in sums over 100 percent of the yearly net earnings. This suggests that non-FBs tend to benefit stockholders in the short term as they manage market value, which is not the case for FBs, which are founded with a long-term vision in mind. Thus, the challenge for non-FBs remains in finding ways to build wealth. Other research I performed (Yunis, 1999, 2000, 2001), in which 280 FBs were analyzed between 1992-1995 and 1996-2000, concludes that FBs place the sustenance value first on creating wealth with a clear view of persisting into future generations. It will be hard for FBs to comprehend the crucial need to build wealth; nonetheless, these figures illustrate why FBs persist longer than non-FBs. In summary, FBs capitalized dividends on a constant ratio 2:1 compared to non-FBs.

## *Financing Structure*

A noticeable difference may be observed in FBs' and non-FBs' financing structures. FBs mainly fund themselves through operative resources, and as this study shall conclude, FBs have increased their operational liabilities by tenfold.

In contrast, the non-FBs have greater access to financing through banks, showing an operational liability improvement of only 88 percent.

## *Bond Issues*

Bond issues may be another perspective from which to observe financial attitudes on both industries. Thirteen public FBs issued bonds totaling US$1.4 billion and fifteen non-FBs for US$2.5 billion, with no interest rate differences. On the other hand, this study secured information on privately held companies which placed bonds for six FBs and thirteen non-FBs for amounts totaling US$825 million and US$1.9 billion, respectively.

# COMPARING CHILEAN AND LATIN AMERICAN FAMILY-OWNED BUSINESSES WITH PEER BUSINESSES IN DEVELOPED COUNTRIES

## Quality Criteria Used for Comparison

FBs in developed countries as well as in Chile and Latin America may be compared in some areas; in others they simply cannot. In Latin American countries, FBs are in a more precarious standing. Europeans and Americans are eager and decisive when dealing with strategic progress in the business field but do not have the same attitude when dealing with family values.

FBs in developed countries, on the other hand, are stronger in terms of their business organization. Latin American FBs are lacking in modern technology and haven't conveniently adapted to the competitive adjustments imposed by globalized markets or the necessary management standards required. Notwithstanding these limitations, Latin American FBs are evolving at a slow pace today; some technological improvements have been implemented to improve efficiency at lower operational costs, and the need to be aware of international markets has been raised.

In fact, strengthening companies necessarily depends upon the emphasis the business environment sets on professionals in charge of managing the businesses, that is, their professional excellence. Today, one does not need to be a large company to compete in the global market; what is needed are top-notch professionals who are capable of competing and succeeding, an edge small family businesses are betting on. Large companies confuse huge financial resources with efficiency, and they neglect the basic values of management FBs concentrate their efforts on. In time non-FBs will realize this and may stumble because of their lack of vision.

Five years ago we surveyed representative businesses in six countries in South America (Chile, Peru, Bolivia, Uruguay, Paraguay, and Argentina), interviewing leaders of 974 FB s. Seventy-nine percent felt that companies they managed needed to urgently strengthen management, 74 percent indicated the decision-making process within their companies required improvement, and 56 percent indicated an urgent need to improve competitive advantages. They recognized that success is instigated; failure is accidental.

Another published survey conducted in September 1997, which included data collected on 250 FBs from ten Latin American countries,[3] showed unexplainable behavior. Only 5 percent of these businesses (twelve companies) had formally constituted a board of directors. Most of these companies resolved issues on a daily basis and make rash decisions on last-minute critical variables, without pondering or analyzing each critical success indicator professionally.

Another study carried out in 2003 by Santiago's Chamber of Commerce indicated that 2 percent of the Chilean market is involved in e-trade, which certainly increased their risk of failure. Most of these companies trade in the domestic commercial arena, a small and highly competitive environment, in a permanent tug-of-war for the same piece of the pie.

## WATCHFULNESS OVER ORGANIZATIONAL LIFE IN FAMILY-OWNED BUSINESSES

### A Consultant's Challenge to Implement Strategic Factors, Manage Competitive Risks versus Organizational Family Misalignments

The following was based on various consulting experiences (Yunis, 2000) and documents as well as the research conducted by the author: A strategic viewpoint is essential, but not enough for a family-owned corporation to achieve success (Rosin & Berger, 1991). A misalignment between business styles and market requirements is the difference between successes and reaching an untenable position. This occurs due to the lack of academic background of most family-led businesspeople.

In fact, most owner-executives often confirm that what keeps them up at night is not their lack of strategies, but rather their inability to implement them within their organizations. A few months ago, at a meeting with a dozen clients, most believed that approximately 70 percent of all failures experienced acting as executive chairmen were due to strategic implementation flaws.

Following from this idea, the more fundamental questions that Latin American businesspeople should ask themselves are as follows:

> *Should strategic business models be redefined?* Yes, I strongly recommend it.
> *Why does a good company made up of supposedly bright people, in touch with their products and customers, have problems implementing strategies successfully?* Because family members do not allow their executives to manage their organization.

When these questions are considered, the search for progress takes a completely different course. What distinguishes excellent performers is the manner in which they manage to realize their goals. That is, they should become organized to recognize the direction they need to take to participate in a specific market. Many of the struggles they face are symptomatic of dynamic and complex problems that are embedded in their organizational models. Corporate leaders of family-owned businesses tend to believe that their company personnel behave irrationally. These are tough problems to solve, as they are deeply rooted in their economic logic, hindering family-owned businesses from making effective and timely decisions. Likewise, when family members are capable of transforming strategic proposals into compatible organizational management, they achieve competitive advantages for their companies. In summary, families acting in this manner share certain features: they understand the nature of the challenges they face, they recognize them, and they plan designs and adapt them to their needs.

The key to improving on performance is not modifying the goals or exhorting the organization to work better. On the contrary, the solution is to change the organizational environment and attitude of the entire group, with the purpose of favoring a decision-making process in line with their main goals.

To conclude, most family organizations analyzed have evolved in time by intuition, by individual efforts, stress, circumstances, and internal power struggles (McKinsey & Coo, 2004). Today, consultations under way in Latin American companies are performed on a more in-depth personal basis, which has led me and my team to understand that we must increase our efforts through various public talks to motivate change as a requisite for family-led companies.

## NOTES

1. Family office: At present, family offices are not common practice in Chilean firms. Perhaps there may be an extensive need for these within the next five years, although this is not yet on the horizon.

2. Although individual consultants exist in various countries in Latin America, EQUITY is the sole family-owned business consultant firm in the entire region.

3. The ten surveyed countries are Mexico, El Salvador, Guatemala, Honduras, Venezuela, Colombia, Ecuador, Peru, Chile, and Argentina.

## REFERENCES

Adizes, I. (1998). *Corporate life cycles.* Upper Saddle River, NJ: Prentice Hall.
Damodaran, A. (2001). *The dark side of valuation.* Upper Saddle River, NJ: Prentice Hall.
McKinsey & Company (2004). ICARE Business Conference: Potenciar el gobierno corporativo de las empresas en Chile.

Medel, L. (1999, November). Dinastías de empresas familiares. *Revista Capital,* *91*(106).

Medel, L. (2002, August). Empresas familiares vs. sociedades de capital: En la cancha macroeconómica, entrevista a Jorge Yunis. *Revista Capital, 90*(76).

Rosen, R. and Berger, L. (1991). *The healthy company: Eight strategies to develop popular productivity and profit.* Los Angeles: G.P. Putnam.

Schwager, J.D. (1999). *Technical analysis.* New York: John Wiley & Sons.

Yunis, J. (1998, September). Empresas familiares Chilenas cotizan en la bolsa desde 1993 [Press release].

Yunis, J. (1999, 2000, 2001). *Equity-Chile.* Santiago, Chile: Equity-Chile.

Chapter 9

# Ireland

Marcus Spillane
Bill O'Gorman
Naomi Birdthistle

The island of Ireland is located on the northwestern edge of Europe. Politically, the Republic of Ireland consists of twenty-six counties, while the remaining six northeastern counties all form Northern Ireland, which is part of the United Kingdom of Great Britain and Northern Ireland. Where the word *Ireland* is used in this chapter, it is to be taken to mean the *Republic of Ireland.* Ireland has been a member of the European Union (EU) since 1973. According to the Central Statistics Office (2003), Ireland has a population of 3.9 million, with approximately 29 percent below the age of twenty. Ireland is a small, modern, trade-dependent economy with growth averaging a robust 8 percent during the Celtic Tiger years, 1995 to 2002. The country has moved from a predominantly agrarian society to a focus on industry, services, and foreign direct investment (FDI). Although exports remain the primary engine for Ireland's growth, the economy has also benefited from a rise in domestic consumer spending, construction, and business investment.

## *FAMILY BUSINESS DEFINED*

Family business is a relatively young field of academic inquiry, and as such, academics, consultants, professionals, and practitioners have struggled to define the term. The difficulty with the definition of a family business is compounded by the finding that family business relationships change according to the structure and size of the business (Birley, 2000). The husband-wife business is vastly different from a large family business in terms of the participation of family members in ownership and day-to-day management. Gersick, Davis, McCollom-Hampton, & Lansberg (1997)

*Handbook of Family Business and Family Business Consultation*
Published by The Haworth Press, Inc., 2006. All rights reserved.
doi:10.1300/5491_09

propose a three-dimensional view of family business, taking into account the position of a company in terms of family, ownership, and business life cycles. Handler (1989) identifies four dimensions used by writers in family business literature to define the family firm: degree of ownership and management by family members, interdependent subsystems, generational transfer, and multiple conditions. She observes that although there is no consensus as to what uniquely defines a family business, there seems to be a general agreement that the dimensions to be considered are the first three.

In an attempt to define the term *family business* from an Irish context, the John C. Kelliher Family Business Centre (JCKFBC), which was established in 2002 at University College Cork, conducted a survey of businesses in Cork city and county. Cork is the largest county in Ireland and accounts for 11 percent of the total population. The results of the survey identified that 73 percent of respondents considered themselves family businesses, of which 97 percent of these respondents own more than 50 percent of the voting shares of their respective businesses. In addition, 84 percent identified that family members are directly involved in managing the family business. Fifty-six percent of the businesses were being run by the first generation, and 88 percent of total respondents stated that they intend to pass on the business to the next generation (Buckley & O'Gorman, 2003). Based on these findings, the authors of this chapter have adopted the following definition as the interpretation of what constitutes a family business in Ireland:

> A family business is a business where one family holds more than 50% of the voting shares, supplies a significant proportion of the company's senior management and is effectively controlling the business, where there is evidence of more than one generation working in the business and/or intention to pass the business on to the next generation, and that the family regard the business as a family business. (Buckley & O'Gorman, 2003, p. 6)

The terms *family business* and *family firm* are used interchangeably in this chapter.

## FAMILY BUSINESS LANDSCAPE

No official statistics exist that identify how many family businesses there are in Ireland. In order to determine a figure that would give an estimate of the number of family businesses in Ireland, it is necessary to examine the data pertaining to the overall business landscape in Ireland and to use the results from other European sources for the calculation of this estimate. The

European Commission (2003) found that some 20.5 million enterprises operate in the EU, and 70 percent are classified as small and medium-sized enterprises (SMEs). In European terms, an SME is an enterprise that employs less than 250 people. The European Commission further subdivides this definition to explain the difference between micro, small, and medium-sized enterprises: a micro enterprise employs fewer than than ten people, and a small enterprise employs more than ten people but fewer than fifty. According to Riehle (2003), of the 20.5 million enterprises in the EU, some 17 million are owner managed and/or family businesses in the fields of manufacturing, commerce, and services. In an Irish context, the National Competitiveness Council (1999) identified that 89.8 percent of businesses are classified as micro businesses, 8 percent are small businesses, 1.6 percent are medium, and 0.6 percent are large enterprises. Thus, 99.4 percent of businesses in Ireland are classified as SMEs.

Using these statistics, one can deduce that, since the majority of businesses in Europe are SMEs and the majority of these are family businesses, 83 percent of businesses in Ireland are owner managed and/or family enterprises. This estimate is supported by Wrixon's (2002) comments that approximately 75 percent of all businesses in Ireland are family businesses. From these estimates it can be clearly seen that family businesses play an important part in the Irish economy.

## HISTORY OF FAMILY BUSINESSES

Traditionally in Ireland, family businesses have been associated with produce from the land, such as brewing, distilling, milling, tanning, and other agri-related businesses. Some family businesses have all but disappeared; the name continues, but the extent of ownership by the family has been greatly diluted. For example, the most famous Irish family business, Guinness, took over other family brewing businesses such as Smithwick's and McArdle's in the 1980s. Then Guinness merged with Grand Metropolitan to form Diageo, a public company, in late 1997.

Many family businesses dating from the eighteenth and nineteenth centuries still exist in Ireland today, such as Waterford Wedgewood (1759), Punch Industries Limited (1851), Johnson and Perrott Motor Group (1820), and the Musgrave Group (1876), to mention but a few. However, the vast majority of family businesses, with an existence of more than two generations, are ones that have been founded since the creation of the Irish Free State in 1922.

Two major issues have impacted family business longevity in Ireland—economic policies of successive Irish governments and the growth in competitiveness and globalization. As stated earlier, many of the older family businesses were operating in traditional industry sectors. With the advancement of globalization and increased competitiveness in the Irish economy, most of these traditional sectors came under threat in the last fifteen years of the twentieth century. Despite this, approximately 50 percent of family businesses in Ireland have revenues greater than $13.1 million (€10.0 million using a dollar/euro exchange rate of 0.77 at time of writing), and 41 percent have revenues in excess of $26.2 million (€20.0 million) (PricewaterhouseCoopers, 2004, hereafter PwC). However, family businesses have not had a long tradition of uninterrupted development in Ireland, as compared to other countries. For example, if the results of the JCKFBC survey are extrapolated, then approximately 56 percent of family businesses in Ireland are in their first generation (Buckley & O'Gorman, 2003). This may contribute to the fact that research into the family business sector is only beginning in Ireland and therefore the support services available to family businesses are also in their infancy.

Anecdotal evidence suggests that only a relatively small percentage of family businesses survive to the third generation. The limited research conducted to date suggests that the majority of family businesses have no procedures in place for addressing issues of governance or succession. For example, the PwC *Irish Family Business Report* (2004) indicates that 53 percent of family businesses in Ireland never prepare strategic development plans, 3 percent never prepare management accounts, and only 31 percent prepare accounts annually. Without regular structured management information, owners and managers may not be aware of valuable opportunities for the business in time to take advantage of them, nor will the owners and managers be able to take timely or corrective actions when and where needed. The report also identifies that the lack of planning for succession is still a major issue for family businesses in Ireland.

## FAMILY BUSINESS RESEARCH

A paucity of family business research exists for Ireland. Some of the large professional service firms have performed the bulk of commercial research, while two tertiary-level educational institutions have performed the majority of academic research that exists to date. Only over the past five years has an increase in research into the family business sector occurred. For example, PwC produced the *Irish Family Business Report* in 2002 and 2004. The findings suggest that the vast majority of family businesses in Ireland have no procedures in place for addressing governance issues and that family politics and lack of succession planning were identified as both short- and long-term constraints.

Academic research conducted by Birdthistle (2004) specifically examined family businesses as SMEs and analyzed their learning strategies. She found that the majority of family businesses in Ireland are established as private limited companies and that they are closely held organizations in which multiple generations and/or a number of family members serve as employees or are dependent upon the business for financial support. An analysis of the learning and training environment in Ireland yielded results indicating that learning and training opportunities are sparse and if family business members wish to avail themselves of training they primarily go abroad. Sending members of the management team to formal training programs is not a common practice carried out by family SMEs. This suggests a lack of formal training initiatives for family businesses in Ireland. The findings identify that as the business grows in size, so too does the level of importance of training family members. Informal training strategies are more commonplace among micro businesses, as they find the cost of formal training prohibitive.

With this landscape in mind, this chapter is based on the evidence that exists to date, namely the research performed by commercial entities, research conducted by this chapter's authors, plus interviews with members of family businesses and research available from the University of Limerick and the JCKFBC.

## FAMILY COUNCILS, FAMILY OFFICES, AND PHILANTHROPY

Family businesses in Ireland have grown significantly over the past several years, and demographics suggest that more and more multiple generations are now actively involved in the management of family businesses; the sector is still not sufficiently developed to warrant these various structures.

The setting up of family councils to facilitate the interaction of the family with the business is only now becoming more common. Along with the setting up of a family constitution, this is often the starting point for family business consultants when they are advising clients.

Although rare, family offices, which enable the family to invest their wealth as a group with centralized financial planning, are becoming more prevalent, as the wealth that has been generated in Ireland by family businesses is now being extracted. The term *family office* is somewhat grandiose for the current structures in Ireland, which are somewhat informal. There has yet to be collaboration among families to embrace the wider concept of multiple family offices, though this is where some of the professional service firms feel the opportunities lie for the future.

Philanthropy, in relation to family businesses in Ireland, for the most part does not exist as it is understood globally. However, family businesses in Ireland are very much the bedrock of local communities. Frequently these businesses are very active in sponsoring and promoting local causes ranging from sports teams to youth community centers. Rarely is professional advice sought in these cases; in essence, contributions and sponsorships are provided on an ad hoc basis and according to the whim of the families themselves. To be more specific, it is generally one member of the family, who is somehow associated with the sporting or social activity being sponsored, who makes the decision.

In general, the Irish market is still far from having a critical mass for family councils, family offices, and philanthropy to be significantly beneficial. In due course, like in other mature markets, these structures will become more commonplace, but for now most of the professional service firms have indicated that there is little interest in, or understanding of, these structures among their clients.

## FAMILY BUSINESS CONSULTATION

O'Gorman (2003) found that many people in Ireland, including members of family businesses, consider family business consultation to be merely advice to family businesses on issues of taxation, accountancy, and legislation. The authors of this chapter suggest that family business consultation is more than this—it is consulting on every aspect of the family and the business and the interaction of both. It should be based on a clear understanding of the dynamics of families and families within businesses. Based on the authors' research it is evident that heretofore the needs of many family businesses were not adequately satisfied by domestic family business consultants. As a result, these family businesses often sought advice, such as conflict resolution and succession planning, from consultants and professional service firms from abroad. Fortunately, a number of the larger professional service firms in Ireland are now beginning to provide these services. In addition, many of the banks, accountancy, consultancy, and legal firms now have dedicated teams to serve their family business clients. However, few of these firms engage in research, and only one produces regular reports on their research findings.

Based on discussions with professional services firms, for this chapter, the authors noted that the family businesses engaging these firms would generally have revenues in the range of $2.6 million (€2 million) to $6.5

million (€5 million) and upward. However, all the firms agreed that they have family business clients spanning the entire range from micro enterprises to large family-run public companies.

Some of the larger professional services firms run family business seminars to which they invite both clients and nonclients, at various locations around the country. Part of the reason for these seminars is to educate members of family businesses on specific family business issues. In addition, these seminars provide a forum for families to interact with one another, which leads to a realization that many family businesses face similar issues and that there is a benefit to be gained from engaging a family business consultant.

Most of the professional service firms in Ireland tend to market their family business services through the sponsorship of conferences and/or the publication of research in the family business sector. This can be differentiated from academic research in that it is more commercially focused, but it still provides useful data pertaining to the family business landscape in Ireland. Today media coverage in relation to the family business sector is increasing the awareness of the special issues and dynamics associated with these businesses.

Until 2004 none of the state enterprise support agencies had a particular focus on family businesses, even though there has been a movement toward recognizing the importance of this sector. Similarly, the Small Firms Association (SFA), a national organization representing the needs of small enterprises in Ireland, when contacted, stated that they do not distinguish between SMEs and family businesses (Birdthistle, 2003).

One of the more proactive organizations that provides support and advice to family-owned and -managed businesses is Plato Ireland, another business support forum for owner-managers of SMEs. Through a unique partnership with large "parent" companies, Plato provides SMEs with facilitated group learning, specialist expertise and advice, networking opportunities, and business development training.

Unfortunately, it is evident that even today the majority of advice being provided to family businesses in Ireland primarily relates to business issues, with little focus on family issues. Also, in most cases, the advice is based on long-standing and close personal relationships between the founder of the family business and his or her advisor. This relationship, initiated when the family business was much smaller, in most cases can no longer provide the specialist support that is now required. In addition, younger generations who are now involved with the family business have a jaundiced view of the support and advice these advisors can provide to their families and businesses. This statement is supported by O'Gorman (2003), who identified that 71 percent of family businesses indicated that they ask their accountants for advice only when making critical business decisions. However, this advice seems to be primarily fiscal in nature. Interestingly, 28 percent of the respondents stated that accountancy firms do not have enough expertise to deal with broader business issues. In relation to the legal profession, 92 percent of the respondents stated that they use their solicitor/legal representative only "in times of difficulty."

With the significant growth experienced by family businesses during the Celtic Tiger years and the resulting increase in personal wealth, and the changing demographics in Ireland, the primary issues facing family businesses in 2006 are (1) succession and (2) how to realize wealth and diversify. Thus the role of the family business advisor is becoming increasingly important to the development and sustainability of family businesses.

Because of this increased importance, the first Family Business Center in Ireland, the JCKFBC, was established in 2002. The focus of this Center is to perform family business research and to educate family members, consultants, and advisors involved with family businesses. The Center also provides a networking facility whereby members of family businesses can discuss their issues in a confidential, cooperative, supportive, and nonthreatening environment.

## REPUTATION OF FAMILY BUSINESS CONSULTANTS

It is apparent to the authors of this chapter that the status of family business consultants has improved significantly over the past few years. Much of this is attributed to an increased awareness of the functions and skill set of family business consultants. Family business clients are keen to see that their advisors have the required soft skills and empathy for their family business issues. Despite this, O'Gorman's (2003) research suggests that families still feel some reluctance to actually engage advisors to help with sensitive family issues. Part of this is due to family members' inabilities to admit that they have these dilemmas. As the whole family business sector gets more exposure through education, media, and the activities of family business consultants, families may become more open to engaging such consultants.

Though, as has been mentioned previously, awareness is increasing about the part that family business consultants play, there is still reluctance in Ireland to be proactive about engaging a family business consultant. It appears that families are still very much reactive and will seek out and engage a family business consultant only when faced with specific family business issues or a crisis. This, of course, is not ideal and often makes an equitable solution all the more difficult to attain.

The chapter authors think that there is a feeling among some larger family businesses in Ireland that domestic service providers are not sufficiently skilled or experienced in dealing with family business issues to warrant hiring them. As a result, these businesses look to family business consultants from abroad, in particular to the United Kingdom, where the discipline is much more developed. In addition, the authors have identified a number of family businesses whose preference is to use the services of consultants from abroad. One of the arguments for this is that it safeguards their privacy. They see most attempts by Irish professional services firms to sell family business services as an invasion of privacy. Anecdotally, the feeling is that in Ireland everyone knows everyone else's business. In short, much education and confidence building still must occur before family members of family businesses feel comfortable dealing with and accepting advice from family business consultants in Ireland.

## TRAINING PROGRAMS FOR FAMILY CONSULTANTS

The big professional service firms currently perform most of the family business consulting in Ireland. These firms are able to draw on best practices and a body of knowledge developed in-house by their international offices. Most of these firms have designated family business teams. These multidisciplinary teams are composed of trained family business consultants from separate divisions within their organization, such as accounting and tax. They look after the firms' family business clients and come together as required, depending on the family business client's needs. Each of the team members are additionally trained in family business issues, such as succession planning and family dynamics. This training is part education, which is normally sourced abroad, part on-the-job mentoring from senior professionals, and the provision of in-house courses and seminars. Unfortunately, as already stated, the focus of family business consultants in Ireland is still more on business rather than on family issues. However, the authors of this chapter are convinced that the JCKFBC and other tertiary-level institutions will perform a central role in family consultants' education and understanding of family business dynamics in the future.

## INTERNET USAGE AND FAMILY BUSINESSES

Research conducted by Griffin (2002) examined the factors influencing internet adoption and usage rates among SMEs in Ireland. He found that small firms operating in the business services, wholesale and retail, construction, and manufacturing sectors do not believe that the Internet is ready for e-commerce activity in their industries due to the dynamic nature of these sectors and the subsequent cost and maintenance implications of advanced Internet adoptions. This leads to the conclusion that a small firm in a more dynamic environment may be less likely to adopt advanced Internet technologies than one in a more stable environment. The most common Internet application being used was e-mail, and the main benefit being leveraged through Web sites is currently the provision of information to customers.

From a family business perspective, research conducted by Birdthistle (2004) found that information technology ("IT") systems are prevalent in the majority of small and medium-sized family firms in Ireland. In addition, these small and medium-sized family firms tend to maintain a database of employees' skills, thus indicating a constant use of IT systems within the firm. Communication is conducted in these family businesses using traditional methods and/or e-mail. However, micro family firms in Ireland tend not to have IT systems, nor a database of employee skills established, and two-way communication is very much on an informal, ad hoc basis. The overall conclusion that can be derived from Griffin's (2002) and Birdthistle's (2004) research is that the Internet is not being adopted as a means of conducting e-commerce but is primarily adopted as a communications tool.

## THE IRISH EXPERIENCE
## OF FAMILY BUSINESS CONSULTING

The following three case studies are fairly indicative of the consultancy process for family businesses in Ireland. As the authors of this chapter have already demonstrated, the profession of family business consultation is not yet fully developed in this country. What the authors now show are three levels of consultancy engagement by family businesses in Ireland. The first case study, Shannon Ale House, is based on two generations being involved in the family business. Two-generational family businesses are the most common form of family businesses in Ireland. The second case study, Burren Limited, is a family business that is in its third generation. This would be typical of a small number of family businesses in Ireland. The third case study, Four Provinces Limited, is based on a multigenerational family business in which several generations make up the shareholding and the business is professionally managed.

## Case 1: Shannon Ale House

Shannon Ale House is a micro family business. The business was established in 1964 by David O'Connell. It has nine employees and a well-established reputation. In 2004 David decided that he needed to make arrangements for his future and the future of the family business. The catalyst for this decision was his recent surgery and the recommendation of his doctor to reduce his stress levels. His daughter Kate had been involved in the family business for several years, but there was no formal agreement as to her range of duties and responsibilities. Kate always envisaged herself as her father's successor.

## The Consulting Relationship

Having considered his situation, David decided to contact a family business consultant based on an article he read in a local newspaper. David suggested that the initial meeting be arranged off-site because he did not want his daughter to know what was going on.

According to David, "I was looking more for someone to listen to my concerns and issues rather than answers. I knew a lot of the answers, but I wanted to bounce them off someone before I implemented them. The atmosphere with the consultant was very relaxing and it was great to know that she knew what I was going through. I saw the consultant more as my 'business doctor' than a consultant."

Despite the high regard he had for the consultant, David refused to take her advice of involving Kate in the meetings, because he was undecided about Kate's future within the business. David felt if Kate had been part of the meetings she would possibly have assumed that she would be his natural successor. However, David was not ready to hand over control of the business to his daughter.

Initially the consulting arrangement was based on a preagreed number of meetings on a fixed-fee basis. Halfway through the engagement David decided to sell the business so that he could retire. This decision changed the relationship with the consultant from being a family business advisor to being more of a financial advisor. Over the following eighteen-month period the consultant advised David with regard to the sale. During the entire engagement David did not inform Kate of the consultant's involvement nor of his plans for the future of the business.

The Shannon Ale House was sold to a local publican. The relationship between David and Kate has seriously deteriorated.

## Case 2: Burren Limited

Burren Limited is a medium-sized family business that has more than fifty employees. The business was founded in the 1940s by Billy Tell. Billy and his four sons, John, George, Alex, and Patrick, managed the business together until Billy's death in 2000. Alex recently retired as managing director of the business. Upon his retirement, the youngest of the four sons, Patrick, left the family business and formed his own company. John, the eldest son, and George both remain in the business. George's eldest son is now the managing director. Today three generations are working in the business, including the spouses of family members.

## The Consulting Relationship

Alex Tell initiated the idea of hiring a family business consultant because more and more third-generation children were becoming involved in the business. Alex was perceptive enough to realize that he and his brothers needed to consider succession planning. According to Alex they "had an annual general meeting, the focus of which was reviewing the past year's performance and planning subsequent years. Discussions about family-related issues, however, were usually under the heading of 'any other business.'"

The family hired its bank manager to act as the consultant. The bank manager was well regarded in the region for his financial acumen. The payment for the consultancy was added to the business's ongoing bank charges. As was later to become evident, the consultant, although competent with respect to financial advice, was inept with respect to family business issues. Alex believes "the consultant underestimated the complexities of the nature of family business." Despite this, the consultant's interventions facilitated the successful restructuring of the business. In addition to facilitating the restructuring of the business, the consultant also introduced a succession plan, as well as formalizing weekly meetings and an annual weekend retreat for the directors. While the consultancy experience was positive, Alex firmly believes that if he were to start the process again, he would engage a consultant who had recognized family business skills.

## Case 3: Four Provinces Limited

Four Provinces Limited is a large family business in its fourth and fifth generations. During the 1990s the directors of the business, all of whom were members of the family, decided that the business needed external family business advice. They engaged the services of a well-regarded family business consultant whom they had heard presenting at a family business conference. The business is now entirely run by professional managers. Family interests are represented at the board level by a number of family members.

## The Consulting Relationship

At the initial meeting with the family business consultant, some family members were skeptical. Nevertheless, the family business consultant was engaged based on his reputation and experience. Any remaining skepticism evaporated as soon as the family business consultant began to work with all parties. He employed a variety of techniques, including one-on-one meetings with family members, group meetings, and retreats. A key element was the structuring, establishment, and implementation of a family constitution.

When asked, by the authors of this chapter whether the family business consulting experience was positive, there was general agreement that it was.

The family were also inclined to extend the consultancy engagement and to use the family business consultant to facilitate key sessions in the future and to coach future generations on important issues relating to the family business.

## SUMMARY

This chapter and the case studies presented herein highlight the authors' view that family business consultation is still in its infancy in Ireland. However, the impact of demographics, the boom years of the Celtic Tiger, and a heightened awareness of the unique issues surrounding family businesses have brought about an increasing willingness to consider the idea of engaging a family business consultant. Families now seem to be more comfortable with the benefits of utilizing such consultants. Thus, consultants are finding they have more business opportunities in this sector, that there is a greater need to focus on the family business consultation process and to provide more comprehensive services to family business clients. All of this, coupled with the establishment of a National Family Business Centre and a Chapter of the European Family Business Network (FBN) in Ireland in early 2006, indicates that the discipline of family business consulting in Ireland is maturing and becoming more important to the continued vitality, sustainability, and succession of family businesses in Ireland.

## REFERENCES

Birdthistle, N. (2003, November). Educating the family business: An investigation into centers of excellence for family businesses and family business educational programs. Paper presented at the SME's in the Knowledge Economy ISBA Conference.

Birdthistle, N. (2004). Small family businesses as learning organizations: An Irish study. Unpublished doctoral thesis, University of Limerick, Ireland.

Birley, S. (2000). *PRIMA international research report on family businesses.* Imperial College, London: Grant Thornton.

Buckley, N. & O'Gorman, B. (2003). Analysis & results of the family business questionnaire, October 2003. Working paper. JCKFBC, University College Cork.

Central Statistics Office. (2003). Population and vital statistics for Ireland. Retrieved September 9, 2003, from Central Statistics Office Dublin Web site, http://www.cso.ie/statistics/popnbyage2002.htm.

European Commission. (2003). Competence development in SMEs. Retrieved August 12, 2003, from http://europa.eu.int/comm/enterprise/enterprise_policy/analysis/doc/smes_observatory_2002_report2.en.pdf.

Gersick, K.E., Davis, J.A., McCollom-Hampton, M., & Lansberg, I. (1997). *Generation to generation: Life cycles of the family business.* Boston: Harvard Business Press.

Griffin, J. (2002). An examination and analysis of the internet adoption experience in SMEs in the Republic of Ireland. Unpublished doctoral thesis, University of Limerick, Ireland.

Handler, W. (1989). Methodological issues and considerations in studying family businesses. *Family Business Review, 23,* 257-276.

National Competitiveness Council. (1999). *Annual competitiveness report.* Dublin: Stationery Office.

O'Gorman, B. (2003). Supporting family businesses now—A foundation for future generations. Paper presented at the STEP Seminar, November 3, Cork, Ireland.

PricewaterhouseCoopers. (2004). *Irish family business report 2004.* Dublin, Ireland: PricewaterhouseCoopers.

Riehle, H. (2003). Family businesses in an enterprise economy. Retrieved March 21, 2004, from http://www.asu.de/www/doc/c41c0323dd77add26d14610doc7b6f33.pdf.

Wrixon, G.T. (2002). Keynote speech, launch of the MComm in Family Business Direction at University College Cork (UCC), July 16.

# Chapter 10

# Korea

Ji-Hee Kim

## BACKGROUND OF KOREAN HISTORY
## AND ECONOMIC DEVELOPMENT

Korea has a long history. The legendary beginning of Korea is fixed at 2333 BC, with the establishment of the first kingdom. Historians refer to this earliest era of Korean history as the Ko Choson (Ancient Choson) period. This was followed by the Koguryo, Paekche, Silla Kindgom, and Koryo periods, and ended with the Choson period in 1910.

From the late 1500s until 1876, when it was forced open by Japan, Korea had shut itself off from foreigners and foreign influences. China, Russia, and Japan all coveted its territory, but Japan's victory in the Russo-Japanese War led to the end of Korean independence with its annexation by Japan in 1910. The Japanese occupation of Korea was cruel and complete. Koreans were forced to take Japanese names and forbidden to speak the Korean language, celebrate Korean holidays, or wear Korean festival costumes (*Compton's Encyclopedia,* 1958).

As "Japanese" territory, Korea's future was tied to the outcome of World War II. In the waning days of the conflict, the Soviet Union declared war on Japan. By agreement between the United States and Union of Soviet Socialist Republics, Korea was occupied by Soviet forces north of the 38th parallel and by U.S. forces south of the 38th parallel.

Thus began the division of the Korean peninsula into two political states. It must be remembered that the Koreans are one ethnic family and, despite the efforts of the Japanese colonial masters, speak one language. Such homogeneity has enabled Koreans to be free from ethnic tensions and to maintain a firm solidarity with one another.

*Handbook of Family Business and Family Business Consultation*
Published by The Haworth Press, Inc., 2006. All rights reserved.
doi:10.1300/5491_10

## ONE PEOPLE WITH TWO POLITICAL
## AND ECONOMIC SYSTEMS

In November 1947, the United Nations (UN) General Assembly adopted a resolution that called for general elections in Korea under the supervision of a UN commission. However, the Soviet Union refused to comply with the resolution and denied the UN commission access to the northern half of Korea. The UN commission assembly then adopted another resolution calling for elections in areas accessible to the UN commission. The first elections in Korea were carried out on May 10, 1948, in the areas south of the 38th parallel.

On June 25, 1950, North Korea launched an unprovoked full-scale invasion of the South, triggering a bloody three-year war. The entire peninsula was devastated by the conflict. A ceasefire was signed in July 1953.

The Republic of Korea was organized in the south. A Stalinist state, the Democratic People's Republic of Korea, arose in the north.

### The Democratic People's Republic of Korea: North Korea

Under its founding leader Kim Il-Sung, North Korea adopted Ju Chee, a policy of diplomatic and economic self-reliance, as a barrier against too much Soviet or Communist Chinese influence. Political, economic, and military policies were incorporated around a core ideological aim: eventual unification of Korea under North Korean control. Kim's son, the current ruler, Kim Jung-Il was officially designated as Kim's successor in 1980 and took on a growing political and managerial role until his father's demise in 1994, when he assumed full power. He encountered no opposition.

Following decades of economic mismanagement and the misallocation of resources, North Korea has relied greatly on international food programs to feed its population since 1995 while continuing to allocate its resources to maintaining a standing army of about 1 million (CIA, 2005).

Ju Chee and communist political ideology drive economic development in North Korea. Accoriding to the CIA World Factbook (2005), today this country is one of the world's most centrally planned and self-contained economies. It is besieged by desperate economic conditions. Industrial capital stock is beyond repair as a result of years of underinvestment and parts shortages. Industrial and power outputs have also decreased enormously.

The nation has suffered a decade of severe food shortages attributable to collectivization of agriculture, a lack of arable land, weather-related problems, and ongoing shortages of fertilizer and fuel. At this time, large segments of the population suffer from long-term malnutrition and horrific living conditions. So far the government has complete control over the populace. However, some minor market reforms, such as relaxed restrictions on farmers' market activities, were instituted in 2003 (CIA, 2005).

The enormous military budget consumes funds desperately needed for investment and civilian consumption. Recently North Korea announced that it possesses nuclear weaponry, an announcement met by much consternation by most of the world.

### The Republic of Korea: South Korea

The partitioning of Korea at the 38th parallel gave South Korea 75 percent of the Korean population but little industry. In addition, the Korean War left 1.5 million South Koreans dead, 100,000 orphans, and millions homeless and separated from their families (*Compton's Encyclopedia,* 1958).

In the immediate postwar years serious social disorder continued under the government of aged President Seung-Man Rhee. South Korea's democracy was not mature, and the country experienced tremendous difficulties. President Rhee stepped down in April 1960.

The second republic was established in August 1960. The need for rapid social and economic development led President Park Chung-Hee to adopt a strong central government. The Park administration aimed at ensuring political stability and national revival through socioeconomic policies under authoritarian presidential leadership. Japan served as South Korea's economic development model. As with Japan, Korea's economic revival favored *chaebols* (large conglomerates), close business/government relationships, limiting imports, and promoting exports. Under Park's tenure the so-called "Miracle on the Han River" came to pass. (The Han River flows through Seoul, South Korea's capital, and along its banks the bulk of the country's modern industry flourished.)

A succession of military-backed presidents followed Park. Economic policy favored big business with some incremental changes. With time South Koreans demanded democracy and a representative political system. With political changes came a new awareness of a more democratic brand of economic development.

### Korean Economic Performance

During the past forty-five years, South Korea has accomplished a great deal in terms of economic growth and integration into the contemporary high-tech world economy. Forty years ago South Korea's gross domestic product (GDP) per capita was comparable with that of the poorer countries of Africa and Asia. In 2003 South Korea's GDP per capita was US$17,800, or eighteen times North Korea's and equal to that of the poorer economies of the European Union.

South Korea's success through the late 1980s was brought about by a system of close government/business ties that favored big business and included directed credit, import restrictions, sponsorship of specific industries, and strong control of labor. The government promoted the import of raw materials and technology at the expense of consumer goods; savings and investment were fostered more than consumption (CIA, 2005).

Long-standing weaknesses in South Korea's development model came to the fore during the Asian financial crisis of 1997-1999. Some of those that were exposed in the glare of the debacle's spotlight included high debt-to-equity ratios, an undisciplined financial sector, and huge foreign borrowing. Growth plummeted to –6.6 percent in 1998, then catapulted back to 10.8 percent in 1999 and 9.2 percent in 2000. Growth dropped again to 3.3 percent in 2001 because of the sluggish global economy, declining exports, and the fact that much-needed corporate and financial reforms had halted. Robust consumer spending and exports led to impressive growth in 2002 of 6.2 percent, despite weak global growth, followed by moderate 2.8 percent growth in 2003.

As a part of its early efforts to catch up with advanced countries, South Koreans were exhorted to work extremely hard. During this time South Koreans referred to the hardworking Japanese as "the lazy Asians." Times have changed. As evidence of its graduation to developed wealthy country status, in 2003 the National Assembly approved legislation reducing the workweek from six days to five.

## THE BACKBONE OF KOREAN ECONOMY: FAMILY BUSINESS, SMALL AND MEDIUM-SIZED ENTERPRISES, AND ENTREPRENEURSHIP

### Korean Family Business and Small and Medium-Sized Enterprises (SMEs)

To Westerners, Korean business means the giant chaebol conglomerates. However, it is also a country in which family businesses are the backbone of the economy.

Even for Koreans, the phrase, *family business* conjures up an image of very small mom-and-pop enterprises. Although most Korean small businesses are family owned, not all family businesses are small. Large and internationally well-known family-controlled firms include Samsung Electronics, LG Electronics, and Hyundai Motors.

The Korean Small and Medium Business Administration (KSMBA) and politicians are very interested in promoting and facilitating family business start-ups and enhancing entrepreneurship in SMEs. Therefore, an understanding of Korean SMEs and entrepreneurship is critical to understanding family businesses in Korea.

In general, Korean SMEs are classified into small and medium-size enterprises depending on the number of regular employees (or the size of sales volume for those with fewer than 300 employees). As of 2002, the number of SMEs in Korea is about 2.95 million, with 900,000 medium-sized enterprises (50 to 300 employees), 240,000 small enterprises (ten to fifty employees), and 2.62 million micro enterprises (fewer than ten employees). SMEs are the backbone of the Korean economy; they represent 99.8 percent of all private enterprises and employ 86.7 percent of the total private employment workforce, or 13.09 million employees.

From 1997 until 2002 (corresponding to the Asian economic crisis and recovery period), the number employed by large enterprises dropped by 1.25 million while SMEs increased their employees by 2.13 million. According the Korea National Statistical Office (2003), more than 2.7 million Korean enterprises (or 86.55 percent of total enterprises [3,187,916]) meet the quantitative and qualitative criteria for classification as a family business—that is, a business owned by one person or a family. In 2003, the number employed by family businesses represented 45.5 percent (6,708,597) of the total number employed by all businesses (14,729,166).

## Korean Family Business and the Entrepreneurial Spirit

According to the *Global Entrepreneurship Monitor (GEM) 2002 Executive Report* (Ewing Marion Kauffman Foundation, 2002), South Korea ranks sixth of forty-one nations in entrepreneurship. This implies a very high degree of enthusiasm for entrepreneurial activities. As a country, South Korea is globally competitive in twenty-four industries and is a leader in shipbuilding, steel, and semiconductor production.

Anecdotal evidence suggests that many young Koreans begin their careers working for larger companies with the idea of leaving and starting their own businesses. In South Korea's sophisticated and competitive business climate, enthusiastic Koreans readily realize their dreams by starting up their own enterprises. Entrepreneurial activity and spirit have a statistically significant association with subsequent levels of economic growth, and in the case of South Korea, improved economic conditions are strongly correlated with entrepreneurial activity.

## Korean Entrepreneurship: A Human and Social Capital Explanation

What drives South Koreans to be so active in entrepreneurial activities and why do they harbor such an entrepreneurial spirit? Perhaps the Korean context offers explanations.

South Korea occupies the southern half of the Korean peninsula. The country is midway between Japan to the east across the East Sea (Sea of Japan) and China to the west across the Yellow Sea. It is slightly larger than the U.S. state of Indiana, with a total land area of 98,480 square kilometers, and hosts a population of 48,598,175 (July 2004 estimate), almost all of whom are ethnic Koreans. It has little arable land, few remaining forests, and no petroleum. It does mine coal, tungsten, graphite, molybdenum, and lead and has some hydropower potential.

Enclosed by potentially hostile neighbors and lacking sufficient natural resources, the Koreans have abundant human and social capital. South Koreans are characterized as being hardworking with strong family relationships and values and unusually strong group solidarity.

In addition, Koreans value education. South Korea has built an outstanding and rigorous educational system, and large numbers of Koreans pursue graduate and postgraduate work in the United States and Europe. Today South Korea has a well-trained, technologically competent workforce. Unlike some of its Asian neighbors, Koreans are considered to be creative and innovative. Thus, opportunities abound and well-prepared South Koreans are able to link these opportunities to action leading to competitive advantage in the knowledge-based global economy.

## Korean Entrepreneurship: A Life Cycle Explanation

As an alternative explanation, the life cycle concept can be evoked to describe South Korean entrepreneurship. During the immediate post–Korean War years, economic development efforts focused on big business over entrepreneurial start-ups. It was big business that received foreign assistance and government sponsorship, and it was during this era that the large family-owned conglomerates—the chabols—took root.

During the 1960s and 1970s, under President Park's military regime, government-led industrialization continued. This again favored big business, and the dynamic activity of big companies created a synergistic effect benefiting entrepreneurs as well. From the 1980s to just before the 1997

Asian financial crisis, changes occurred at an accelerated speed among big companies. The big companies became more diverse and sought to establish their brands in the world marketplace. At the same time, greater democratization and policy efforts were instituted to bridge the gap between the large companies and small and medium-sized firms. This was the beginning of widespread realization of the importance and promise of the SME sector.

With the financial crisis of 1997 the Korean economy was severely tested. Large companies faltered, many downsized, and a number failed. During the crisis, redundant employees and new graduates without employment were forced to begin businesses or seek employment with SMEs.

For example, during the financial crisis period, the number of large business start-ups (companies with more than 300 employees) decreased by 44 percent. Moreover, the large corporations began to force early retirements. As a result, the unemployment rate increased and many households lost their financial mainstay. Consequently, family businesses and small business start-ups were key to overcoming the economic crisis.

Post-financial-crisis Korea is profoundly changed. For big business the trend is away from conglomerate diversification to a focus on core competencies. Postcrisis business reform has created stronger company financials by paring down holdings in diverse industries, emphasizing short-term gains, and, for many large manufacturing companies, moving operations overseas. Thus, big companies are improving their debt-to-equity capital structure and focusing more on innovating rather than research and development to increase annual revenues.

Since the financial crisis, the government realized the importance of entrepreneurship, family business, and small and medium-sized business to South Korea's economy. Now government policy has changed dramatically to support and encourage families to start businesses using family resources as a means to overcome unemployment issues, to enhance entrepreneurial activities, and to aid economic recovery. In short, the Korean government looks to all sectors of society, not just the large businesses, to recapture the country's economic vitality. At last a cooperative environment in which large companies and SMEs can prosper together has been established.

The recognition of the importance of entrepreneurship in Korea has swung in a full arc. Finally SMEs are receiving the attention that their contribution to the Korean economy warrants.

### The Korean Family Business Paradox: Mom and Pop versus the Chaebols

When referring to family businesses in South Korea, there are two extremely contradictory perceptions. Most people think that family business means "mom-and-pop" small and medium-size businesses engaged in traditional sectors. On the other hand, Korea's largest business groups, the chaebols, are family derived.

A *chaebol* is defined as a gathering of formally independent firms under the single common administrative and financial control of one family. Inside Korea the chaebols evoke negative sentiments. These social impressions are of family businesses with strong government support (and possibly corrupt practices), lack of separation between family and company affairs, nepotism, unprofessional handling of succession problems, and poor governance.

By the middle of the 1990s the thirty largest chaebols accounted for over 40 percent of Korean's total output. Large Korean family businesses, including giants such as Samsung, Hyundai, and LG had as many as eighty affiliated companies under their control. These family business groups participated in a variety of industries, including semiconductors, consumer electronics, construction, shipbuilding, automobiles, import/export trading, and financial services.

Chaebols served three primary functions that were particularly well suited to the realities of the immediate post–Korean War economy. First, the chaebol is a directed network of companies whose organizational structure can access and benefit from imperfectly marketed inputs such as capital and information. Second, chaebols offer an alternative to portfolio diversification; that is, equity investments in Korean publicly traded companies were nonliquid and not transparent, and were not managed in the best way.

Chaebols eliminate problems arising from the structure of postwar Korean industry—that is, dealing with monopolies or oligopolies by the use of vertical integration. The outward orientation of Korean chaebols was strongly influenced by two factors. First, the market imperfections and increased transaction costs faced by Korean firms encouraged them to pursue internalization. Second, the Korean government emulated Japanese development and pushed an aggressive, export-oriented development policy. To stimulate exports, the Korean government provided various supports and subsidies to large Korean family business groups, further distorting the market mechanism and thereby inducing more expansion.

In spite of the negative general impression of chaebols, these family businesses' contribution to Korea's economic development has been tremendous. If anti-chaebol sentiment is to be countered, these companies must respond with higher standards of ethical management.

## A New Appreciation for Family Business in Korea

Recently, it has become increasingly obvious to all that family businesses are very important players in the Korean economy. This awareness began to grow as the Koreans recognized the better performance of family businesses during the recession period, including stability of ownership as one of the advantages of family businesses. Thus, advancement of the family business sector is a key to revitalizing the economy in the long run and they are currently back in fashion in Korea. Well-run family businesses think strategically for the long term; their owners are willing to put up with occasional lean years. Moreover, stable ownership protects them against undesired takeovers, and management continuity creates a sense of trust with customers and employees. Furthermore, a relatively flat hierarchy and uncomplicated decision-making structure mean greater flexibility.

In conclusion, family businesses form the majority of all Korean companies. They provide the largest number of jobs and create the lion's share of Korean GNP.

## New Directions in Korean Family Business

Since the Asian financial crisis, business confidence has weakened in Korea, bringing uncertain business conditions, labor disputes, youth unemployment, forced retirements, and unnecessary costs. Therefore, economic revival in Korea hinges on dynamic and renewed family businesses.

Family businesses have the ability to use their human and financial resources to solve serious unemployment issues arising from early forced retirement of the parents' generation and the high rate of youth unemployment. A new movement in Korean family business start-ups has begun. It involves the transformation from the mom-and-pop family business engaged in traditional low-tech industries into high-tech knowledge-based family business start-ups. In this model the financial resources and business skills of the parents are combined with the skills and resources of their future-oriented, technology-savvy, college-educated children. Together the two generations are starting firms, building wealth, creating employment, and forging a new future for Korean family business.

In addition, Korean family businesses are becoming more professional. They are introducing professional management, using strategies to increase performance, and becoming more market driven.

### Reunification of Korea and the Potential Role of Family Business

Another unique facet of Korean family business relates to its potential role in the reintegration of North and South Korea. Reunification remains the long-cherished but elusive goal of all Koreans. Some progress was made in 2000 when the Republic of Korea's President Kim Dae-Jung made a historic visit to Pyungyang, the capital of North Korea, to meet with Kim Jung-Il. Also, North and South Koreans marched under one banner in the opening ceremonies of the 2000 Olympiad in Sydney, Australia. However, many obstacles still remain.

Although North Korea's philosophy of Ju Chee has failed to provide adequate food, fuel, and goods, it has imprinted the country with a fierce independence. This independence is maintained by an unassailable internal security apparatus, a powerful army, and the possession of nuclear weapons. The potential for North Korean aggression and the compassion of other countries in regard to its starving citizens have so far forestalled collapse. A widely held belief of South Koreans is that North Korea should not now be pressured but it will eventually implode. Thus, it is believed that reunification will come.

Taking the experience of Germany and its reunification as a model, the unification of the Korean peninsula will be even more expensive. The economic gap between the two countries is far more extreme, since North Korea on a per capita basis produces just six percent of South Korea's per capita GDP.

In the south, government and family business research scholars have begun to develop a family business model for the future Korean reunification to enhance economic development, to reduce reunification costs, and to provide entrepreneurial opportunities for the North Koreans. This model includes providing basic business-knowledge education, family business education, and training programs for business start-ups. This model has been piloted, refined, and successfully used to integrate North Korean refugees into the South Korean economy.

## ACADEMIC RESEARCH IN THE FIELD OF FAMILY BUSINESS

When working within a family business, it is easy to recognize that the business is a family business. However, when looking at many businesses from the outside, it is often difficult to determine which is a family business and which is not. Different criteria and definitions have been discussed for more than a decade, often leaving academics, consultants, and, most of all, family business owners and managers without a reliable answer. How should we define family business? This is not so easy to answer, as surprisingly little literature has been produced on the subject in Korea. There is even disagreement over the term. Many writers insist that ownership and management have to be in the hands of one person or one family, while others are satisfied if the family leaves its mark on the company.

Although more than 86.55 percent of all businesses in Korea are family businesses by virtue of ownership and control, the awareness of family business issues in Korea is quite recent. In the mid-1990s some of the top researchers in family business studies recognized the importance of family business research and started defining the concepts, characteristics, and dynamics of family firms. Some major scholars (Ji-Hee Kim, Sook-Jae Moon, Young-Ho Nam, Young-Keum Jeong, etc.) contributed to bringing a holistic and systemic approach to family business analysis. In the beginning stage, family business research topics have included the importance of family business in the Korean economy (Kim & Moon, 1997a), defining "family business" (Kim & Moon, 1997a; Hong, 2000), developing conceptual frameworks and models (Kim & Moon, 1997a, 2001; Kim & Stafford, 2002), the importance of family members and kinship relationships (Kim & Kim, 2000), the family business system (i.e., family, ownership, and management), and family business functions (Kim & Moon, 1997a; Kim, 1999; Kim & Moon, 2001; Kim & Hong, 2000b).

The idea that the family and kinship relationships are critical variables and key factors in Korean family business studies and that the heart of the field is about understanding the reciprocal impact of family on business and business on family has begun to crystallize in the research (Kim & Moon, 1997a; Kim, 1999; Kim & Kim, 2000; Cha, 2001). This perspective is acceptable in so far as family and kinship ties are an important consideration in hiring staff and acquiring funds to get enterprises started. At the point of its creation, control of a company remains in the hands of the founder and key family members who play a crucial role in setting its style of management.

Broad-based models of sustainable family businesses that take into account the reciprocal relationships between family and business systems in an effort to foster the simultaneous development of functional families and profitable firms have emerged (Kim & Moon, 2000; Kim & Stafford, 2002). Some studies found that the success of family firms depend more on effective management of the overlap between family and business than on resources in either the family or the business system (Jeong, 2001b; Joung, 2002). The advantages of family businesses, such as strong family relationships, shared values, similar beliefs and vision, common goals, a strong sense of mission, the family spirit, common positive perceptions of the family name, flexibility, long-term commitment, and entrepreneurial culture, are well accepted in Korea, as demonstrated in the recent Asian financial crisis.

Other research has been conducted focusing on founder characteristics and economic performance of the chabols by explicitly addressing group-wide resource sharing and internal business transactions (Lee, 1997; Chang & Hong, 2000). Since the 1997 financial crisis, some researches have focused on how to improve investment environments for family business and venture enterprises with entrepreneurship education, government policy to promote and enhance family business start-ups, how to more effectively use family resources in family business settings (Kim & Moon, 2001; Jeong, 2001b), providing effective financial service for family business (Kim & Hong, 2000b), enhancing family business education and curriculum development (Kim & Moon, 2001; Jeong, 2001), female-owned family business (Jeong, 1999), succession issues (Jeong & Cha, 2001), performance of family along both family and business dimensions, and comparison studies between family businesses and nonfamily businesses (Jeong, 1999; Kim & Moon, 2000; Kwak & Rhee, 2000; Jeong, 2001b; Jeong & Cha, 2001; Joung & Song, 2001; Kim & Stafford, 2002).

Research about family business has gathered considerable momentum, particularly in the past several years. However, many challenges still face researchers. The challenges are based on the following issues: developing common definitions, a comprehensive research model, and theoretical foundation. The theory of family business must explain why family firms exist, what determines their scale and scope, and how family firms might differ from nonfamily business firms. Family business research in Korea has not investigated the following areas: compensation, governance, non-family executives, preparing successors for leadership, strategic management, family business policy, family councils, family business consultation, financing transitions, professional family business advisors, shareholders, professionalization, globalization, and innovation. Thus, the array of research topics needs to be broadened.

A further challenge is gathering empirical data at the national level. The data used in research have had relatively small sample sizes, and the result of such studies does not represent the entire population of Korean family businesses. No family business research institute or center has been established yet in Korea to encourage research and create networking among researchers, family business owners and members, consultants, practitioners, and policymakers to promote family businesses. In addition, the situation is extremely challenging in regard to collaborating with professionals in other fields.

## HIGHER/PROFESSIONAL EDUCATION
## IN FAMILY BUSINESS

As an academic field, family business faces many challenges in the Korean higher educational system. Few universities offer family business curricula. In 1999, Ewha Women's University offered the first graduate family business course in Korea. Since then only a few universities offer family business courses at the undergraduate and graduate levels. These are Soongsil University, Kunkuk University, the Catholic University of Korea, Taejon University, and Sungshin Women's University. To support academic ventures, Kim and Moon (2001) and Jeong (2001a) developed model family business education programs and curricula.

In 2004 the KSMBA and the government sponsored the establishment of the Korean Graduate School of Entrepreneurship (KGSE). Family business courses have been included in KGSE's entrepreneurship major.

### How Should Family Business Management
### Be Taught?

As an answer to this rhetorical question, family business courses should be specifically directed toward the unique characteristics of family businesses in general and Korean family business in particular. Thus, courses should involve the "familialization" of business as well as investigating the dynamics of the family system. For example, in the family business management course, students should be first exposed to the traditional issues arising from family relationship, family culture, parent-children interactions, sibling rivalry, gender, ethnicity, and conflict topics. Then coverage should be given to family business systems and structure, dual functions (family function and business function) of family business, business strategies, business governance and control systems, organizational behavior, leadership, professionalization, and succession. In addition, functional area strategies in operations, management, marketing, finance, accounting, human resources management, management information, innovation, and entrepreneurship should be covered. Finally, empirical family business field research should be included in family business management studies. Within each of these topics, the substance of discussion will be about how, due to family dynamics, family firms may be different from nonfamily firms in terms of objectives, constraints, alternatives, and typical practice and performance.

The first and only Korean-language family business textbook was published by Ji-Hee Kim in 2001. Therefore, it is important that researchers, educators, and professional service providers publish additional articles and textbooks on family business and family business consultation guides.

Because family business is a very new academic field in Korea, it is important for academics to collaborate with researchers, practitioners, and family business owners to acquire and disseminate a better understanding of family businesses in Korea. Education of family business practitioners and potential practitioners must be addressed through formal and informal education, and on-the-job training. It is also critical that the government, universities, research institutes, professional organizations, and media understand and stress the importance of family business and successfully communicate this to society. The participation of all facets of society is needed to promote family business education pursuits.

## FAMILY BUSINESS CONSULTATION

Family business consulting is extremely new in Korea. Currently no professional family business consultation organization exists in this country. Most family business consulting and advice has been provided through SME support organizations such as KSMBA, the KSMBA's Small Business Development Centers (SBDC), and the Korean Federation of Small Business (KFSB), a small business owners' organization.

The KSMBA and SBDC are government organizations created to support SMEs. Since its establishment in 1996, the KSMBA has been actively providing support for SMEs to ensure their stable growth in the new economic environment. KSMBA has both service and policy-making functions. Until recently KSMBA's policy-making function belonged to the Ministry of Commerce, Industry, and Energy. KSMBA's service function was strengthened with a reorganization that created its Office of Planning and Management, SME Policy Bureau, Management Assistance Bureau, Venture Business Bureau, Technology Assistance Bureau, and Marketing Assistance Bureau. This reorganization was part of a move toward smaller and more efficient government.

The SBDC provides outreach for the KSMBA and was established in 1998. It provides consulting, assistance for start-ups, financial support, education and training, technology, and globalization advice for SMEs.

The KFSB's purpose is to support small business policy making, marketing, financial support, training, small business digitalization, publishing, product liability advice, globalization of small business initiatives, networking, and cooperation with large corporations. The KFSB hosted the first Korean National Family Business Forum in 2003.

Another route for obtaining professional family business consultation in Korea is through online family business columns and consulting Web sites. A family business column, Family Business Column and Consulting, has been posting regularly by Ji-Hee Kim at the Web site of the Korean Small Business Development Center (2003), which is part of the KSMBA government home page. The purpose of this site is to provide professional family business knowledge and family business advice, to introduce government policy promoting family business start-ups, and to provide one-on-one online family business consulting. Another online family business column and consulting Web site was created by Sehoh Kang (2001), current CEO of Unisys Korea Ltd, former CEO of Samsung Networks Inc. (2002), and former CEO of Samsung Unitel Co. Ltd (2001). This site consists of academic family business lectures, a professional family business column, one-on-one family business online consulting, family business information, definition of family business concepts, a development model for high-tech-driven family business start-ups, and a family business question and answer site. This Web site is unique and provides professional family business lectures and a column by Dr. Kim, the family business model development by CEO Kang, and the one-on-one free family business consulting by Dr. Kim and CEO Kang.

Another new trend in family businesses is media coverage in a business/economic magazine, an IT (information technology) weekly economic venture magazine, and a venture newspaper. Private consulting groups have started offering family business executive training and educational programs in conjunction with universities.

Even though no professional family business support organization exists in Korea, interest about family business is growing rapidly. This is especially true for information technology–focused family business start-ups.

In conclusion, Korea needs a family business support organization and a family business research and development center. From these can grow a strong research and practitioner support mechanism, including the collection of a national family business database, family business roundtable meetings, and family business forums.

## SUCCESSFUL FAMILY BUSINESS CASES

Since there are no available Korean family business consultation cases, I will describe instead two successful family businesses as illustrations of large family conglomerates. These cases have been discussed in the public media, so there is no issue regarding confidentiality of information. Historical details were taken from www.samsung.com (Samsung Group, 2005) and www.hyundai-motor.com (Hyundai Motors, 2005).

## Samsung Group

Samsung means "three stars" in Korean. Samsung is the largest family business chaebol in Korea. According to *Family Business Magazine,* it is the third largest family business in the world. Samsung had revenues of US$98.7 billion in 2003 and employs about 175,000 worldwide. Its flagship is its Samsung Electronics Division. Samsung Electronics is one of world's largest makers of computer memory chips, home and consumer electronics equipment, mobile phones, and microwave ovens. Other Samsung divisions are involved in life insurance, securities, and import/export trading ("World's 250 largest family businesses," 2004).

What makes Samsung one of the world's leading family business companies? Since it was founded in 1938, Samsung has continually refined its mission statement to respond both to change in itself and in the world. Its corporate slogans over time have been "Economic contribution to the nation," "Priority to human resources," and "Pursuit of rationalism." Each slogan represents significant moments in Samsung's history, reflecting different stages of the company's growth from a domestic industrial leader into a global consumer electronics powerhouse. In the 1990s, Samsung once again acknowledged the need to transform its mission statement to keep pace with its growing global operations, rapid changes in the world economy, and escalating competition from well-established rivals. Samsung's management philosophy is "We will devote our human resources and technology to create superior products and services, thereby contributing to a better global society." Samsung's management philosophy represents its strong determination to contribute directly to the prosperity of people all over the world as a single human society. Key to Samsung's efforts is its people, whose talent and creativity are dedicated to doing their best at all times. Technology also plays an important role in making it possible to achieve higher standards of living. Superior products and services are what it is all about. Samsung believes that the success of its contributions to society and the mutual prosperity of people across national boundaries truly depend on how it manages the company. Samsung's objective is growth— a perpetual challenge—but always working within the context of cooperation and inclusion of its customers (http://www.samsung.com).

### Samsung's Beginnings (1938 to 1969)

On March 1, 1938, founding chairman Byung-Chull Lee started a business in Taegu, Korea, with 30,000 won. At first, Mr. Lee's little business was primarily in trade, selling dried Korean fish, vegetables, and fruit to Manchuria and Beijing. But in just over a decade, Samsung came to have its own flour mills and confectionery machines, its own manufacturing and sales operations, and ultimately became the roots of the modern global corporation that still bears the same name today.

## Samsung's Industrial Era (1970 to 1979)

Throughout the 1970s, Samsung laid the strategic foundations for its future growth by investing in the heavy, chemical, and petrochemical industries. The company's second "Five-Year Management Plan," announced in August 1973, targeted these industries and also introduced Samsung to the shipbuilding industry. During this time, the company took steps to enhance its competitive position in the world's textile industry, integrating its manufacturing processes from raw materials to end products. As a result, many new companies were created, including Samsung Heavy Industries Company in 1974, and Samsung Shipbuilding Company (created when Samsung acquired Daesung Heavy Industry Company) and Samsung Precision Company (now Samsung Techwin) in 1977.

## Entering the Global Technology Marketplace (1980 to 1989)

The late 1970s and early 1980s represented a time of increasing diversification and global growth for Samsung's core technology businesses. In 1978, Samsung Semiconductor and Samsung Electronics became separate entities as new products were introduced to the global market. Samsung produced semiconductors only for the domestic market until the successful development of a 64K DRAM (dynamic random access memory) VLSI chip in December 1983, when it became a world leader in semiconductor products. Samsung Precision Company (established in 1977) laid the foundation in another high-tech industry—aerospace. Renamed Samsung Aerospace Industries in February 1987 (now known as Samsung Techwin), Samsung has been developing its aerospace capabilities with unprecedented speed ever since. Future plans include the development of future space stations and even space facilities for the moon and Mars in the early twenty-first century. The mid-1980s also saw Samsung entering the systems development business, establishing Samsung Data Systems in 1985 (now known as Samsung SDS) as a leader in information technology services, including systems integration, systems management, consulting, and networking services. Samsung's increasing focus on technology led to another key development in the mid-1980s with the creation of the company's two research and development (R&D) institutes, Samsung Economic Research Institute (SERI) in 1986, and Samsung Advanced Institute of Technology (SAIT) in 1987. Together, these two pioneering R&D organizations have helped Samsung expand its reach even further into electronics, semiconductors, polymer chemicals, genetic engineering, optical telecommunications, aerospace, and new fields of technology innovation from nanotechnology to advanced network architectures.

On November 19, 1987, Samsung's founding Chairman Byung-Chull Lee passed away after almost fifty years at the helm of the company. His son, Kun-Hee Lee succeeded him as chairman. On the fiftieth anniversary of Samsung's founding in 1988, he announced the "Second Foundation" of the company, directing Samsung's growth toward becoming a world-class twenty-first century corporation. For this "Second Foundation," Samsung challenged itself to restructure old businesses and enter new ones with the aim of becoming one of the world's top five electronics companies. The merger of Samsung Electronics and Samsung Semiconductor and Telecommunications was undoubtedly a key strategic moment in the progress toward this goal. For the first time in the group's history, Samsung was now in a position to maximize its technological resources and develop value-added products. The integration of overlapping projects also reduced costs and efficiently utilized capital and labor. By the late 1980s, Samsung's efforts to consolidate its electronics and heavy companies started to pay off with a well-regarded reputation matching the high-tech products the company was known for.

## Leaping onto the Global Stage (1990 to 1993)

The early 1990s presented tremendous challenges for high-tech businesses. Mergers, coalitions, and buyouts were common while competition and consolidation flourished. Companies were pressed to rethink their technology and services offerings. Business began to flow across borders between countries and companies. Samsung's response to these opportunities was its "New Management" program.

## The New Management Era (1994 to 1996)

New Management was more than a mere reengineering of Samsung; it was an entire revolution dedicated to making world-class products, providing total customer satisfaction, and being a good corporate citizen. In retrospect, New Management was a decisive turning point for Samsung, the moment when the entire company was repositioned on the basis of "quality first." During this period, seventeen different products from semiconductors to computer monitors, liquid crystal display (LCD) screens to color picture tubes leaped into the ranks of the top five products for global market share in their respective areas. Twelve others also reached top market rankings. Ever since entering the LCD business in 1993, Samsung has been the undisputed world leader. Samsung Heavy Industries' drill ships have captured 60 percent of the world market since their introduction. Part of Samsung's success is due to its rigorous enforcement of quality control at all of its plants across the world. Thanks to the "line stop" system, any employee can shut down the assembly line when inferior products are discovered. Production is simply halted until the problem is solved. Samsung also adheres to the "six sigma" concept of total quality management.

New management is about not only quality products but quality people. Wherever Samsung does business, its Human Resources Development Center conducts customer service training sessions for personnel who come directly in contact with customers. Even Shilla Hotels and Resorts, Samsung's world-class hotel in the center of Seoul, participates by offering lessons on etiquette and customer service to Samsung employees as far-flung as Samsung Life Insurance, Samsung Securities, and Samsung Card. Samsung has also streamlined its internal infrastructure to be more consumer friendly, establishing Samsung Corporation's forty-eight-hour Home Express system and Samsung Cards' service guarantee system.

Being number one also means recognizing corporate social obligations, whether the cause is social welfare, environmental conservation, cultural events, or sports. Indeed, Samsung actively participates in sports marketing, and as a result of its intensive efforts, its chairman, Kun-Hee Lee, was selected as a member of the International Olympic Committee (IOC) in July 1996, greatly enhancing the company's image as a key contributor in world athletics.

## Digital Frontier (1997 to 1999)

1997 was a dark year for nearly all of Korea. That year, nearly all companies in Korea shrank. Samsung was no exception. The company restructured by reducing the number of its affiliated companies to forty-five (the standard of affiliates number is according to Fair Trade Law), decreasing personnel by almost 50,000, and improving the soundness of its financial structure, lowering 1997's 365 percent debt ratio to 148 percent by late 1999. The company sold ten business units to overseas companies for $1.5 billion, including Samsung Heavy Industries' highly acclaimed construction equipment business unit to Volvo AB of Sweden and its forklift business to Clark. Although the news was bleak, Samsung was one of the few companies able to continue growing thanks to its leadership in digital and network technologies, and its steady concentration on electronics, finances, and related services.

## Pioneering the Digital Age (2000 to Present)

With the start of the second millennium, Samsung began its second century. People must now successfully manage the opportunities and challenges resulting from the new and quickly changing digital paradigm with equally revolutionary changes in the rules it uses to do business. Currently, Samsung Group is again undergoing changes in its business structure, management perspective and systems, and corporate culture to meet a global standard. It is a time of intense competition; fortunes can be made or lost in the blink of an eye. This is one reason Samsung believes that it is perfectly positioned to be one of the world's recognized leaders in digital technology. Its commitment to being "world's best" has succeeded in securing the number-one global market share for thirteen of its products. Its target is nothing less than to have thirty number-one "world products" by 2005, adding digital TVs, IMT 2000, and printers to its current world market leaders—semiconductors, TFT-LCDs, monitors, and CDMA mobile phones. At the same time, it is making historic advances in research and development of its overall semiconductor line, including flash memory and nonmemory, custom semiconductors, and DRAM and SRAM. For example, Samsung Electronics, which has been among the world's top ten in U.S. patents for four consecutive years, has 13,000 researchers representing a US$ 1.7 billion investment in research and development.

In the financial market, Samsung is also committed to being the world's best. Samsung Card has been selected as the "Best Card Company in the New Millennium" by Master Card, the result of securing more than 1 million members within one year through the release of Aha Loan Pass, the first loan-only card in Korea. Euromoney has also selected Samsung Securities as the "Best Security Company" for the third consecutive year. Samsung Life Insurance has ranked as the tenth largest company by Fortune's "Global 500" in the life/health insurance category. Samsung is also actively promoting its brand value, a key engine of business growth. Samsung's brand value increased to US$ 8.31 billion in 2002 from US$ 6.37 billion in 2001 and was recognized by Interbrand Corporation as the fastest-growing global brand. How was Samsung able to work such astounding progress in such a short time? One answer is that this company is perpetually engaged in achieving global competitiveness through continually improving its financial structure and profitability and looking at its organizational structure. Reducing production costs and working hard to maintain brand image have also contributed to this surge. Accordingly, Samsung Electronics has secured a nation's credit rating from standard and poor's (S&P) and Moody's. Samsung Fire also has been recognized by S&P for its stability and growth potential and has received its second consecutive "A" rating. Another clue to the quick pace of development goes to the heart of the management philosophy—devote human resources and technology to create superior products and services, thereby contributing to a better global society.

As a worldwide Olympic partner in the wireless equipment sector for the 2000 Sydney Olympics, Samsung provided 25,000 advanced digital wireless telecommunication devices, including mobile phones. It also served in that capacity at the 1999 Nagano Winter Olympics, and will be a worldwide Olympic partner in the 2006 Torino Olympics and 2008 Beijing Olympics. It actively participated as a contributor in the Asian Games, Samsung Nation's Cup Riding Competition, Samsung Running Festival, Samsung World Championship (a U.S. LPGA Tour), and many other sporting events around the world.

## *Hyundai Motors*

Hyundai Motors is also a chaebol group. Hyundai means "the present time" in Korean. Hyundai Motor is one of Hyundai's biggest groups. Hyundai was broken into five groups by the Korean government to diminish the influence of its founding Chung family. Hyundai Motors considers itself independent. Founder Ju-Young Chung died in 2001.

Established in 1967, Hyundai Motor Company has grown into a leader in Korea's automobile industry. In 2003, Hyundai exported over 1 million vehicles and surpassed the US$ 10 billion mark in export sales. In the glow of such remarkable performance, Hyundai is intensifying its efforts and taking on the challenges necessary to achieving global top-five automaker status by 2010. Hyundai is well aware that its growth would not have been possible without the support and the loyalty of its customers. Breaking away from the traditional image of a corporation as an entity motivated only by profit, Hyundai will redouble its efforts to become a company that honors customer support, wins trust through transparency and ethical management, and faithfully fulfils its social responsibilities. In 2005 Hyundai plans to take a further step toward becoming a global enterprise by such management policies as global management acceleration, brand value enhancement, sustainable management capabilities development, and human resources-focused management.

Quality and brand power are the two priorities for Hyundai Motor Company as it prepares for the future. No longer content to follow and learn, Hyundai is now seeking to lead the motor industry in shaping the evolution of motor vehicles. With Hyundai's publicly stated goal of becoming one of the top five car makers in the world by 2010, the Hyundai brand will require careful repositioning. Management realizes that achieving this goal will require strong determination and above all, stronger public confidence in the Hyundai name. It will also carry with it a new set of responsibilities, such as greater transparency in management and the environmental, social, and economic facets of sustainable development.

By publicly announcing a new global environment management body last year, Hyundai reiterated its commitment to leadership in the social sphere. In reinforced its place as a top-rated carmaker by winning the 2003 Global Automotive Shareholder Value Award presented by Price Waterhouse Coopers and Automotive News. For the second consecutive year, Hyundai captured top honors in the Consumers' Satisfaction Survey conducted by J.D. Power and Associates which also rated the Hyundai Sonata first in its 2002 and 2003 Initial Quality Survey. By active implementation of four management policies in 2004, Hyundai will accelerate the speed of development. These policies are as follows:

1. Step up global management by establishing local support systems across the globe to maintain momentum as a growing global player, and expand overseas manufacturing bases and raise R&D capabilities above the industry standard.
2. Reposition its brand identity to be known as a maker of refined and elegant automobiles to enhance its brand value, and improve its product development system.
3. Maintain its sustainable management capabilities, by devoting itself to fulfilling social responsibilities as a global carmaker through development of safer and more environmentally friendly vehicles while respecting fundamental values, striving for ethical management and expanding contributions to social causes.
4. Attach greater importance to human resources.

Hyundai will expand the recruitment of engineers and multilingual talented individuals who are at home anywhere in the world. Hyundai Motor will reinforce its position of strength and confidence by continually improving its management capabilities. And by promoting the development of national and international coprosperity, the company plans to raise its net value.

## Vision of Hyundai

To become one of the top five global automakers. The company initiated a far-sweeping corporate restructuring program while bolstering its R&D efforts to produce automobiles that meet every higher standard of quality, safety, and environmental friendliness. Making the best use of synergy effects with Kia Motors, Hyundai Motor Company has set its sights on providing the finest customer service, up-to-date technology, flawless quality, and the best value in the industry. In addition, the company will focus its R&D efforts on the development of more environment-friendly technologies, while at the same time more aggressively implementing its "Six Sigma" quality improvement campaign that will earn the greater trust of its customers and ultimately contribute to improved business profitability.

## New Technology

Pristine natural environment is a birthright and is perhaps the most important legacy Hyundai can bequeath to our children and future generations. Hyundai's efforts to develop greener technologies are unrelenting as Hyundai seeks new ways to protect the planet from further environmental damage. The company is placing increasingly greater effort on the development of environment-friendly power plants which are powered by a variety of alternative fuels and which emit less pollution than conventional combustion engines.

## Future Car Development

Hyundai Motor Company's ambition to become one of the top five global automakers would be impossible to achieve without continuous investment into the development of future-oriented concept cars that have come to serve as barometers of competitiveness, technology, and creativity.

## SUMMARY

It is anticipated that family businesses, small, medium, and large, will continue to expand and thrive in South Korea and be looked upon favorably by the government. We can also expect that research efforts will be accelerated into the areas alluded to previously that have not yet been investigated, and that the need for consultants will be slowly recognized as South Korea becomes more and more involved in the larger world business scene.

## REFERENCES

Central Intelligence Agency (CIA). (2005). *The world factbook.* Retrieved 2005, from http://www.cia.gov/cia/publications/factbook.

Cha, S.L. (2001). A study on the satisfaction with occupation and family living of couples involved in the family business management. *Journal of Korean Home Economics Association, 39*(9), 121-135.

Chang, S.J. & Hong, J. (2000). Economic performance of group-affiliated companies in Korea: Intragroup resource sharing and internal business transactions. *Academy of Management Journal, 43*(3), 429-448.

*Compton's Encyclopedia* (1958). Korea—A divided land torn by war (Vol. 8, pp. 75-79). Chicago, IL: F.E. Compton & Company.

Ewing Marion Kauffman Foundation. (2002). *Global entrepreneurship monitor: 2002 Executive report.* Retrieved 2004, from http://www.emkf.org/GEM2002.

Hong, S.H. (2000). Theoretical framework for the research on family business. *Journal of Korean Home Economics Association, 38*(9), 19-32.

Hyundai Motors. (2005). Home page. Retrieved 2005, from http://www.hyundai-motor.com.

Jeong, Y.K. (1999). A study on the family business as an alternative for women's employment. *Journal of Korean Home Economics Association, 37*(11), 125-138.

Jeong, Y.K. (2001a). The development of family business education program through the evaluation of curricula. *Journal of Korean Home Management Association, 19*(6), 129-143.

Jeong, Y.K. (2001b). A diagnoses on the actual management status of small family business. *Journal of Korean Home Management Association, 19*(4), 121-135.

Jeong, Y.H. & Cha, S.L. (2001). A study on succession of the small-scale family business. *Journal of Family Resource Management Association, 5*(1), 70-95.

Joung, S.H. (2002). An analysis on the factors related to the family business performance. *Journal of Family Resource Management Association, 6*(1), 103-115.

Joung, S.H. & Song, J.Y. (2001). A study on transformation factors to family business establishment—Focusing on pre-wage earner group. *Journal of Family Resource Management Association, 5*(2), 13-27.

Kang, S. (2001). Family business column and consulting. Retrieved 2004, from http://www.kangseho.com/familybiz.

Kim, H.Y. & Kim, S.H. (2000). A family system of family business: Participation within a family in a small family business. *Journal of Korean Home Economics Association, 38*(7), 1-12.

Kim, J.H. (1999). Bivalent attributes and dual functions of family business. *Journal of Korean Home Management Association, 17*(1), 1-15.

Kim, J.H. & Moon, S.J. (1997a). Theoretical approach to the family business management. *Journal of Korean Home Economics Association, 35*(6), 317-334.

Kim, J.H. & Moon, S.J. (1997b). Theoretical approach to the home-based business using the family resource. *Journal of Family Resource Management Association, 1*(1), 43-55.

Kim, J.H. & Moon, S.J. (2000). Work and family characteristics of family business in Germany—Based on the interview with female business manager in the family businesses. *Journal of Korean Home Management Association, 18*(2), 77-91.

Kim, J.H. & Moon, S.J. (2001). A study on the development empirical research areas and curriculum model on family business. *Journal of Family Resource Management Association, 5*(1), 123-140.

Kim, J.H. & Stafford, K. (2002). Family resource management pattern by dual role manager of the family business in Korea and the United States. *Journal of Korean Home Management Association, 20*(2), 43-56.

Kim, S.M. & Hong, S.H. (2000a). The financial status of family business: Comparison of home-based family business with onsite family business. *Journal of Korean Home Economics Association, 38*(10), 181-197.

Kim, S.M. & Hong, S.H. (2000b). The financial status of household and business in the family business. *Journal of Korean Home Economics Association, 38*(7), 13-26.

Korea National Statistics Office. (2003). Report on the census on basic characteristics of establishments. Retrieved 2004, from http://smba.or.kr.

Korean Small Business Development Center. (2003). Home page. Retrieved 2004, from http://www.sbdc.or.kr.

Kwak, I.S. & Rhee, K.H. (2000). A study on the work environment and location of family-owned small business. *Journal of Korean Home Economics Association,* *38*(7), 27-37.

Samsung Group. (2005). Samsung's digital world. Retrieved 2005, from http://www.samsung.com.

The world's 250 largest family businesses. (2004). *Family Business Magazine.* Retrieved 2004, from http://www.familybusinessmagazine.com/topglobal.html.

Chapter 11

# Lebanon

Josiane Fahed-Sreih

## CHARACTERISTICS

Usually family businesses are not given their due importance in world economies, and this also applies to Lebanon, where family businesses account for the majority of the contribution to the private-sector economy. The private sector in Lebanon is considered a pillar for economic growth.

Family businesses in Lebanon constitute 85 percent of the private sector, while the private sector constitutes 90 percent of the economy, leaving only 10 percent to the public sector. Family businesses play an important role in creating employment opportunities. The private sector in Lebanon provides 1.05 million out of 1.24 million employment opportunities, and thus the public sector provides only 190,000 positions.

### Distribution of Employment by Sector

Of the employment in the private sector, the distribution of employment is shown in Table 11.1.

TABLE 11.1. Distribution of employment by sector.

| Sector | Percentage |
|---|---|
| General trading and tourism | 38 |
| Industry | 10 |
| Public sector | 15.6 |
| Construction | 9 |
| Agriculture | 8 |
| Unemployed | 19.4 |

*Handbook of Family Business and Family Business Consultation*
Published by The Haworth Press, Inc., 2006. All rights reserved.
doi:10.1300/5491_11

Lebanese family firms prefer to remain as family businesses and avoid an initial public offering, knowing that outside forces and the threat of globalization could lead to enormous financial and managerial changes. These family companies favor protectionism, conservatism, and a high level of secrecy, which is contrary to what is entailed in the flotation of shares on public financial markets.

As global markets have evolved and imposed certain challenges on organizations, the same challenges have been placed on family businesses. The characteristics of family businesses make it even more difficult for them to adapt to the world changes, because the growth of family business is always tied up with the fear that the business will loose its family identity and will not remain a source of income for the family's future generations.

### Family Business Contribution to GDP

The contribution of the various economic sectors of family businesses to the gross domestic product is shown in Table 11.2.

The percentage of family businesses in Lebanon per sector is as follows:

| | |
|---|---|
| Agriculture | 60 percent |
| Manufacturing | 53 percent |
| Trade and services | 62 percent |
| Lebanese banks | 43 percent |
| Operating banks | 24 percent |

Family businesses make up the major percentage of businesses in all sectors except in the banking industry, due to the capital-intensive nature of this sector. The number of operating banks in Lebanon is sixty-seven, of which nine are foreign banks and six are Arabic banks. Ten are Lebanese with a majority of Arab ownership, and five are Lebanese with foreign majority ownership. Of the thirty-seven purely Lebanese banks, sixteen are

TABLE 11.2. Family business contribution to GDP.

| Business type | Percentage |
|---|---|
| Agriculture | 8 |
| Industry | 16 |
| Commerce and services | 67 |
| Construction | 9 |

family owned, which means 43 percent are family owned, and 24 percent of the operating banks are family owned. These family-owned banks employ 29 percent of those working in the banking industry. In agriculture the percentage goes up to 60 percent, and of the employment in this sector, 78 percent is made up of family members. In manufacturing, 55 percent of the total salaries are paid to employees in this sector.

## HISTORY

Consulting in Lebanon is quite a new function, whether it is consulting to achieve high quality standards, human resources consulting, or family business consulting. Until recently, most of the consulting was financial, performed by experts working in financial companies and banks. Consulting was performed by international experts and international companies. The field of family businesses was never considered a separate field here until the Lebanese American University (LAU) created the Institute of Family and Entrepreneurial Business (IFEB) in 1999. The Institute was launched in May 2000 with its first workshop titled "Pressing Issues Facing Family Firms." In summer 2000, LAU invited two experts, Drs. Joyce and Bob Brockhaus, from the United States to lead the first seminar on "Understanding the Unique Challenges Facing Family Firms." This seminar and workshop were the starting points on the topic of family business in Lebanon. A few organizations had offered programs on family business in the Middle East, but none were academic. The LAU, with its Institute of Family and Entrepreneurial Business, is the first academic center in Lebanon and the Middle East to develop educational programs in the field of family businesses and to conduct research in the area. The Institute houses a data bank on family firms in Lebanon and the Middle East.

Few big organizations have consulted with international experts on issues they confront, since most of the family businesses in Lebanon were initiated in the 1950s and 1960s, and most passed smoothly to the second generation. However, those who are about to embark on a transition to the third generation find it very difficult, as the number of shareholders has increased tremendously, and hence are now seeking outside help to find solutions.

In Lebanon, it has been a tradition to divide all the assets, including the business, among the brothers. Sisters are always excluded from the equation, as female family members are looked at as future mothers. It is assumed that they will get married and raise their own children and economically will not be responsible for the family like the brothers are. So the inheritance goes to the sons, having in mind that they, as men, will take care of their parents economically when they grow older. In wealthy families, the female heirs will be given some money in the form of real estate or fixed assets. They are usually excluded from inheriting the family business. In diversified businesses, every brother will be in charge of a segment of the work, and sometimes, the diversification follows the number of children involved in the business. Thus businesses are created according to the number of children who will be capable of running them.

Now, with the changing role of women, and the globalization phenomenon which causes competition to intensify, family firms are more concerned about issues of a family business nature, such as the transition in the business, leadership and control in the family, and the role that females should play. They have to face intensifying competition and chose among the heirs for the leading position in the business. They usually deal with these in a nonprofessional way, and they have no clear ideas as to what the solutions should be. The media usually focuses on dysfunctional occurrences in family businesses in Lebanon, especially those that lead to disputes.

It is believed in Lebanon and the Arab countries, more than anywhere else in the world, that family businesses are a way to enhance a family's social standing rather than an impersonal, money-generating activity or a market-driven activity. This special way of managing a business in these countries relates to the socioeconomic and cultural backgrounds of these families (Ali, 1993). The culture here in general refers to a system of governance that is headed by the father, the only money provider in the family and the patriarch. The system functions according to seniority leadership and male authority; thus males usually are destined to take over the business and leadership is transferred into the hands of the oldest male. This accepted scheme eliminates sources of conflict, as it will be accepted as part of the culture: it is something they always have lived with.

The challenge in Lebanese family businesses is one of complexity, as families have become increasingly diverse. Families are experiencing greater geographical dispersion, more divorce, and more freedom of choice, as well as changing gender roles in the family and their businesses. Succession situations are not openly discussed, as this would create tension. Senior-generation leaders tend to stay in office as long as possible and resist turning over the leadership to juniors. The mismanagement of continuity could be at the heart of many problems in family companies. Senior leaders have to acknowledge that they have to leave office for the younger generation to take over, which is always difficult. Many refuse to retire completely, which is another critical issue facing family firms in Lebanon.

## THE USE OF THE INTERNET

Family firms in Lebanon exhibit characteristics that bode well not only for their own longevity and growth but also for the prosperity and stability of the country and the region. The family firms we studied tended to take the long view, exhibit perseverance and self-reliance under pressure, invest in technology, and express optimism. Firms in Lebanon have gone through the harsh years of war and survived in spite of the heavy shelling and uncertainties facing not only their businesses but the country at large. These firms are doing well and still growing, and they show a high level of stability. These family businesses are survivors. The average life span of family companies here is forty years, and 75 percent of those firms are now managed by the second generation.

The use of technology is considered to provide an important route to business success. Our research shows that Lebanese family firms are embracing information technology. Those interviewed said that IT investments have helped them boost productivity (58 percent), enhance customer service (55 percent), manage quality control (43 percent), achieve competitive advantage (42 percent), and improve responsiveness (29 percent).

Further, most of those interviewed said they viewed continued investments in technology as essential to their development. Nearly half (45 percent) said investments in information technology are "very important" to achieving their business goals, while another 46 percent said those investments are "important" or "somewhat important. The findings are drawn from 106 interviews conducted during 2003 at the Institute of Family and Entrepreneurial Business at LAU with CEOs and senior executives of family firms in Lebanon.

Given the evidence that family firms are using technology to progress and modernize, any government policies that encourage additional investment are likely to pay dividends in improved competitiveness, higher employment, increased exports, and a bolstered tax base.

The current low levels of debt among Lebanese family firms suggest that these companies have the capacity to borrow money for investment. Special incentives that encourage incurring debt in order to grow and modernize would support those firms, the banking industry, and the entire Lebanese economy.

## RESEARCH

### Family Firms: A Leading Force in the Lebanese Economy

Family businesses constitute a majority of all firms in Lebanon, and many are large, dominant companies. More than one-quarter (27 percent) of respondents interviewed reported annual revenues of US$10 million or more. In fact, ten respondents—9 percent of the total sample chosen—reported more than US$1 billion in annual sales.

Further, nearly half (46 percent) of family businesses are growing. Over the past five years, 9 percent of respondents experienced annual revenue increases of 21 percent or more. More than one-fifth of respondents (21 percent) generated annual revenue increases of 6 to 20 percent, and another 16 percent of interviewees reported modest increases of 1 to 5 percent annually.

Predictably, optimism is strong among family-business leaders here. More than two-thirds of the respondents we interviewed (69 percent) anticipated annual revenue growth over the next five years. In fact, one-eighth of all respondents (12 percent) predicted growth of 21 percent or more per annum.

As employers, family firms are very important. Five-person companies are typical in the industrial sector, but many family Lebanese enterprises employ far more. Among respondents, one-quarter employ more than 100 people full-time. In the industrial sector alone, our research shows that family firms employ some 14,000 people, or 12 percent of the industrial workforce in Lebanon. (Research conducted on 500 companies in Lebanon—2003 IFEB.) Further, more than half of respondents (53 percent) expected to increase employment over the next five years, suggesting that family firms are likely to play an important role in reducing Lebanon's 18 percent unemployment rate.

## PROFILE OF THE CONSULTANTS

### Training

On a yearly basis, the Institute of Family and Entrepreneurial Business at LAU organizes conferences and seminars in the field and hosts international experts and consultants from the United States and Europe. These speakers have the opportunity to make contacts with owners and members of families of different generations seeking help or just interested in the topic. These contacts usually result in a future interest in consulting. The image of international consultation is usually high in the minds of the Lebanese; however, they are always skeptical about how much this applies to the culture of the Middle East. Family firms in Lebanon and the Middle East have more confidence to work with international consultants because they believe that the secrets of the family will not be disclosed in their communities. They usually take their professional advice but are not fully convinced that the complete details given by international consultants are applicable here and want to adapt it themselves to their own culture and traditions, which they think that international consultants cannot fully understand. According to our research, the majority of Lebanese firms consult with their accountants (55 percent), their financial advisors (30 percent), and bankers (27 percent). Some 17 percent would ask their children for advice, while 16 percent of them would ask their business peers (see Appendix). None of these consultants have the appropriate family business management background, and their advice is centered on their respective field only.

## Background

Family businesses in Lebanon that have survived for more than three generations have consulted mainly with their accountants and with their lawyers. They focus on the legal and transitional aspects without really looking at the family side and the implications of the decisions on the family. Families that have been successful have the legal framework all set properly, and in certain cases the birth order in the family makes the divisional aspect easier to handle and very clear, which results in a successful transition.

The family business owners interviewed prefer local consultants by far (90 percent versus 10 percent for foreign consultants—see Appendix). Those that have recruited foreign family business consultants were satisfied with their input. Their inclination to use consultants from abroad is mainly due to the secrecy issue and to the widespread belief that international consultants can bring an added value to their businesses. It is also believed by some that foreign consultants have better skills if they come from Europe or the United States. In general, European consultants are believed to provide the best service, since their culture is thought to be closer to the Lebanese.

It is very hard for some Lebanese companies to reveal the kind of problems they have, or even to ask for a consultant, as this would mean they have family problems. It is also believed that if they admit to problems in the family, then this would affect the business, the image of the company, and the confidence of the stakeholders in the market. The majority would even refrain from participating in a seminar on family businesses, claiming that they have no problem whatsoever. In general, those who refrain are those who really need a consultant.

Consultants should have a family business background with communications and relational skills. They should speak the language (Arabic) and should know the culture of the country. Their work will also add value if they understand the culture behind different religious groups, the inheritance aspects inherent to the religions, and the culture of the family regarding gender and traditions. Some family business consultants have a psychology background, some others have a management background, and some others are lawyers. When asked about the professional who has been very instrumental in succession planning (see Appendix), family firms in our sample responded that accountants were most helpful, with a 37 percent response rate, followed by lawyers (less than 20 percent) and family business consultants (less than 20 percent).

In Lebanon, the inheritance rules of families follow the religion. For Christians, the inheritance rules and culture are different from those for Moslems and Druzes (Fahed-Sreih, 2004). So, for proper consultation in this country, the consultant should know the laws surrounding inheritance for the different religions existing in the country (approximately seventeen different religions) and also know the legal framework for companies.

### Roles and Functions Performed by Consultants

Family firms in Lebanon often overlook the dangerous "soft issues." They postpone attending to the family business issues until it becomes urgent to tackle them or until the tensions mount and the problems blow up. They consider mildly important issues of influences, such as that of a spouse, on the business dynamics and the relationship between the brothers. They disregard the level of pay of family members versus nonfamily employees in the same position. Family firms here need to adopt a more proactive approach to contingency planning, such as a "dying scenario" in which one can consider what will happen if the founder or the leader of the firm is dying or sick, or just disappears from the scene, and try to plan for the next period. The culture in the Middle East makes it very difficult to anticipate death or major illness.

Instead, family firms need effective contingency planning. They need to think in terms of a wider perspective and avoid insurance-based approaches and narrow thinking. Family firms have to go through regular risk analysis and embrace "broader thinking" strategies. Consultants should make sure they understand and tackle the problems encountered in the businesses and help solve them, keeping in mind the family's culture and religion, its social standing, and its perception of the participation of in-laws and females. The solutions found should work at least for one generation to come.

## Compensation

In Lebanon, consultation was not highly valued. Companies will not pay a high amount to consultants and will not seek consultation unless there is a very important need for it. Hence, the compensation for consultants is not great. They believe that intensive work to create a family document is not an important task and that the consultant should not be paid more than $5,000 total. Consultation to establish quality standards for companies with 1,000 employees is done by international companies located in Lebanon, for sums ranging between $5,000 and $10,000; it is considered important, as it helps them achieve quality standards and hence gives them a competitive advantage. Family consultation is not usually viewed as a necessity to conduct proper business or to create and sustain a competitive advantage. It will become a necessity when the family members perceive a severe family problem.

## Consultants As Employees

There is a common belief that consultants should become employees so that family members can have control over them, and most of the consultants do end up becoming employees in the family companies. It is believed that when they become employees they will maintain secrecy and become more loyal to the business. A consultant needs to gain the confidence of all parties in the family and work on a full-time basis for the company. The compensation of a consultant is usually negotiated, especially when they require high fees. Reputable lawyers would set their fees at $1,000 per hour. Reputable family business consultants should set their fees at the same level. However, when setting fees, consultants should take into consideration that the lowest salary in Lebanon is 350,000 Lebanese pounds, which is equivalent to $233, and the average salary is around $600 per month. The compensation, be it on a per hour, per project retainer, or per day basis, will be negotiated by the family company.

## KEY CONFLICTS OF FAMILY BUSINESS MEMBERS

### Problems Encountered in Lebanese Family Businesses

Problems faced by Lebanese family businesses most commonly arise from issues pertaining to transparency, power delegation, and planning. Family social standing is mostly associated with family name and identity. Due to the close-knit and interrelated socioeconomic networks in Lebanon, family business members are very conscious of the direct impact their actions might have on the image of their businesses and the public perception of their entire families. The separation between the family business, the business environment, and the family is a daily struggle to which family businesses have to accommodate. Thus, Lebanese family businesses tend to try to preserve their "hermetically sealed" organizational structure and their business secrecy.

Power delegation is another major concern for these family businesses. Family members, regardless of the size of their business, rarely delegate full responsibilities. Decision making is a sacred responsibility of the family members running the company. Accordingly, recruiting employees for key positions from outside the closed family network raises trust issues.

Last but not least, problems related to lack of planning are most noticeable in the absence of established human resource policies as well as more general family business policies.

## Problem Solving

Family business tensions are very often handled with dysfunctional and short-term approaches. There are no tension-solving system structures that channel family members' concern at home and at work simultaneously. Lebanese family business leaders solve tensions through the following ways:

1. Maintaining secrecy from employees, family members, and other owners
2. Excluding from the decision-making process family members or shareholders who, in their opinion, are the cause of tension, and alienating them from important roles in the organization
3. Hiring noncompetent and overpaid family members when it will help reduce the tension among disagreeing family members, an expensive attempt to create harmony and maintain power
4. Bestowing concerned family members with titles which in reality carry no executive power

## Succession Problems

Although succession planning is a major issue for family firms in Lebanon, 63 percent of family firms have not yet chosen their successors. Succession problems are mainly related to the imminence of leadership change. Thirty-nine percent of the respondents to the 2003 American Family Business Survey stated that their family companies anticipate leadership change within the next few years (Simmon, 2003). This percentage is quite in line with the percentage revealed by Lebanese family firms. Succession planning requires CEOs to accept leadership loss/succession and thus a transformation in business dealings. In general, there is a psychological barrier to the acceptance of succession planning. As a result, indecisive founders or CEOs of family firms are in the process of negotiating a co-succession, a transition from an absolute power to a shared one.

Even with the appointment of a successor, the founder's and/or leader's executive power and authority determine, off the record, the dynamics of the family business. Succession in Lebanese family firms takes the form of passing leadership from the CEO-father to his eldest son. In practice, nonetheless, decision making remains the privilege of the old leaders, who never or rarely retire. The involvement and even the physical presence of the older generation characterize Lebanese family firms; it is very rare to see a complete succession or a complete "passing of the baton" stage. Even in the case of a planned succession, older CEOs going through the transition phase with their successors intentionally complicate the process and tirelessly attempt to instill their irreplaceable guidance and knowledge, underestimating their successors' future leadership (self-perceived).

## *Governance Structures—Possibilities for the Future*

Family firms should seek outside help and consultation to establish a governance system that clearly outlines the duties, responsibilities, and rights of family members, shareholders, the management team, and the board of directors.

They should implement governance structures in order to enable

- effective communication,
- ongoing planning,
- shared decision making, and
- expression of shared values.

The advice of a consultant in the creation of the governance structure is usually very instrumental. These structures relate to three entities:

- The ownership governance structure
- The family governance structures
- The business governing/governance structures

It is suggested that each structure, whether related to ownership, business, or family, have its own set of meetings and family forums to deal with the important issues the family may be facing and to provide the right framework for proper governance. Shareholders' meetings and board of directors' meetings decide the ownership structure. Family meetings, family retreats, the family constitution, and family councils determine the family structure, whereas the management development team and the board of directors draw the business structure.

## The Family Council

Very few family firms in Lebanon have formal family councils. First-generation family members usually exercise their control to determine how to solve issues pertaining to the family. Respect for seniors and the older generation make this work effectively.

## Family Philanthropy

Philanthropic activities in big family firms are generally/usually set and carried out by their family foundations. In smaller family firms, donations are made to social organizations in the community at the family member level rather than at that of a family foundation. They do not follow a preset program with agreed on objectives and strategy. Philanthropic duties/activities are done in conjunction with the social environment and community needs. Our research shows that no family firm has a philanthropic committee on the board of directors.

## Family Offices

Creating family offices is a phenomenon gaining more importance in Lebanese family businesses. Family firms are more aware of the role the family office can have in avoiding as well as dealing with existing problems.

## The Family Assembly

The family assembly brings the family together to discuss business issues and/or make decisions on key issues. The formation of family assemblies is not a common practice in Lebanese family businesses. In contrast, it is considered wise to discuss such important issues with key individuals on a one-to-one basis away from the influence and feedback of all family members. This accepted scheme allows family members who are working in the business to feel more comfortable about their decisions.

## Family Meetings

Family meetings are very common and essential for harmonious work and family environments. Usually such meetings take place at the family/parents' house on a Sunday for Christians and on Friday for Moslems (the Holy Day). Another common practice is family reunions every Christmas or holiday season, where all family members are expected to be present and participate. Business might be informally discussed, and such family reunions are essential to keep the family together and to share family issues. Family reunions are at the heart of a proper family governance system. In my opinion, it is unfortunate that modern families are not very keen on preserving the tradition of family reunions.

## Board of Directors

Boards of directors in family firms do not seem to abide by the set/required professional requirements. Our findings show that 40.5 percent of the interviewees believe in the constructive contribution of the Board of Directors, while only 19.8 percent perceive the contribution of the Board to be outstanding. The Board of Directors is executive by nature: 34 percent of the committees are executive and 17 percent are audit committees. The audit function in Lebanon is a legal requirement for all the organizations/firms that have a formal board of directors. Accounts should be reviewed by a formal/registered/certified auditor and, for certain types of organizations, by two formal financial auditors. It is worth noting that most of the boards do not meet regularly: 17.9 percent never meet, 33 percent meet one to two times per year, 11.3 percent meet three to four times per year, 6.6 percent meet five to six times, and 6.6 percent meet more than six times. The majority of family members who are not members of the board of directors do not attend board meetings (56 percent), while 11.3 percent always attend. It is reported that 20 percent have an advisory board (see Appendix). As for compensation, around 40 percent receive no fees for attending board meetings, while 53.7 percent receive annual fees.

## CASE STUDIES

### Case 1: Overcoming Religious and Cultural Gender-Related Hindrances

This case embodies how family businesses can, through proper consultation, solve religious and cultural issues. In Lebanon, the diversity of religions makes it more difficult to deal with inheritance aspects in family businesses. For Sunni Moslems, in the absence of sons in the conjugal family, the inheritance would go to the males who carry the family name in the extended family, that is the sons of the brothers, and not the daughters. This case centers on a successful Lebanese entrepreneur who has only one daughter. After long years of hard work, starting as an office boy in a big transportation company, he started his own company. The company grew remarkably. The father's main concern was to pass on the company's leadership to a successor whom he deemed worthy of the inheritance. However, the mother insisted that the business should go to their only girl. As a result, the father transformed his business to a corporation (SAL Corporation, Societe Anonyme Libanaise), in which its shares belong to the bearer. He also needed to change his religious sect to Shia. As a Shiite Moslem, the father guaranteed the rights of his only daughter to be his successor/heir. By implementing participative management and by imposing her physical presence in a culturally female-hostile shipping port environment, the daughter was able to turn her father's company into a multi-million-dollar company with branches worldwide in Cyprus, Syria, Turkey, Algeria, Egypt, Jordan, and Kuwait, to list but a few. Today, as she is married to a Christian, the daughter's task will not be as hard as her father's was. Her three children, one son and two daughters, all have equal inheritance rights.

### Case 2: Brothers Turning into Enemies

The Fishers is a well-known family business operating in the household electric and kitchen appliances industries in Lebanon.* They have been operating in the Lebanese market for more than forty years and have a reputation for their competitive prices and state-of-the-art designs. The father founded the business; after his death, his two sons inherited it. These brothers conflicted about the way the business should be run. The older brother wanted to invest more money in the company, while the younger brother wanted to invest the company's assets outside the company (i.e., stock market). However, after consultation, the older brother decided to borrow money from the bank and buy his younger brother out of the business. Though this solution was meant to help the business survive leadership tensions and spare the family destructive animosity, the younger brother, after losing the money he settled for and not succeeding in blackmailing his brother for more, resorted to horrible criminal ways against his own blood. He attempted to kill his brother with a grenade. This sad story ends with the older brother recuperating in a hospital and the younger

---

*The case is a true story but the names used are fictitious.

brother serving time in jail. Later the older brother withdrew his accusation to save his brother, but the younger brother is still inculpated by civil law.

This tragic development in the family business makes us wonder about the initial consultation effort that led to the split. The question remains whether the arranged consultation was fair or not. No doubt the settlement was fair; otherwise, the younger brother would not have accepted it. One might question the fairness of the implementation of the settlement process and its follow-up mechanism, and whether it took into account the younger brother's personality.

## CONCLUSION

Consulting for family firms is different from consulting for nonfamily firms, as the dynamics of a family business necessitate special attention. Systems thinking is crucial to family business consulting. For the systems approach to offer working and practical solutions, it must accommodate to the family culture context. In the Lebanese context, religious as well as gender issues need to be understood and addressed. The foundations of any consulting activity require the consultant to build strong bonds with the family, and these bonds should be based on trust. Holding a family retreat, for example, gives the consultant an opportunity to highlight a number of issues that need to be solved. In addition, he or she needs to orient and make clear to the consulting family business what its options and possibilities are. Consultants should be role models, teachers, and coaches, and should have the ability to convince their clients as to which are the best choices. In certain cases, using a multidisciplinary team of consultants may help families solve and avoid important problems, and break dysfunctional family patterns.

Family business consultants should understand their own family patterns before doing any outside consultation. They should do their own genograms and understand how their experience in their own families has affected their own lives (Kaslow and Ridenour, 1984). Consultants should stand on higher ground to be able to help their clients deal with their family conflicts/family business conflicts. They should be knowledgeable about the culture of the country and check concerned family members' reactions to possible solutions. Consultants should be aware that one size doesn't fit all and that a cookie-cutter approach is a recipe for failure. Every family firm has its own dynamics, its own culture, and its own issues, and the same type of solution will not work for all. The case illustrations show that not all cases are a success and a solution that might seem to fit one would turn into a disaster for another.

Consulting for family firms is absolutely not easy but it is very rewarding, especially when the consultant's efforts blossom into a healthier family business and enable a wealthy family and a family firm to grow beyond family disputes/misunderstandings. The foundations of consulting for family businesses remain the same in all countries; however, consulting for companies in Lebanon and the Middle East requires a specific cultural, religious, and gender awareness and, most important, awareness of patterns of relationships within a given family.

## APPENDIX A

### *Who Are Your Most Trusted Business Advisors? (Rank Your Top Three with 1 Being the Most Trusted.)*

| Set | Accountant | Banker | Business peer | Children | Religious people | Financial advisor | Friends | Insurance agent | Lawyer | Spouse | Other consul | Parents | Blank | Total |
|---|---|---|---|---|---|---|---|---|---|---|---|---|---|---|
| 1 | 4 | 1 | 0 | 0 | 0 | 4 | 0 | 1 | 2 | 0 | 1 | 1 | 4 | 18 |
| 2 | 6 | 1 | 0 | 1 | 0 | 4 | 0 | 0 | 5 | 1 | 5 | 1 | 6 | 30 |
| 3 | 5 | 3 | 2 | 2 | 1 | 5 | 0 | 0 | 2 | 1 | 1 | 4 | 4 | 30 |
| 4 | 6 | 4 | 2 | 1 | 0 | 3 | 2 | 2 | 4 | 3 | 1 | 1 | 1 | 30 |
| 5 | 6 | 3 | 3 | 1 | 0 | 4 | 1 | 2 | 7 | 1 | 0 | 2 | 0 | 30 |
| 6 | 4 | 4 | 2 | 0 | 0 | 1 | 3 | 0 | 3 | 1 | 3 | 4 | 5 | 30 |
| 7 | 6 | 2 | 1 | 0 | 0 | 3 | 0 | 0 | 4 | 0 | 1 | 2 | 11 | 30 |
| 8 | 3 | 2 | 1 | 3 | 0 | 3 | 0 | 0 | 2 | 1 | 1 | 3 | 11 | 30 |
| 9 | 3 | 2 | 1 | 1 | 0 | 1 | 2 | 0 | 2 | 2 | 3 | 4 | 7 | 28 |
| 10 | 5 | 3 | 2 | 5 | 0 | 2 | 2 | 1 | 3 | 3 | 1 | 2 | 1 | 30 |
| 11 | 7 | 2 | 1 | 3 | 5 | 0 | 0 | 0 | 3 | 1 | 3 | 2 | 3 | 30 |
| Total | 55 | 27 | 15 | 17 | 6 | 30 | 10 | 6 | 37 | 14 | 20 | 26 | 53 | 316 |

Survey funded by the Institute of Family and Entrepreneurial Business at the Lebanese American University: ifeb@lau.edu.lb, www.lau.edu.lb. Findings are drawn from 106 interviews conducted during 2003 with CEOs and senior executives of family firms in Lebanon.

## Who Are Your Most Trusted Business Advisors?

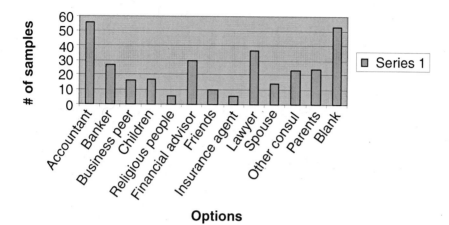

## What Is Your Preference Toward the Nationality of Your Consultant?

| Set | Foreigner | Local | Blank | Total |
|-----|-----------|-------|-------|-------|
| 1 | 0 | 10 | 0 | 10 |
| 2 | 2 | 8 | 0 | 10 |
| 3 | 0 | 9 | 1 | 10 |
| 4 | 0 | 9 | 1 | 10 |
| 5 | 2 | 7 | 1 | 10 |
| 6 | 1 | 9 | 0 | 10 |
| 7 | 1 | 9 | 0 | 10 |
| 8 | 1 | 9 | 0 | 10 |
| 9 | 1 | 9 | 0 | 10 |
| 10 | 2 | 8 | 0 | 10 |
| 11 | 1 | 5 | 0 | 6 |
| Total | 11 | 92 | 3 | 106 |

## *What Is Your Preference Toward the Nationality of Your Consultant?*

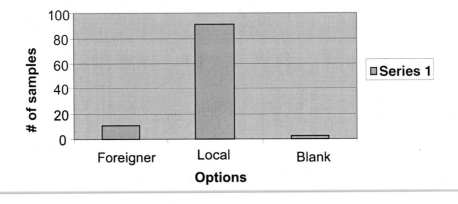

## *Have You Participated In or Attended Seminars Related to Family Business in the Past Year?*

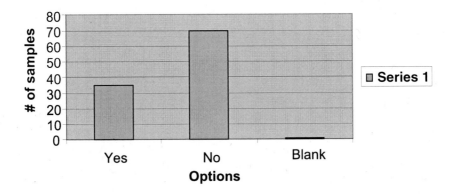

## Which One of the Following Professionals Has Been the Most Instrumental in Your Succession and Estate Planning?

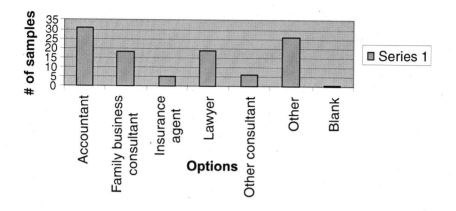

## Do You Have an Advisory Board?

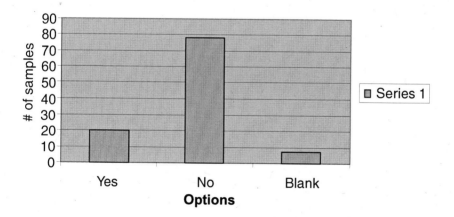

## REFERENCES

Ali, A.J. (1993). Management theory in a transitional society: The Arab's experience. *International Studies of Management and Organization, 20*(3), 7-35.

Fahed-Sreih, J. (2004). *Facts and figures concerning family businesses in Lebanon.* Arlington, TX: Franklin Publishing.

Kaslow, F. & Ridenour R. (1984). *The military family: Dynamics and treatment.* New York: Guilford.

Simmon, R. (2003, March 11). Bailing out of the retirement plan: Survey on family business. *Wall Street Journal.*

Chapter 12

# Mexico

Salo Grabinsky

## BACKGROUND

Families have been starting their own businesses and working together in them the world over for centuries, perhaps even millennia. In fact, most enterprises on the planet today are owned and managed by families, according to IFERA (2003). Latin America is no exception. Countries such as Argentina, Brazil, Colombia, and Mexico are the home of huge numbers of thriving family enterprises of every size and in every field.

Mexico has undergone a major transformation since the end of World War II, evolving from a rural-oriented economy with enormous natural resources, scant industries, and little infrastructure into the world's eleventh largest economy. The country's pool of companies, numbering only a few thousand prior to World War II, has burgeoned to nearly 2.8 million firms at present, according to Mexican census figures (INEGI, 1999). Most are small family-owned shops, factories, and service companies generally operating at the break-even level. However, families also control some of the nation's major enterprises. For example, nearly 35 percent of the EXPANSION 500 companies for 2004 are owned and managed by families. (The Expansión 500 is the Mexican equivalent of the Fortune 500 and includes government-owned companies and the subsidiaries of such multinational firms as Wal-Mart and Ford.) This is also true of the hundreds of large, family-run private companies not included on the EXPANSION 500 list ("Las 500 empresas más importantes en México," 2004). Over 80 percent of the 100 most powerful businessmen in Mexico work in family-controlled businesses, and another 10 percent of these men are large stakeholders in their enterprises or groups ("Los 100 empresarios más importantes de México," 2003). It is a proven fact that the vast majority of private-sector companies in Mexico are comprised of millions of family-owned businesses, in comparable percentages to these types of companies

*Handbook of Family Business and Family Business Consultation*
Published by The Haworth Press, Inc., 2006. All rights reserved.
doi:10.1300/5491_12

found in the United States, Asia, and Europe. This means that the field of studies on family-owned and family-managed firms, as well as consulting in this sector, has become a top national priority.

The growth of the Mexican economy has not been without setbacks. The country has undergone a number of major crises over the past fifty years that have weakened the nation's economy and impacted the personal income of many Mexicans. This has forced those enterprises that survived to modernize in order to be in a position to effectively handle the challenges of technological advances and globalization which the world is experiencing.

However, many of these companies were not prepared to deal with the internal upheavals related to succession and continuity in their firms, which are forces that may be unleashed upon the retirement or death of the founder-patriarch (most businesses are in the first- or second-generation stages and are run by men), due to an acute lack of rules of governance and structures for the management and control of the firm and the issues related to wealth and the inheritance conflicts that will arise from the owner's demise. The enormous challenge and opportunity that this situation entails presently rests on the shoulders of a minuscule number of professionals dedicated to providing consulting services to those few families that have become aware of the perils that lie ahead and are willing to take preventive actions to adapt and be prepared to meet the challenge. Therefore, most family businesses are literally sitting "on top of a volcano," and the tremors portending an impending eruption should be a cause of concern for everyone.

## *DEFINITIONS USED IN THIS CHAPTER*

Although the literature contains dozens of valid definitions of what a family business is, the one I use here encompasses many characteristics of these firms: "A Family Business is one which is owned, managed and controlled by a family or group of relatives. The members of these families make major operational, strategic and management decisions ASSUMING TOTAL RESPONSIBILITY for their actions" (Grabinsky, 2002, p. 9).

The key point is that the decision-making process in family enterprises has been a source of enormous strength for them due to the owners' flexibility, freedom, and adaptability, versus the relative rigidity of the decision-making situation prevailing in more structured and bureaucratic institutions. Moreover, decisions in family businesses are made and the risks are taken precisely the way they are because there is no superior who has to be consulted nor has time been of the essence. These factors are important in defining a family business in its inception and early stages. This broad definition has proven useful in advising all kinds of firms, including those operated among close relatives, in-laws, and parents with children and grandchildren, using a family systems approach.

## OUR CONSULTATIVE MODEL AND PHILOSOPHY

I strongly believe in the value of a structured universe, and the prime example is perhaps our solar system, where planets follow predetermined orbits, moving in coordination, which avoids turbulence and collisions. Nevertheless, this system is obviously not perfect, since natural disasters such as hurricanes, eruptions, earthquakes, and tsunamis do disrupt normal activities on Earth.

By analogy, family business systems must also be structured and governed by principles that predict some disruptions and other cyclical events. It must be assumed that throughout its existence, an enterprise will be subject to both growth and recession, fierce competition, and periods of profitability. Moreover, the involvement of the owner and his family in the business and the stages they happen to be at in their own individual life cycles will have a profound effect on the firm's remaining sustainable over time. Each family business is unique and necessitates a custom-made approach, which involves sensitivity, creativity, and knowledge on the part of the consultant, just as much as the willingness of the owner, his or her family, and key executives to agree to implementing the required changes.

The matter of trust is an essential ingredient for the success of any consulting endeavor. As Kaye and Hamilton state (2004), the consultant has to find a person within the family circle who will be the trust catalyst (or else a trusted nonfamily professional or executive) and interact with him or her in order to be able to gain full access to the family business system and to be assured of having the family's cooperation throughout the entire process. Advisors themselves, in turn, should try to become a trusted catalyst to all their clients who look to them for guidance, communication, and sometimes simply for a word of comfort. This attitude creates a solid foundation for a long-term relationship among all parties, which is highly beneficial to the continuity of the firm.

Another key element is that of the internal cultural issues which are always present within a family, based on its traditions and social and educational background. It is just as important for a consultant to have a free-flowing interaction and empathy with the clients' values and beliefs as it is to be conversant with the family's business and financial matters. The family business consultant brings not only an impartial and objective attitude to clients but also an open mind as to what makes that particular family tick.

The two parties' value systems may differ somewhat, but a sufficient common ground of cultural identity should guarantee that both formal and tacit messages from the client's family are recognized and taken into consideration to help design a feasible project. I have learned to be on the lookout for any signs of hidden conflict in seemingly functional families and address them head-on to clarify and weigh their degree of importance in the overall picture. In short, cultural factors really do matter, and I have to stay alert to any major differences between the client's perceptions and my own, because when the differences are too great, it is better to simply decline to be their advisor. In Mexico, even owners from the higher social echelons and educated classes (many of them graduates of U.S. colleges and of prestigious universities in other countries) will reject a practitioner who does not fit into their social group or does not understand their inner feelings, values, and attitudes. The Latin mind has particular qualities that differentiate it from other cultures, such as the Japanese or the Caucasian, and I find it quite difficult as a consultant to be of any real assistance in delicate issues if I have no in-depth understanding of my clients and their cultural background and context.

We must be clear as to who is the boss and why, in order to center our work on assuring that we will have his or her support and can count on the ultimate implementation of our recommendations. A common mistake is to accept a consulting assignment, when requested by a relative of the owner, without first finding out whether the key decision maker is backing up the entire process and fully agrees with the choice of consultant. The consulting process is such a sensitive one that requires clarity, support, and common goals from the outset.

At the beginning of my practice I was mostly involved in creating Boards of Directors for small and medium-size family firms and in helping them modernize their management practices and decision-making process. Gradually, after gaining more experience and becoming increasingly aware of our clients' needs, my firm had to evolve and tackle other areas, and this is when the systemic approach to consulting became paramount in our practice.

A family business should be viewed as a system which operates under certain predetermined precepts and rules governing each subsystem in a particular manner. Four different forces are directly at work in a family-owned enterprise, often involving conflicting and even opposite goals: *the business* as a for-profit enterprise, *the family* as owner and manager of the business, also serving as the cohesive bond between its members, *company management,* which may or not consist of family members, and, finally, *ownership and wealth,* both within the company and the external assets comprising the owner's family estate.

These disparate subsystems, each revolving within its own orbit, are subject to multiple external and internal factors that interact in a myriad of ways. Disruptions are frequent, stemming from, among other factors, the passage of time, the economic conditions of the country or region, the increased complexity of the family and the business, the life cycles of the founder and successors, and the respective psychological issues which, at any given time, may converge in the family business system, creating problems, instability, and a series of conflicts and crises that can sink the entire enterprise (see Figure 12.1).

This unavoidable and often unexpected scenario of turmoil and even chaos may stem from one or several subsystems or from external factors and requires going through a tactful, often time-consuming and costly, multidisciplinary process. Results are often dependent on the willingness of the various family stakeholders to negotiate among themselves, sometimes despite long-standing animosities and resentments, regarding how to manage the company skillfully through rough economic downturns and protect the firm's wealth from recessions and even prolonged economic stagnation. No wonder we hear an often-quoted Spanish saying that in a wealthy family, "The father is a merchant, the son a gentleman, and the grandson a beggar" ["Padre comerciante, hijo caballero, nieto pordiosero"] (Kaye & Hamilton, 2004).

Taking into consideration that each family business system is not only unique but also that it will be subject to constant disruptions, we apply a

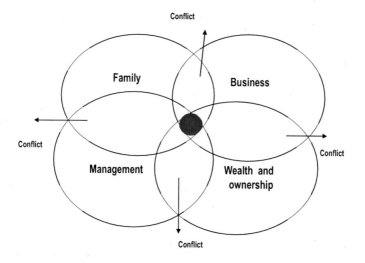

FIGURE 12.1. The family business as an unstable system.

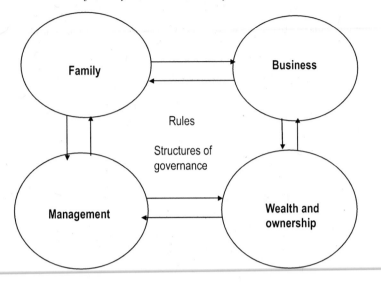

FIGURE 12.2. Family business system model for consulting.

model for family business consulting that focuses on a preventive framework to reduce the degree of potential damage and crisis to manageable levels by strengthening the system's core values: family unity, business continuity, and the preservation of wealth (Grabinsky, 2001).

This model consists of helping the client design the rules and structures for each particular family-owned business and then getting the client started in putting them into effect on a step-by-step, systemic basis (see Figure 12.2).

This consulting model follows these stages:

1. Initial evaluation and diagnosis by the advisor in collaboration with key members of the family business, prior to formalizing the consulting process and implementation plan. This diagnosis is obtained on both the personal level and with the aid of Internet-based simulation questionnaires.
2. Family dynamics session with key stakeholders and, when needed, referral to psychologists, well-trained and credentialed therapists, or institutions specializing in mental health services.
3. A session to prepare the first draft of the Family Constitution or Protocol. The Protocol is a document that clearly establishes all the procedures and rules to be followed by the family members in the event

of a crisis, based on their hierarchy or some other agreed-upon structure, and aids in steering them through situations that could set off a major family conflict but which the existence of and compliance with the Protocol largely defuses. Internal review of the Protocol is necessary to resolve doubts and achieve the full acceptance of key family members prior to formalizing it.

4. Evaluation of the strengths and the financial and market situation of the firm in order to complete a business diagnosis prior to establishing the Board of Directors. This includes interviews with key executives and board members to assess the company's overall situation.

5. Meetings to set up the rules governing the Board of Directors, including a formal session with the advisor acting as a moderator and facilitator.

6. Formalizing the Family Protocol, which also includes a mission statement.

7. Setting up the Board of Directors or Advisors, as called for in each case.

8. Analysis and evaluation, with the support of attorneys and financial planners, of ownership issues, wills, legacies, and inheritances. The succession process and wealth preservation measures are based on rules and guidelines contained in the Family Protocol.

9. Special key issues which require the attention of the family business consultant and need to be clarified and/or resolved prior to concluding the process.

10. End of the formal intervention by the consultant.

11. Follow-up and other postconsulting arrangements agreed upon by both parties to preserve the relationship on a semipermanent but nonbinding basis.

In many instances advisors find that they have to get deeply involved in a specific issue and the entire process is changed. Although this may be unavoidable, I prefer to follow the model delineated here, which has proven to be effective for most of my clients.

### A CASE STUDY:
### CASA STRAUSS S.A.—"THE PALACE OF MUSIC"

This company* was founded early in the twentieth century by two cousins, Johann and Paul Strauss, who initially emigrated from Germany to South

---

*Permission received to use this company as a case study example.

America, where they worked as sales representatives for a large European musical instrument manufacturer. Later they decided to settle in Mexico, based on the country's relatively solid development and stability under the rule of dictator Porfirio Díaz. The European manufacturer offered to be their capitalist partner, so that the two cousins decided to go into business together and opened a small store as distributors of musical instruments in Mexico City.

The nation's stable situation was short-lived, however, due to the outbreak of the Mexican Revolution not long afterward (1910-1921), which created widespread chaos and ultimately led to over 1 million deaths. Nevertheless, the partners decided to stay on and took advantage of the capital's cultural scene, as well as the opportunities to be had in the provinces with the local folk brass bands, a centuries-old tradition still alive today in thousands of villages and cities. These groups needed musical instruments to play, as well as sheet music to read.

After the Mexican Revolution, the company, now renamed Casa Strauss, continued to prosper, and after a certain time, the two cousins decided to purchase an important stake from the European manufacturer and turn their business into a family-owned firm. The partnership was then divided on a 60/40 basis. The 60 percent majority was inherited by Johann's two sons, Albert and Kurt Strauss, while the remaining 40 percent was owned by Paul's son, Erick.

During the post-Revolutionary years, the company continued to grow both in the downtown area and the new residential districts of Mexico City, as well as in the provinces.

Mexico's entry into World War II, as part of the Allied effort against Nazi Germany and the other Axis countries, caused a serious but temporary disruption of activities. Due to the German origin of the Strauss family, the Mexican authorities impounded their businesses, since in this period the government kept strict control over foreign nationals from enemy countries. At the end of the war the family's properties were returned and Casa Strauss continued to grow.

During the second half of the twentieth century, the second-generation family members, Albert and Erick, and third-generation William were fully involved in the management of the firm, and by the twenty-first century, as of May 2004, the organization was structured as follows:

> *Branch A:* Owns 30 percent, under the leadership of second-generation Albert Strauss, as general manager.
> *Branch B:* Owns 40 percent, headed by second-generation Erick Strauss, who is sales and public relations manager.
> *Branch C:* Owns 30 percent, directed by third-generation William Strauss, who assumed leadership upon the death of his father Kurt in representation of his family branch. William, who is several decades younger than his two cousin-partners, held the position of administrative director until recently.

The two second-generation cousins, Albert and Erick, both of whom are now in their seventies, have maintained a civil but distant relationship for nearly fifty years. William, who is an intelligent and easygoing individual, has been acting as a catalyst and mediator between his two elder cousins.

The Strauss group of companies presently consists of eight enterprises, which are engaged in running several retail stores, owning valuable real estate, as well as operating a corporate office and a rope manufacturing company. The group's revenues are in the US$25 to 30 million range and the enterprise employs 200 people.

## Our Consulting Assignment

In 1998, two third-generation members of the Strauss family attended the Diploma Course on the Professional Management of Family Businesses (© 1997 Salo Grabinsky) coordinated by our office and the Mexican Chamber of Industry. Strong personal ties developed between us during these classes, as a result of which the Strauss family requested our services to achieve the following goals:

1. Help strengthen communications among the current partners and facilitate the incorporation of new family members in an orderly and efficient manner.
2. Design and implement a set of rules to be included in a Family Protocol.
3. Help coordinate the succession process, including the planned retirement of the two second-generation partners.
4. Aid in the initial setup of the Board of Directors, together with its Rules of Governance.
5. Assist one family branch (the one headed by Erick Strauss) in dealing with its estate planning (not fiscally or tax related) to ensure a just and planned will for those family members who are not involved in the group.

Finally, and quite importantly, several members of the group have repeatedly asked us to mediate, as trusted advisors, in order to reduce tension among themselves and help the family achieve a common goal. This mediation has become key to any consultant who realizes that to help the different members, you have to narrow their differences and hopefully help them to settle on a common ground.

A major transition took place in 2004, which was monitored and mediated by our consulting office. Both Albert and Erick retired from the day-to-day operations of Casa Strauss and received a fair and adequate financial settlement for their decades of work there, while retaining their stature as directors on the board. Moreover, Erick Strauss also decided to sell part of his 40 percent stake to the two other branches, for liquidity and estate purposes, retaining a small (10 percent) percentage for his son Edward Strauss, an expert in musical instruments, who has worked with Casa Strauss for over twenty years.

As of this writing (August 2004), the third generation has assumed full operational control of the Strauss group. The three family branches are present and working in a highly coordinated way. William Strauss has assumed the role of managing director, and Erick's son, Edward, is active in the purchasing area.

Albert's two siblings, George and Tania Strauss, are rapidly developing into key executives, working together with nonfamily professionals to create a dynamic, capable team that will be a major factor in ensuring the continuity and strength of the family firm.

Another matter of note is that we assisted in the valuation of Erick Strauss's 30 percent stake (with full disclosure and the prior approval of the other two branches), and we had the great satisfaction of learning that the counteroffer made by the purchasers was only minimally lower (less than 5 percent) than the figure we proposed. Thus, the purchase agreement was executed without a glitch and all the parties were satisfied.

The four third-generation cousins of Casa Strauss are now committed to carrying out the following actions:

1. Further professionalize their decision-making process with an efficient Board of Directors consisting of both family and nonfamily directors, who are trusted by everyone. At present the company uses the services of advisors, who are helping the Board make key decisions.
2. Strictly adhere to the Family Protocol to prevent potential conflicts.
3. Work in coordination among themselves and with other executives to maintain and strengthen a high-caliber top management team.
4. Engage in a formal strategic planning process.

### *The Consulting Process in This Case*

Following our systems approach, we first focused on family dynamics, detecting various minor but solvable issues, such as the long-standing superficially polite but nevertheless trying rivalry between the two second-generation cousins. In addition, we learned that Edward Strauss, Erick's son, was often rebellious, he failed to comply with company discipline, and he rarely attended meetings, which created a tense situation among his uncles and cousins.

Both issues have been satisfactorily resolved through the sale of Erick's 30 percent stake to his two cousins and by assisting Edward to negotiate a working agreement. Edward is currently fully committed to his job responsibilities and communicates extremely well with William and his other cousins, and everyone agrees that he has now become "a member of the team." In this case, we saw no need to refer any of the family members to therapists or other specialists.

Then we focused on the Family Protocol, which was created by consensus and is a document created to provide guidelines to members when they need to deal with potentially thorny issues. One example: No family member can hold shares in Casa Strauss unless he or she holds a full-time job in the group and has been approved by the Board upon fulfilling certain requisites related to education and experience outside the firm.

The next step was to assess the businesses and have the Board of Directors establish certain policies, budgets, and controls. This task was not fully completed because the two second-generation cousins preferred to retain a Board whose function was merely to act as consultants but to hold no real power, since they themselves preferred to make major policy decisions. I am convinced that the new generation will be more amenable to using and empowering the existing Board as the key structure and have been promoting this idea among the younger family members.

Finally, Erick Strauss asked us to evaluate his estate, as a result of which he and his wife Martha changed their wills, adjusting them to the rules of the Protocol. Moreover, this assessment helped him to retire with a compensation package commensurate to his position of having been a key employee in Casa Strauss for half a century.

These steps began with his selling most of his 40 percent stake in the business, retaining only a 10 percent stake, to ensure a comfortable financial situation upon retirement, and also by planning ahead for a just distribution of his liquid estate among his other three siblings, who are not connected with Casa Strauss. No tax issues were involved in our work, since Mexican estate tax laws are presently very simple and also because Erick's own attorney and tax accountant handled these matters. The family has told us that they are quite satisfied with the results.

As is usually the case with family business consultants, even after a given consulting process has ended, former clients keep in touch and regularly request our assistance in handling various key developments. This profession is a highly rewarding one with many fascinating facets. For me, the conclusion of many consulting processes usually marks the beginning of a long and fruitful relationship with my client-friends.

## THE MOST IMPORTANT ASPECTS
## OF THE CONSULTING MODEL

After years of consulting work, we have found that our model is most applicable when the case in hand responds to a preventive project, which has the complete support of the owner(s)-patriarch(s), where the following generation is fully aware of the perils and complexities that their families and the business will have to face in the not-so-distant future and are willing to cede power in order to institutionalize and achieve a structured company. If these key premises exist, our consulting effort is helpful for medium-sized to large enterprises or groups. However, when the opposite is true, this model is not fully productive and has failed with families already embroiled in long-standing conflicts, involving attorneys, or when inheritance issues make it difficult to define and obtain the support of the key players. Traditional entrepreneurs who are not interested in or willing to loosen their grip on their excessive power and control over their families, business, and wealth will most likely interfere in the process and will probably derail it.

Finally, very small family companies that have no formal management in place and are run in an old-fashioned or rudimentary way by the founder-owner may find the system model too sophisticated and impractical, so that a different approach is called for. (We usually accomplish this by acting as a friend, offering tips and opinions as required, usually on a pro bono basis. In addition, we have developed a simplified model for smaller family firms, which is currently being applied, and have a growing network of advisors under our firm's supervision and control.)

As mentioned previously, over the course of my years of practice, I have learned that one distinctive and key aspect that characterizes a family business consultant is the practitioner's personality and ability to establish immediate rapport and trust among the various and often quarreling members of the owner's family. Although these traits are also necessary in other professions, not all fields demand the same level of ongoing involvement that a family business consultant must commit to. Stated simply, family business consultants act as friends, confessors, and even surrogate relatives whom clients feel secure about turning to because they feel assured of receiving impartial advice and getting help in making up their minds about totally disparate issues. I always introduce myself by stating what I am not: I am not a lawyer, therapist, priest, or rabbi. Rather, I hope to become a trusted and impartial friend who will help create sustainable structures, will set logical rules of governance, and can be counted on to offer sound, independent advice. This requires certain personality traits that are not commonly found in many practitioners.

I strongly urge people interested in entering this exciting and challenging field of providing advisory services to family-owned and managed firms to first do some honest and profound soul-searching to determine whether their level of empathy, ability for personal involvement, and, of course, knowledge and capacity are such that these characteristics will further their careers. As shown in the case of the Casa Strauss family, where deep rivalries and life cycle matters posed potential problems and turmoil, the presence of an advisor-friend with high ethical standards, who became close to all the members of the three owner branches, was fundamental to achieving the desired results.

Among the distinctive features of the consulting model we use is that it has been replicated in countless cases, it follows a structured and easy-to-understand schedule, and it is based on a step-by-step process. It has also proven to be practical and valid as the starting point in repositioning the family firm for the future. The model helps clarify issues, based on an initial assessment and the use of diagnostic tools, and guides the client in seeking professional advice from specialists in carrying out a multidisciplinary effort. One client-friend summed up our work by stating: "Salo, you're not only a close friend but are also our advisor of advisors" in helping build a solid and dynamic family enterprise.

## CONCLUSION

I have been very fortunate in becoming passionately involved in the revolutionary field of family businesses in Mexico and throughout the world. This is a fast-evolving profession which requires more valuable research, the sharing of practical experiences, and networking among professionals, and it needs more practitioners who have both the knowledge and the particular personality characteristics that enable them to become fully committed to their clients on a long-term basis. It is a highly rewarding profession with an enormous potential for the right kind of person. I am happy to report that I have found that many members of our Family Firm Institute have these traits.

Finally, one last fact we have to keep in mind is that our profession is still in its infancy, which means that fortunately we still have a great deal of work ahead of us!

## REFERENCES

Grabinsky, S. (2001). *Dinámica y conflictos en las empresas familiares* [Dynamics and conflicts in family businesses]. Mexico City: Del Verbo Emprender.

Grabinsky, S. (2002). Prologue to the fifth edition. In *La empresa familiar* [The family business] (p. 9). Mexico City: Del Verbo Emprender.

IFERA. (2003) Family businesses dominate. *Family Business Review, 16,* 237.

INEGI. (1999). Censos económicos [Economic censuses]. INEGI 13, CD-ROM, Mexico.

Kaye, K. & Hamilton, S. (2004). Roles of trust in consulting to financial families. *Family Business Review, 17,* 151-163.

Las 500 empresas más importantes en México [The 500 largest companies in Mexico]. (2004). *Expansión, 35,* 190-227.

Los 100 empresarios más importantes de México [The 100 key executives and entrepreneurs in Mexico]. (2003). *Expansión, 34,* 87-93.

# Chapter 13

# Saudi Arabia

Joseph Paul
Zaher Al Munajjed
Haluk Alacaklioglu

The Kingdom of Saudi Arabia is a very family-oriented country populated by family businesses that are rooted in ancient tribal systems. A tribal sense of family and patriarchs, sometimes with multiple wives, creates a far more complex web of family relationships than we see in the West. This complex web of extended family relationships, inheritance laws that are precisely defined by *Sharia,* an indulged successor generation, a recently more volatile sociopolitical environment, many families with poorly prepared successors, the intrusion of Western lifestyles and values into an ultraconservative religious society, gender issues, and the shared family ownership of large portfolios of often unrelated businesses are all variables that interact to create challenges for Saudi family business leaders, as well as for their consultants. A case study portrays a scenario of these interacting variables, and examples are given of the issues facing an interdisciplinary and culturally diverse consulting team in a country that is both very ancient and very modern.

## THE SAUDI BUSINESS LANDSCAPE

The concept of *family business* has meaning only when these organizations are compared with companies that are not controlled by families. However, in countries such as Saudi Arabia, the vast majority of businesses are family owned. Although many multinational companies engage in business in this country, they all had, until recently, to conduct this business within the context of partnerships with Saudi family businesses. Thus, since Saudi Arabia is a kingdom, the country itself has a profound influence over

*Handbook of Family Business and Family Business Consultation*
Published by The Haworth Press, Inc., 2006. All rights reserved.
doi:10.1300/5491_13

many of the traditional family businesses within the kingdom through the political system and through deeply rooted Bedouin traditions.

In this context some specifics regarding the royal family and the history of the country are noteworthy. The U.S. Central Intelligence Agency (CIA) World Factbook Web site (2004) provides the following description of recent Saudi Arabian history: "In 1902, the founder of the modern Saudi dynasty, Abdul Aziz bin Abd al-Rahman Al Saud, captured Riyadh and set out on a 30-year campaign to unify the Arabian Peninsula." In the 1930s, the discovery of oil transformed this old culture and new country into a petroleum-based economy.

"The current chief of state, Abdallah bin Abd al-Aziz Al Saud is both the King and Prime Minister. He has been in power since August 1, 2005. The Crown Prince and First Deputy Prime Minister Sultan bin Abd al-Aziz Al Saud is the half-brother to the monarch and the designated heir to the throne since June 13, 1982. The Kingdom has both a Council of Ministers that is appointed by the monarch, and a consultative council, also appointed by him."

"Following Iraq's invasion of Kuwait in 1990, Saudi Arabia accepted the Kuwaiti royal family and 400,000 refugees while allowing Western and Arab troops to deploy on its soil for the liberation of Kuwait the following year."

"This is an oil-based economy with strong government controls over major economic activities. Saudi Arabia has the largest reserves of petroleum in the world (26 percent of the proved reserves), ranks as the largest exporter of petroleum, and plays a leading role in OPEC. The petroleum sector accounts for roughly 75 percent of budget revenues, 45 percent of GDP, and 90 percent of export earnings. About 40 percent of GDP comes from the private sector. Roughly 5.5 million foreign workers play an important role in the Saudi economy, for example, in the oil and service sectors." The government in 1999 announced plans to begin privatizing the electric companies, which follows the ongoing privatization of the telecommunications industry. "The government is supporting private-sector growth to lessen the kingdom's dependence on oil and increase employment opportunities for the swelling Saudi population." Priorities for government spending in the short term include additional funds for the water and sewage systems and for education. However, water shortages and rapid population growth constrain the government's efforts to increase self-sufficiency in agricultural production (CIA, 2006).

## *HISTORY*

### *Early Leaders*

Family business consulting is very new to the Middle East, a region which has not known family-specific advisory services (even in marital issues). Until recently any attempts to provide family-business-related services in Saudi Arabia were usually made by the business and investment consultants who had already earned a family's trust over years of prior service.

Saudi Arabia was not ripe for specialized family business consulting services until recently, as most of the business patriarchs who founded the businesses were only in their fifties and sixties. They were alive and well and still in charge, and they had no precedent for specialized family business services. Only when this group of founders began to grow elderly during the 1990s did issues of succession and governance start to come to light.

Most of the advising at that point was done by business consultants from outside of Saudi Arabia who were already affiliated with a family and operating locally. Also, bankers and lawyers from abroad who had previously only handled issues that fell within their professional scope of practice began, on a limited basis, to provide mediation and advice to address family issues. But, as in North America, these lawyers, financiers, and management consultants found themselves in the emotionally charged atmosphere of the family system and it became increasingly clear that more specialized consultation services specific to families in business were necessary.

A generic version of family business consulting was introduced by certain universities (Harvard) or consultants (McKinsey). Nevertheless, only since the late 1990s have conflicts within family businesses become a "hot" issue. This increasing phenomena has largely been due to a number of notorious family conflicts exploding into the public eye. These internecine family business conflicts sometimes pulled in the government, chambers of commerce, or members of the royal family, who mediated between siblings. This is not to say that all Saudi family businesses are unprepared for the challenges of succession. Obviously a number of families are ahead of others in structures and governance. However, many who have created technical solutions still stumble on sibling relationship issues.

In recent years specialized services to Middle Eastern families in business have been provided by consultants already practicing in the West. One of the very first to begin this work in the region was David Bork. He has been working in Istanbul since 1988. His entry into this part of the world came through speaking engagements at international gatherings of the

Young Presidents' Organization in Istanbul. (A description of his work in Turkey appears elsewhere in this book—see Chapter 16.)

Bork's work has been followed in the region by a few Western consultants who have backgrounds in the professions of law, behavioral sciences, management consulting, and finance. However, only a handful of consultants from outside the region provide services regularly, and only a few specialists living in the area (two in Israel, one in Lebanon, one in Pakistan, one in Saudi Arabia, and two in Turkey) are members of the Family Firm Institute (FFI, 2004).

As is true elsewhere, some consultants are product focused (e.g., financial instruments both domestic and offshore) and others deliver services in the context of process consultation. One group from PriceWaterhouse uses a bicultural team approach. These consultants have received training from Dr. Ivan Lansberg, a "thought leader" in the field of family business consulting.

Although there is a degree of competition among the few family business specialists working in the region, they also know and respect one another and often share the podium at regional family business conferences in Dubai, Kuwait City, or Jeddah. For instance, the Institute for International Research (IIR) has hosted the Family Company Management Conference for the past eight years in Dubai, in addition to offering smaller family business workshops through out the region. More recently, the regional magazine *MEED* has offered such a conference in Saudi Arabia.

The authors of this chapter are also among the consultants in this area. Our group is known as Global Family Business Consultants. GFBC is an international partnership founded by Haluk Alacaklioglu (Turkish-German national) and has one Saudi (Zaher Al Munajjed) and two American (Joe Paul, David Bork) partners. Haluk Alacaklioglu and Zaher Al Munajjed have been working for more than twenty years in the Middle East and Europe advising numerous family firms. Together with their American partners, GFBC provides services around the globe (United States, Holland, India, Turkey, Saudi Arabia, United Arab Emirates, United Kingdom, Kuwait, Egypt, Germany, Ireland, Columbia, Nepal)

Global Family Business Consultants is also in a strategic alliance with the Aspen Family Business Group (AFBG), one of the first consulting groups in North America to specialize in family businesses.

### Training and Philosophy of Consultants

The partners in GFBC come to this work from different backgrounds. David Bork has worked in the Middle East since 1988. Zaher Al Munajjed and Haluk Alacaklioglu were born in the region and have been working there professionally since the early 1980s, and Joe Paul began working in the Middle East in 1999.

Al Munajjed is a graduate in business administration from Harvard Business School (MBA, 1982) and also holds a master's in French international law from the St. Joseph University in Beirut (1978). He started his career as a corporate account officer at Citibank in Riyadh before leaving for graduate school in the United States. Upon his return he established CBM, the Consultants for Business and Management, in Jeddah and spent more than twenty years working for or advising family business leaders.

Alacaklioglu is also a graduate of Harvard Business School (MBA with honors, 1983). While working as an executive at Deutsche Bank, First National Bank of Chicago, Procter & Gamble, and Philip Morris (Marketing Director, Middle East) he worked in a variety of countries and cultures, in Germany, the United States, Switzerland, Saudi Arabia, Bahrain, and Turkey. He then joined Egon Zehnder International as a consultant. This company is the world's leading privately owned, global, top executive search and management assessment firm, with more than fifty offices worldwide.

Paul graduated summa cum laude with a BS in psychology and later received an MS in clinical psychology in 1978 from the University of Idaho. He has been licensed as a family therapist since 1990. He is a director emeritus of the Family Firm Institute, an international professional association for family business consultants and advisors. He was honored by FFI with the status of Fellow because of his contributions to the field. He is the co-author and author of several family business assessment devices, including The Aspen Family Business Inventory, The Family Wealth Management Inventory, and The Aspen Family Foundation Inventory (Paul & Jaffe, 2004).

Bork is one of the world's leaders in the field of counseling family businesses. Since 1970 he has had in-depth, long-term involvement with more than 350 families in business. He has assisted them in charting their way through every imaginable family business issue, including succession between generations, death of the founder, sale of the business, and the complexities of dealing with wealth. He is a proponent of the family systems approach to family business and pioneered the integration of family systems theory with sound business practice. Bork is the author of *Family Business, Risky Business: How to Make It Work* (Bork, 1986), and co-author of *Working with Family Business: A Guide for Professionals,* the first book of its kind in the field (Bork, Jaffe, Lane, Dashew, & Heisler, 1996).

At Global Family Business Consultants, we believe that our clients are best served by a multidisciplinary team. Although it is unrealistic for one consulting firm to provide every possible service that might be required by a family in business, we believe that a core set of skills are necessary. And, when needed, the core skills of this team should be complemented by other advisors brought in because of specific needs of the client. The core skills that GFBG provides are a knowledge of family systems theory and intervention based on this knowledge, conflict mediation, organizational design, executive development and evaluation, and creating and improving governance structures.

Besides having these basic professional skills, it is essential that at least one of the team members be "culturally competent." And, whenever possible, it is important to use professional simultaneous translators to interview in languages that the consultant cannot speak. The skills of a simultaneous translator are far more subtle than being merely bilingual. Their insights into the nuances of both languages and into culturally unique nonverbal communication are a critical resource when discussing complex issues. Their unusual ability to simultaneously speak in one language and listen in another allows for a dialogue flow approaching that of a conversation in one language.

We believe that it is essential that all of our services be grounded in one or two of the many family systems theories. The two theories that are most influential in our work are the Bowenian theory of Murray Bowen (Bowen, 1978) and the contextual theory formulated by Ivan Boszormenyi-Nagy (Boszormenyi-Nagy, Grunebaum, & Ulrich, 1991). The contextual orientation assumes that the consultant's leverage in all interventions is anchored in relational determinants and that a comprehensive approach addresses these determinants via the four interlocking dimensions of (1) facts, (2) individual psychology, (3) behavioral transactions, and (4) relational ethics. This approach never loses sight of the goal of both benefiting individuals and promoting change within the system. The contextually oriented consultant enters the system with a focus on the existing level of trust in the family and a sense of fairness among the family members (Boszormenyi-Nagy et al., 1991). Interventions are designed to build trust whenever possible in order to open the system to new possibilities that do not exist in a low-trust environment.

The insights from these theories combined with many years of working with families in business all over the world have led us to some of our own insights that we believe might qualify as general principles of family business consulting across cultures:

1. Regardless of the consultant's discipline of origin, there is a meaningful distinction between *family business consultants* and *consultants to families in business.* The former works with unique kinds of businesses; the latter works with unique kinds of families. Signifi-

cant differences in assessment and intervention flow from this difference.

2. Assessments and interventions need to be grounded in an understanding of individual psychology, family systems theory, and organizational development.

3. The level of trust in the family and in the business defines what is possible, and interventions need to be based on an assessment of the level of trust in these systems and the basis of the mistrust, when it exists.

4. Of the factors that make a family business work, we have found that trust is more important than love.

5. Commitments to rational agreements and contracts among family members typically will not control the family dynamics that drive behaviors, especially when mistrust or a sense of unfairness is prevalent among family members. Generally speaking, problematic family issues need to be dealt with directly by the consultant if he or she feels competent to do so, and not indirectly via documents that have not addressed underlying family issues.

6. A family-owned business is often weakened when a family leader uses the business to try to manage the problematic psychological issues of an individual family member, or the problematic relational issues in the family itself. The more serious the issue and the longer it goes on, the more likely it is to damage the business. If, for instance, a leader maintains an incompetent family member in an executive position only to keep harmony in the family, the business is bound to suffer. The longer it lasts, the more damage it does.

7. The interventions of consultants need to be based on an assessment process that integrates the interactions of family dynamics, management requirements, and ownership concerns.

8. Consultants should not take sides until they are sure they know why they are doing so. The initial responsibility of the consultant is to create a context that is safe enough for the family to have the conversations they have been avoiding. To do this the consultant must be seen as trustworthy in the eyes of as many members of the client-family as possible. This means that it is important to avoid being unwittingly co-opted by the politics of the family early in the engagement and before a strategic plan for the engagement has been developed.

9. Much of the change that happens as a result of successful consultation shows up first in the way people communicate. Sometimes this means talking about issues they have avoided, and sometimes this means that they simply must learn to be more civil.

10. Resistance to change is a natural part of a system's way of surviving. Whenever possible, this resistance should be honored and reframed by the consultant as an individual's attempt to preserve something important. It is the consultant's responsibility to monitor the balance between the forces for change and the homeostatic forces that preserve what is familiar to the family. Interventions should be managed accordingly.

11. Most successful interventions lead to
    —Increased differentiation of some family members as effective fiduciaries, or "accountables," e.g., managers, directors, and/or trustees. We describe this process as "finding your voice" in a new role or business responsibility.
    —The differentiation of organizational subsystems within the family and business that will carry significant responsibilities, e.g., creating a Family Council, a Board of Directors, a Management Team, a Shareholders Group, etc.
    —The ability of individuals and subsystems to morph from one role to another in an orderly way.

12. One of the most important intangible assets of a family in business is the ability to think clearly together. The most common factor that interferes with the ability of the family to function intelligently is family politics. The assessment process needs to identify those factors that keep the family from thinking clearly.

13. Avoid rushing to solutions early in the consulting process. To do so is often an indication that the consultant has been co-opted by factions within the client system or by personal (sometime unconscious) issues of the consultant.

14. The consultant needs to develop a standardized assessment process that integrates objective assessments and clinical interviews. The consultant should also attempt to include all individuals in the family who have, or will have, either a direct or indirect influence on the family's decision-making process. This means that it is important to include spouses who do not work in the company or own stock.

In Saudi Arabia, as well as many in other places in the world, there is a culturally based resistance to including women in the assessment process. Indeed, for traditional Saudi families, it would be unthinkable for a male consultant to interview a female family member without her husband, brother, or father attending the interview, if such an interview is allowed to occur at all. However, it is important to know that the women in Saudi Arabia have significant, albeit indirect, influence on the men's decisions about business. For this reason we try to include at least the women who are part owners or potential owners of the family business, as well as those who are wives of owners, in the assessment process.

The assessment protocol and intervention strategies used in Saudi Arabia and elsewhere in the Middle East and Europe by GFBC have been strongly influenced by the service delivery system developed by AFBG. For instance, an assessment device created by AFBG called The Aspen Family Business Inventory (Paul & Jaffe, 2004) has been translated into Arabic and Turkish (Alacaklioglu and Paul, 2004) and modified for use in the region. This assessment device has become the foundation of GFBC's assessment protocol and interventions. Specifics of this assessment device and the Aspen Family Business Consulting model are discussed elsewhere in this book (see Chapter 3).

## IMPORTANT ELEMENTS IN THE FAMILY BUSINESS FIELD TODAY

Our typical Saudi clients have thus far been families with companies in the second and third generation of the business existence. These families often employ three to seven brothers in senior management and/or in board positions. They each tend to have a diverse portfolio of companies. Many of the second-generation family members have been educated in the West, with a larger portion of the third generation having Western undergraduate and graduate educations. An increasing number of third-generation successors have also worked in other companies in North America or Europe before coming home to work for their family in Saudi Arabia. It may be that having a Western education is the most critical variable regarding the family's inclination to use consultants with a family business specialization.

Our engagements tend to be project oriented, and the client's selection of a consulting group is often based on competition that was initiated by a request for proposal announced by the family or one of their agents. Compensation is negotiated at the time of acceptance of the proposal and is typically provided incrementally based on predefined milestones in the project.

The specific role of the consultant varies from one provider to another, just as it does in the West. And as in the West, the differences in services tend to be based on whether specialized family-based services are provided. Traditional management consulting firms tend to provide technical solutions to financial or legal questions, and they tend to assume that troubling family dynamics can be managed by these technical interventions. In contrast, family business specialists tend to precede technical solutions with an in-depth analysis of the family dynamics that drive the family and the business. These family business specialists also tend to have psychologically or family systems trained members on the consulting team who collaborate with partners from financial, management, or legal backgrounds.

Families in Saudi Arabia are able to enjoy the benefits of seasoned senior professionals trained in the West who are partnering with local professional partners. The unique challenges tend to be based on linguistic and cultural issues. However, it must be said that regional political unrest limits the number of Western consultants willing to work in Saudi Arabia (U.S. State Department, 2004).

The more progressive Saudi families tend to have already engaged top-notch management consultants prior to seeking out specialized family business services. However, their governance structures tend to be informal, somewhat improvisational, and prone to being driven by family dynamics, just as in Western countries.

In Saudi Arabia and throughout the Middle East there is a conflict between values that are held at the cultural, country, and family levels. This conflict is between the traditional Islamic and Bedouin values and the values of Europe and North America. We can see this competition for hearts and minds happening at the geopolitical level and all the way down to individual family members in conflict over business issues. It is not uncommon during assessment interviews to hear that a family member, a branch of the family, or a generation of the family has become "too Western." It is very important for the consultant to be aware of these philosophical and religious issues and be prepared to help family members skillfully discuss them.

Most family business conflicts everywhere in the world come down to differences in the way individuals or groups prioritize their values. Frequently the values are the same or similar, but there is a difference in the way the values are ranked in terms of importance. For instance, two people in a family business might say that preferential treatment of close family members and professional accountability are both important values. But the two may have a serious conflict with each other because they rank them differently in importance. Thus, it is always essential for the consultant to families in business to be comfortable with these kinds of discussions, and it is especially true in the cultures of the Middle East.

## IMPORTANT STRUCTURES

### Family Councils

The Saudi concept of family involves a large web of extended family relationships. In the West we would consider such a large group a clan instead of a family. It is not at all unusual for a weekend family gathering to include

350 family members who see one another regularly. Thus the introduction of the concept of a Family Council is rather easily received by Saudi family leaders. The family's activities in a Family Council would, however, differ from one family to another on the basis of factors such as what they perceive as the legitimate role of women. Those non-Saudi consultants who have been invited into the private compounds of the families have seen gender relationship variations from the very traditional, where no women are allowed into the room with the men, to relaxed settings where the women are dressed in the most stylish Western attire and fully participate with their male relatives in business-related discussions with the consultants.

### Family Philanthropy

There are two types of Islamic charity. There is *Zakat,* which is obligatory, and *sadaqah,* which is voluntary. The word *Zakat* itself means "purification," and the purpose is to purify legally earned wealth. The Koran teaches that as Allah provides wealth to the rich, they also have a responsibility to see to the needs of those less fortunate. Thus *Zakat* is not merely an act of generosity but a religious obligation. *Zakat* stipulates that the poor are entitled to 2.5 percent of a wealthy person's net worth every year. *Sadaqah,* on the other hand, is the voluntary form of charity which depends on need and the amount of excess wealth (Athar, n.d.). Because of the close relationship between religion and government, the Saudi government has the prime responsibility for the public welfare and wealth redistribution. Thus both civil and religious obligations are satisfied simultaneously.

Athar identifies three basic concepts that form the basis of Islamic philanthropy:

1. Charity has to be from lawfully earned money; there is no concept of Robin Hood-like acts in Islam.
2. The concept of ownership of wealth in Islam is that all wealth, after necessary personal and family expenses, belongs to Allah. It is up to the individual to decide how much of this excess wealth he should give back to the cause of Allah.
3. "All philanthropy should be for the pleasure of God alone" (Athar, n.d.)

These principles, of course, represent the ideal, and as in any culture, there is a wide range of ways that families address charitable giving.

Philanthropy has not yet been a focal issue of our work with our Saudi clients. This is probably because all of our Saudi clients are already engaged in charitable giving, as prescribed by their religion.

In addition, because of their Western educations, many Saudis are donors to their alma maters in Europe and North America, and a few sit on the governing bodies of their former universities.

Much international attention has been given of late to the channeling of funds to terrorist organizations via Islamic charities. This of course would be a great concern to GFBC, if it were the case with any of our clients. To manage this issue we rely on our Saudi partner's knowledge of the major business families in the country.

### Family Offices

Family offices are only beginning to be considered by Saudi families. However, many of the functions of a Western family office are performed by the staff of the companies owned by the families.

### Board of Directors

The typical Board of Directors is composed of brothers from the second generation of the family business. They tend to function at a relatively informal fiduciary level. Sometimes task forces or a management committee emerge from the more professionally trained members of the third generation to compensate for the continued informality of the elder family members who sit on the board of directors. However, the real influence these successor-generation committees have is often frustrating to the younger generation, since no real authority is given to their group.

## CULTURE-BASED ISSUES ENCOUNTERED BY CONSULTANTS

### Sharia

Estate planning in Saudi Arabia is defined by *Sharia,* which is the legal system of much of the Islamic world and the legal equivalent of English Common Law or Napoleonic Law. However, the underlying principles of inheritance are quite different. In English Common Law the inheritance is based on the testament or desire of the deceased. In Sharia inheritance is based on a sense of the well-being of the family.

The rather complex application of Sharia to inheritance is based on concepts articulated in the Koran (Hussain, n.d.). Although the rules of Sharia are comprehensive, the principles that define the inheritance rules involve only a few verses. These verses have led to specific defining details that have been interpreted over the centuries by the legal reasoning of Muslim clerics. The specific verses that are the foundation of the Sharia rules of inheritance are shown here:

1. "Allah commands you regarding your children. For the male a share equivalent to that of two females" (Koran 4:11).
2. "If [there are] women [daughters] more than two, then for them two-thirds of the inheritance; and if there is only one then it is half" (Koran 4:11).
3. "And for his parents for each of them there is one-sixth of the inheritance if he has a child, but if he does not have a child and the parents are the heirs then for the mother one-third" (Koran 4:11).
4. ". . . but if he has brothers [or sisters] then for the mother one-sixth" (Koran 4:11).
5. "And for you there is one-half of what your wives leave behind if there is no child, but if they leave a child then for you there is one-fourth of what they leave behind . . ." (Koran 4:12).
6. "And for them one-fourth of what you leave behind if you did not have a child, but if you have a child then for them one-eighth of what you leave behind . . ." (Koran 4:12).
7. "And if a kalala man or woman [one who has neither ascendants nor descendants] is inherited from, and he [or she] has a [uterine] brother or [uterine] sister then for each of them [there is] one-sixth. But if they [uterine brothers and sisters] are more than that then they are sharers in one-third [equally]" (Koran 4:12).

Sharia prescribes which survivors receive shares from an estate based on their relationship to the deceased and the relationships of the other surviving family members. Sharia is also considered sacred in Saudi Arabia and much of the Arab world. And the consequences in the afterlife of not following it are severe, as can be seen in the following passage:

These are limits [set by] Allah [or ordainments as regards laws of inheritance], and whosoever obeys Allah and His Messenger will be admitted to Gardens under which rivers flow [in Paradise], to abide therein, and that will be the great success. And whosoever disobeys Allah and His Messenger, and transgresses His limits, He will cast him into the Fire, to abide therein; and he shall have a disgraceful torment. (Koran 4:13-14)

## Examples of the Effect of Inheritance Laws

The following scenarios of inheritance reflect variations based on differing sets of relationships among of survivors of the deceased. As will become obvious, the differences are strongly influenced by the variable of gender.

To illustrate the various permutations of the inheritance rules we will begin with the case example of "Bin Typical." If Bin Typical is survived by his mother, his three wives, nine sons, and seven daughters, their respective inheritances of shares would be as follows:

His mother receives 16.67 percent.
The three wives each receive 1/3 of 12.5 percent.
The nine sons each receive 1/9 of 51 percent.
The seven daughters each receive 1/7 of 19.83 percent.

But if he was not survived by his mother, then the remaining survivors would have the following inheritance:

The three wives each receive 1/3 of 12.5 percent.
The nine sons each receive 1/9 of 63 percent.
The seven daughters each receive 1/7 of 24.5 percent.

If, however, Bin Typical had three wives, nine sons, and one daughter who survive him, then the following distribution would ensue:

The three wives each receive 1/3 of 12.5 percent.
The nine sons would each 1/9 of 82.89 percent.
The one daughter would receive 4.61 percent.

Lest one believe that the daughters always get the short end of the stick, suppose that in a last scenario that Bin Typical is survived by one wife and three daughters only. In that case the distribution would be as follows:

The wife receives 12.5 percent.
The three daughters each receive 1/3 of 87.5 percent.

Given these permutations you might accurately imagine that in some families, there is concern about who will inherit the controlling interests of multibillion-dollar companies.

## THE ISLAMIC BUSINESS ENVIRONMENT

As in daily life itself, business life in Saudi Arabia is inseparably linked to the principles of Islam. Many Westerners are surprised to learn that the Saudi economy is one of the most open in the world and that Saudi family enterprises are among the most freewheeling. This somewhat surprising fact makes sense when one considers that *Hanbali,* a school of Islamic law that is dominant in Saudi Arabia, is a bit paradoxical. It is one of the most liberal Islamic legal theories concerning commercial and economic matters, while at the same time it defines an ultraconservative approach to social and legal matters.

### Attitudes About Wealth

Saudi attitudes toward wealth are substantially different from those in the West. It is believed here that God (Allah) almighty is the Creator of all things, both spiritual and material, and no "guilt" is attached to accrual of private wealth. Since Allah has so bountifully blessed and provided for Saudi Arabia, there is no disgrace attached to each Saudi's obtaining as much bounty as possible. And counter to Western stereotypes, the Islamic world sanctioned women's owning and inheriting property long before the West did, and some Saudi women now are counted among the wealthiest in the world.

### Charging Interest

One of the most formal Islamic restrictions on economic activity is *riba,* which is collecting interest. It is considered to be usury and banned by Sharia. The Saudi banking system, however, has found ways to eschew this restriction, for instance by charging "fees" rather than interest and by offering "profit participation" rather than "paying interest."

### Successor Competency and Entitlement

In some families the responsibilities for the family companies will be passed to younger family members who have never really been held accountable in a business context. In the worse-case situations, there is sometimes an additional factor of a sense of psychological entitlement that results from being raised in an extravagant and indulged way, without accountability. Another version of this is seen when one or two members of the successor generation are competent to the run companies, yet have siblings who are not but who have been lavishly indulged by their parents. These indulged siblings will expect the same treatment from their more competent siblings that they were accustomed to from their parents. Some of the more competent successors see this as an untenable scenario.

### Traditionally versus Professionally Managed Companies

As indicated earlier, some Saudi families have had a tradition of sending their children to the West to be educated for the past two or three generations, and sometimes have required the younger generation to work in Western publicly held companies. This pattern for grooming successors gives these families a significant competitive advantage in the Saudi (and global) marketplace. If these differing patterns of preparing successors continue into the next decade, many of the more traditionally managed companies will be acquired under duress by a relatively small number of the more professionally managed family businesses. This will result in a concentration of ownership into the hands of fewer and fewer families.

### Intrafamily Socialism

Intrafamily socialism a phrase coined by the authors to describe the pervasive value among Middle Eastern families by which the leaders try to ensure that all family members enjoy basically the same lifestyle regardless of their level of responsibilities. In assessment interviews we sometimes comment to the client that the family/business system they are describing sounds like a family that "works like capitalists in the marketplace but lives like socialists within the family." This always makes the client laugh at the ironic truth of the phrase.

### CASE STUDY

The following is a composite of many family business scenarios in Saudi Arabia. It was first presented by Zaher Al Munajjed as "The Bin Typical Family" case in April 2004 at the 8th Family Company Management Conference in Dubai, sponsored by the Institute for International Research (www.iirme.com). It is meant to portray a typical history of situations in a family business story. Consultants might have been engaged at any point in the story.

> Once upon a time in Saudi Arabia there was a businessman called Abdul Rahman Bin Typical. . . .

## Company Background

His was a trading company established in the 1950s, like most other businesses in Saudi Arabia. His two eldest sons worked side by side with their father, sacrificing their chances for a formal education. His seven younger sons graduated from college. In all he was blessed by Allah with nine sons and seven daughters by his three wives.

## Company Development

The father and his sons worked very hard. They built a distribution network and diversified their product offerings. During the 1970s and 1980s the company grew with the boom years into a multimillion-dollar company. At the death of the father the two elder sons became de facto successors as leaders of business and family. The women kins' shares in the company were bought as is traditionally done. A limited liability company was then established among the nine brothers.

## Management Style

Management control was solidly in the hands of two elder brothers. All major decisions were made unilaterally. Below the two sheik brothers the organizational chart included only middle- and lower-level staff. Senior positions were held by younger brothers (administration, finance, operations), but little authority was delegated to them. A foreign minority partner was brought in to help with external contacts. All young male family members worked in the company during summers and upon their graduation from a university.

## Interesting Facts

International consultants were intermittently brought in to recommend how to structure the organization and jobs, but all studies were shelved. All working brothers (shareholders) were paid no salaries but have liberal allowances. Then one day a serious health issue pushed brother number one out of day-to-day management and into the chairmanship. But he still indulged himself in micromanagement at will. An unofficial, unstructured management system emerged among the other brothers, with some acting as conduits of information to others. Younger brothers became more vocal as owners over time. With time the third generation began to enter the company as executives.

## Bird's-Eye View

Elder brothers had a strong sense of ownership. There was extreme centralization with very little authority delegated to others (brothers or employees). There was a lack of transparency in business decisions. There was an absence of accountability. No governance or management structures were really functioning. The younger brothers from the second generation and the men from the third generation felt stifled and frustrated.

### The Magic Safety Valve Appears

A pattern began to emerge in which independent business subsidiaries were financed for disgruntled family members. We found the following:

- Four members of the third generation who were working in the mother company exited to set up independent companies.
- Brother four of generation 2 set up the first independent subsidiary.
- Brothers five and six set up the second independent subsidiary.
- Brother seven set up an independent small business.
- Financing for all of these companies came from the mother company (at the elder brother's initiative).
- Ownership in the mother company was unaffected.
- These independent businesses became the private playgrounds for the younger brothers.

### Crisis and Triggers

After several years of great successes Subsidiary 1 hit major problems due to unplanned expansion and the "one-man show" attitude of the company leader. The red ink reached tens of millions. The issue remained tucked away. The situation was initially tolerated, then ignored, then eyed with worry. The troubled business became the object of unspoken tension among the brothers, and this required a group of brothers to exert direct pressure.

### "Heartbreaking" Questions for the Elder Brothers

- Do you hold your brother personally responsible for a financial loss he created?
- To what extent should you endure such a loss, and when do you put an end to the policy of denial?
- When does the business interest supersede the family emotional bonds?
- Should you replace your brother at the helm with a hired nonfamily member?
- Can you trust a nonfamily member in a position of responsibility?
- Do you want to pay the high costs associated with professional senior management?

### Making the Hard Decision

After four years of agony, professional management was brought into the ailing subsidiary with the following assignment:

1. Assume carte blanche leadership to turn around the financial situation
2. Create viable systems and structures and hire professionals as needed

3. Assume that family members have no immunity from performance standards, and if they do not meet the standards, then they must leave the business

## The Value of Red Ink

The separation of family loyalties and business requirements was forced by the pain of seeing the red ink. The crisis and the potential loss of face for the whole family created a consensus for change, including the agreement of the brother responsible for the independent subsidiary. Yet the handling of the new arrangements with the professional management were not imposed, and in fact were assigned to the underperforming brother to implement so that he would feel included in the process and would save face. Classic implementation difficulties and the brother's resistance to stepping aside created a situation in which

1. staff report only to the problematic brother;
2. the grapevine dominated communications;
3. the benefactor sheikh syndrome regained its grip on everyone; and
4. financial discipline and personal commitment to accountability disappeared again.

## Two Years Later—A Positive Ending

The brother in charge of the subsidiary moved voluntarily away from the business and devoted himself to new endeavors. A professional team set structures and procedures and achieved a turnaround in the business. The lessons of the experience slowly began seeping into the mother company.

## Business Conflicts Within the Bin Typical Family

- Intergenerational disputes (older versus younger brothers)
- Role conflicts (chairman as micromanager)
- Communication problems (tradition and respect suffocate healthy business communication)
- Conflict created by using shared resources of mother company
- Rivalry within the business
- Personal problems played out in the business

## Remaining Family Business Issues Within the Bin Typical Case

- Issues of ownership succession were only partially handled in advance (women kin were bought out and LLC created at death of father).
- Issues of management succession remained untouched (possible remedies: governance structures, management team, advisory board).
- Issues of the succession of authority were barely touched (possible remedies: transfer of authority, executive coaching, professional development).

- Relationship transformations were embryonic (possible remedies: family meetings, interventions, written agreements, mediation, family councils, family mission statement).
- Knowledge transfer was incomplete (possible remedies: executive knowledge harvest, developing a knowledge management strategy).

## SUMMARY AND CONCLUSION

The challenges of consulting outside one's culture of origin can be greatly mitigated by use of an interdisciplinary team with culturally relevant knowledge and experience. Although the majority of family business issues are quite similar all over the world, the subtle cultural, religious, and legal differences are very important in assessments and interventions.

Bin Typical's is an example of a company stuck in the informality of the entrepreneurial phase of family business development. It is a situation that could and does happen all over the world. We see a successor generation of siblings sharing ownership but not power, strong centralization defining decision making, and no functional governance structures in existence. It is a recipe for disaster for the family and business anywhere.

The subsidiary crisis was an opportunity to start to reform and organize management and family issues in a way they could be used as a springboard to tackle the informality of the mother company.

In summation, the principles that contribute to a successful family business in Saudi Arabia are the same as those for family businesses anywhere. Among these are the following:

- Recognize the differences between the business requirements and the family dynamics.
- Create the structures and processes that reflect the two different purposes that each system serves.
- Identify and groom those who are best suited in the family to serve in the role of "accountables" (executives, directors, etc.).
- Develop trust and a shared vision among the family members who serve as accountables.
- Recruit and retain nonfamily accountables who will complement the skills and experience of the family members and who can contribute to the realization of the long-term strategic plan.
- Apply international best business practices.

The transition from informality to the implementation of these principles and practices is like an expedition into unknown territory for many families. As consultants we are much like guides for the family on their expedition.

We are responsible to lead them at times, to help them lead themselves at others, and sometimes to protect them as they travel from one stage of family business development to another. Although the landscape of the journey may be familiar to the guide, it is often strange and frightening terrain for the family.

We are now at a stage in the development of our field where some consultants are using the guiding skills they have learned in the West in cultures that they barely know. Although much of the new family business landscape looks familiar, that familiarity can also be misleading. The oasis you think you saw may be a mirage, or the map you have may be inaccurate. We sometimes find ourselves to be truly in situations where we do not know what we do not know.

At professional gatherings such as the Family Firm Institute we profess to place a high value on collaboration with other disciplines. The form of that collaboration varies quite a bit from one practitioner to another. But if it is important to collaborate within one's culture, it is even more essential when working outside of one's culture of origin. There is a unique richness in the cross-cultural/cross-disciplinary work we are doing through our firm. It has the excitement of working on the outer edge of what is familiar. We all feel very fortunate to work with one another and with the fascinating families we serve in Saudi Arabia and elsewhere.

## REFERENCES

Alacaklioglu, H. & Paul, J. (2004). Consulting services (online). Retrieved November 29, 2004, from http://www.family-advisor.com/services.html.

Athar, S. (n.d.). *Islamic philanthropy: For the love of God* (online). Retrieved October 23, 2004, from http://www.islamfortoday.com/athar21.htm.

Bork, D. (1986). *Family business risky business: How to make it work.* New York: AMACOM.

Bork, D., Jaffe, D., Lane, S., Dashew, L., & Heisler, Q. (1996). *Working with family businesses: A guide for professionals.* San Francisco: Jossey-Bass.

Boszormenyi-Nagy, I., Grunebaum, J., & Ulrich, D. (1991). Contextual therapy. In A. Gurman & D. Kniskern (Eds.), *Handbook of family therapy,* Vol. 2 (pp. 200-238). New York: Brunner/Mazel.

Bowen, M. (1978). *Family therapy in clinical practice.* New York: Jason Aronson.

Central Intelligence Agency, USA. (2003). *Saudi Arabia—World factbook.* (online). Retrived October 23, 2004, from http://www.cia.gov/cia/publications/factbook/geos/sa.html.

Family Firm Institute. (2004). *Yellow pages: A resource guide for family business professionals.* Boston, MA: Author.

Hussain, A. (n.d.). *The Islamic laws of inheritance* (online). Retrieved October 23, 2004, from http://www.zawaj.com/articles/inheritance_hussain.html.

Paul, J. & Jaffe, D. (2004). Publications: Family Business Inventory (online). Retrieved November 29, 2004, from http://www.aspenfamilybusiness.com.

U.S. Department of State. (2004, August 12). Travel warnings (online). Retrieved October 23, 2004, from http://travel.state.gov/travel/saudi_warning.html.

# Chapter 14

# Scotland

Bill Gordon
Kenneth McCracken
Barbara Murray

## *FAMILY BUSINESS LANDSCAPE*

Prior to 1994, there had been no research or general awareness of the stock of family firms in Scotland. This was recognized by Barbara Murray (then Dunn) at Glasgow Caledonian University and at the same time by Scottish Enterprise, the U.K. government's economic development agency in Scotland. Murray, who was then a faculty lecturer in strategic management with a background in consulting to family businesses, acquired funding from Scottish Enterprise to conduct the first ever comparative academic study examining the quantitative and qualitative features of family businesses in Scotland and Northern Ireland, including the attitudes of professional advisers to family business clients (Dunn, 1995a).

This inaugural survey, in which 1,085 firms responded, demonstrated that in Scotland over 99 percent of firms are privately owned, 85 percent of which are wholly owned by the family, and in 95 percent, the family owns 75 percent or more shares. The survey covered all generations and sizes of business, and most sectors, especially manufacturing and distribution, but excluded the financial sector. Attitudes to ownership succession revealed that 73 percent of respondents wished to remain as private, family-controlled businesses for future generations, yet less than 29 percent had planned for this. Fifty percent of the sample stated they had made a will, and it is likely that this was the only step taken toward ownership succession planning (as distinct from management succession planning).

Fifty percent of the firms that responded were at the first-generation stage (G1), after which family ownership trailed off, with 29 percent at G2, 12 percent at G3, and 8 percent at G4 and beyond. They were also, at the point of the survey in 1994, reluctant to seek out help with imminent family

*Handbook of Family Business and Family Business Consultation*
Published by The Haworth Press, Inc., 2006. All rights reserved.
doi:10.1300/5491_14

succession issues, which were affecting the family and the business (see Exhibit 14.1).

Looking inside the family business revealed how closed they tended to be at the level of power and control, with the average Board of Directors containing two family executive directors and occasionally a family non-executive member. Very few Boards had any outside influence at all, although in Northern Ireland there was a tendency to have a relatively larger Board (see Figure 14.1).

---

## EXHIBIT 14.1. Introversion Toward Management Succession Planning

### *Scotland: Management Succession*

- Ninety-five percent have five or fewer full-time family members in the business.
- Next successor will be
  - — Family                          71 percent
  - — Nonfamily                    29 percent
- Discussed with family?      26 percent
- Have a plan?                      8.5 percent
- Preparation of successor?  2.5 percent

---

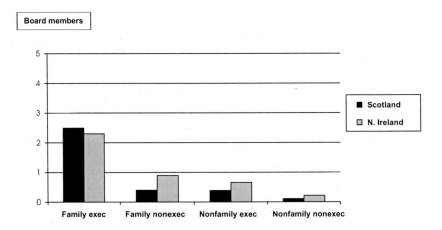

FIGURE 14.1. Family business governance: The board closed to outsiders.

This inaugural survey was followed by a comparative analysis of the attitudes of governments to family businesses in the United Kingdom, Sweden, Norway, and Spain (Bursary, 1995). With the exception of Spain, in which the Instituto de la Empresa Familiar was blazing a trail and encouraging the formation of GEEF (European group lobbying in Brussels for more supportive tax regimes), the research at that time reported an absence of recognition of the importance of family entrepreneurship, as well as an absence of development programs and services which took into account of the differences between family and nonfamily firm behavior.

A long-standing and pernicious philosophy—unspoken as well as spoken in some quarters—was evident, which assumed that taking (or leaving) the family out of the family business was a prudent objective, because when families controlled businesses their model of success usually led to firms which were small, inefficient, and nepotistic—also assumed to be a bad thing. On the positive side, also emerging at that time were some curious people and institutions which were open to being convinced that family businesses may be a misunderstood phenomenon which, given the right conditions, could prove themselves to be a considerable strength and resource in economies seeking growth—if the families owning these firms also acknowledged the challenges they would need to overcome to be sustainable business entities in the long term.

This research project proved to be the start of the process of family business recognition—and self-recognition—in Scotland. This was a feature of good timing: Scottish Enterprise was proactively promoting business start-up, growth, and continuity. The research demonstrated the importance of segmenting firms not just by size, sector, age, or other economic variables—but by using the variable of ownership form and demonstrating the importance of understanding ownership attitudes, which equate to business aspirations and related competitive strategy and behavior. The impact of family emotional and relational dynamics on business growth and aspirations was also highlighted. Business development agencies, professional service providers, and educators, as well as the families themselves, were challenged to undergo education, training, and development to integrate into the development of advisory and educational services the factors which originate in ownership attitudes and family dynamics (i.e., to cease denial). Business families were challenged to come out of the woodwork and be less secretive and more open to information and ideas, to respond to events and programs designed to help them, and to be receptive to the knowledge and ideas being developed at that time, mainly in the United States, Canada, and Switzerland.

Further research over the next eight years looked at these themes in greater depth. An argument was developed, with the support of Scottish Enterprise and the London Stock Exchange, for recognizing the potential for economic growth and development of family enterprises and factoring this into the conditions being created for flotation on the interim public market for smaller firms that did not necessarily wish to forego control of the business (Dunn & Hughes, 1995). Cases were selected to create a theoretical basis explaining the origin and foundation of the identity of a family enterprise, highlighting the continuity of philosophies and practices over generations of continued ownership (Dunn, 1995b). These views led to a perspective that family businesses in fact made up a "special sector" in their own right in the United Kingdom and beyond, meriting the design of specific proxies for analysis and for business growth development strategies and interventions (Dunn, 1996).

## RECOGNITION AND SELF-RECOGNITION
## OF FAMILY BUSINESS SIGNIFICANCE

The original research data were instrumental in creating a stakeholder alliance which was to put family businesses on the map in Scotland. The findings were informative, scaremongering statistics which were used to challenge "the system" in Scotland to change its ways. To do nothing was tantamount to standing by and watching firms decline, when something positive could be done instead (see Exhibit 14.2).

The research highlighted the challenges facing Scotland's family enterprises and their discouraging prospects unless some—very feasible— changes were made by all the stakeholders involved in the system (as listed in Exhibit 14.2) with leadership for such a process being taken in the education sector (Figure 14.2).

The study also focused on the emotional dimension of family ownership, leadership, and continuity of the business, and stressed the importance of gaining more understanding of these factors if really meaningful help was to be offered by educators, professional advisers, and business development agencies.

## DEVELOPMENT OF THE HOLISTIC
## FAMILY BUSINESS SYSTEMS APPROACH

The key outcome of the research, though, was the creation by Murray of the United Kingdom's first Centre for Family Enterprise in Glasgow. In 1994-1995, Murray had toured university-based family business centers and programs being offered in the United States and Europe (Loyola, Chi-

## EXHIBIT 14.2. The Challenges Facing Scotland's Family Enterprises in 1994

1. Scotland (and the rest of the United Kingdom) has a systemic socio-macro economic, a problem which all stakeholders are unknowingly colluding to perpetuate: family enterprises and their developmental and continuity needs are not understood, leading to unacceptable levels of failure of these businesses.
2. All stakeholders (families in business, educators, government, professional service providers) share responsibility for addressing the problem in an integrated, collaborative way.
3. FBs are emotional-economic systems, so relationships influence and drive governance, structure, and strategy.
4. System dynamics and evolution of family business systems are biologically driven as well as economically driven and are inevitable and predicable.
5. At any one time, 25 to 30 percent of firms expect their succession to be complete within five years: a churning effect is going on.
6. Very little evidence exists of preparation by families; pain or aging are often the key triggers to action.
7. Advisors are underprepared and underserve clients; branding and professional constraints get in the way.
8. Educators are seriously lagging behind in the United Kingdom: undergrad, postgrad, doctoral, and executive education.
9. Local and national policy focuses on start-up and clusters rather than sustainability and continuity.
10. A little support goes a long way (CFE and IEF/GEEF prove this).
11. Sustainability of the family enterprise sector in a healthier form requires healing what is currently a "sick" system through a holistic, integrated, multiple-stakeholder approach to policy, strategy, know-how, and resources.

cago; Northeastern, Boston; Baylor, Texas; Durham, New Hampshire, Centre for Family Enterprise, Montreal; and IMD, Lausanne). From this, the Centre for Family Enterprise (CFE) at Glasgow Caledonian University was launched in 1995.

The CFE was based on a stakeholder-funding model in which Scottish Enterprise, professional service providers, the university, and family businesses themselves funded the world-class programs and speakers, services, and conferences. The teaching and learning philosophy for the programs

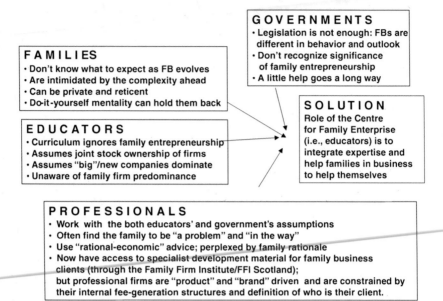

**GOVERNMENTS**
• Legislation is not enough: FBs are different in behavior and outlook
• Don't recognize significance of family entrepreneurship
• A little help goes a long way

**FAMILIES**
• Don't know what to expect as FB evolves
• Are intimidated by the complexity ahead
• Can be private and reticent
• Do-it-yourself mentality can hold them back

**SOLUTION**
Role of the Centre for Family Enterprise (i.e., educators) is to integrate expertise and help families in business to help themselves

**EDUCATORS**
• Curriculum ignores family entrepreneurship
• Assumes joint stock ownership of firms
• Assumes "big"/new companies dominate
• Unaware of family firm predominance

**PROFESSIONALS**
• Work with the both educators' and government's assumptions
• Often find the family to be "a problem" and "in the way"
• Use "rational-economic" advice; perplexed by family rationale
• Now have access to specialist development material for family business clients (through the Family Firm Institute/FFI Scotland); but professional firms are "product" and "brand" driven and are constrained by their internal fee-generation structures and definition of who is their client.

FIGURE 14.2. Holistic, multiple-stakeholder approach led by education sector.

and services was ultimately systems theory, incorporating family systems theory, family business governance, human and organizational development, and transitions theory. This was an important factor in the development of the family business consultation process to be described in this chapter.

Supporting the CFE was attractive to professional firms because the variables of ownership form and family dynamics opened up new market segmentation possibilities. The sponsorship model enabled participation by staff of these professional firms in the programs and the development of the analytical skills required to understand and work with businesses which were also acknowledged to be emotional systems. Since professional training for accountants, banks, and the legal professions did not cover handling family business clients per se, the firms which took part were then able to use the knowledge gained, both from the programs they attended with families and those designed specifically for advisers, to refine and develop services directed at specific market segments, and to deliver the services from a more informed base. The CFE offered a more robust alternative to the customary course of family business client experience, which usually came through an accumulation of case experience, so that after several years sufficient knowledge from trial and error or war stories was gained, which could then operate as a personal database for working with family business clients.

The CFE also offered a means for a small number of firms (one from each discipline) to gain a market lead through differentiation in this newly defined niche segment. The key approach taken to integrating the knowledge and expertise of the professions into the continuity planning of family enterprise is shown in Figure 14.3. This model helped families in business understand the work that lay ahead to achieve continuity and was useful for designing family business educational programs and interventions.

The CFE's partners also recognized and appreciated the thorough academic grounding upon which the Center's model and activities were developed. In parallel to the experiential education activities the CFE provided, academic research deepened and in so doing, informed the objectives, the content, and the interactive delivery style of the programs offered. Murray's doctoral research (Murray, 1999) spawned a series of publications demonstrating the emotional underpinnings of succession-related decision making in firms during succession transitions (Dunn, 1999) and the nature of the stages in the succession journey which the family enterprise system, as an emotional and commercial entity, undertakes (Gersick, Lansberg, Desjardins, & Dunn, 1999; Murray, 2003) with the implications for all of the stakeholders who are involved in this journey. Although academia usually does not manage to engage the attention span of entrepreneurs, practitioners, and business development agencies for long, the conversion of these

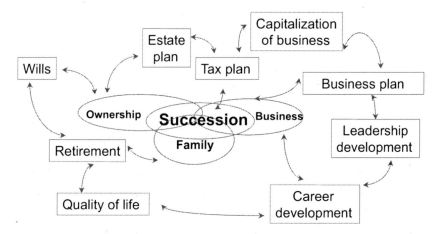

FIGURE 14.3. Model for integrating family business system continuity tasks with professional advisory services.

findings into what has become known as the "pracademic" approach meant that the work was truly grounded in cybernetic systems theory and at the same time concerned with the practical steps required to help firms and individuals to understand and focus their efforts on doing what was needed to remain successful family enterprises for their foreseeable futures (Figure 14.4).

With funding from sponsors and an annual fee for families who joined the CFE, a creative annual program of seminars was offered each year, attracting the field's world-leading practitioners and presenters to address specifically the topics that challenged family businesses—emanating from family ownership and family dynamics. An annual conference was also held to market the Center and the program.

### SCOTLAND AS THE HUB OF FAMILY BUSINESS ACTIVITY IN EUROPE

The CFE's focus between 1994 and 2001, under the leadership of Director Barbara Murray, was to work in an action research capacity with family businesses, delivering a mix of education and consultancy. Family firms taking part received an initial audit, the education program customized to

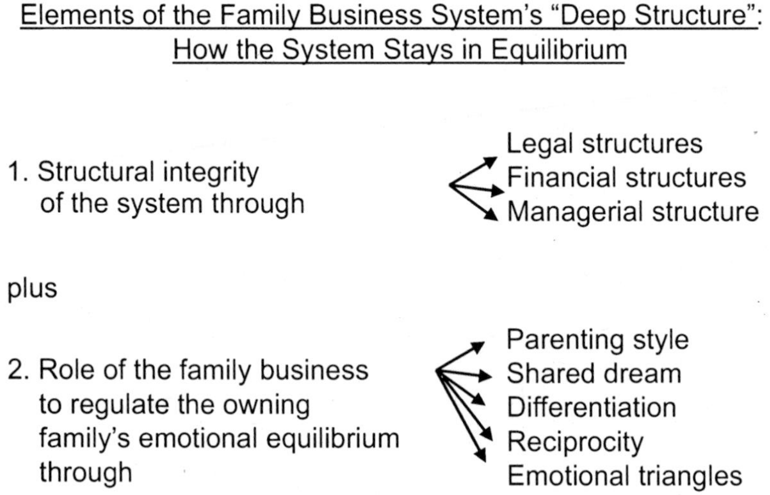

## Elements of the Family Business System's "Deep Structure": How the System Stays in Equilibrium

1. Structural integrity of the system through
   - Legal structures
   - Financial structures
   - Managerial structure

plus

2. Role of the family business to regulate the owning family's emotional equilibrium through
   - Parenting style
   - Shared dream
   - Differentiation
   - Reciprocity
   - Emotional triangles

FIGURE 14.4. Theoretical and practical underpinnings of "pracademic" approach to family business support and interventions.

the needs of each annual cohort, and ongoing interventions to provide the impetus for the change they agreed was needed.

During this time, the seeds were sown for what was to become a national, holistic approach to helping family businesses through educating not just the families but also professional service providers, educators, and business development agencies. Just as families and their family enterprises were regarded as a system which was open to inputs and therefore open to change, at the Scottish national level, the system whose deep structure was made up of the business development, education, and advisory services was also opened up to the potential for new knowledge and skills shift to increase the capacity of the system to serve the needs of these clients better. The idea behind it all was that if everyone in the system, including the family businesses themselves, are open to using the knowledge and skills made available, then real change can be achieved and the old pernicious attitude about inefficient family firms can be changed—from within the system.

When the CFE was first established in 1994, it became established as the Scottish Chapter of FBN (the Family Business Network)—the worldwide association for family businesses. There are sixteen chapters of FBN worldwide, enabling international family business members to visit one another, network, and learn together. By bringing the FBN Annual World Conference to Edinburgh in 1996, Scotland's activities were put onto the global map and this ensured the quality of education and interaction with family businesses at home in Scotland was world class and never parochial. This undoubtedly raised the esteem of family businesses, which enjoyed having the "gurus" visit and work with them and contributed enormously to the ongoing recognition and self-recognition of this sector.

Similarly, the CFE became the locus for developing the analytical and intervention skills of professional service providers, with courses taking place around the country to develop the ability of family business professionals to become personal family business advisors. This led to interest among professionals in forming a Scottish Chapter of FFI (the Family Firm Institute—world association of professional service providers to family businesses) and the U.S.-developed program "The Launching Pad" which lays the foundation of a family business education, took place in Glasgow.

By 2000, Scotland was well served by a number of family business relationships: the CFE's academic and application role, the presence of FBN and FFI chapters serving family businesses and the advisory community, respectively, government-sponsored research and other universities beginning to include family businesses on their curricula—albeit at the visiting lecture level, and the launch of Family Business Solutions as a specialist consultancy working exclusively with family businesses. Scotland was becoming the European hub of applied family business activity.

## RESULTS OF THE NATIONAL EXPERIMENT

A great deal transpired between 1994 and 2004. With the coming and going of the key people and the changing of policies and internal restructurings that are the normal features of institutional life, the original idea had not changed, but the form of delivery had. Throughout the ten-year history, each of the stakeholder groups involved underwent a degree of change which affected how family business development was delivered, but the overall trend was very positive, because each stakeholder had taken from the experiment what it needed to specialize in what it does best.

In 2001, a second important survey was commissioned by the government's business development agency, Enterprise Ayrshire. Ayrshire is one of Scotland's most important commercial areas and has undergone significant regeneration from traditional industries, such as mining and shipbuilding, to electronics and biotechnology. One issue emerging from this revolution was that the incoming industries were satellites of global firms with their headquarters and research and development functions based elsewhere, so although the new jobs were welcome, they were in effect vulnerable to uncontrollable forces outside Scotland. For this reason, Enterprise Ayrshire wished to know more about how to develop its indigenous stock of businesses, and following the buildup of interest in this sector in previous years, suspected that family businesses, with their long-term orientation and track record, were an important element requiring a strategic approach to development and continuity (Exhibit 14.3).

---

### EXHIBIT 14.3. Significance of Family Enterprises in Ayrshire, Scotland

1. The total number of jobs: 2,300
2. Overrepresentation in job-based sectors: manufacturing, construction, communications
3. Well-established firms (over half established more than twenty-five years)
4. Fifty-nine percent of firms in peripheral location—long-established firms providing the main source of employment after the public sector
5. Commitment and support/philanthropy attached by family business employers to their local economy (83 percent agree this is important)
6. Growth rates generally satisfactory or encouraging; however most rely on doing business locally.

The sectors in which family businesses predominated were mining and quarrying, manufacturing, and transportation—traditional sectors with long-established businesses, mostly trading locally. This raised questions about the future sustainability of these firms after the current leader retired, when the successor would have to contend with strategic issues and market challenges as the local and national industrial landscape changed.

A "vulnerable" subgroup of family enterprises was identified in the form of those expecting the retirement of the CEO in the next one to five years (but with limited planning for the transfer of power and leadership to the successor): 31.6 percent expected the retirement of their CEO within one to five years; a further 14.6 percent anticipated the CEO retiring in the succeeding five years. This amounted to 46.2 percent of firms undergoing major change in the next ten years, and profound change in a family business system, involving

- change in leadership and the figurehead of the business;
- decisions about changes in the ownership of the business;
- change in the locus of power, authority, and responsibility (may lead to strategic change);
- different processes for decision making (usually from unilateral to shared);
- uncertainty for nonfamily staff, customers, and suppliers;
- differences in the relationships and expectations of professional advisers; and
- an urgent need to plan for liquidity: to fund retirement, growth, and inheritances.

However, it became evident from this sample that the succession "solution" was usually a compromise between tax efficiency, family harmony, and business requirements, in that order of priority. The most consulted advisors, even one to five years before the retirement, were the accountant and the lawyer. Evidently planning within the family was informal and ad hoc, and therefore left in the hands of those who held the power and decision-making authority. Since most successors were found to be between the ages of thirty-one to forty-five, it was expected that there would be some misgivings on their part about the decisions being made which affected their lives, families, and careers.

Continuing with the theme of tax efficiency, the role of the spouse in the family business was illuminated in the research (Figure 14.5). Although almost 70 percent said the role of the spouse was important, on further scrutiny this role (almost exclusively the wife) had two dimensions to it. The

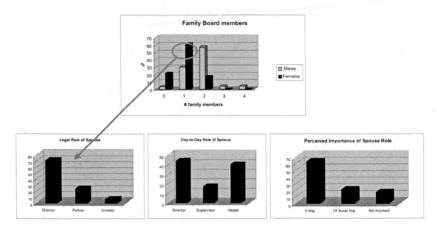

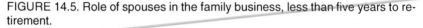

FIGURE 14.5. Role of spouses in the family business, less than five years to retirement.

first was the formal legal role in which 95 percent were either directors or partners. Less formally (meaning in the everyday reality of work in the business), 63 percent of spouses functioned in a supervisory or helper role. This was most likely a response to the tax regime in which there are benefits to be gained from having the spouse registered as a director.

There are some important implications from these findings from the perspective of family business consultation. As the senior generation ages and succession comes into full and urgent focus for the marital couple demanding solutions to the transfer of power, control, and wealth to the next generation, often the "silent partner" finds her voice in a business relationship. This is often neither expected nor wanted, and the enormity and complexity of succession as a systemic task then dawns on the family and the business, this not being anticipated by the traditional professional advisors.

The survey analyzed behavior in those businesses that expected CEO retirement within five years and found that in many cases, the business was largely the pension of the seniors, and so retaining control over their postretirement income was the most obvious driver behind the seniors' stated misgivings about the lack of readiness and ability (but not the willingness) of successors.

Finally, the survey reinforced the extra dimension that family involvement and family orientation brings to society and the local economy in general. Table 14.1 highlights the attitude of the owners of family businesses.

The CFE has survived the founding director's exit, mutating through the university's focus shifting from direct involvement with family businesses

TABLE 14.1. Family involvement and orientation.

| Attitudes and positions | Percentage |
| --- | --- |
| Plough profits back in for the long term | 96 |
| Happy there is a business in the family | 84 |
| Actively support local community | 82 |
| Forego rewards now to allow growth | 54 |
| Worried: if business can support the family in future | 52 |
| Regard the business as "the pension" | 48 |
| Family put venture capital into one or two new ventures | 26 |
| Feel trapped in the family business | 13 |
| Family's attitude to risk a constraint | 0 |

*Sample:* 84 firms with less than five years to retirement.

toward further interdisciplinary academic research and teaching. Scottish Enterprise and its local agencies have developed programs for family businesses support, succession, and growth over the years, and at the strategic level involve family entrepreneurship in their planning considerations.

The family businesses themselves who attended the programs and conferences recognized the benefits of learning about family-business-specific matters together with their peers, and are currently in the advanced stages of incorporating their own independent Scottish Family Business Association, with the support once more of Scottish Enterprise.

The final part of the story was spun out of Family Business Solutions. This consulting firm is a collaboration between Barbara Murray and Wright Johnston & Mackenzie LLP, the legal firm which was a founding sponsor of the CFE. Using the holistic, family business systems approach, the firm now has considerable longitudinal experience of working with family enterprises not only in Scotland but throughout the world. The model is being enhanced and developed through working with business families at all stages of evolution and through working in different cultures across the globe.

Scotland is now well served with a strong infrastructure led by educated and informed leaders in its academic, entrepreneurial, professional, and economic development sectors.

## TRANSFORMATION OF A LAW FIRM'S PERSPECTIVE ON THE FAMILY BUSINESS CLIENT

Wright Johnston & Mackenzie LLP (WJM) is a full-service law firm based in Scotland's major cities, Edinburgh and Glasgow. In 1995 WJM became a founder sponsor of the CFE. Initially the reasons were a combination of Murray's vision for the CFE which was supported by her research, as well as the usual marketing benefits associated with an exclusive sponsor's arrangement. However the enduring benefit of the association between WJM and the CFE has been a law firm that has absorbed a systems approach to working with family businesses and the formation of a separate consulting business.

The initial challenge for WJM was how to combine the idea of the family business as a complex system of interacting interests with the conventional view of the successful lawyer as being an expert adviser who develops a deep, but often narrow, technical specialty. The expert model requires the client's needs to be broken down into a series of technical problems to which there are technical solutions. The family business system perspective immediately cast doubt on this as always being a helpful approach, especially as it ignored the emotional needs of the client and often seemed to result in the expert advising one part of the system, leaving clients to work out how to combine technically sound ideas for their business with further technical input from other advisers.

It also occurred to WJM that the expert model had led them—and other firms—to organize their business around the technical preferences of the lawyers rather than the needs of the client. Putting all the tax specialists together made sense for several reasons, but not quite as much sense to clients when they wanted help with the wide range of family and business issues that arise during an intergenerational transition in ownership and leadership.

The spur to WJM to act on these insights was provided by repeated requests for consulting help from families attending the CFE. The challenge was how to create two interdisciplinary teams, one among the WJM lawyers with different technical specialties who were excited by the opportunities offered by this new area of practice, and another between the CFE and WJM.

By 1999 WJM had become the CFE's most enduring supporter and it was agreed between Murray and WJM's family business champion, Ken McCracken, to form a joint venture consulting company that was separate from WJM and the CFE. Family Business Solutions Ltd (FBS) would be able to focus on providing consultancy help without detracting from the responsibilities of Murray and McCracken to their host institutions, both of which supported this new venture.

### The Family Business Group: Specialization of Specialists

Inside WJM the challenge was to build on the enthusiasm among the lawyers who had attended the CFE educational program. The WJM management board intuitively grasped that application of family business know-how was an opportunity to become the market leader in potentially the largest unrecognized market for legal services. More resources were then invested in attendance at the CFE as well as international family business conferences.

In several of the firm's existing practice groups the development of new services for family businesses became a prominent strategic objective, with each group having its own champion to lead these initiatives. A new Family Business Group, comprised of these representatives from the other practice groups, ensured that the family business know-how was being fed into this process. This structure ensured a multidisciplinary atmosphere in which new services could be developed that combined traditional legal expertise with family business systems thinking.

Another major decision for WJM was to ensure that it had its own succession plan for this new service from the outset. McCracken was joined by lawyers at all stages of their careers so that a family business orientation was developed at every level in the firm. Like many of its family business clients, WJM is in this for the long term.

WJM is now acknowledged as the market leader in family business in Scotland. Their strategy is based on having a cadre of family-systems-informed experts who are working with their specialist colleagues to provide a unique full service for families who are in business together. This group is also working with FBS to develop services in relation to family business governance and transitions.

FBS, meanwhile, has grown strongly. The company works with clients across the United Kingdom as well as in Northern Europe, Central America, and the Middle East. They now have three full-time consultants: Murray, McCracken, and Bill Gordon, as well as a research assistant from WJM. Gordon joined FBS after running the Family Council in his own family business, Wm Grant & Sons Ltd, for five years. His experiences, and the unique perspective of the "insider" in an evolving family business system, have added a great deal to the depth and breadth of FBS.

## EMBRACING FAMILY BUSINESS GOVERNANCE

Over the past ten years, we have witnessed the emergence of more formal family governance structures in family-owned enterprises in Scotland. It is difficult to pinpoint the exact mix of factors that have contributed to this development but it is likely to be a combination of the following.

First, networking among family businesses was a direct result of increasing interest and attendance at the Center for Family Enterprise events. These events spread the awareness of the benefits that a more formal system of family governance could create.

Second, a parallel "education and enlightenment" program was going on which was led by a small number of larger family enterprises such as Wm Grant & Sons Ltd, who sent their shareholders to the "Leading the Family Business" course at IMD in Switzerland.

Finally, there was a coming together and sharing of insights and experiences between these larger enterprises and smaller family-owned businesses led by Barbara Murray, whose enthusiasm and passion for family businesses to learn from one another sparked great things.

The formation of Family Councils, Family Forums, Shareholder Councils, and Family Assemblies is now more commonplace in Scotland, with the degree of formality varying among families and their businesses. The formation of these structures has become a prime focus of family business consultation—the aim being to encourage clients to embrace family business governance and aim for world-class governing standards within structures which are practical and feasible for their size and evolutionary stage.

For small families, regardless of the size of business, holding simple family gatherings suffices, as long as these have a well-planned agenda and are coordinated and led by someone other than the business leader. Larger family businesses in which there are multiple branches with their own interests to protect require a more formal arrangement such as a formal Family Council or even a Family Office—but the aim in all cases is to maintain and strengthen family linkages and to reinforce the family's commitment to its investment and its legacy.

This is absolutely right, as there are no hard and fast rules about how the family governance system should be constituted. Having said that, it is preferable and more beneficial to see these bodies professionalize their modus operandi to become truly integrated additions to the business governance.

Organizations such as the Institute for Family Businesses based in London, founded in 2000, are working hard to encourage a more formal and professional approach toward family and business governance, which is a powerful catalyst for raising their game. The Scottish Family Business Association will help Scotland's family businesses to remain at the forefront of these developments.

In the same way that family businesses are becoming more structured and professional in their approach to family governance, the same trend is evident in their approach to philanthropy. We see family values being extended into the business and into their policies on philanthropic support, all through the family governance system. This approach has resulted in philanthropy evolving from what was in the past a primarily business-driven function to a more broadly based family- and business-driven activity that is more professional in all aspects of delivery.

As with governance of the family, there is a firm size and developmental dimension to their approach to philanthropy, as we have seen smaller firms and those with charismatic leaders taking personal control of philanthropic activities in the form of support for local charities, sports clubs, etc. Most of these prefer to keep their donations anonymous. When the business becomes more substantial, and when siblings or cousins are involved, often a more formal and professionalized approach is taken, with a separate structure such as a charitable trust being established and governed by family who are not involved in the core business. Communication, through integration of these governing structures, is essential because the activities of the charitable trust can impact on the visibility of the family's name or on the product brand, and likewise, the activities of the business can impact on the works of the charitable trust. Thus, quite often we see charitable working groups within family offices or councils whose task is to implement and monitor the philanthropic policy on behalf of the family.

After a ten-year buildup, what matters is that these bodies are now in place and are on the increase—which is encouraging for the United Kingdom and for the field of family business. The litmus test will be their effectiveness within a more dynamic economic environment.

## REFERENCES

Bursary, J. C. (1995). European business development initiatives for family enterprises—A comparison of macro and micro conditions in Norway, Sweden, Spain and the UK. Presented by Scottish Enterprise, August.

Dunn, B. (1995a). *The challenges facing Scotland's family enterprises.* Glasgow: Center for Family Enterprise.

Dunn, B. (1995b). Success themes in Scotland's family enterprises: Philosophies & practices through the generations. *Family Business Review, 8*(1), 17-29.

Dunn, B. (1996). Family enterprises in the UK—A special sector? *Family Business Review, 9*(2), 139-156.

Dunn, B. (1999). The family factor: Impact of family relationship dynamics on progress by business-owning families during ownership and leadership transitions in family enterprises. *Family Business Review, 12*(1), 41-60.

Dunn, B. & Hughes, M. (1995). Themes & issues in the recognition of family enterprises. *Family Business Review, 8*(4), 267-292.

Gersick, K.E., Lansberg, I., Desjardins, M., & Dunn, B. (1999). Stages and transitions: Managing change in the family business. *Family Business Review, 12*(4), 287-297.

Murray, B. (1999). Emotional and developmental influences on the management of generational transitions by business-owning families. Unpublished doctoral dissertation, University of Stirling.

Murray, B. (2003). The succession transition process: A longitudinal perspective. *Family Business Review, 16*(1), 17-34.

Chapter 15

# Trinidad and Tobago

Annette Rahael

## BACKGROUND

The twin island state of Trinidad and Tobago is known around the world as the country where the only new musical instrument of the twentieth century, the steel-pan, was invented. The islands are the southernmost islands of the Caribbean, visible from the northeast coast of Venezuela. Trinidad is by far the bigger island, covering a total of 1,864 square miles, with the sister isle of Tobago situated on 116 square miles of land just off the northeast coast of Trinidad. Christopher Columbus first set foot on Trinidad in July 1498 and wrote (as cited by Besson & Brereton, 1991) that "the fields and foliage likewise were remarkably fresh and green and as beautiful as the gardens of Valencia in April." In the ensuing five centuries, Trinidad was ruled by the French and the Spanish, and was a colony of Great Britain until independence in 1962. Despite the proximity to mainland South America, the first language of the country is English and the political and civil institutions are modeled after those of the former colonial masters. Socially and culturally, however, the country has been heavily influenced by the United States, and American brands have infiltrated every aspect of life on the islands.

Trinidad and Tobago boasts the richest economy in the Caribbean, buoyed by significant reserves of oil and gas. The country experienced ten years of economic growth from 1993 to 2003. Growth in real gross domestic product in 2003 was 4.1 percent, compared with 2.7 percent in 2002, and the prognosis is for continued robustness. At present Trinidad and Tobago is the second largest producer of liquefied natural gas in the Atlantic Basin and likely will remain in the top three for the foreseeable future. This augurs well for the economy of the country, which has been spared the ravages of major hurricanes in the past because of its southerly location. Indeed, the geographical position of the country adds heavily to its strategic importance

*Handbook of Family Business and Family Business Consultation*
Published by The Haworth Press, Inc., 2006. All rights reserved.
doi:10.1300/5491_15

to the United States, which is the country's largest trading partner and is the biggest consumer of Trinidad's energy products.

The bulk of the investment in oil and gas is foreign, but there has been some local private-sector input and the current government is keen to encourage local participation. The phenomenal growth in the energy segment of the economy has had a ripple effect in other areas, and in 2003 the transport, storage, and communication industries experienced growth of 6.9 percent; distribution, 5.9 percent; and construction, 4.8 percent. The country enjoys a balance of payments surplus, a floating but stable exchange rate, a political democracy, and a highly literate labor force. These factors make for fertile business conditions, and the landscape is replete with commercial and residential construction projects in various stages of completion. The government has undertaken some housing projects and maintains a handful of state enterprises, but the nonenergy economy is mostly in the hands of private investors and businesses. Regrettably, the Central Statistical Office maintains no statistics as to the type of ownership of establishments over and beyond the classification as private, government, and foreign, so no official figures are available to indicate the percentage of businesses that are family owned. The prevailing view among observers, however, is that outside of the energy, insurance, and financial segments of business activity, the majority of the business firms are family owned and operated.

No meaningful discussion of local business in Trinidad and Tobago can occur without some discourse on the ethnic composition of the country and the distribution of ownership among the different ethnic groups. The Central Statistical Office (2002) reports that according to the 2000 census, the total population of the country was almost 1.3 million, of which 37.5 percent is of African descent, 40 percent East Indian, 20.5 percent classified as mixed, 0.6 percent white, 0.3 percent Chinese, 0.3 percent other, and 0.8 percent not stated. The ancestors of this diverse mix of peoples arrived on the island at various times and for differing reasons. Most of those of African origin are the descendants of slaves brought by the Europeans to work on the agricultural plantations from the seventeenth to nineteenth centuries. After slavery was officially abolished in August 1838, the freed blacks did not continue to work on the sugar plantations in sufficient numbers and the foreign planters faced a labor shortage crisis. In collaboration with the local authorities, they devised a plan to bring immigrant labor into the country, but they had to ensure that the immigrants worked in the agricultural estates. As a result, a scheme of indenture was adopted, bringing Indian laborers who were required by law to work for a prescribed period on the land before being "freed" to perform any other jobs or return to India. The first arrivals landed in Trinidad in 1845.

The Chinese had already been here in very small numbers since the early nineteenth century, but between 1853 and 1866 over 2,000 more arrived under the indenture system. The whites are descendant of the Europeans. Numbered among the "other" is a group of Syrian Lebanese immigrants who fled their homeland for religious and economic reasons, and although not statistically significant enough to record in the population statistics, they are major players in the economy of the country.

When the slaves were freed they were given a small plot of land to grow their own food but were not able to attain enough acreage to compete with the plantation owners of the day. Many of their descendants were able to acquire additional plots of land in sufficient size to operate agricultural businesses, and others developed craft and artisan businesses. These enterprises were unable to expand for a variety of reasons: some of the landowners did not have proper title to the land, many died intestate, and in other cases the land was sold or abandoned due to squabbles among the surviving family members. With no access to collateral, the agricultural and trade businesses failed. The blacks migrated to the urban districts, gained an education, and obtained jobs in the Civil Service.

The freed Indian workers did not return to India in the anticipated numbers and remained on the island, which they recognized as being their new home. They did not have easy access to the professions or civil service, and so became farmers and landowners. The Chinese did not stay in agriculture and went on to become the shopkeepers of the day. Their competitors were the Portuguese business owners who had emigrated here in the first half of the nineteenth century, supposedly to provide labor for the plantations. They were not able to withstand the harsh life of agriculture and had set up small business enterprises. The Syrian Lebanese community is the latest immigrant group, and arrived in Trinidad early in the twentieth century. Although a very small numerical presence on the island, they are substantial business owners and have infiltrated practically every area of enterprise in the country. In the research paper "Entrepreneurs in Trinidad and Tobago: A Sociological Survey," Dave Ramsaran (1994, p. 147) concluded that the Syrians are "over-represented in the field of business when compared to other ethnic groups," and while the representation of Indo-Trinidadians "in the entrepreneurial sphere seem to be in proportion with their numbers in the wider society" the Afro-Trinidadians were "highly under represented." This predominance of Eastern cultures in the business environment of Trinidad is an influential factor in the determination of some of the issues that confront family businesses on the island.

## FAMILY BUSINESS AWARENESS

The *Annual Economic Survey* compiled and published by the Central Bank of Trinidad and Tobago for 2003 shows that the energy sector contributed 31.4 percent of GDP, with the remaining 68.6 percent originating from agriculture (1.7 percent), manufacturing (10.0 percent), construction (11.5 percent), financial services (23.5 percent), and other (21.9 percent) (Central Bank, 2003). Outside of the energy and financial subdivisions, it is widely believed that the other contributing firms are primarily family businesses. Despite the lack of available data, a viable assumption is that the bulk of private businesses in Trinidad and Tobago are family owned and controlled. Among the thirty-five companies on the Trinidad and Tobago Stock Exchange, which now lists some regional companies, it can be safely argued that at least 35 percent are family controlled.

The information gaps indicate that no research has been conducted to date on the incidence, type, or economic contribution of family business in the country. There is no family business center at any of the regional campuses of the University of the West Indies or at any private institution. A survey of the theses and papers submitted and kept at the local campus at the university yielded no published studies of family businesses and their impact on the society. There is an interest in entrepreneurship as it relates to ethnicity, and a widespread belief that the family structure of certain ethnic groups is a key facilitating factor in the growth of family businesses. Family business is not a course in any of the management studies programs at any of the country's tertiary institutions, and only a single one-day workshop has been hosted by the University Institute of Business in Trinidad in 1998 that focused on family business.

There is no family business section or column in the weekly business news supplements published by the newspapers. Over the past few decades the newspapers have very occasionally carried a human interest story on the founder or successor of a family business but these are not frequent nor do they necessarily report on the "familyness" of the business being highlighted. In fact, the newspapers report almost exclusively on family business fights that reach the courts and on practically nothing else about family business. In the past decade two major family business battles have been waged in the courts, and only recently, on November 28, 2004, the front page headline of one of the country's three newspapers featured a family business dispute that had found its way into the legal system (Joseph, 2004a). Warner Grain Mills Limited is a leading supplier of chicken in the country and was founded in 1973 by Assic Mohammed, who has since died leaving the company to his wife, four sons, and daughter. One of the sons, Fareid Mohammed, contends that he was forced out as a company director on January 31, 2000, and since then has not seen financial statements of the company nor been paid any dividends. He claims that at the time of his enforced departure there was an agreement in place that he would receive gratuity, but he is yet to do so. Mr. Mohammed says the matter has now become urgent as he has a rare form of cancer and desperately needs the money for surgery. The company has filed an application to nullify Mr. Mohammed's claim since they contend that the matters in the current lawsuit were raised in another matter in 2002 and that has been settled already (Joseph, 2004b). At the time of writing the case is still before the courts.

Other such disputes do reach the courts but manage not to receive the publicity that this one has. Apparently Mr. Mohammed actively sought the media's involvement in an attempt to gain some leverage over the family and the company, since most family businesses, indeed nonfamily businesses as well, are desperate to avoid this kind of public exposure. This may be a strong motivating factor in out-of-court settlements of family business disputes.

Despite the media's tendency to highlight the larger corporate and often multinational companies, there is some awareness of the importance of family firms to the economy. As much as a couple of decades ago, a letter to the editor claimed that "the backbone of this country is the family business, regardless of size" (Scott, 1986, p. 8).

## FAMILY BUSINESS CONSULTING

At present only two other members of the Family Firm Institute (FFI) live in Trinidad. Dr. Shafeek Sultan recently joined FFI and has within the last year formed the Caribbean Family Business Institute. This company has held no workshops or conferences, nor conducted any research or published information regarding its activities. Dr. Jean Griffith, another FFI member since 2000, researched two local family businesses for her doctoral thesis at the California-based Fielding Institute, but that paper is not available to the public. Dr. Griffith lists on her business card family business consulting as one of the services she offers and says that about 30 percent of her clients are family businesses. The FFI confirms that the author is the Caribbean's only recipient of the Certificate in Family Business Advising that the institute awards and which she received in October 2004.

The island boasts many competent legal and business professionals who have either established their own consulting firms or work in the international accounting firms which offer consulting services. In his responses from 168 entrepreneurs, Ramsaran (1994) found that 49 percent used consultants, although the majority of those businesses were mostly manufacturing concerns which employed external technical support. There are professionals who have provided advice to family and nonfamily companies with regard to issues of organizational behavior, finance, marketing, human resource management, accounting, and other disciplines. The survival and growth of so many local businesses speak not only to the entrepreneurial spirit of the founders but also to the quality of advice they receive. Yet a prominent family business owner, Harry Sooknarine (1998), said that "professionals are not always prepared to deal with the special nature of family companies." My conversations with some lawyers and accountants on the island seem to support this assertion as they openly admit that they would rather not deal with any of the background emotional issues that beset family businesses. The prevailing attitude among those to whom I spoke is illustrated by the statement of one lawyer that "we can do whatever they like, but they must come knowing exactly what they want."

The existing advisors are unable to ignore the unique challenges facing those businesses even if they are reluctant or perhaps ill equipped to handle the demands of the family business system.

## THE ISSUES

The lack of information on the specific issues facing local family businesses is lamentable, especially since the business environment is rich with so many diverse family firms. Family-owned businesses are present in every stage of development, owned by people of distinct ethnic backgrounds. Although the challenges that they face may well be universal, they nonetheless provide fodder for research that will inform the local consultant in the field.

Although there has been no research or publications dealing with the specific concerns of consulting to Trinidad businesses, family managed or not, I gleaned feedback from some of those working in the field.

### Professional Management

While many of the businesses are in the expansion phase, Dr. Sultan Khan says that there is painfully slow movement toward the institution of professional protocols and standard organization features, and speaks of family executives who "manage by the seat of their pants." This supports the view generally expressed in the field that family businesses spend far less time, money, and energy on human resource management and strategic planning than do nonfamily businesses. One business consultant says that our family business leaders "trust people, not systems" and while there is no statistical confirmation, empirical evidence suggests that even as our family businesses employ nonfamily professionals, practically all the executive posts are held by family members whether they are suitably qualified or not.

Indeed, family business owners are often reluctant to expand until their siblings or children join the business. The children of family business owners may attend a university abroad but return immediately to take up fairly senior positions in the company, usually without having worked elsewhere. In my own discussions with families, even when they are convinced of the wisdom of having the successor generation work outside of the company, the problem has been in obtaining reasonable jobs on the island. The population is so small and the business fraternity so well-known to one another that people are wary of hiring those who have easy access to capital since they view them as potential competitors, even if the family businesses are unrelated. The corporate businesses are reluctant to invest in training young graduates whom they know they have no chance of retaining.

Even among the bigger family businesses, some of which have set up subsidiary companies in other islands and have employed nonfamily professional management, there is a tendency to concentrate and centralize the decision making in the hands of the family chief executive. Many of the consultants to whom I spoke lamented the flawed decision-making processes of our family businesses. They believe that many company decisions are not made on the basis of business intelligence, data, and analysis but rather on the whims of the founder or purely based on family considerations.

This suggests a lack of implementation of the recommended structures for dealing in an integrated and meaningful fashion with family issues as distinct from business issues. It is this failing as well as a perception that there is a glass ceiling for nonfamily employees that has made it challenging for family businesses to attract the best talent. It is most telling that none of the consultants interviewed could identify a single family-owned business in which family members no longer participated in top management, leaving the firm in the hands of nonfamily professionals.

### Succession

A few family businesses on the island span more than three generations, but by and large, existing businesses are either run by founders or founders with their children or sibling teams. There have been successful transfers from the founders to sibling teams, although there are enough instances in which the founder has simply vested different businesses in separate companies and split the "loot" among the offspring, rather than risk the possibility of crippling conflicts. An increasing number of businesses are run by siblings who are now introducing their own children into the business. My own experience to date suggests that the sibling teams function fairly well but that there are serious concerns among the owners as to whether the business will make the transition to cousin consortiums.

The one common issue that reared its head in every single interview I conducted was succession planning, or rather the lack thereof. Nothing seems to consume the minds of these professionals and indeed the owners they advise as much as to whom and how to cede management and ownership control. In the Chinese and Arab communities, the prevailing practice with regard to leadership succession seems to have been primogeniture, but even when a cultural norm dictates the passage of power, the transition is not proving easy. There is a movement on the part of younger people not to accept such an automatic anointing of leadership, and since there is seldom any published criteria of the skills and qualifications needed for the job, mediation of such disputes is not an easy task for any advisor not schooled in family dynamics.

In discussion with me, Dr. Griffith indicated that in her experience, succession planning was not institutionalized in local nonfamily businesses either and subject to similar difficulties there as well. Most other advisors with whom I spoke felt that the problem was compounded in family businesses by the lack of discipline prevalent in our family businesses. This may be attributed to the relative youth of these businesses when the founder may still be around or at least his or her influence remains very strong and direct.

Respondents spoke of the lack of transfer of skills and authority from one generation to the other, even as the succeeding generation members are accessing far more tertiary education than their parents have. It would seem that founders and even second generation members are experiencing the usual fear of letting go. This may well be attributed to the business climate of this small country where businessmen seem to believe that it is their names and networking abilities which open opportunities far more than the capabilities of their businesses. This is the view even when the businesses are ostensibly well organized and professionally run.

### Role of Ethnicity and Gender

As noted earlier, the majority of family businesses in Trinidad and Tobago are owned by people of Indian, Syrian, European, and Chinese descent. A rising number of African descendants are establishing their own businesses, but these are predominantly founder businesses. Although the descendants of the Eastern immigrants are assimilating into the diverse melting pot of Trinidad, enough distinct characteristics and traditions of the founding forefathers remain that strongly influence the conduct of the family and the family business.

In the absence of any research studies, all claims are subject to refutation, but I concur with the consultants who ascribe distinct behavior within businesses to the ethnic origin of the family. The prevailing view is that the Syrian Lebanese maintain the strictest and tightest family structures that translate into the most closely held businesses. There is a culture of obedience to a patriarch which influences the nature of business decision making. There have been suggestions that this conduct is also observed among the Chinese who adhere to the traditional values of respect for generational authority. The Indians have not been so rigid and there appears to be more conflict, or at least more publicly acknowledged disagreements and consequences thereof among family business members.

Ethnicity is closely correlated to gender issues among our family businesses. The Eastern cultures are predominantly patriarchal and there are major concerns among family business owners about giving shares to a daughter who may then introduce her husband into the boardroom. Indeed many businesses are named "founder's name and sons" even when the founder has daughters who work in the business. I have found it be one of the most emotive issues when talking with business owners who do not share similar fears about daughters-in-law. They may worry about their sons' wives being divisive but feel that the family is better able to manage the women and shudder at the thought of their son sharing authority with another man's son. There has been a tendency in the past to "take care" of daughters by disbursing property or cash, but not shares in the business.

The stage is set for a change in that custom as more women qualify and work in the family business and challenge the historical practice. There is a movement toward equality, and business owners easily acknowledge the talented contribution of their daughters, but it remains to be seen whether they will translate that recognition into objective selection of leadership and more evenhanded distribution of shares.

### External Input

There is a legal requirement that limited liability companies have at least two directors, hold meetings to pass certain types of resolutions, and submit annual company returns. Once a business attains a reasonable size, the preferred legal structure is a limited liability company, and family businesses tend to choose that mode of association. The process of searching the registration of companies to determine which businesses have more than the token two directors is painstaking and time-consuming, and it was not feasible to undertake such a task for this publication, but a safe assumption is that most family businesses have a rubber stamp board which exists for legal purposes only. My limited survey reveals that few family companies have external directors. There may be members of the owning family who do not work at the company and occupy a seat on the board. Even if a family business has a more active and bigger board of directors, chances are that there are minimal numbers of outside directors and those are drawn from the company's lawyer, accountant, or even management consultant. Often, most, if not all of the family members who work in the business are board members, as are some of the senior nonfamily managers.

Strategy is generally determined by family members working in the business and succession planning is a matter for the owners. As the businesses grow and need to access more capital, the banks are beginning to take a more critical look at core issues; I have recently been approached by the CEO of a bank on the island to deliver some talks to family businesses about the need for proper family and business structures. At the first presentation, some interest was displayed in the idea of active boards with external directors which may suggest that it is an idea whose time has come. In the interim, it appears that families have a trusted family friend or advisor or long-standing professional consultant who fills a variety of roles for the family and business. In most cases, this person functions as sounding board for business strategy and/or conflict mediator and/or family confidant. I was able to speak to a couple of these chosen ones and they indicated that the families are very unwilling to trust other outsiders even when it is obvious that additional input is needed.

Although my presentation to the bank's customers was well received, the bank's CEO is lamenting the reluctance of his clients to embark upon the process of implementing the desired processes and attributes the unwillingness to proceed to the same emotions that cause so many people to procrastinate on making a will.

The following case illustrates some of the issues facing local family businesses.

## CASE STUDY: THE ABC COMPANY

I received a call from my friend Mike who knew of my interest in family businesses. I had worked in a senior management position in a second-generation family business for two decades and was about to begin a formal course of study toward obtaining a certificate in family business consulting. Mike had been most encouraging of my efforts and was very excited at the prospect of referring me to my very first client. "George is a good man," he said, "and really wants to organize his business." George was a second-generation Middle Eastern immigrant. Mike gave me George's number and told George that I would call. I made the call and George responded with real interest and enthusiasm. He invited me to meet with him at his company's offices. In the interim I spoke to Mike about the nature of the business and his impressions of the family. I learned that the business was a small distributor of pharmaceuticals and was a relatively successful business. It had been in operation for over twenty-five years and was engaged in some repackaging as well as distributorship of some established brands. Mike could tell me little about the family dynamics except to say that he knew that some of the children worked in the business.

I went to George's office and was immediately struck by the obvious lack of organization within the physical space. The building, which the company owned, was in good repair, but the office layout was not well thought out and there was more than a hint of chaos in the air. It did not lend an impression of order and efficiency. However, the receptionist was expecting me and I was immediately ushered into George's office. George was keen to share with me his plans for divesting his shares in the company to some of his children. He had six children, four of whom resided in Trinidad while the others lived in North America. While we were talking, his son Brandon blew into his dad's office like a whirlwind, looking for a document.

George introduced me as a consultant and said that I would be helping the company and family "get organized." I had no chance to respond to that characterization or explain my role as Brandon was polite but distant and quickly left the office, leaving his father to comment that "the boy is always rushing around, attending to too much detail, if you ask me." I spent some more time with George in his office getting the bare basic history of the business. He was more interested and anxious in having me "get started" as he put it and was ready to engage me on the spot. I asked if we could meet again, at my office this time, and he agreed not to discuss my role with any member of his family until then. A couple of weeks later, we were finally able to meet and I got a more coherent and cohesive view of the family and the business.

George had started the business from his home on an absolute shoestring budget about thirty-five years earlier. His living room was the warehouse and his bedroom the office. During the day he visited his customers and at night he did the paperwork. His wife, Joyce, had little input in the business and was busy having and rearing children. The family and the business grew simultaneously. Within five years of starting the business George acquired a building in which he housed the offices and warehouse and was no longer operating from home. The business had grown to include some light manufacturing and packaging, but the mainstay of the business remained the distributorship. The company employed almost 100 people.

Of the four children who lived in Trinidad, two sons worked in the business along with one daughter. The other child, a daughter, had married well and had no connection to the business. The daughter and son who lived abroad were both specialist medical doctors who worked at prestigious facilities in North America and had absolutely no desire to ever return home. To George's mind, this translated into no interest in the business, and he had already helped them financially to acquire nice homes in North America. As far as George was concerned, he had discharged his responsibility to the children who were not working in the business and was concerned only with exploring how he would organize the business for the three family members who worked in the business and how he would provide for his and his wife's remaining years. He did let slip that his wife disagreed with the approach and wanted to "leave something" for the other children, but he was not entertaining her position. She was a nominal shareholder in the business and one of two other directors besides George. Fred was the family lawyer and was a legal director on the board, which George said never met but simply fulfilled legal requirements.

According to George, his younger son Brandon was the brighter of the two boys and had recently obtained a first degree in business administration from a North American university. He had joined the company two years before. Andrew was older by eleven years and had joined the business ten years ago directly out of high school. He had attended a number of short courses, workshops, and seminars in a variety of business topics, but had no university education. His daughter, Catherine, had obtained some local certification in accounting but functioned mostly in administration and had been working in the business for seven years.

George was concerned that Brandon was appointing himself the leader and that both Andrew and Catherine resented their younger brother's assumption of authority. George said that he wanted to retire and was ready to pass on some of his shares in the company but was worried that the children were not getting along. He was concerned that Brandon was brash and would not consider the views of his siblings in the running of the company, even if he gave the boys equal shares. Andrew had recently married, and George was not sure whether his wife would "know her place," as Joyce did. He explained that his intention was to provide a separate inheritance, perhaps some property that he and his wife now owned, for Catherine but to mandate that she would have a job for life, if she so desired. The company had some nonfamily middle management but no human resource policies or other professional structures.

I held an orientation meeting with George and his three children and they all agreed that there was need to introduce some formal and documented procedures into the business. I subsequently conducted individual interviews with the four working family members and key personnel within the company, including two outside advisors—the accountant and the information technology consultant. George resisted my attempts to meet his wife, insisting that she had "nothing to do" with this, a position not inconsistent with the view of men of his era and ethnicity.

The picture that emerged was that of a solid business that was beset by both organizational and family issues. Family relationships were strained. Andrew had worked in the company as "chief cook and bottle washer," as he put it, for ten years and his role was usurped by Brandon who had only just joined the company. Catherine felt that because of her gender, her ability and dedication had never been recognized as she was constantly shunted into administrative positions for the time that she had been there.

There were some defined departments and division of labor, but often roles were confused and difficult to identify. Some functions seemed to be organized enough, but many tasks were ill defined and repetitive. Employees were fairly happy but wished for more structure in their jobs. The external advisors recognized that the company had long needed some professional input but said that George had only now agreed to get help. Using the Taguiri and Davis three-circle model (as cited by Gersick, Davis, Hampton, McCollom, & Lansberg, 1997), I identified in each system a list of desired outcomes:

**Business Dimension**

The implementation of the following:

1. A human resource management function
2. Documented operational procedures
3. A formal strategic plan
4. Regular and reliable financial reporting
5. An effective management team

**Ownership Dimension**

Preparing documents or contracts for

1. legal distribution of shares,
2. shareholders' agreement, and
3. formation of a Board of Directors.

**Family Dimension**

1. Improved communication
2. Setting up regular meetings

Since we had already established the need for the business to implement structures and procedures, I started in this area. George agreed to my recommendation to engage a human resource management consultant who worked under my direction to initiate a human resource function. I have expertise in operations and logistics and launched into a very comprehensive program of producing procedure manuals. We both put in long hours on-site working with family members and employees. This phase went fairly smoothly and we received adequate cooperation in our implementation of some basic business systems and procedures, but I was not making any significant headway into family relations and communication.

George continued to talk about liberating himself from routine operations but would still hold daily operational meetings with his three children, who all seemed to be vying for the position of chief executive officer. The departmental structures and job descriptions for the middle and lower management of the company were completed, but we were having difficulty in producing any formal roles or compensation policies for the family members. Andrew could not handle all of the new systems but wanted to remain as he had been before, involved in or overseeing what he considered the critical business functions. Brandon appropriated for himself all the financial and purchasing decisions, to Andrew's dismay, and Catherine sought to expand her area of influence over and above the administrative work.

The children were comfortable with their salaries, which were determined by George who had striven to be fair and balanced by giving each sibling what he thought would make them comfortable in their current lifestyles. George was totally ineffective in resolving the conflicts. The human resource consultant and I made numerous suggestions as to possible organizational structures, but we faced many stumbling blocks which all seemed to revolve around "who is in charge of whom."

We finally got an ostensible division of labor among the three, but they each reported to George in his now weekly briefing sessions that involved only the family members. We did manage to put in place a management team which included some nonfamily managers and that team met monthly, but despite a comprehensive generic agenda, the nonfamily members were not totally in the loop and it was clear that the more serious business decisions were made at the weekly briefing sessions.

George thought that the best way to have harmony was to give the boys equal shares of 24 percent each until his death and that of his spouse, when they would get the remaining shares. He was considering giving Catherine a smaller percentage of the shares as she had signaled to both her parents that she was unhappy not being a shareholder, although she fully expected that each of her brothers would own a far greater amount than she did. Indeed, the quantum of the shareholding did not matter to her as much as the fact of it. She told me that she wanted the shares to give her similar status to her brothers' wives and their yet-unborn children. In the interim George did legally transfer a total of 45 percent of the shares equally to the two sons but there was no shareholders' agreement covering buy-sell arrangements.

I held some discussions, mostly with George, about the need for a Board of Directors with at least one-third of the members drawn from external sources. George gave some lip service to the suggestion but was clearly not going to implement this. I raised the issue at one of the meetings with the three children, but George dominated the discussions and the next generation deferred to him on the issue.

I had originally contracted for one year, as I was due to leave the country on a one-year sabbatical, and the contracted period came to an end. When I returned, I called George to see how things were going. He said that the systems were implemented and operations were much smoother, with resultant growth in business, but that he wished for better relations among the three children. He did give Catherine 10 percent of the shares and she was happy with that. He talked about restarting the process. I told him that I was available and he is to call when he is ready. I have been back in the country for one year now and he is yet to call.

My recommendations did address the desired outcomes in the business dimension, and that would undoubtedly position the company to take advantage of additional expansion opportunities. The distribution of shares gave the next generation a tangible sense of ownership, but there is more to be done in the areas of family communication and structures. There is a need for the three siblings to operate more effectively as an ownership and management team and this would require a different type of intervention on my part. This family will benefit from a properly constructed board, which in many cases can be of great assistance in stabilizing family dynamics.

## CONCLUSION

There is much work to be done in Trinidad and Tobago and, I daresay, the Caribbean with regard to disseminating the knowledge of the special characteristics of family businesses. The survival and growth of these businesses are critical to the economy and, regrettably, the collective learning is diluted when firms continually close down and new ones crop up to fill the same need. Indeed, it could easily be argued that unless a large portion of the existing family businesses make a successful transition to more professionalism and resolve the ownership and management succession issues, then the forces of globalization will sweep them away. This will leave a vacuum which will easily be filled by the multinational corporations which are already encroaching beyond the oil and gas industry and into the traditional family business spheres of retailing, manufacturing, and real estate development.

There is need for research to at least document our experiences, if not also to test any of the existing theories. Foreign-based statistics may well be universal, but it will be more authentic if we are able to access our own data. The agencies that collate business statistics will need to review and revise their classifications to allow for the recognition of the role of family businesses in the economy. It is a cause that I intend to pursue.

Family members and the society at large have a stake in recording the stories of our successful family businesses and understanding the economic benefits of multigenerational firms. It is equally worthwhile to reflect on their demise and attempt to identify their failings. There is real interest and concern among the few family business members with whom I have directly engaged, and the challenge is to educate the stakeholders so that the awareness is translated into action.

It is a mission of serious proportions, and as I launch my own career in the field, I am aware of the differing areas that require attention. I am gratified by the positive response that I have received from the bank's customers and other family businesses with whom I have come into contact. I have been curious as to whether my gender or even my ethnicity (I am a child of Syrian immigrants) would be a deterrent in obtaining consulting jobs. It is a little premature to draw any conclusions, but indications are that my gender may be a positive factor in obtaining jobs since the male owners appear to be more comfortable sharing their emotional anxiety with a woman. My membership in a community where the businesses are primarily family businesses is reassuring to business owners who feel confident in my ability to address issues because I "have lived it" according to one client.

The consulting practice will reach some, but we need to host seminars, workshops, and lectures that widen the audience. Thankfully the local university is supportive of the need and has already contracted with me to develop and teach a course in family business dynamics; perhaps that will generate enough interest to encourage researchers and consultants in the field.

# REFERENCES

Besson, G. & Brereton, B. (1991). *The book of Trinidad.* Newtown, Trinidad: Paria Publishing Company Ltd.

Central Bank of Trinidad and Tobago. (2003). *Annual economic survey, 2003.* Trinidad and Tobago: Author.

Central Bank of Trinidad and Tobago. (2004, May). *Economic bulletin.* Trinidad and Tobago: Author.

Central Statistical Office. (2002). *Pocket digest 2002.* Republic of Trinidad and Tobago: Author.

Gersick, K.E., Davis, J., Hampton McCollom, M., & Lansberg, I. (1997). *Generation to generation: Life cycles of the family business.* Boston: Harvard Business School Press.

Joseph, F. (2004a, November 28). Cancer victim sues family for $30m. *Newsday,* p. 3.

Joseph, F. (2004b, December). Delay in $30m court battle. *Newsday,* pp. 1, 9.

Ramsaran, D. (1994). Entrepreneurs in Trinidad and Tobago: A sociological survey. In S. Ryan and T. Stewart (Eds.), *Entrepreneurship in the Caribbean* (pp. 119-173). St. Augustine: The University of the West Indies.

Renwick, D. (2004, September 30). T&T's proven strength in the Atlantic Basin. *Business Guardian,* p. 19.

Scott, S. (1986, October 6). Backbone is the family business: Letter to editor. *Guardian,* p. 8.

Sooknarine, H. (1998, November 12). "Presentation to UWI students" in seminar "Crises at the millennium—Strategies for human success and development" at the Department of Management Studies at the University of the West Indies.

Chapter 16

# Turkey

David Bork

This chapter addresses the most important challenges presented to an American when consulting to family businesses in Turkey. It discusses the complexity of the Turkish context and how the author modified a collection of consultation procedures that were grounded in early work in the United States that began in 1970 and was refined over the intervening years. When I began working in Turkey in 1988, the presenting task was to create a family business consultative process that would work in that culture. A core concern was how to create a safe, trusting environment in which leaders of Turkish family-owned business would be open to use the services of a consultant not familiar with the Turkish culture. It identifies a range of elements in the Turkish culture and business climate that combined to shape the modifications.

## THE CHALLENGES OF UNDERSTANDING A NEW AND DIFFERENT CULTURAL CONTEXT

### Challenge 1: Becoming Known in a New Culture

I have worked with family-owned businesses in Turkey for more than fifteen years. Some engagements have gone on for nearly four years and in every case there is some kind of continuing relationship, be it formal or informal. The first client came to me after a family member heard me speak at a YPO International University. (Young Presidents Organization is an organization devoted to "Better Leaders Through Education and Idea Exchange." www.ypo.org) The issues and outcomes in that first case were unusually dramatic. Family members were very public and vocal about what had been accomplished. The "word of mouth" exposure led to one after another of the

*Handbook of Family Business and Family Business Consultation*
Published by The Haworth Press, Inc., 2006. All rights reserved.
doi:10.1300/5491_16

country's leading businesses seeking me out and engaging me to work within their systems.

## Lesson 1

The best way to build a client base in Turkey is by "word of mouth" from satisfied clients. This is probably true the world over.

## Challenge 2: Dealing with the Complexities of Cultural Differences

Consulting to family-owned business in Turkey has been an enormous intellectual challenge akin to attempting to complete a complicated jigsaw puzzle. Imagine that you have finished all the puzzle edges and a good part of the body. You think you have exhausted the search for the missing piece that will allow you to go forward; you are almost certain that the piece, pieces, or whole sections of pieces you seek are missing, gone. Suddenly insight strikes. "Voila!" The missing element is revealed and you understand how the piece that is in your hand fits into what has been completed, that already exists. This is the mind-set that will open the doors and show the way.

## Lesson 2

All the pieces are present when you arrive. It is the eye and the mind that must be trained to see them.

## Challenge 3: Opening Up Emotionally to a New Culture That Has Different Values

Each of us is a product of our culture and the experiences we have had in it. It shapes our manner of thinking about everything—our views of fairness, equality, how to consider alternatives when solving problems, how we think in the present, and our hopes for the future. Within any culture there are significant differences, and between cultures those differences can be a chasm without bridges. When traveling in another country it is possible to be a detached observer, but when working in that same country, detachment is no longer an option. One's mind and heart must be open to the people and the culture. It is necessary to learn what is important to the people. Openness to learning about *everything* is the required orientation, taking care to see things in their context and not pass judgment on what you see. When this is the orientation of the consultant, great opportunity lies ahead.

*Lesson 3*

Passion for a people and a culture is essential for a successful engagement. If consultants are not open to "embrace the people, the culture and the land," then it is likely they will have a higher level of success working elsewhere.

## OLD AND NEW CLASH IN UNEXPECTED WAYS

### Challenge 4: To Rapidly Develop a Working Knowledge of the Turkish Ethos Imbedded in Centuries of Historic Events

The "dawn of the Democratic Republic of Turkey" was in 1923. It began with Kemal Ataturk, known today as a "leader and nation builder." Photos of Ataturk are ubiquitous in Turkey. In every commercial business, every office, every restaurant, in homes—no matter how grand or meager, there is reverence for this man and a photo to prove it. His leadership inspired the Turkish people at a time when many had no hope of ever being anything but the doormat to armies of the world. Ataturk changed the course of history for the Turkish people, and for that reason he is held in great regard. Under the Ottomans the people suffered greatly for a very long time. At a time when many wanted to give up, Ataturk brought them hope and a vision of a better life than they and their ancestors had experienced. It was not without a price. There had been centuries of turmoil as the armies of the then-known world fought on and trampled their land and their dreams. In Ottoman times, the intelligencia were the military and many of the advisors and viziers were from foreign lands. Often the foreigners brought knowledge of the extant world along with skills in commerce, managing, administering, controlling, and directing. There were vizers who urged their sultan to reach out and conquer more. At its zenith, the Ottoman empire extended from the Atlantic Ocean to the borders of India, the Balkans, the Arabian Peninsula, and much of what we know today as the "Middle East." Its splendor is legendary, its ambition unequaled and its dark side, disturbing.

Every sultan had numerous wives in his harem. The politics of both palace and harem were very complex. When the sultan aged and his end was imminent, his wives, advisors, and viziers all jockeyed for positions of dominance, advocating their "pasha" (prince) as the sultan's successor. To say that it was an intense environment would be an understatement. After the selection had been made, things settled down in a special way. It was simple. The previously competing pashas were all murdered in their sleep, a fine but strong silk cord having been tied around their necks. Sometimes advisors and vizers got the same treatment. Succession in modern Turkish businesses no longer includes use of the silk cord, but you can be certain that the memory of jockeying for positions of dominance is in the very DNA of the modern Turk.

Under Ataturk, a democracy was created, use of surnames adopted, a governmental structure created, a written language defined, an economic process determined, and schools created. Orientation to the West was decreed, and it required wearing Western attire and included banning men from wearing of the fez. Everything changed, yet beneath the surface much remained the same. Books are written of this, but it must be known that Ataturk, with his band and their followers, with the support of the people, seized control. They literally yanked Turkey out of the Ottoman period and into the second quarter of the twentieth century. They were determined to catch up and run with the modern world, as they understood it. In my experience, the sense of urgency that I understand to have characterized that time continues to permeate the business culture today. So much of what took place during that period continues to play a critical role in defining the context of the modern Turkish business climate. Analysts, historians, and revisionists are likely to suggest that different courses of action should have been taken on controversial human, social, religious, and ethical issues. They may be right, and of course hindsight is always 20/20. Ataturk was a visionary, an extraordinary leader who mobilized the Turkish people. (For comprehensive information about Ataturk, see Kinross, 1964; Mango, 1999.)

Visits to important historic sites and structures was one way to learn to understand the culture. After visiting the primary tourist sites, I found the places that were special to the Turks. One of the best guidebooks is by the late Hilary Sumner-Boyd, professor of humanities at Roberts College in Istanbul, and John Freely, a well-known writer about the history of the area (Sumner-Boyd & Freely, 2003). The fact that I even knew about the Turks' special places conveyed to my clients the message that I had a genuine interest in the history and culture of Turkey. I could discuss what I had seen with family members and draw them out so as to learn why they felt the site or structure was important.

*Lesson 4*

Going beyond the level of the casual tourist deepens and enriches one's understanding of the people and the culture.

## A NEW WAY OF GOING

The Turkish governmental structure created by Ataturk and his followers is a parliament. The people elect the political parties and then members within those parties elect the parliamentarians. If one party gets the majority in parliament, they select the prime minister. If there is no majority, then the parties try to build a coalition which then selects the prime minister. In the first seventy-five years of the Turkish Republic there were fifty-two governments, depending on how you count them. One could make a case that the dynamics of the Ottomans simply has a new alliteration in this system. The structure they created set the stage for a perennial attitude of unpredictability: "Be ready, dramatic change is imminent." The unpredictability is reflected in the simultaneous inflation and devaluation that Turkish businesses have had to accommodate at various times. Instead of building cash reserves for future development, many businesses put their money into tangible assets as a hedge against devaluation. As a consequence, when they needed cash, they often did not have it. The net effect is the need to simultaneously keep everything "open and on the screen" so they are prepared to react to the dynamic economy.

*Lesson 5*

Don't get fixated on the way things are because changes can come without any notice.

## SOME BUSINESS PRACTICES ARE UNIVERSAL

At the outset of the Republic the federal government of Turkey regulated and/or owned critical business sectors. Finance Minister Kemal Unakitan, citing his experience as a child getting bread, milk, and margarine from the state, says that Turkey was the most communist member of NATO. In the context of 1923 it would seem to make sense that in orchestrating the transition from the Ottoman way to democratic order, control was the real issue. The events of 1923 continue to influence the way the economy functions, even today. If you were an entrepreneur at the beginning of the Republic, you had to "work the system." You wanted to succeed and to do so in a business arena regulated or controlled by the government, so you got "cozy" with the regulators. You lobbied the government representatives who regulated your sector or you hired them when they tired of being in the government or saw that by working in the private sector they could earn considerably more money. It is no different from current practices in many other countries. Often the former regulator, a government employee, was hired to be the titular head of all or part of the business. Over time this manner of operation produced management systems in which decision making became relationship based and highly politicized, rather than criteria or data based, as is found in a merit- or competence-based systems. Any effort to effect change in a politicized system is likely to have an impact on sacred cows within the system. This also encouraged the formation of deeply embedded loyalties, which often proved to be barriers to change. In Turkish businesses it is not unusual for loyalty to take precedence over competence. This means resistance to change is often systemic. This can be said about family businesses in other parts of the world too, but the degree to which I found this to be true in Turkey is higher than in many other places.

*Lesson 6*

The importance of networking was not invented in modern times. In Byzantine times, in the Ottoman empire, and in the modern Republic of Turkey, who you know and how you know them can and will impact on your fortunes.

## "NOT INVENTED HERE"

This was the Turkish business mantra for many years. At the outset of the modern economic period, Turkey did not possess the technology for many types of products. Enterprising Turkish businesses partnered with foreign businesses who had proprietary interests in the technology or products. This took place in almost every industry, and the products were as diverse as automobiles, toothpaste, pharmaceuticals, and blue jeans. The offshore businesses were motivated to partner with Turkish businesses because they saw a market, customers for their products, but did not know how to access the market in a country like Turkey. This created a mind-set that "we don't invent the product" and encouraged dependence on off-shore suppliers of methodology and technology. Many of these off-shore partners are now ending or have ended these relationships because they feel that they no longer need a Turkish partner to access the Turkish market. This means that the Turkish business must scramble to reinvent itself. Once the beaming bride, that same business has become the "would-be bride," left at the altar. There were situations when a higher level of inventive history would have produced solutions more rapidly and assured long-term continuity of product ownership.

## BE BETTER THAN THE OTHER GUYS

In Turkey, if your business is any kind of a market force in terms of your product, then some globalized business with highly sophisticated operations is coming after your market. This means that, even though yours may be a very solid, well-funded business, you are up against a global corporation with huge resources, product development staff, and funding far greater than is available to you. The size of your principal competitor may be many multiples of your business with vast resources, yet to survive you have to be at least as good as they are, hopefully better.

## *GOVERNMENTAL CONTROL AND PRIVATIZATION*

Governments of the past twenty-plus years have all said they were going to end federal control of various industries and privatize the government-owned sectors. Progress on this very important objective has been slow, at best, and viewed by many as deleterious to the national interests. For a very long time there has been an open economy which is recorded and taxed, side by side with a "black economy" that operates outside the taxable structure. This creates problems at the governmental level because it does not have access to the true potential tax revenue from all sources that is needed to operate and modernize the entire country. It has been said that even today, the open and black economies of Turkey are of equal size. Thus, when you play by the rules, you are up against competitors who do not, and that gives them an advantage because they pay no taxes!

Stephen Kinzer, former Istanbul bureau chief for *The New York Times,* has written about many parts of this matrix, based on insight garnered during his tenure in Istanbul (Kinzer, 2002). This is an excellent resource for understanding the era prior to the election of the current prime minister, Recep Tayyip Erdogan.

> Turkey has lately undergone profound transformation in its social, economic and political life. Two-thirds of Turkey's population lives in large cities where 80% of GDP (Gross Domestic Product) is produced, accentuating large income disparities. Agriculture employs a third of the workforce, but produces only about a tenth of the GCP. (JP Morgan, 2004)

The average age is twenty-six, nearly 32 percent of the population is under the age of fifteen, while the adult literacy rate is 86.5 percent (*The Economist,* 2005). From this very brief collection of facts and impressions the reader can develop some insight into the Turkish economic, social, and political complexity.

On December 17, 2004, the European Union voted to start membership negotiations with Turkey on October 3, 2005. This will be the beginning of a process that could take years and carries the potential of transforming the political and social landscape of both parties to the process. As Turkey moves forward it will be evaluated on multiple criteria, including its ability to contribute to the EU's goal of becoming the "most competitive and dynamic knowledge-based economy in the world." The start of accession talks represents an inflection point for Turkey's economy and will be a driving force in the policymaking agenda. It is quite likely that this process will be a dominant factor in further stimulating internal reforms and opening the door for substantial economic growth.

*Lesson 7*

Because they face a far more complex matrix of issues than found in other economic systems, the level of business skill and acumen of Turkish business men and women is high.

## *MYTH OR REALITY?*

Kayseri is a place in central Turkey. It is said that when a boy is nine years old he is given something to sell on the streets of his village. If he is successful, he is brought into the business. If he is not successful, he is encouraged to enter the university. Whether this story is myth or reality, it accurately represents the cultural attitude toward commerce.

No matter where you go in Turkey there is a vendor who wants to sell you something. The "Covered Bazaar" in Istanbul is a window on how deeply the intensity of the sales ethic is imbedded in the culture. Under one roof are thousands of booths or shops with an incredible range of goods waiting to be sold. Vendors are almost exclusively male. They look at your shoes while they "rolodex" through their options and decide what language to use in addressing you. When they find the language you understand, they make their "pitch" with an intensity that many visitors simply cannot resist. If they discover that you want something slightly different from what they have in stock, they plead with you to wait a moment while they send a minion to get what you seek from "my friend who has just what you want." They do not want to hear you say "No," and do all in their power to make the sale, dropping the price or offering a product of different quality.

It is not likely that these businesses are looking for a family business consultant to help them shape their future, but this story conveys something of the intensity with which Turkish businesses seem to operate, their commitment to "doing the deal," and selling what they have to offer. It is a reflection of the Turkish "culture of commerce" and the attitudes present in all businesses. Adjacent to the antiquities, push carts, the fish markets, and street vendors is an Istanbul as sophisticated as London, Paris, New York, or Tokyo. Shops and department stores have goods on par with comparable stores anywhere in the world. On the surface those shops may look like something you have experienced elsewhere, but that is only the exterior impression. Underneath is a passion for making the sale that is uncommon anywhere in the world. This is the passion that drives Turkish businesses.

*Lesson 8*

Turks have an uncommon passion for closing the sale.

### *ALL IN ONE ROOM, ALL IN ONE FAMILY*

Imagine that you are seated in the conference room that belongs to one of the leading Turkish businesses. On the walls are photographs and paintings of the founder, probably born early in the twentieth century during the waning years of the Ottoman empire. Beside the various images of the founder is a photo of Ataturk. The parents of the founder may well have been Anatolian sheep herders in central Turkey. The formal education of the parents and the founder are likely to have been meager at best. Also in the room are several of the founder's children, probably born in the mid to late 1920s. With no gender bias, the founder has probably made his children equal owners of the business. That is where the equality stopped. Despite the fact that all the founder's children are highly intelligent, only the sons were well educated by the standards of that generation. The daughters may have graduated from a "proper" Turkish high school but the door to college was often closed to them. They may be elegantly turned out in the latest fashions, but often their thought processes are a reflection of their being deprived of the learning behind the doors they could not access. The grandchildren of the founder are also in the room, and for them, no opportunity has ever been spared. In their nurseries they had nannies from foreign lands, and as they grew up, they learned Turkish from their family and the foreign language of the nanny. Whether in Turkey or in distant lands, they went to fine private secondary schools with high academic standards where they probably learned still another language. Some went on to the prestigious colleges and universities of Europe and America. A few earned advanced degrees in business, finance, engineering, or chemistry. All of the people in the room share common ancestors and, to be sure, each has strong opinions. The challenge is that each of them is grounded in a different set of premises and has different ways of thinking about the present as well as the future. Those with recent business educations are well versed in "participative management," something either not yet introduced or not fully implemented into their family's business. Regardless of generation, all revere and defer to the most senior founder. It is possible that after careful examination of an issue and discussion of excellent alternative solutions, they will defer to the wishes of the founder, even when they might like to do otherwise.

*Lesson 9*

Don't be misled by surface appearances and assume everyone operates with the same assumptions or thinks in the same way.

### *"THAT YOUNGER MAN IS MY UNCLE"*

Another configuration in the room might be as follows: There are two senior men, Mehmet and Turgut, approximately the same age. The father of Mehmet was the eldest son of his family. Turgut and the father of Mehmet were brothers, having come from a family of many, perhaps a dozen. Turgut is the youngest member of that large family, and while about the same age as the other senior man in the room, Turgut is the uncle of Mehmet. The family norm requires that the nephew, Mehmet, defer to his uncle, Turgut. In this case, the uncle, Turgut, was of an earlier generation, ultraconservative in his thinking and behavior. His business experience and acumen had serious limitations. In spite of those limitations, the more progressive senior man, Turgut's nephew, Mehmet, who was reared with a far more progressive mind-set, felt compelled by family norms to defer to the wishes of his uncle, or at least soften his advocacy of more progressive courses of action. The modern economic history of Turkey is represented in these profiles and other configurations I will leave to the reader to imagine. As the outside consultant, you must find a way to communicate with all of these people in a manner that positive change can be effected.

*Lesson 10*

Understanding the unique, complex social structure of Turkish families, the hierarchy, and the traditions of the families is essential to all interaction with them.

During my long career serving family business in North America, Europe, Africa, Asia, and the Middle East, I have moved through the evolutionary stages that defined this emerging field. Sometimes I was privileged to participate in developing innovative, "never before" solutions (Kinkead, 1980; Bork, 1986). The fact that I had many years of experience in the field made it possible to bring Turkish family businesses state-of-the-art family business technology and procedures. The challenge was to chart an acceptable path so the Turkish family business systems could "leap frog" over many of the evolutionary stages required elsewhere and go directly to "international best practices for family businesses."

## MODIFYING ONE'S METHODOLOGY TO FIT THE CONTEXT

Chapter 3, "The Aspen Family Business Group Consulting Process," is an exposition of a family business consultative model, grounded in my work with family business, beginning in 1970. Over the past seventeen years it has been fully developed, refined, and added to by my partners in the Aspen Family Business Group (Bork, 1993; Jaffe & Paul, 1998; Bork, Jaffe, Lane, Dashew, & Heisler, 1996). The model described in that chapter has a number of principles built on a foundation of family systems theory and organizational development (Bowen, 1978). In this chapter I have stressed the importance of understanding the Turkish context. It is equally important to view this consultant's comments and efforts *in the context of his professional development,* for it occurred at a time when there was no clear path for consulting with family-owned businesses. (For early practices in the field, see Danco, 1975.) It was a process of developing and defining myself as a family business consultant and learning how to address this niche market in business consultation. Thus, a few specifics about my professional development are relevant.

## MY PROFESSIONAL BACKGROUND

My initial organization development training was in the mid-1960s through National Training Laboratories–Institute for Applied Behavioral

Science, at the feet of the men and women who founded the organizational behavior field (www.ntl.org). The early pioneers at NTL were Kurt Lewin, Ron Lippitt, Kenneth Benne, and Leland Bradford. The field had its beginnings in 1946 under Dr. Bradford's leadership when he was director of the Adult Education Division of the National Education Association. (For more information on NTL, see www.ntl.org/about-history.) I started my consulting business in 1968 and my first family business client came to me in 1970. I used 1970 state-of-the-art organization development principles and sound business practices to achieve what was requested, then came away from the engagement saying, "None of my organizational training prepared me to work with groups of family members." I searched for an organized body of knowledge about family functioning in a business setting and did not find one. This launched a personal practice that has served me well for nearly thirty-five years.

*Lesson 11*

When I wanted to know something about accounting, business law, finance, psychology, or any other matter, I would identify the very best professional who knew what I needed to know, then pay them to educate and coach me in my work. This process is how I found Dr. Murray Bowen and his theories about family systems (Bowen, 1978, 1988; Kerr & Bowen, 1988). As I studied family systems theory and simultaneously worked with family business, it became clear to me that one could work with a client system to craft an elegant business solution, *but* almost always, the keys to implementation of that solution were "locked" in the family psychology. Thus, if one failed to address the elegance of the business solution *and* the psychology of the family, nothing could be implemented. In 1988, the "Ten Qualities of Families Who Remain Positively Connected and in Business" were identified as a template against which families in business could be measured. For me, it represented an improved clarity about families in business (Nelton, 1991). The ten qualities have since been validated through the research of McCann, DeMoss, Dascher, & Barnett (2003). In *Adaptation to Life,* Dr. George Valliant postulated stages of adult development that proved to be valuable to me in understanding families in business (Valliant, 1977). Donald Super of Columbia University provided me with insight into career development (Osborne, 1997).

It was also necessary to do my own work to understand my family system, including my place and role in it. I believe "doing one's own work" is essential for all family business consultants. Failure to do so risks complicated transferences when working with client families. The importance of this is well documented by Bowen (1988) and Kaslow (1995). (Transference is what occurs when the consultant is working on a problem or issues within a family, had the same problem or issue in his or her family of origin, and deals with it from that basis rather than as an objective professional.)

It was with the mind-set of the ten qualities, the various referenced concepts, and other methodologies developed over many years that I began to work in a culture I knew nothing about. I began with what I knew at that time, and one by one tested the fundamental premises and methodology I had been using in Western countries which have cultural foundations different from those in Turkey. Some of the premises and methodology proved valid for use in the Turkish culture, while some did not work at all. Turkish culture-specific methods were invented as the need arose.

*Lesson 12*

Begin with an open mind, see what works, engage the client system in determining what works for them, and make the modifications necessary.

## THE CULTURAL COACH

### Challenge 4: How to Create a Methodology That Would Compensate for the Gaps in My Understanding of the Turkish Culture

What you have read thus far is a sampling of the complexity in the Turkish culture. I began each engagement by directly confronting with the client my lack of knowledge and experience in the Turkish culture. The fact that Turkey is a "low trust" society is a big handicap for business. International studies and comparisons show that the level of trust in the Turkish society is comparatively very low. Turkish people do trust the people of their own families, village, and town. This is due to the many "fault lines" that run through the society (Turks versus Kurds; Sunnis versus Shiites; Islamists versus secularists, etc.). This lack of trust toward people who are not "one of us" presents challenges for establishing partnerships, hiring professionals, delegating authority, *and hiring outside consultants!*

I settled on the notion of "the cultural coach" as a method of addressing this problem. It became my practice at the outset of an engagement to request that the client family appoint a person they feel is widely trusted within the system. The decision is left to the family and can be a family member or trusted advisor. The cultural coach must not be the patriarch nor a family member most often thought of as the "out front" leader. If the cultural coach were to be one of the excluded categories, it would completely compromise the concept.

The task of the cultural coach is to meet with the consultant at various points throughout the engagement. In these meetings, ideas about various interventions are shared along with proposed actions or recommendations under consideration. The purpose of this exchange is to explore the potential consequences of an intervention under consideration. In those exchanges the *cultural coach does not pass judgment on the efficacy of the concept* itself, but rather helps the consultant understand the consequences and risks of the concept if/when implemented within the culture. This is especially important should the proposed action be an egregious violation of cultural norms. (Hopefully the reader has not made that mistake!) Conversations between the cultural coach and the consultant were kept confidential and private. Through this process the family was assured that any concept that made its way from consultant to family had been vetted by the cultural coach and that I fully understood what might be at risk in any given action. A side benefit of this interaction is the building of a high level of trust with the cultural coach, a person within the system who has been selected because he is trusted within the family and company. This accelerates the consultant building high trust throughout the system.

*Lesson 13*

If your consultant team does not include a Turkish national or a person who truly knows the culture, create a cultural coach.

## LANGUAGE, UNDERSTANDING, AND BUILDING TRUST

At the outset of nearly every engagement, everyone in each client system *claimed* to be bilingual and to fully understand English. I soon learned that their claims notwithstanding, the level of English comprehension varied widely. Rarely did a family member openly admit that they did not comprehend everything. It was only in the private individual sessions that it was possible to "gently test" the understanding. To do so in a group session would risk potential embarrassment for the individual who did not understand. If you do this, you may sabotage yourself and soon be back on the airplane! Once one has a sense of the various levels of comprehension, it is then possible to adjust one's presentations to fit everyone. In many cases, it is the same as the "individualized instruction" you would find in the best of educational systems. Working with an individual in a private setting is an opportunity to address the issue of understanding and is one more opportunity to build interpersonal trust. The typical situation for contemporary Turkish families is that they are multilingual and at ease in several languages, but facility with multiple languages is not present in every generation.

*Lesson 14*

When the client is working in a secondary language, the consultant's language, the consultant faces the dual challenge of assessing the client's comprehension of the language and their understanding of the business or family concept being presented. The consultative process must be modified so it fits with and accommodates the conditions in the system. I also identified the importance of using simultaneous translators when necessary.

## ENGAGING THE ENTIRE SYSTEM

### Challenge 5: What Process Will Enable You to Get the Right People in the Room?

From my earliest days working with family business I have begun the process with a daylong seminar that includes as many family members as I can convince the engagement managers to involve (see Table 16.1). There are several reasons for doing this.

1. One can send people printed material but you never know who reads what. A seminar allows for subtlety and nuance in explanations that can be tailored to the case. Printed matter tends to be more generic and less useful as a teaching tool. The seminar also presents opportunity for interaction with family members the consultant may not have met yet. All who attend get a chance to experience the consultant, and conversely, the consultant has an opportunity to observe the interactions within the group. In this process both the client and the family can determine if there is a "fit."

2. The seminar presents an opportunity for the consultant to put a very large amount of information into the system, rather than present to a few who may or may not chose to share it with others in the system who are not directly involved in the business. The consultant can be certain that the "others" already have opinions, that they can form new opinions and most certainly they carry influence within the system. The influence may be direct or indirect, such as the influence of a business savvy spouse not normally involved. Often the younger generation will resonate with the progressive concepts that they hear in the seminar then, behind the scenes or at their family dinner table, become advocates for positive change.

TABLE 16.1. Eight core principles of Aspen Family Business Group consulting process.

| Principle | Generalization about modification for use in Turkey |
|---|---|
| Engage the entire system. | This was a new concept for most families. Often the patriarch or his surrogates controlled the flow of information to women in the family. |
| Complex systems require interventions based on a wide range of behavioral science and knowledge interventions. | Among Turkish families, there is a wide range of readiness to embrace certain interventions, structures, and concepts. It was generally true that if the patriarch favored that which was proposed, most other family members followed suit. |
| Attend to the family's advisory system. | The advisory system is rarely formalized. Putting a collection of advisors together in the same room may be viewed as "novel." When it came time for written agreements, I found the pragmatic route was to draft the agreement, meet with the attorneys who would convert it according to the Turkish legal code, then have it translated back into English and assure that document reflected the original intent. |
| Help individuals and systems move in positive direction. | The fundamental principle of accepting people and systems where they are in their respective stage of evolution, then helping them to formulate goals and move most expeditiously toward the goal is a universal principle. |
| Help clients reframe their experience in a constructive light. | This is an essential skill and practice but has some special implications in the Turkish culture. |
| Change requires trust, integrity, and communication. | The role of trust is paramount in all relationships. The process of building trust between consultant and all members of the client system is complex. |
| Focus on differentiation and individuation of people and subsystems. | It is fair to suggest that Turkish families are far less likely to be willing to discuss these matters, especially if psychological terms are used. The best way I found to approach this was through the language of boundaries. Developing clarity about all types of boundaries—between individuals, by position or role in family, between the business and the family and between those who work in the business and those who do not, etc., was readily grasped, understood, and put into practice. |
| Follow the time frame of the system, not the advisor. | This may be one of the trickiest elements since every case is different. |

3. When moving into a patriarchal or hierarchal system, which is most often the case in Turkey, the introduction of a broader group of players is, in itself, an important intervention. It sends a clear message that "something different" from past practice is about to happen. Depending on the generation, the gender mix in family business meetings will differ. In my Turkish experience, if someone was born after 1955, they are included in business

discussions regardless of gender. If born between 1925 and 1955, it will vary by family norm, with women of this generation often not included. I am personally committed to opening doors and creating opportunity for everyone, regardless of gender. It has always seemed foolish to ignore talent in a system, wherever it might be. However, every consultant must exercise caution not to transfer their values into the client system before it is ready to embrace them. It is a delicate, cross-cultural matter that must be thoughtfully and carefully orchestrated. (Paul, Al Mumaajed, & Alacaklioglu, speak to the gender issues in Chapter 13 on Saudi Arabia.) Broad involvement of the family members was a new concept for most Turkish families. Often the patriarch or his surrogates controlled the flow of information to all in the family, regardless of gender.

*Lesson 15*

"We haven't done that before" should never deter the consultant from introducing alternative methodology to achieve desired ends.

## PERSONAL CONSULTATION TECHNIQUES

### *"Executive Squares"*

As part of the diagnostic phase, it is useful to see how the family operates under different circumstances. I use two exercises for this purpose, "Executive Squares" and "Lost in the Wilderness." The former is designed for five participants. If there are more than five family members in the group I either repeat the exercise or run more than one simultaneously. This is a nonverbal exercise with carefully prescribed rules on how to function during the exercise. The underlying concept is that it is necessary for all parties to see the problem as a group problem, thus encouraging a broader view of matters. Five people are seated around a small round table. They each receive an envelope with pieces of a puzzle. The instruction is given as follows:

This is a group task. You will be finished when everyone has a square of equal size in front of you. During this activity you may not speak, point or gesture to another person. You may give your pieces to another person but you may not reach and take pieces from another person. You may not out of frustration simply dump your pieces in the middle of the table and you are not to speak until the task is completed.

This entire activity, including the instructions, is recorded on video, then analyzed by the group to determine what can be learned about their existing problem solving process. The recorded behavior of individuals can be very revealing, even symptomatic of the interactions in the group that are barriers to going forward effectively. In this exercise there are times when four of the five participants have completed squares in front of them while the fifth person sits pondering what to do with their perceived jumble of pieces. Often the solution lies in simply turning over one or more pieces to see the solution. This is a very powerful demonstration of real life situations when looking at a set of issues from a different angle or another perspective produces new insight into the solution. This important concept is recorded on video and is a potential learning all can grasp from observing their own behavior rather than be told they did something by a family member or the consultant. During the processing of the video someone invariably says, "Well, if we could have talked, we would have found the solution more rapidly." That is a set up for the next exercise.

## *Lesson 16*

Never underestimate the power of looking at a problem from another perspective.

### *"Lost in the Wilderness"*

Several different exercises are available that present a crisis situation for a group to solve. There is no need to have expertise within the group to do the exercise; as a matter of fact, situation-specific expertise can be a barrier to the best learning outcomes. The stated task of this exercise is to complete a group ranking of the items listed as available to work with in the crisis situation. Of the "Lost" family of exercises, I find "Lost in the Wilderness" to produce the best learning opportunities.

The situation presented is this: a small prop plane in which all have been traveling has crashed in Northern Minnesota. It is the dead of winter with all the concomitant problems. All passengers are in city clothes and they are eighty miles from a town. Both pilot and copilot have been killed and the survivors must chart a course of action. To do this, they must determine the order of importance of the fifteen items listed that have survived with them. First each individual makes his or her private ranking, then the group discusses the problem and produces a group ranking. The entire exercise is recorded on video for analysis later. The interactive instructions are quite general, allowing the normal dynamics of the group to surface. When they are finished with the group ranking, each individual is instructed to identify the person they thought to be most knowledgeable about the situation as well as the person they thought was most effective in moving the group to the solution. Then, individual and group scores are compared to the expert ranking of the items, in this case, leaders from the National Outdoor Leadership School (NOLS). The quality of the group score is dependent on how well they used the resources in the group. There have been instances in which there was a highly knowledgeable person in the group with a score near the NOLS score, yet the group score was far worse because the group did not use that resource. Conversely, in groups that work together effectively, the group score often exceeds the best individual score. Success in this exercise hinges on the group's fundamental assumption to either stay at the crash site and wait to be rescued, the optimum choice, or to strike out for the distant town. In every case in which I have used this exercise, it is referenced at some point later in the engagement when seeking to understand the fundamental assumptions in real-life business issues.

The notion of doing this type of exercises was foreign to my Turkish clients but it turned out to be a very effective teaching tool. Through the group analysis of the video they see some of the problems inherent in their manner of interaction. Using these data it is possible to build an agenda to address interactive skills they need to learn if they are to become a more effective work group. When people participate in building an agenda, "buy in" usually goes with it. In some cases there is a sense of excitement and playfulness, enabling the consultant to witness how humor is used in the family. Space limitations preclude full development here, but I wish to mention that video recording can be very useful in communications training as well.

*Lesson 17*

We as human beings are constructed such that we cannot truly see ourselves. Our eyes are positioned looking forward and thus, "blind by design." Use of exercises that produce interaction around problem solving, coupled with video recording this interaction, followed by group analysis of the playback makes it possible for client and consultant to more objectively see various patterns of interaction and then consider options for improving that process. It is one more chance to get "buy in" on the developmental agenda.

### Building Trust Is the Principal Challenge in Any Culture

Trust is built one person at a time. It is necessary to create a process in which the consultant has the opportunity to listen carefully to each client, then paraphrase to the client what they understand to be the client's concerns. During and after the seminar one can make assessments regarding the family functioning. As part of the seminar, interviews are scheduled with everyone. Sometimes there is "push back" from a family member about participating in the interviews. I have learned not to give in to this "push back" on interviewing everyone. Invariably at least one of the persons in the room not normally involved in business discussions is the family "truth teller," and in their interview puts their finger on one or more critical issue that might not be surfaced in other ways. If the consultant sets the stage and is perceived as trustworthy and truly listens *and hears,* the people in the system will tell the consultant everything he or she needs to know.

When the Aspen Family Business Inventory (Jaffe & Paul, 1998) became available in 1998, it was translated into Turkish for early tests. Specialists in the Turkish language did the early translations, and as it was used with Turkish families, they too had input into refining the language of the instrument. The result of this process is an instrument that has linguistic credibility in the Turkish language. The Inventory business section is grounded in "International Best Practices for Family Business." The specific questions in the section on family function reflects the "Ten Qualities" which I previously found to be a relevant way of assessing family functioning in Turkey. Prior to the availability of this instrument, all data were anecdotal and gathered through individual interviews, using my less than scientific process of comparing the data to the Ten Qualities profile. Since it came online, the inventory is administered as part of the family seminar, scored, and available for discussion in the individual interviews. This makes it possible to codify the presenting issues at a higher level and discuss the individuals views on issues that might not have come out in the interview had they not been "tagged" by the instrument. The net effect is that it is possible to move the system more rapidly to agreement on the issues and an appropriate problem-solving process.

Fundamentally, the inventory identifies "differences that make a difference." One engagement goal might be to narrow the band of differences in the system and raise the median. Administering the inventory at the outset of an engagement and then after a year presents the opportunity to compare the results and objectively validate shifts of attitude and viewpoint in the system.

*Lesson 18*

Think of every interaction as an opportunity to build trust within the client system.

## *Advisory Systems in Turkish Businesses*

It was Leon Danco who first advocated pulling the entire advisory system together as an effective intervention to coordinate various activities within the client system (Danco, 1975). It is a very important concept that I have embraced since first learning about it. In all of my experience in Turkey I have never been successful in organizing such a system, even though I tried. The AFBG consulting model speaks to forming a variety of agreements that guide and govern different structures in the comprehensive family business system. With Turkish clients, it was not always clear if I could get all the different structures implemented, so I found it useful to try to wrap as many elements and principles as possible into a single agreement. The pragmatic route was to work with the principals to develop procedures or make decisions, then draft an agreement containing these elements. This was followed by a meeting with the attorneys who would convert it according to the Turkish legal code. When finished, the attorney's document was translated back into English and vetted by the consultant to assure that document reflected the original intent. Often more than one of these cycles was required. Along the way other advisors might be consulted, but if an advisory system similar to international best practices for family businesses was in operation in Turkish businesses, I never saw one and could not get the principle adopted.

## *Reframing Issues in a Positive Light*

I believe that the ability to take a complex or not so complex matter and reframe it positively is one of the most important skills in the consultant's toolbox. The ability to do this in any setting cannot be underemphasized. I was interviewing a Turkish entrepreneur who started his business soon after the founding of the republic. His business paralleled the modern economic history of Turkey. He spoke about his concerns and said, "You know, we may own this business and of course our family will have plenty of money for generations, but this business belongs to our nation." This viewpoint is unusual anywhere. In the context of Turkey it is extraordinary! After some time of reflection, I reframed his thought into a mission statement for his very substantial company: "We are committed to being a strong economic force in Turkey for the next 100 years."

At least ten years have passed since this statement was adopted, and it has proven to be a very effective tool in guiding the direction of this company. They may not have been as effective had the issue not been reframed in a manner that allowed them to look at their circumstance in a different light, in this case, the long-term light.

### Shifting from Process Consultant to Content or Expert Consultant

The AFBG model is one of process consultation. In that process, the consultant facilitates client system activities that identify issues, develops an analysis of the issues, and then alternatives for addressing them in the context of the client's priorities. This process is built on the principle that the people who have the problem also have the skills to create the solutions. The process consultant often must teach many of those skills as the work progresses.

As I attempted to use this methodology with Turkish clients I found that often their bank of information, education, or life experience did not include the same breadth of experience and options one might find in a more Western group. In part, this was due to the generational matters addressed in All in One Room, All in One Family. Further, because of historically operating as a hierarchal and patriarchal system, they often wanted to defer to "the authority" rather than risk offering an option. Thus, when I tried to use the same methodology I used in the United States, I could not draw out of the Turkish problem-solving group a choice of options as diverse as I knew existed. This reality meant that I often had to directly or indirectly supply more of the options for consideration than I might have offered in another culture. Doing this gave the group more choices and allowed them to push forward to what might be "international best practices" of cutting-edge solutions. I found this a challenge because in process consulting one seeks to get the group to "own the product produced by the group," not a solution seen as invented by the consultant. One of the most important by-products of process consulting is individual and group "buy in" and commitment at every stage of development. This begins with identification of the critical issues, development of the criteria by which successful outcomes are defined, followed by identifying a broad range of alternatives. The criteria that describes the successful outcome(s) then is used to select the most efficacious alternative and determine a specific plan of action. Through this process the group becomes responsible for the outcome. In a "pure" process consultation model, the consultant works with the ideas and suggestions from the group, uses the Socratic method to draw them out, but rarely offers specific suggestions. Because of the cultural norms, I often found it was necessary to add ideas, suggestions, even fully developed plans for consideration, thus departing from the process consultation model. This enabled the group to move forward at a faster pace. It is a matter of being very pragmatic in working with the group. If it is not possible to move them to an optimum course of action using one method, then it is necessary to be inventive and find some alternative process or methodology that will achieve the same end result.

## *Follow the Time Frame of the System, Not the Advisor*

This AFBG principle flows out of the process consulting model. It may be one of the trickiest elements to deal with when working in Turkey. There are times when a consultant is invited into the system for a specific purpose. The client had the mind-set of "Come and fix this . . ." In other circumstances, the client looks to the consultant to manage the time frame. I have learned that in managing the process of planned change, it is necessary to keep an appropriate level of momentum or activity going to keep the system moving toward the desired goal(s). If the system gets "overheated" and moves too fast, it creates anxiety within the system and leads to events occurring that are counterproductive to the desired goal. If the process of change moves too slowly, there is little or no change and results in an inadequate level of motion or progress toward the goal. It does not happen. I believe that managing this process is a delicate art that requires keeping your fingertips on the pulse of the system, moving or "tweaking" each and every intervention so there is a "dynamic tension" between those elements or practices that characterize the past and the desired goal. The Turkish client has asked you to travel thousands of miles and is paying you very substantial fees to achieve a given result. Those factors mitigate in favor of an agreed-upon time frame and a plan of action that is carefully benchmarked.

Keeping one's finger on the pulse of the system requires "provident proximity." You have to be present to do this. Generally I schedule some type of intervention about every six to eight weeks. This could be a series of follow-up meetings to monitor progress on various elements of the action plan, a special event that was to culminate in some announcement or decisive action. While working with the largest company in Turkey, I found it necessary to remain in-country for ten to eighteen days at a time. Being physically present and on the scene allowed me to personally tweak the change process and keep it on course. If someone was having difficulty completing a task or was off course, it was possible to give assistance of make a "course correction." When I was not physically in-country, I remained in regular communications with all principals in the system, either by telephone or e-mail. This allowed me to coach the principals in implementing the change, and if necessary, return for specialized assistance, delivered in person. The tweaking is just one more effort to orchestrate the dynamic tension of planned change.

*Lesson 19*

Dynamic tension between past and future is the "engine" that pulls the system forward to the goal.

It is useful when working anywhere in the world to establish a calendar and sequence of events. Since I advocate taking a very long view, then planning and managing for the short and mid-term, the calendar may run out for many years. At the top of the calendar I list the names of all the players and their present and subsequent ages for the entire calendar. There have been times when the age listed for an individual at some future date is fairly absurd *but* it helps to make the point, emphasizing the urgency of making certain decisions while one can or even while one is still alive! The reader might ask, "Whose time frame is driving the work?" and the only answer is that it is a mix of the system, the consultant, and the process of effecting planned change.

## IF IT WERE ONLY THIS SIMPLE

The metaphor that compares a family business consultant and an orchestra conductor speaks volumes to me. The conductor begins with a careful analysis of the composition he or she will present in concert. He understands the themes and counter point as they play against each other, reflects on the intentions of the composer, and finally makes a decision on his interpretation and how he will conduct the work. He then gathers the best instrumentalists he can find and they come to rehearsal ready to play their parts. When it is time for the public performance, the conductor raises his baton and, with the down beat, sets the meter for the work. As the composition unfolds under his baton, he pays special attention first to one section and then another as each carries the theme, answers back with a counter theme, and punctuates the message of the work. Sometimes for effect he dampens or accentuates the tone of one section to make a point or allow still another section to be heard. He cues a soloist when it is time to come in, then gives clear direction for unison accents as the substatements of the work are reached.

At last the finale! It is the crowning moment when the conductor ties everything together in a resolution that completes the statement we heard in the beginning theme of the work.

*Lesson 20*

Family business consultation is akin to the work of the orchestra conductor. It is both art and science, but it is the art that lifts the spirit!

## REFERENCES

Bork, D. (1986, 1993). *Family business, risky business: How to make it work.* Basalt, CO: Bork Institute for Family Business.

Bork, D., Jaffe, D., Lane, S., Dashew, L., & Heisler, Q. (1996). *Working with family businesses: A guide for professionals.* San Francisco: Jossey-Bass Publishers.

Bowen, M. (1978, 1988). *Family therapy in clinical practice.* New York: Jason Aronson.

Danco, L. (1975). *Beyond survival.* New York: Reston Publishing.

The Economist. (2005). *Pocket world in figures, 2005 edition.* London: Profile Books.

Jaffe, D. & Paul, J. (1998). *Aspen Family business inventory.* Ft. Worth, TX: Aspen Family Business Group.

JP Morgan Chase Bank, Economic Research. (2004, November 19). Turkey's roadmap for EU entry. [Internal document.]

Kaslow, F. (1995). *Projective genogramming.* Sarasota, FL: Professional Resource Press.

Kerr, M. & Bowen, M. (1988). *Family Evaluation: An approach based on Bowen.* New York: W.W. Norton.

Kinkead, G. (1980, June 30). A family business is a passion play! *Fortune,* p. 70.

Kinross, L. (1964). *Ataturk: A biography of Mustafa Kemal, father of modern Turkey.* New York: Quill/Wm. Morrow.

Kinzer, S. (2002). *Crescent and star: Turkey between two worlds.* New York: Farrar, Straus and Giroux.

Mango, A. (1999). *Ataturk.* London: John Murray Ltd.

McCann, G., DeMoss, M., Dascher, P., & Barnett, S. (2003). Educational needs of family businesses: Perceptions of university directors. *Family Business Review, 16*(4), 283-291.

Nelton, S. (1991, April). Ten keys to success in family business. *Nation's Business,* p. 44.

Osborne, W. L. (1997). *Career development, assessment, and counseling: Applications of the Donald E. Super C-DAC approach.* Alexandria, VA: American Counseling Association.

Sumner-Boyd, H., & Freely, J. (2003). *Strolling through Istanbul.* London: Kegan Paul International Ltd.

Vaillant, G. (1977). *Adaptation to life.* Boston: Little, Brown and Company.

Chapter 17

# United Kingdom

Juliette Johnson
Mark Jones
Peter C. Leach
Francis Martin

In researching this chapter we have conferred widely with both suppliers and consumers of family business consulting services across the United Kingdom (which, for the purposes of this chapter, should be construed throughout as excluding Scotland). Our main conclusion is that, in comparison with the fully developed marketplace in the United States, family business consulting in the United Kingdom, although growing fast, has still some way to go to reach maturity. Awareness of specialist family business consultants in the United Kingdom is increasing, but acceptance as a consulting discipline in its own right has only relatively recently taken root. There are grounds for optimism, but as yet the pace and extent of future growth remain unclear.

A distinction needs to be drawn at the outset between the "soft" side of family business consulting—areas such as conflict resolution, mediation, and the development of family business governance structures—as opposed to the "hard" side, covering, for example the technical aspects of family estate planning, legal and tax advice, and pension provision. Throughout this chapter "family business consulting" refers to the "softer," more broad-based advisory work features.

The authors would like to thank the many organizations and individuals who have contributed to this chapter. In particular, Andrew Drake (Partner, Boodle Hatfield); John J. Freeman (Director, Business Analytics consultancy); Grant Gordon (Director General of the Institute for Family Business, UK); Susan Kaye (Managing Director, Challenge of Excellence group); Alexander Scott (Executive Chairman, Sand Aire Limited); Rupert Merson (Partner, BDO Stoy Hayward); Daniel Sacerdoti (BDO Stoy Hayward); Simon Perry (consultant editor), and Business Link advisory service.

*Handbook of Family Business and Family Business Consultation*
Published by The Haworth Press, Inc., 2006. All rights reserved.
doi:10.1300/5491_17

Several distinctions should also be drawn between the typical U.S. approach to family business consultation and the U.K. perspective. The U.S. preference tends to be to work with pools of specialist professionals who all approach their work from a detailed understanding of the dynamics of family businesses. A family business consultant in the United States—who would often be someone with a psychotherapy background or attached to an academic institution—would want to build his or her support team from (as required) lawyers and financial planners who also specialize in family business work.

In the United Kingdom, on the other hand, family business consultants usually hail from a nontherapy professional background, and their approach tends to be to draw on lawyers, tax and pension advisers, and property and insurance experts as needed to successfully complete the assignment. Typically they would choose from the general pool of quality advisers available, not specifically looking for family business experience or expertise. Yes, they need to have some understanding of family businesses in general, and the sensitive issues that affect the client in particular, but much of this will be achieved via initial assignment briefing sessions before their work starts. These people are providing "hard" advice (such as on the legalities of writing a shareholders agreement or how to have the death of a shareholder covered by life insurance). It is not expected that they come with any of the "softer," conflict resolution or mediation skills required, for example, when the task is to draw up a family constitution or shape a family council structure.

One final point concerning U.K. terminology. The authors are uncomfortable with the use of the word "consultant" in the context of family business advisory work. Consultant, especially in the United Kingdom, carries connotations of problem solving by outside professionals—of visiting a client, collecting the relevant facts on problem issues, and then going away and writing an expert analytical report including "solutions." But this is not the way that family business consulting works; rather, clients are offered expert facilitation, trust-building, support, and guidance services that help families arrive at their own solutions and their own consensus as to the best way forward. However, despite these reservations, and despite a preference for terms such as "adviser" and "facilitator," in the interests of consistency across this book the authors have adopted "consultant" throughout the chapter.

## FAMILY BUSINESS LANDSCAPE

Just over 76 percent of U.K. companies are family owned (BDO Stoy Hayward & London Business School, 1990), and clearly these businesses represent a vital component of the national economy. Many people, when they think "family business," also think "small," but there are many very large family enterprises (see Table 17.1). Also, it has been estimated that over 50 percent of people employed in this country, outside the public sector, work for family businesses.

Although family firms are to be found in every sector of U.K. commercial activity, their special strengths mean that they flourish best in fields in

TABLE 17.1. A selection of large U.K. family businesses ranked by turnover.

| Rank | Company (location) | Owning/ controlling family | Turnover 2003 (£m) | Employees | Sector |
|---|---|---|---|---|---|
| 1 | Caudwell Holdings (Stoke-on-Trent) | Caudwell | 2,276 | 7,401 | Telecommunications |
| 2 | John Swire & Sons (London) | Swire | 1,948 | 83,081 | Shipping transport |
| 3 | Specialist Computer Holdings (Birmingham) | Rigby | 1,884 | 4,569 | IT systems |
| 4 | Stemcor (London) | Oppenheimer | 1,535 | 322 | Steel trader |
| 5 | Wilkinson Hardware Stores (Worksop) | Wilkinson | 1,045 | 19,310 | Retailer |
| 6 | C. & J. Clark (Bristol) | Clark | 943 | 13,933 | Footwear manufacturer and seller |
| 7 | JCB (Rocester, Staffordshire) | Bamford | 902 | 4,233 | Construction equipment manufacturer |
| 8 | Sir Robert McAlpine (Hemel Hempstead) | McAlpine | 835 | 2,240 | Construction |
| 9 | European Metal Recycling (Warrington, Cheshire) | Sheppard | 829 | 1,363 | Metal recycler |
| 10 | Bestway (London) | Pervez | 754 | 1,715 | Wholesaler |
| 11 | Shepherd Building Group (York) | Shepherd | 603 | 3,530 | Builder |
| 12 | Food Brokers (Portsmouth) | Cracknell | 392 | 350 | Consumer goods distributor |

*Source:* Adapted from JP Morgan Bank (2003). "Focus: The Top 100 Family Businesses in the UK," *Families in Business,* November-December, pp. 50-58; numerical data updated by BDO Centre for Family Business. (*Note:* This organization was launched in 1992 as the United Kingdom's first organization dedicated to serving the needs of the family business community; today it operates from a network of ten regional centers across the United Kingdom.)

which their advantages can be fully exploited. Typical characteristics of family business are

- owner-manager;
- entrepreneurial;
- cash rich; and
- niche/knowledge based.

Thus family businesses tend to do well in sectors in which the owner-manager feature is important, particularly in the service industries; for example, most hotel chains in the United Kingdom were originally family owned. Family firms are also found in activities where entrepreneurial drive remains a key ingredient of success; there is a great tradition in the retail sector, for instance, of businesses being passed on from one generation to the next.

An above-average representation of U.K. family businesses is found in sectors where cash flow is good. Cash is critically important in the financing of family companies, and the history of industrial development highlights, for example, food processing, which has traditionally been a good cash generator, with many long-established companies still in family hands. (In a recent ranking of the top 100 family businesses in the United Kingdom [JP Morgan Bank, 2003], no fewer than twenty-six operated in one subsector or another of the food industry, including manufacturing, processing, importing, restaurants, and supermarkets.) Similarly, family businesses tend to do well in niche sectors, often still trading on the genius of someone who founded the company many years earlier, or where the business is based on some specific knowledge or trading secret that represents the key to success.

Mention of firms still trading on the genius of a long-gone founder raises a key factor that distinguishes the U.K. family business landscape from the situation in most other countries—many of these companies are very, very old.[1] Some examples:

- Carver plc, founded in 1778, first operated in the whip industry. Over the years it has diversified in order to maintain a sustainable, international company for long-term family investment. As a seventh-generation family business, Carver today specializes in the development and manufacture of gas and electric heating, cooling, and ventilation equipment.
- C. Hoare & Company was established by Richard Hoare in Cheapside, London, in 1672, and is the last survivor of England's seven-

teenth- and eighteenth-century private deposit banks. Today the bank is run by members of the tenth and eleventh generations.

• Founded in 1591, R. Durtnell & Sons is the oldest building company in the United Kingdom. The firm, based today in Kent, has been handed down from father to son for twelve generations.

• The United Kingdom's oldest family firm is believed to be John Brooke & Sons, in business since 1541. During its first 450 years the company manufactured fabrics, including uniform cloth for British, French, and Russian troops. Faced with intense global competition in the late 1980s, the firm closed its traditional woolen and worsted mill, and the fifteenth generation is now transforming the mill complex into an entrepreneurial development park.

## HISTORY AND EVOLUTION
## OF FAMILY BUSINESS CONSULTING

Family business as a distinct and specialized field of business consultation was introduced and pioneered in the United Kingdom in the late 1980s by Peter Leach, a partner with the accountancy firm Stoy Hayward (now BDO Stoy Hayward LLP). Peter had been working with family businesses in the United Kingdom for a number of years, but during his travels in the United States from the mid-1980s onward he had become interested in the way that conceptual thinking about family companies had begun to take hold there among both advisers and family businesspeople, spurred on by focused academic research about the unique issues faced by these companies.

Influential figures working on researching and analyzing family businesses in the United States at the time included Peter Davis (then at Wharton Applied Research Center), Ivan Lansberg (at Yale School of Organization and Management), and Harry Levinson (at Harvard), with more practical input from established consultants such as Benjamin Benson and Leon Danco. During his U.S. travels, Peter Leach studied the work being undertaken by such individuals. He "shadowed" Wharton's Peter Davis on the latter's assignments advising some major U.S. family businesses, and also attended many family business seminars and conferences which, by the late 1980s, were becoming increasingly popular all over the country. Witnessing this growing activity, he became convinced that it was a valuable area of theoretical and practical study, and indeed of commercial value, and set about organizing its adoption in the United Kingdom.

Starting from a blank canvas, the first step was to commission two studies, supervised by the London Business School, designed to review and quantify family business activity in this country (BDO Stoy Hayward & London Business School, 1989, 1990). These included the key finding referred to earlier that 76 percent of U.K. businesses are family controlled. Next, Peter wrote a book called *The Stoy Hayward Guide to the Family Business,* which was published in March 1991 by London publisher Kogan Page. The book is currently in its third edition—now jointly authored by Peter Leach and his colleague Tony Bogod (Bogod & Leach, 1999)—and has sold some 60,000 copies in English, plus many foreign translations distributed around the world.

In 1991 and 1992 Peter Davis was invited to help launch the various U.K. initiatives, and he was the keynote speaker at a series of sell-out seminars (organized in conjunction with venture capital group 3i) which took place around the country. The seminars (each attended by some fifty to sixty family businesspeople) raised the profile of the sector significantly.

It rapidly became clear that taking a fresh look at family businesses was an idea whose time had come. Nevertheless, a degree of skepticism was encountered from certain people who noted how this initiative was being spearheaded by a firm of accountants, so in 1992 the Stoy Centre for Family Business was founded, designed to provide some separation and independence from the main firm. Since its foundation, the Stoy Centre—recently rebranded as the BDO Centre for Family Business (BDO CFB)—has published a regular newsletter, organized seminars, and developed its own identity.

In view of the successful launch of family business consultation in the United Kingdom, there were expectations that accountants and other consultants would expand their services in the field, but in fact, for most of the 1990s this did not happen. In Northern Ireland, for example, BDO CFB was able to break new ground, organizing research in conjunction with the Ulster Business School (part of the University of Ulster) to provide academic foundations for its growing family business consultancy practice in that province. It was not until late in the decade that another accounting firm—Grant Thornton LLP—began to build a presence in U.K. family business consulting, followed by PricewaterhouseCoopers LLP.

More recently there has been an expansion of non-accounting firm "boutiques" devoted exclusively to advising family businesses, which are often run by family business consultants from an academic background, reflecting the fact that educational institutions and business schools have started to incorporate family business studies into their curricula, providing another boost in awareness of the issues faced by U.K. family businesses.

An important event in 2001 was that the annual conference of the U.S.-based Family Firm Institute (FFI) took place in London—the first time the conference had been held outside the United States. In the same year the Institute for Family Business (IFB), the U.K. chapter of the international Family Business Network (FBN) was founded. IFB is an independent not-for-profit association established by families for families; it is governed by a membership-elected Trustees' Board supported by a full-time secretariat. The IFB, which has an Advisory Council drawn partly from among the consulting community, is devoted to sustaining a successful family business community in the United Kingdom via regular educational programs and research initiatives.

## BACKGROUND OF TODAY'S CONSULTANTS

### Who They Are and Who They Work For

At an individual level, family business consultants in the United Kingdom generally come from professional backgrounds; they are mostly accountants, management consultants, lawyers, and bankers, plus some (although not many) psychologists and therapists. An interesting recent development has been the increasing involvement of family business owners or ex-owners in consultancy and educational activities.

This quite long list of categories should not, however, be allowed to disguise the fact that very few advisers are working as "family business consultants" in the terms we defined earlier—i.e., working on the "soft" side of family business advising. In an informal survey of knowledgeable specialists conducted during research for this chapter, the question, "How many people do you consider to be experienced family business consultants in the United Kingdom?" drew average answers of around twenty.

The very limited scale of involvement of psychologists and therapists in family business consulting here versus in the United States highlights a marked social and cultural divide between the two countries. The "Frequently asked questions" section of the United Kingdom Council for Psychotherapy's Web site includes a revealing question: "How does UKCP feel about the general public's mistrust in psychotherapists?"—an essential issue for UKCP to address in this country, but not an issue that is raised often, if at all, in the United States. So U.K. family businesspeople are on the whole very reluctant to consult with therapists about family business issues.

This does not mean that knowledge of family psychology can be dispensed with by U.K. consultants—on the contrary, it is vital because behind the business problems there are almost always deep-rooted family issues and tensions, and the former cannot be resolved without addressing the latter. U.K. family business consultants must have a broad understanding of these emotional and psychological issues, but they must avoid following the U.S. psychology- and therapy-based model too closely.

The issue therefore has practical implications for the day-to-day work of family business consultants in this country versus those in the United States. The point has been made that consultants here tend to come from a "traditional" professional background—people who, on the whole, are very comfortable dispensing commercially valuable, professional advice as experts to clients. But family business consultancy work is different—technical expertise is clearly needed in order to resolve these specific issues, but nontechnical input is also required from specialists who are good at facilitating potentially difficult family discussions on sensitive issues (see Exhibit 17.1).

It is important to understand this distinction, because a good family business consultant in this country will not give advice but will facilitate the family's arrival at solutions, letting them achieve this as a family. There is an acceptance in the United Kingdom that psychotherapy is not a discipline that is going to be well received in the commercial context (nor, the research

## EXHIBIT 17.1. Family Business Consultancy Requires a Unique Perspective

This case throws into stark relief the difference in approach between family business consultants and other types of specialist advisers in the area in the United Kingdom. It arose at a seminar designed to discuss the techniques of both groups. The case was presented by a lawyer who headed up the family department at a large firm of solicitors (that is, he worked with families who own businesses), and it concerned a business owner who had left his wife, with whom he had had one son, and married his secretary, with whom he had had another son. The solicitor presented the firm's solution involving working only with the owner of the business to find a very correct and powerful technical solution based on setting up trusts to deal with the future ownership. But a family business consultant would not begin to approach the case in that way. He or she would see that the facts here potentially indicate an emotional minefield and would recommend that if, rather than just the business owner, the whole family become involved in the process of finding, and becoming part of, a solution. The company might technically be the client, but a family business consultant would recommend that everyone in the family and key players in the business had a voice in the process. This allows a solution to be found that is understood and accepted by everyone affected by it, if that is indeed the wish.

suggests, in many other contexts), and therefore input on it has to come from the professional world, but there are limits on how many people will do it because it is so far outside the usual comfort zone of professional advisers.

### Training for Family Business Consulting Work

Some prestigious educational institutions have begun incorporating family business studies into their curricula—for instance, the University of Gloucestershire researches family business issues and offers an MBA and short courses in this area.[2] Courses are also planned as part of the London Business School's "Leadership in Family Business Research Initiative." But these, like the entrepreneurship and family business management courses at the Institute Européen d'Administration des Affaires (INSEAD)—based at Fontainebleau in France but with a U.K. and, indeed, an international following—are intended more for people who work in family businesses rather than being designed to "train" family business advisers. Currently there is no UK body charged with certifying family business advisers.

The Family Firm Institute does organize training courses for family business consulting work. They tend to run most of their training in the United States where they are based, but they have also run U.K. conferences and more are planned here. They have a two-year Certificate in Family Business Advising program, with participants assigned to a mentor who advises and assists them through the training.

Some firms are setting up their own internal systems to ensure that their staff are suitably qualified in family business consulting work. For example, no one can undertake consultancy work for BDO CFB until they qualify under its licensing procedures, comprising defined standards for

- minimum periods of experience shadowing and carrying out family business advisory assignments, and
- level of "continual professional development," including personal study and training course requirements.

More broadly, there is evidence of a growing belief among family business consultants and others working in the field that the establishment of a nationally recognized qualification could be advantageous in differentiating family business consultants from other types of advisers.

## *Philosophical Outlook and Skills Needed*

Detailed skill sets are discussed in the next two sections, but perhaps the most important factor to emphasize here is that serious listening underlies the skills of the best family business consultants. Listening to what is being said and developing the ability to pick up the signals of what is truly being communicated are vitally important in working effectively with family businesspeople and in building their trust.

Another interesting view on skill requirements, that would enjoy wide support, was provided by one of the contributors to the research underlying this chapter, John J. Freeman (personal communication, 2004), who heads up the Business Analytics consultancy:

1. The ability to remain independent, to be able to understand one's own limitations and the ability to realize when one's own experiences could influence the intervention. The first breeds confidence and trust in the family members, the second will stop you getting into areas you are not qualified to deal with, and the last will stop you imposing solutions based on your prejudices.
2. Knowledge of different solutions and possibilities so as to be able to facilitate discussions on how the family can look at a problem in order to find the solution that suits them.
3. The ability to realize when the family, or a large subset of it, does not want to solve a problem because the only solution might cause the family to disintegrate and thus be left in a worse state.

## *FAMILY BUSINESS CONSULTING ACTIVITIES*

### *Do Consultants Compete or Collaborate Across Fields?*

"Both" is probably the most accurate approximation of an answer to this question. Competition exists, but it is limited in the context of the relatively underdeveloped market for the provision of family business consultancy services in the United Kingdom. But at the same time, this recognition of a new market with considerable scope for growth encourages quite a significant level of collaboration among consultants.

Collaboration takes a variety of forms, in particular cooperation among consultants in their joint support for, and sponsorship of, educational and networking initiatives such as business school courses, research, workshops, seminars, and conferences. Many family business owners still do not realize that this area of expert advice exists, and the way providers tend to operate is to raise awareness of the field by "planting a seed" at these educational and networking events while knowing that most probably assistance will not be sought immediately. But the idea may resurface years later when developments take place that make people realize that their family needs this process—in short, family businesses will seek out consultants at a time when they are ready.

This should not be taken as implying a completely competition-free environment. An element of competition does exist and providers do sometimes have to bid for assignments. Referrals are an important source of work—for example from investment banks such as JP Morgan or the family department of law firms, who are not trying to compete with the main providers of broad-based family business consultation. Many referrals also come from commercial banks, because they understand that it is the "softer" family business issues that tend to bring these businesses down and lead them to default on their loans.

In addition, government agencies are a source of assignments, such as Business Link, which tends not to provide specific advice on "soft" issues but does have family business planning as one of its portals. Also, in Northern Ireland, much of BDO CFB's family business consultancy work is underpinned by its recent appointment as sole supplier of such services under the government-sponsored "Invest NI" development initiative (a program that subsidizes family firms seeking the assistance of family business consultants).

### Companies Most Likely to Utilize Consultancy Services

Many companies still do not realize that specific family business consulting expertise is available in this country, so they naturally fall into the category of companies that are unlikely to utilize such services, and, even for those who are aware, there has historically been a specific U.K. cultural problem—the fact that consultants do not enjoy a glowing reputation among small to medium-sized businesses generally and, perhaps, among family businesses in particular. There has been a common belief that consultants are excellent at "examining your watch and telling you the time"— in other words, in providing you with an erudite compilation of your problems but offering little beyond the obvious, or indeed impractical, in the way of constructive advice about how you should go about solving them.

However, as competitive pressures and growing complexity bear down on today's businesses, evidence indicates that this anti-consultant predisposition may be on the decline. Parallel with this has been a marked increase in the past decade in publicity and education about the importance of family businesses, their potential strengths and weaknesses, and the problems that can afflict them. As mentioned, the government-sponsored Business Link system that assists the small and medium-sized enterprise (SME) sector has become more active in learning about consulting to family businesses, while the European Union has been alert to family business needs and has been pumping money into trying to improve the succession of SME businesses to the next generation. These developments, the growth of the IFB, and the low-key but persistent promotional activities of consultants themselves are all increasing awareness.

### Types of Skills Consultants Should Have

A detailed model of the qualities and competencies of good family business consultants is presented in the next section but, in more general terms, perhaps the three most important skills for a consultant in this field are listed here:

1. *Communication.* Discussing family strengths and weaknesses is a sensitive minefield, and it is vital to have communication skills that enable the consultant to pick up on the undercurrents of what is being said—to be a "developed listener"—and to know when it would be better *not* to say anything.
2. *Ability to build trust.* This leads on from the first point and is a critical skill. The consultant must build trust with the family quickly—the family must come to understand at a very early stage that the consultant is acting on behalf of the business and the family as a whole, not for one particular individual or group at the expense of others.
3. *Facilitation.* Family business consultants must be able to probe the difficult issues and develop discussion of a family's problem areas in a subtle and sensitive way that minimizes the possibility of friction and confrontation.

## ROLES AND FUNCTIONS OF CONSULTANTS

### Multigenerational Family Business Consulting

Approaches to family business consultation vary from consultant to consultant in the United Kingdom, but one methodology that BDO CFB has found works well with larger family businesses, particularly where many members of the younger generation are involved, is best described as a multigenerational approach to consulting. This means that the firm aims to divide its consulting teams in a way that mirrors the age structure of the family members they are meeting. So if two generations are playing key roles in the businesses—say on average one aged in their fifties and the other in their twenties—they try to ensure that the ages of consultants on the assignment matches this profile. This helps both to establish working relationships and to set up good communication more quickly than would otherwise be the case, because people of similar ages relate to each other more easily. In the right circumstances, this multigenerational structure can be a very powerful approach to consulting and will evolve naturally as businesses respond to the need for specialist advice for all generations in order to achieve longevity.

### A Model for the Roles/Functions of Family Business Consultants

Underlying the model set out in Exhibit 17.2 is the overriding importance for family business consultants to remain independent from family members, and the need to provide a solid foundation of trust that explains and informs the consultant's role and objectives. One of the contributors to the research underlying this chapter, Susan Kaye (personal communication, 2004), who is a therapist/family business consultant and managing director of The Challenge of Excellence group, made the following telling points on how consultants can help maintain their independence:

- Say what you will do . . . and do it.
- Say what you will not do . . . and don't do it!
- If working with individuals or subgroups, emphasize confidentiality at *each and every* meeting. You have to work at avoiding any sense of partiality being perceived.
- Avoid being used as a messenger. Instead encourage family members to send their own messages, exploring with them the pros and cons of so doing, and coaching them to discover for themselves the best ways to send "difficult" messages.
- Keep a professional distance yet maintain warmth and a sense of humor.

Family members must trust consultants implicitly and have complete faith in their independence and in the fact that they are working in the interests of the family as a whole, not for, or favoring, particular family members or groups (see Exhibit 17.3). This helps ensure that all family members feel party to all decisions that affect the family business.

## EXHIBIT 17.2. A Family Business Consultancy Model

### *Research*

Information gathering about the company and family:

- Historical background
- Family tree
- Company structure
- Share structure
- Family culture, vision, and values
- Family aspirations and preferences

### *Counselling*

The consultant needs to do the following:

- Be a good listener.
- Build trust.
- Maintain confidentiality.
- Be professional.
- Be objective and independent.

### *Facilitating*

In order to encourage and maintain effective communication the consultant needs to do these things:

- Be able to chair family meetings.
- Communicate with people who have varying levels of understanding.
- Identify and introduce sensitive issues into the process in a tactful and effective way.
- Maintain control, particularly in an emotionally charged environment.
- Guide the family through a process to reach the desired goals.
- Keep everything transparent.
- Allow the family to come up with their own answers.

### *Consolidating*

The family business consultant consolidates the results of the consultation process:

- Confirming the action plan that the family has come up with
- Confirming that everyone's opinions have been correctly heard and interpreted

- Helping the family to resolve any unexpected implementation issues
- Providing an ongoing "hand-holding" role into the future

## EXHIBIT 17.3. Independence: Don't Be Taken for a Ride

After an apparently successful proposal visit to a large family business, during which the concept and importance of adviser independence and neutrality were explained, the adviser innocently accepted a lift to the airport from one of the family. He was spotted, and word soon spread among the other family members. Subsequently he was perceived as being "in the pocket" of the person who gave him the lift, and therefore not suitable to carry out such a sensitive assignment. The consultancy work did not go ahead.

## *TYPES OF INTERVENTION*

Broadly, there are two types of intervention, defined by the motivation of the family business seeking advice—one is reactive and the other is preventative (see Exhibit 17.4).

### *Reactive Intervention*

Some firms—especially smaller family businesses—seek help as a reaction to a particular event that has happened or an issue that has developed. For example, family shareholders may come to realize that a family managing director is not up to the job and they decide they want to replace him, or sibling rivalry may be negatively impacting on the performance of the business. Such consultation assignments are particularly challenging because the issues are already established and people have taken "positions".

### *Preventive Intervention*

Preventive interventions tend to be more prevalent with (but not exclusively) larger family businesses where there is a recognition that certain issues may (or are certain to) arise in the future, and the family wants to put in place appropriate processes and procedures to avoid problems and manage

## EXHIBIT 17.4. Reactive or Preventive Intervention?

This consultancy project began when four brothers, working together in a second-generation family business, commissioned consultants "to help us plan and manage the firm's transition to the next and future generations." The brothers explained that they had no current problems but were worried about the looming complications of multifamily ownership in the third generation, and wanted help setting up plans and structures that would ensure family harmony going forward. After many group and individual meetings set up and facilitated by the consultants, it became clear that some problems and issues for the brothers were very much in the here and now rather than the dim distant future. They had imposed a rule that no members of the younger, third generation could work in the business until they were thirty-five years old, and, rather than just affecting new joiners, the rule was applied to some third-generation family who had already been working for the firm for several years. These family members had to leave the business and find another job, which predictably caused big problems and upset in the family. So what began for the consultants as a preventative intervention turned out to have a significant reactive dimension. Nevertheless, the consultants were able to put structures in place to help deal with future transitions while also addressing the current challenges facing the family.

the situation when the time comes. They are being cautious and have decided to adopt a course that enables them to deal with issues before emotions become involved. For example, the current generation may want to draw up policies that govern whether and on what basis the next generation can join the business, and they decide to do this while the children are still relatively young, rather than when the possibility of them joining has already become imminent.

### Resistance to Intervention

Initial intervention is an important and delicate area, because usually it is instigated by a single member of a family, or a single family group, rather than the whole family. Care must be taken about what is said at this preliminary stage. Generally consultants should broadly only take on an assignment based on a unanimous family appointment; there are too many cases in which they are prevented from acting because someone in the family objects.

## Guidelines on Intervention

The more experienced U.K. family business consultants have adopted internal guidelines incorporating standardized procedures and a code of conduct that applies to all interventions in family businesses. Consulting firms generally present the details of their standardized procedures to the family as a whole at the beginning of every assignment, and it is made clear that the provisions and processes set out in the code are to be rigorously applied and adhered to throughout the work.

The basic procedures as applied in a typical U.K. assignment would cover

- educational seminars;
- one-to-one meetings with family members (see Exhibit 17.5);
- individual meetings with key nonfamily directors;
- group-facilitated sessions (e.g., with family groups or smaller shareholder groups); and
- two- or three-day family retreats, with the family gathering in a quiet environment away from the everyday surroundings of work and home (see Exhibit 17.6).

It should be emphasized throughout that the consultant is not there to provide solutions. Rather, the consultant's role is understanding the issues and

---

### EXHIBIT 17.5. One-to-One Meetings: Some Key Dos and Don'ts

**Dos**

- Do hold the meeting on neutral premises.
- Do emphasize confidentiality and explain how it works.
- Do be aware how tense the interviewee may be.
- Do let the interviewee do 80 percent of the talking.
- Do let the interviewee decide what topics are important.

**Don'ts**

- Don't underestimate how important the meeting is to the interviewee.
- Don't hold the meeting on company premises.
- Don't break any confidences from previous interviews.

## EXHIBIT 17.6. Facilitating Family Retreats:
## Some Key Dos and Don'ts

### Dos

- Do let the family "patriarch"/"matriarch" open proceedings.
- Do agree on clear, unambiguous ground rules and get the "buy-in" of those present.
- Do be patient and let the family arrive at solutions.
- Do be prepared to leave a difficult issue and revisit it later during the retreat.
- Do ensure consensus decisions are written down for all to see.

### Don'ts

- Don't underestimate the time you need.
- Don't go head first into the sensitive issues early in the retreat.
- Don't let anyone object to a proposal without giving clear, logical reasons.
- Don't let anyone dominate the proceedings.
- Don't be prepared to supply answers—this is up to the family, although they will need guidance.

responding to the challenges the family faces by drawing on the consultant's experiences with other families in order to arrive at a tailored approach.

## IMPORTANT ELEMENTS IN THE FIELD TODAY

### Ownership and Management Concerns

Family ownership and commercial management are overlapping—and to an extent incompatible—systems that generate tension and conflict, and, as such, they lie at the heart of family business consultation. Certain issues are primarily ownership focused:

- Governance
- The family council
- Transfer of shares
- Exit routes and share valuation

Other issues are more operational:

- Operating structure
- Procedures
- Jobs and remuneration
- Training
- The board of directors

Overlapping value systems are thrown into particularly stark relief in the field of human resources in family businesses:

| | |
|---|---|
| Recruitment | *Owners* provide opportunities to relatives. |
| | *Managers* recruit those most competent. |
| Remuneration | *Owners* allocate in accordance with needs. |
| | *Managers* allocate salaries according to market worth. |
| Appraisal | *Owners* may not differentiate between siblings. |
| | *Managers* differentiate to identify high performers. |
| Training | *Owners* provide learning opportunities to satisfy individuals development needs. |
| | *Managers* provide learning opportunities to satisfy organizational needs. |

### The Family Constitution (Also Known As the Charter, Protocol, or Creed)

Operational friction and value conflicts arising from these overlapping systems cannot be avoided entirely, but successful consultation activities help families to devise strategies that keep the overlap under control. And it is the process of drawing up a written family constitution (essentially a statement of intent that spells out the family's shared values and its policies in relation to the business) that is often at the heart of consultation assignments—the process under which families begin to face up to the emotional "hot spots" that can be so critical to the future success and survival of their business. The final document will, of course, rarely if ever represent *everyone's* preferred and ideal outcome on *all* the issues included, but at least the rules will have been thought about, debated, understood, and written down during the process of arriving at a consensus.

This does not mean that establishing a family constitution is always the starting point. In smaller firms (say just three or four family members) it may represent overkill, and indeed "family constitution" can sometimes be a rather grand title in situations where a smaller-scale "family action plan" may be more appropriate, setting out policies on just a few fundamental issues. But for bigger family businesses there are serious benefits to be had from a detailed family constitution that lays down ground rules for many years to come. The constitution is a very powerful tool in helping to ensure long-term ownership.

As implied previously, the actual family constitution text that emerges at the end of the consultation process may of itself not be where the real value lies—indeed, there is often the suspicion that once it has been handed over to the family the document may well be tucked away in a drawer to gather dust. But what will not be forgotten is the trust-building process under which the constitution was assembled—getting everyone together (including relatives who previously may never have met), the interviews, starting to think about the "taboo issues," the debates at the family retreat, redrafting the difficult points and learning to understand other family members' points of view—and it is this process that is so valuable. Handled properly by the family business consultant, everyone exits the process feeling that they have had an equal voice and made an equal contribution, which is unusual in a family.

## IMPORTANT STRUCTURES

### Family Council

The family council is a concept that may not be as developed here as it is in the United States. The council operates as a separate forum to bridge the gap between the Board of Directors and the family shareholders, and key points follow:

- It assists communication.
- It operates on a consensus basis, not majority vote.
- It tackles the "forbidden agenda."
- It has no formal power.
- Owners and managers participate.
- It creates the family "glue."
- It enables the family to speak with one voice to the Board.

Thus, rather than large numbers of family members all taking their wish-lists, complaints, and questions to perhaps the sole working family director, a family council is set up as a forum that is representative of the shareholders. For smaller families, the council might well comprise all the family shareholders, but for businesses that have large numbers of family shareholders, traditionally each branch of the family has tended to nominate someone to sit on the family council. Interestingly, however, recent trends suggest that families are beginning to move away from this idea of "family branches," regarding it as an outdated and potentially divisive concept. Currently, in some more mature U.K. family businesses, the new generation has been adopting fresh guidelines that replace branch representation in governance structures with policies and procedures designed to emphasize and foster a unified family approach to the business—clearly a development that places a high premium on establishing and maintaining good intra-family communication. Finally, as regards council membership, there will generally also be a member of the Board on the council—often the family Board member.

Relatively few U.K. family businesses have a family council, but there are some notable examples. In the case of C. & J. Clark, for instance, establishing an effective family council was a key step in saving the business. Currently in its sixth generation, Clark's Shoes is one of the United Kingdom's oldest family-owned businesses and a household name. Some 80 percent of the shares are owned by around 200 individual family shareholders, none of whom owns more than 2 percent, and the balance is owned by employees and institutions. In the early 1990s, years of family feuding came to a head against a backdrop of bad trading results and dividend cuts. In May 1993, the shareholders only narrowly rejected a proposal to resolve the situation by selling the company.

The business that emerged from these crises, although family owned, is managed by nonfamily professionals, and the family council set up in 1993 to help handle the relationship between the family and the Board is regarded as the pivotal governance structure. Features of the council include the following:

- It represents virtually all the family and has its own secretariat paid for by the company.
- There are seventeen councilors drawn from family shareholders and, to be eligible, they require the backing of at least 4.5 percent of the share capital.
- The council meets a fixed four times a year with senior management and the company chairman.
- The council also feeds into the Board via two family members nominated to the Board by the council.
- The council's main role is to inform and educate shareholders and to allow for consultation on issues that require shareholder consent.

Across its twelve years in operation, both insiders and outside observers have become convinced that the family council at Clark's Shoes has worked effectively in securing clarity and a closer understanding and alignment between ownership and management.[3] In 2003 the company won the Family Governance Exemplar at the U.K. Family Business Honours awards.

What happened at Clark's in the early 1990s mirrors the experience at many older family businesses—that as the family grows communication becomes more difficult and can eventually break down. Family directors are dealing with the day-to-day running of the business, so communicating with shareholders is not always their top priority. This is generally fine when the company is performing well, but a distinct change of emphasis is needed when trading becomes difficult and shareholder wealth comes under threat.

### Family Offices

Despite some well-known U.S. models (such as the Pitcairn family office, established in 1923), this concept of how successful family business-people set about organizing the management of their "other" family business—the family's hard-earned assets—is a relatively young one in the United Kingdom.

In the United States the family office industry is substantial and still growing. Multifamily offices (MFOs), which offer services to more than one family, are often formed by a family deciding to open the doors of its single family office (SFO) to other families. This has the advantage of offering the career structure, challenge, and motivation for talented people that the SFO may not, spreading costs and risks across a larger asset base, and providing the opportunity to establish the MFO as a sustainable business.

Compared with upwards of 3,000 family offices (defined in the restricted sense of formal entities "professionally" managing their investment portfolios) in the United States, it is estimated that the United Kingdom has just twenty to twenty-five offices (Close Wins Investment Trusts, 2003). One of the largest UK MFOs is Flemings Family and Partners, established in 2000. Its origins lie in the investment business of Robert Fleming, founded in 1873 and which, as Robert Fleming Holdings, was sold to Chase Manhattan Bank in August 2000. Its target client base comprises family groups, including the Fleming family, individuals, charities, and institutions.

Another well-known example of an MFO is Sand Aire Limited, a privately owned, multiclient family office offering investment management and wealth administration services. Executive chairman of Sand Aire, Alexander Scott explains that the firm was originally an SFO managing the assets of the Scott family, which sold Provincial Insurance in the mid-1990s, and today its stated objectives include the following:

- Helping to develop the vision, strategy, and structures needed for stewardship of wealth
- Providing the professional investment management skills needed to deliver investment performance consistent with clients' objectives
- Coordinating the ongoing financial responsibilities and lifestyle requirements of its clients

The U.K. family office industry covets its privacy and, compared with the United States, very little published information is available. However, it is understood that SFOs are operated, for example, by both the Guinness and Pearson families (Grant Gordon, personal communication, 2005).

## *Board of Directors*

The role of Boards in the governance structure of family-controlled companies has become an important topic for debate in the United Kingdom in the past few years. Recent research has shown that the potential value of a well-structured, balanced, and independent Board is still overlooked by many firms, and that three-quarters of family businesses are run by Boards almost entirely composed of family members (LBS, BDO Centre for Family Business, & IFB, 2003).

Once a family business matures and grows—and becomes substantial enough for shareholder and operational issues to be distinguished—an inability or unwillingness to make use of nonfamily talent at Board level can become a fatal weakness. Family firms are often resistant to change and prone to introspection, and both these traits can be countered by the effective use of outside nonexecutive directors.

So consultants have a key educational role to play promoting and explaining the benefits that independent directors can bring to family businesses:

- Objective and seasoned guidance from successful businesspeople
- Fostering the separation of business policy from family policy
- A more structured and accountable system of corporate governance
- An unbiased sounding-board for family-owned business problems, such as succession
- Mediation, helping the family to resolve disagreements and reduce emotional stresses

- Specialized commercial expertise—either personally or via network contacts—that may not be available internally
- A fresh, creative perspective, helping to generate a climate of trust, openness, and challenge

## MANAGING CONFLICTS AND SUCCESSION PLANNING

### Key Conflicts

The main types of conflict encountered in family businesses can be broken down into four categories: cross-generational; intra-generational; active versus nonactive family members; and family versus nonfamily managers.

- *Cross-generational.* Father-son conflicts are by far the most common type of cross-generational discord encountered and the most difficult to unlock. Psychologists tell us that father-son relationships have a unique potential for conflict, and they represent an area in which the friction between family culture and business culture is brought most sharply into focus. Serious cases of father-son conflict almost always require specialist third-party intervention by a consultant.
- *Intragenerational.* Sibling rivalry and conflicts between husbands/wives and between cousin groups also have the potential to cripple otherwise successful family businesses. It is vital that consultants understand why and how these conflicts develop, and that they are able to communicate this understanding to the parties involved.
- *Active versus nonactive family members.* The outlook, interests, and priorities of family members who actively work in the business are often at odds with those of family members who do not work in it. Nonactive family members interfering in the way the business is being run is always unacceptable. The family puts the Board in place to operate the business and, having done this, their main job is to back that Board and give it full autonomy to do the job it was hired to do. Having a family council can provide safeguards here.
- *Family managers versus nonfamily managers.* Family managers entering the business direct from university and "acting as if they own the place" is a well-known scenario that can generate hostility among nonfamily managers and seriously dysfunctional behavior in a family-owned company. Also, talented nonfamily managers may find themselves running out of opportunities as politics, conflicts, and emotional cross-currents in family firms undermine their work. Fam-

ily businesses have to work extra hard to attract and motivate high-quality nonfamily managers.

## *Managing Succession*

In order to avoid conflict, which can threaten both the business and relationships within the family, it is critical that the basis of any decision on succession—whether succession to key managerial posts or to ownership—be carefully planned and communicated. Those with a stake in the future of the family and the business must be involved in whatever process is used to arrive at these decisions. Key points for consultants are

- start planning early;
- encourage communication and openness;
- promote intergenerational teamwork;
- develop a written succession plan with timescales;
- establish relevant training and mentoring plans for successors; and
- undertake financial and tax planning.

## *EMPHASIS ON SOCIAL AND PHILANTHROPIC RESPONSIBILITY*

This is a subject on which it is difficult to generalize. Some family companies turn over hundreds of millions of pounds a year but give almost nothing to charity, while others with turnover of just £3 million are happy to donate £150,000 to charity every year.

There is, however, a feeling that for family businesspeople in the United Kingdom, philanthropic issues are becoming increasingly important, and a debate is taking place within the family business community concerning the extent to which charitable giving should primarily be a personal or a corporate responsibility. Personal responsibility often wins the day because, although families generally tend to be very supportive of charitable causes, on the whole they prefer to maintain anonymity and a low profile.

The other side of the argument has serious support though, and here there is a cross-over with the broader themes of corporate social and ethical responsibility and corporate citizenship. Some argue that charitable endeavor can and should take place as a corporate initiative, and that, as well as giving money to good causes, no one should feel ashamed if there is also some benefit for the company—for example, "We want to support our community, we can do this by sponsoring community events and, as well as the community benefiting, we should be entitled to make the most of the good publicity we receive in return."

## RESEARCH FINDINGS

The United Kingdom has a limited, although growing, research capability as regards family business issues. Some of the more interesting research findings of recent years include the following:

- *Survival statistics:* Only 30 percent of family businesses in the United Kingdom reach the second generation, less than two-thirds survive through the second generation, and only 13 percent survive through the third generation (BDO Stoy Hayward and London Business School, 1989).
- *Dynastic tendencies:* Within Europe, U.K. owner-managers are the least inclined to establish dynastic family firms and, at fifty-nine years, have the youngest exit rate (Burns & Whitehouse, 1996).
- *The danger of an insular culture:* Three-quarters of family businesses are run by Boards almost entirely made up of family members, and around 60 percent do not have a nonexecutive director (LBS et al., 2003).
- *Anxieties:* Short-term issues of concern for firms surveyed include family communication, struggling with administration burdens, putting off or blocking out unpleasant tasks. Medium-term issues focus on succession plans and skill shortages (BDO Centre for Family Business, 1999).
- *Inadequate preparations for succession:* Although half of the CEOs surveyed expected to retire within six years, 57 percent did not know whether their successor would be family or nonfamily. Most said that if the next generation showed a strong interest, then opportunities would be provided, but there were no plans in place (LBS et al., 2003).

In addition to monitoring such research findings with a view to updating knowledge of their subject, spotting trends, and increasing the effectiveness of their consultancy services, U.K. family business consultants often provide summaries of research reports to their clients. The anonymous and candid responses to researchers' questions they contain can provide insights that help to promote family discussion of difficult and sensitive issues, as well as moving clients toward the liberating realization that they are not alone with their family business problems.

## *FUTURE PROSPECTS*

It is still usually a problem that leads family businesses to seek help, but today they know much more about the subject area than would formerly have been the case—far more information is now available, in the form of books, articles, radio and TV discussion, conferences, and seminars—and this increased sophistication and knowledge bodes well for family business consulting. As explained by one of the contributors to this chapter, Alexander Scott (personal communication, 2004), executive chairman of multi-family office Sand Aire Limited:

> All this extra activity and information will encourage more entrants into the field as family companies capitalize on the assistance on offer. At the same time, the progressively more knowledgeable postwar entrepreneurial generation will increasingly be seeking out support and advice in order to help them ensure successful succession or realization.

Compared with the fully developed marketplace in the United States, family business consulting in the United Kingdom, while expanding fast, has only in the past ten years been accepted as a consulting discipline in its own right. There are grounds for optimism about its future growth and development, but some people point to social and cultural differences that may indicate that take-up in this country is unlikely to approach U.S. levels.

Nevertheless, universities and colleges setting up courses for family members is an excellent sign, hopefully to be followed by the creation of courses specializing in the training of family business consultants. Also, the establishment of a national professional body offering an accreditation system would be a welcome next step in helping to ensure that family business consulting in the United Kingdom achieves its maximum potential.

## NOTES

1. For an interesting recent study examining key success factors and survival characteristics behind some of the U.K.'s oldest family companies, see Tony Bogod, Peter Leach & Rupert Merson (Eds.), *Across the Generations: Insights from 100-Year-Old Family Businesses,* published in 2004 by BDO CFB, London.

2. The University of Gloucestershire launched its family business MBA in 2002, becoming the first U.K. university to offer such a course. John Tucker of Grant Thornton LLP is a visiting fellow at the university and has been closely involved with the MBA course since its inception.

3. This information on C. & J. Clark is based on a presentation given by Judith Derbyshire, company secretary at Clark's Shoes, to the Third National Forum Conference of the Institute for Family Business, London, May 20-21, 2004, and on *The 2003 UK Family Business Honours,* published by JP Morgan Private Bank in association with the Institute for Family Business (UK) and the London Business School.

## REFERENCES

BDO Centre for Family Business. (1999). *Family-owned business: A study of central southern England.* Research report prepared by Bournemouth University Business School. London: BDO Centre for Family Business.

BDO Stoy Hayward & London Business School. (1989). *Staying the course: Survival characteristics of the family-owned business.* London: BDO Centre for Family Business.

BDO Stoy Hayward & London Business School. (1990). *Managing the family business in the UK: A quantitative survey.* London: BDO Centre for Family Business.

Bogod, A., & Leach, P. (1999). *The Stoy Hayward guide to the family business* (3rd ed.). London: Kogan Page.

Bogod, A., Leach, P., & Merson, R. (Eds.) (2004). *Across the generations: Insights from 100-year-old family businesses.* London: BDO Centre for Family Business.

Burns, P., & Whitehouse, O. (1996). *Family ties: A report for the 3i European Enterprise Centre.* London: 3i Group.

Close WINS Investment Trusts. (2003). *UK family offices: A research report produced in conjunction with Cass Business School.* London: Winterflood Securities Limited.

JP Morgan Bank. (2003). Focus: The top 100 family businesses in the UK. *Families in Business, 11*(November-December), 50-58.

London Business School (LBS), BDO Centre for Family Business, & IFB. (2003). *Leadership, culture and change in UK family firms.* Research report prepared by the London Business School. London: BDO Centre for Family Business.

Chapter 18

# United States

Joseph H. Astrachan
Kristi S. McMillan

## INTRODUCTION

Family business has certainly undergone several revolutions since the founding of the field as a separate discipline in the early 1980s, and it is bound to see many more before the legitimacy of the field is taken for granted in the United States. In this chapter we will examine the market in the United States, explore the history of the field, examine the current state of training and the variety of disciplines brought to bear, discuss the many roles consultants adopt in working with family businesses, and finally look at some of the key areas for consulting and prognosticate as to the future of the field. Throughout this article we refer to practices in and features of the family business field and market in the United States, unless otherwise noted.

Family businesses dominate the economic landscape. Astrachan and Shanker (2003) state that using a broad definition of family business (family has effective strategic control of the enterprise), there are 24.2 million family businesses, which represent some 89 percent of all businesses; they employ 62 percent of the workforce, or approximately 82 million people, and account for 64 percent of the gross domestic product (GDP), or about $5.9 trillion. Even using a very narrow definition (multiple family owners, more than one generation of ownership and ownership control), they estimate that 3 million businesses and 29 percent of the GDP are accounted for by family firms. Clearly this is a substantial market.

In their survey of family businesses with at least $1 million revenues and in existence for at least ten years, Astrachan, Allen, Spinelli, & Wittmeyer (2002) found that 39 percent of business leaders expected a leadership change in the next five years and nearly 56 percent expected to experience leadership succession in the next ten years. Given that roughly 30 percent of

*Handbook of Family Business and Family Business Consultation*
Published by The Haworth Press, Inc., 2006. All rights reserved.
doi:10.1300/5491_18

family businesses survive in the family with each generational transition (cf. Ward, 1987), we are faced with a tremendous need for good advice and counsel.

## HISTORY OF THE FIELD

In the 1970s, and to some extent before, a number of consultants and authors identified themselves as primarily consultants to family business. Chief among these are three men, Leon Danco, Harry Levinson, and Richard Beckhard. Prior to these pioneers, there was nary a mention of family business as a form of organization with more than anthropologic merit.

Harry Levinson (1971) applied psychoanalytic concepts to family business. He was an early advocate of the idea that a founder's relationship with his own parents could greatly affect how he viewed and behaved toward his children as well as his motivations for business ownership. Three other authors bear mention: Donnelly published an article in 1964, and Barnes and Hershon published an article in 1976 based on Hershon's dissertation. It could be said of Leon Danco that if there were records in family business consulting, he would have set them all. Among the three pioneers mentioned here, he was the only one to self-identify as exclusively working with family businesses. Danco began working with family businesses sometime following his return from serving in the Navy during World War II. His approach was pragmatic, based in his training in business and economics, and in many ways set the example for the majority of consultants today. By himself, and along with his wife, Katy, Danco wrote many books (L. Danco, 1975, 1980; K. Danco, 1981) that entrepreneurs almost universally felt "spoke to them." Along with his books and articles, Danco also conducted many seminars which began to draw recognition that family businesses had a unique set of challenges and enormous strengths. Danco's many "disciples" include noteworthy "second-generation" consultants and scholars John L. Ward, Don Jonovic, Ross Nager, Francois de Visscher, and Craig Aronoff.

Richard Beckhard had a pivotal role in the development of the field, particularly as it relates to consulting. In the late 1970s and early 1980s he noticed that many of his clients as well as people attending his training sessions at the National Training Laboratories (NTL) were family business based and that they had issues that were different in character from non-family businesses. His approach was based in humanistic psychology and social psychology. He organized, in 1983, what can be considered a pivotal event in the field: a special issue of the journal *Organizational Dynamics* (summer issue) that was entirely devoted to family business (Beckhard &

Dyer, 1983). Later he organized a group of young scholars and family business owners in his apartment in New York and seeded the organization that now serves all who work with and research family companies: The Family Firm Institute, officially started in 1985. Beckhard's many disciples included the first president of FFI, Barbara Hollander; the first editor of *Family Business Review,* Ivan Lansberg; and other second-generation leaders, including Fredda Herz Brown (1998), Gibb Dyer, and Kathy Wiseman. Other second-generation leaders not tied to a particular "guru" include John A. Davis, Ernesto Poza, Nancy Drozdow, Pat Frishkoff, David Bork (arguably a first-generation leader), Nancy Bowman Upton, and many others too numerous to mention (Upton, Vinton, Seaman, & Moore, 1993). (See Chapter 1 for a more elaborate history.)

The field underwent a rapid expansion and intellectual development in part due to a demographic bubble in the United States in which a large number of businesses founded post–World War II had founders rapidly approaching sixty-five years of age or more. In part because of the issues these founders faced and the disciplines of origin of the earliest consultants in the field, the earliest approaches to family business consultation stressed psychological understanding, systems thinking, and an emphasis on a facilitative approach in which families are responsible for making their own decisions and consultants primarily enable conversation and decision making.

Since the mid-1980s the field has grown dramatically. Important events include the founding of the journal *Family Business Review,* which was first published in 1988, the development of ongoing academic programming for family businesses at Oregon State, Baylor University, and Kennesaw State Universities in the mid-1980s, and the development of special interest groups and training in a variety of professions including law, insurance, and accounting. Yet until the mid-1990s, there was scant focus on research and training in family business consulting.

## CONSULTANT TRAINING

Two efforts dovetailed to create better training for family business consultants, but much more is clearly needed. The first book on consulting was by David Bork and his team at the Aspen Group (Bork, Jaffe, Lane, Dashew, & Heisler, 1996). A more recent one by Jane Hilburt-Davis and Gibb Dyer (2002) provides useful reading content for all consultants. The first discussions of organized training and credentialing took place in the Board of FFI as early as 1992. Several consulting groups formed, in part to ensure training and standards of service, including Hubler-Schwarz, Doud-Hausner, the Aspen Group, Metropolitan Associates, Lansberg-Gersick Associates, and The Family Business Consulting Group. In large part, and to varying degrees, these groups took it upon themselves to train and develop their consultants. Much of this training can be characterized as on-the-job training.

A key player in training today, and perhaps the best source of all-around family business consulting training anywhere, is the certificate program developed by the Body of Knowledge (BOK) Committee of FFI. This program involves extensive training in a unified approach to consulting as well as specific education in the many disciplines relevant to the business and family consultative process. The program also includes self-reflection and a formal mentoring program. Various professional organizations also provide some limited training for their members, including associations in law, accounting, and psychology.

The basic approach taken by much of the training in family business consultation is systems based, emphasizing the interacting components of the family business system, including family, extended family, ownership, management, and governance (business and family). The field mostly arose from a psychological orientation, so training tends to emphasize a variety of issues from behavioral and managerial sciences, such as organization development, leadership, and family relations. Generally an emphasis is placed on collaborative training, as much of the work with family businesses requires several specialties.

Much of the training includes is a strong emphasis on balancing family unity and health with business prosperity. One unique problem is determining who the client is. Some stress the entire system; others designate the client as the person or group that retained the consultant; and for others, it is either the business or the family. This is an area in need of further consideration, as it is not clear what the consequences are for focusing on each specific area.

While training programs are developing, outside of traditional legal or accounting work, no process for quality assurance has been established, and there are few models outside of large consulting companies that have their own mechanisms for client feedback and quality assurance. We predict that at some point growing pressures from the market will require a licensing or other quality assurance function that includes knowledge development and continuing education.

## *FIELDS*

At this point in the development of the field of family business consulting, no clarity exists in what fields of origin (law, psychology, accounting, etc.) take precedence (cf. Kaslow, 1993). Indeed, it seems that enough room is available in the market for nearly everyone to define themselves as a family business consultant. It is common to hear stories of older practitioners who state, "I am a family business consultant; I have been working with family businesses for years," or seasoned consultants complain, "Everyone is getting into it nowadays." The variety of fields all have a role in serving the client and perhaps all add significant value. As Cross (2004, p.8) acknowledges, "There is little consensus in the field about how family business consultants can best serve their clients." We now turn to the fields and where they are with regard to family business consultation today.

Marriage and family therapists/psychologists offer a view as to developing family health, repairing family damage and trauma, and improving the family's capacity as a whole to have direct conversations that lead to resolving long-standing conflicts, greater collective understanding, and commitment to the future of the family business. The focus on the family can lead to the view of the business as a problem in the life of a family. At times, the family therapist can use the business and how family members view it as a diagnostic object in the system.

Psychology plays an important role in dealing with individual issues (e.g., alcoholism, substance abuse, narcissism, oppositional defiant disorder), but perhaps plays an overall role in every aspect of the consultative process, particularly as it relates to understanding personality and motivational issues. There have been numerous examples of psychologists seeking to specialize in working with family businesses as an alternative to working with the pressures of the current health care system from which most derive their living. However, as with practitioners from the other core disciplines, many have not acquired the additional specialized training we believe is needed.

Conflict management is a relatively new field that has much to offer the world of family business consulting (Astrachan & McMillan, 2003). It stresses seeking the overlap in interests between disputing groups in order to seek a creative solution. It does not assume that all conflicts can be resolved, but instead makes the point that they can be managed. It also does not assume that disputants can resolve problems on their own.

General management consulting, strategy consulting, and the fields of organizational behavior and organizational development have not yet made great inroads into the family business arena, even though many consultants inherently imply an action-research methodology borrowed from organizational development approaches. These professions do understand that technical and emotional issues run hand-in-hand (Babicky, 1987). It is certainly possible that more integration of these arenas into the family business field can occur. A major obstacle may be that unlike the fields mentioned previously, these disciplines and the ones to be discussed next do not generally lend themselves to thinking about the dynamics of the family dimension.

The "harder" disciplines of law, accounting, and finance have been working with family businesses since their earliest days yet are only recently recognizing in a significant way the importance of the family element as it relates to the business. These specialties are absolutely necessary in every business's life, and the knowledge of these disciplines offers great value for those in the more psychologically oriented disciplines who may not otherwise understand the complex exigencies of business life (Swartz, 1989).

In the many fields that are relevant to family business consulting there is an increasing recognition of the need for and acceptance of family business consulting. There is some confusion as to what family business consulting entails, which we will deal with later. It is clearly more than succession planning. From our observations, family businesses that are older and larger are more likely to engage a family business consultant than smaller, younger ones. In part, this has to do with the price of a consultation and the lack of a body of research that conclusively demonstrates that family business consulting has a positive long-term benefit. On the other hand, it may be that smaller and younger businesses avail themselves of family business consultants less often than their larger and older counterparts because few consultants are available yet, and these consultants are targeting wealthier, larger, and older prospects.

## CONSULTANT'S ROLES

In a recent dissertation examining what it is that family business consultants do, Cross (2004) identifies multiple roles consultants say they have. His first split is between expert advisors and process consultants. He notes that several authors have suggested that an effective family business consultant needs to be both a process consultant and an expert advisor. Expert roles include advice, education, and planning. Among the process roles, Cross identifies several: facilitation, improving communication, and creating structure. Other roles also include mediation, conflict management, and coaching.

The process roles are deemed of utmost importance, with a reliance on the families themselves making the decisions. A widely held belief suggests that the more a family does the research, communicates, and makes decisions, the more the decisions will be agreed with, committed to, and acted upon. We will explore the structure-creating roles in the next section, as the creation of structures seems to be among the most popular of consulting interventions.

No standard for fees has been established in family business consulting. The various roles, levels of expertise, region of the country, and length of time in the field are related to the amount a consultant charges. The range today seems to run from a low of $1,000 per day all the way to $10,000 or more per day. The more the consulting is connected with an accounting or law firm, the more likely it is to fall within their typical standard fee ranging from $100 to $1,000 per hour. Some project price, while others ask a large retainer for unlimited time over the course of a year, negotiated every year. We recently heard of one accounting firm–led project to help unite a family of more than fifty people that included interviews, a report, feedback sessions, and next step implementation that was quoted at over $100,000.

Perhaps unlike other parts of the world, there is no predominant culture of the country. Consultants need to be sensitive to the ethnicity or mix or ethnicities of the families with whom they work. There is a need for more thinking in this area.

Consultants need certain identifiable personality characteristics and skills, including high tolerance for conflict and chaos, empathy and objectivity, listening skills, emotional intelligence, and toughness and compassion. These were all agreed to by the panel of consultants Cross surveyed in his dissertation, and these traits underlie the potentially emotional and conflict-laden context of family business. Cross's panel was composed of consultants that had been in the family business field for at least ten years, and they were all Fellows of FFI. The final fifteen panelists were narrowed from a much larger pool, and their selection was geared to promoting a diversity of disciplines, gender, and age in respondents, and also to ensuring that no two panelists were in the same consulting group.

The field today is still quite diverse and evolving. People are still largely feeling their way forward. Cross's (2004) research shows no widely accepted view exists to define what a family business consultant does or should do. Similarly, no commonly held views of measures are available to gauge the success of a consultation. And perhaps most notably, no studies have explored the long- or short-term efficacy of family business consultation or various interventions.

## TYPICAL CONSULTATIVE PROCESS AND RECOMMENDATIONS

The typical consultation very much follows the classic organization development or action research process. The assignment begins with the contracting phase in which expectations are explored and set, interviews are held in which information is collected and trust between consultant and client are established and reinforced, an analysis of family dynamics and business issues is done, feedback is given in which the consultant reports findings to the system, and action planning and implementation undertaken. Most feedback includes elements of family, management and business strategy, and ownership issues.

A number of common recommendations are often made in the consultative process. The two main categories are processes and structures, and agreements or policies. Of the many structures, recommending the creation of several are generally considered good advice. Some of these actually have a basis in research. For example, Astrachan and Kolenko (1994), in their research on human resources practices, found that Boards of Directors, family meetings, and strategic planning are all correlated with multigenerational succession success and that succession planning was not. We will now look at several frequently used structures before turning to typical policy recommendations. These structures include family meetings, a family council, a family office, a Board of Directors, family philanthropy, and strategic planning.

Family meetings are recommended as a way to strengthen the family and build unity. Their secondary purpose is to provide a forum for the discussion of the business of the family and provide an arena for the family to develop opinions about major business issues and policies. As such, meetings may explore family history and values, the family mission and whether it has changed, communication, education policies, and conflict management (Aronoff & Ward, 2002). Most consultants recommend that family meetings be facilitated by outside professionals.

Closely related to family meetings are family councils. This structure is generally recommended for larger and more sophisticated families. A family council is a representative body that carries out the business of the family, much like family meetings do. Because it is a representative body, it can be smaller and more efficient. It is generally a good idea to have limits set on the council's authority, so that it can make some decisions by itself but the family is clear when a decision is of enough import that it requires the approval of the entire family. Meetings and councils can be funded by the business, but there is not a universally accepted opinion as to whether this is essential.

Family offices provide a more formal mechanism to preserve and protect the family's assets and provide for the family. They are an outgrowth of family diversification, and typically their primary function is to protect the more liquid assets of the family (see Chapter 19 on family offices). They often have a fairly sophisticated investment staff, and common wisdom is that a family should have more than $100 million liquid to have their own office. Some have stated that number should be upwards of $250 million, yet today others are recommending lesser amounts and multi-family offices have been established. In addition to managing family investments, family offices provide a number of key services that help keep the family unified, including coordinated legal and tax services, insurance management, and often a variety of "concierge" services, such as real estate maintenance, travel arrangements, bill payment, purchases, and other related services.

Philanthropic initiatives come in many varieties, from family foundations, directed giving from the business, and coordinated individual charitable giving. All of these activities can have multiple benefits to business-owning families (Danco & Ward, 1990). Most family foundations and coordinated individual giving activities have the need for leaders who coordinate family activity and provide a liaison with the activities and charities with which the foundation and family is involved. These leadership and liaison roles can provide real opportunities for family leadership development. These leadership roles have the added benefit of being both important and not threatening to the family's core assets. Following the activities of the various organizations in which the family has a charitable interest can also provide many learning opportunities for other family members who can become more directly involved in the various organizations. We have already noted the importance of developing family unity, and family members interacting through a family philanthropy can use these common activities to develop greater unity and family harmony. A family philanthropy can also aid the core business in the types of charities pursued and in promoting the family name and reputation of the business. Last, organized philanthropy can provide a mechanism by which the values of the family are promoted, practiced, and transferred from one generation to the next.

A Board of Directors can be one of the most important structures implemented by family business owners. According to Astrachan et al. (2002), of the businesses they surveyed (at least ten years old and sales of more than $1 million), more than 87.5 percent had Boards with at least three members, yet only 29.3 percent of Boards met three or more times per year. Those meeting more often were far more likely to rate the contribution of the Board as being good or outstanding. Fewer than 10 percent of Boards have nonfamily members who are not employees on their Boards. Having a Board provides many advantages. Astrachan, Keyt, Lane, & McMillan (2004), suggest that the primary purpose of a Board for family enterprises is to hold management accountable. As such, a Board provides an important source of credibility to the company which can aid in establishing good relationships between the company and owners and among owners. Boards provide meaningful roles for qualified family members with interests in the business who have pursuits other than business management. Boards can also ensure good strategic planning, revitalize organizational direction, and aid in conflict management.

Strategic planning is the last mechanism to be described here. It involves continuous assessment of the strengths and future of the company. In family businesses this often involves planning for family and business (Carlock & Ward, 2001). Additional benefits of strategic planning, particularly when it involves family owners, is that the family enhances members' commitment to the business and family, and the employees of the company may be motivated to act in a common direction. This, in turn, makes common goals more widely accepted and recognized, which serves to further limit conflicts. Although it is an important mechanism, family businesses report that less than 40 percent have a written strategic plan (Astrachan et al., 2002) and it is likely that even fewer have an ongoing strategic planning process.

A second domain of consulting recommendations is the writing of agreements, which are often represented as policies (Aronoff, Astrachan, & Ward, 1998) or a collection of policies known as a constitution or protocol (Gallo & Tomaselli, 2004). The idea behind the development of policies is that families can communicate and reach agreements before problems occur. It is a good idea to discuss and resolve issues before they happen, otherwise they can become too emotionally laden to resolve. While not conducted on U.S. family businesses, the research of Gallo and Tomaselli clearly shows that the greater the level of family involvement in the development of policies, the greater the satisfaction with them and the greater the efficacy of the policies.

A number of policies are popular currently. For example, Astrachan et al. (2002) report that 28.3 percent of businesses surveyed have entry policies that define the criteria, and sometimes the processes, that family members must meet in order to become employed by the company. They also found that 54.5 percent have shareholder agreements. This relatively high prevalence is most likely because this is a common practice promoted by the legal community. Among businesses, 37.7 percent have formal liquidity agreements in which all issues in the buying, selling, and transferring of stock are defined. Interestingly, they found that only 9.7 percent had existing prenuptial agreements in place that family members are expected to have signed before finalizing plans to get married. Constitutions can contain other policies, such as those that define how decisions will be made, communication rules, codes of ethics and conduct, family mission and vision statements, retirement and exiting from the business, promotion, compensation, dividends, as well as policies about how family members will transact business with one another outside of the business, including investing in one another's ventures.

## MAJOR CONFLICTS

We believe, as Kaye (1991) argued, that in family business conflicts, family members are rarely fighting about what they say they are fighting about. Rather, with each expressed conflict years of other accumulated issues may be involved, causing the emotionalism of the situation. A strong emotional tone tends to characterize family conflicts, particularly those in the workplace (Kaye, 1991). This emotionalism means that standard methods for resolving disputes may not work. Many causative factors may be undergirding emotional reactions, including conscious and unconscious memories of childhood experiences (Astrachan & McMillan, 2003).

One major category of conflict comes from the differences in the ways in which businesses and families operate. Conflict often arises when one party approaches an issue from a family perspective and another from a business perspective. Such issues include norms of equality and collaboration (family) as opposed to norms of merit and competition (business). Another classic example is the norms of relationship protection as opposed to norms of relationships as means to an end. Closely related to this is that family conflicts often spill over into the workplace (Karofsky et al., 2001), and the workplace environment often exacerbates a family conflict and inhibits its resolution.

A related issue is the role of nonfamily employees who are used as pawns in a family conflict, or who stimulate conflict by taking sides with conflicting family members. Even without this dynamic, family conflict with nonfamily employees has a different character.

Among the many other common conflicts in family business are those that emanate from age- and gender-related issues. Older-generation family members reportedly are conflict averse and less willing to let go of power in the family and business systems than younger-generation family members are. This often leads to substantial disagreements, particularly in relation to succession and successor development when next-generation leaders seek opportunities to take risks and to lead. An indication of such succession-related conflict can be seen in the fact that 42 percent of CEOs who expect to retire in five years have not yet chosen a successor (Astrachan et al., 2002).

Gender issues seem to arise in typically male-dominated industries where female successors are not considered or are discounted. We see some attenuation in this typical conflict; in fact Astrachan et al. (2002) found that 34 percent of firms currently report that the next CEO may be female. With 52 percent of firms reporting female family members being employed full-time, one might suspect underlying gender-based preferences are still prevalent. Gender-based conflicts also present themselves in the estate planning process in which a male bias is still common.

## CASE EXAMPLE

This case study exemplifies the struggle to build family unity while maintaining business success, a central theme in a majority of family business consulting assignments. It shows the complex nature of family business consulting, including balancing family relationships while working on keeping the company healthy. Last, it describes a typical five-step consultative process, of contracting, interviewing, diagnosing, giving feedback, and recommending or implementing action.

This family business is a fifty-year-old second-generation trading company located in the Southeast. The youngest of four siblings made the initial contact with the consultant. She was looking for someone who could help professionalize the business by assisting in role clarification as well as the resolution of conflict between two siblings. Recognition of conflict and simple ways to solve it are often presented by consulting prospects during initial contact. But as this case demonstrates, presenting issues and underlying issues are rarely the same.

The four siblings were left to run the business after the sudden loss of their father, the founder. The business did not have a succession plan and the four siblings had equal ownership of the company, with their mother retaining voting control. The mother was very reluctant to step into the battles among her children. Not only was a succession plan lacking, but the conflict between two of the siblings was so deep that one was ready to leave the business; vocal and near-violent arguments occurred frequently. The company was profitable and growing at a modest and steady pace. However, morale had begun deteriorating due to the constant fighting between the two siblings and the lack of a clearly identified leader. The other two siblings felt forced to mediate and try to maintain some sort of peace and calm in the office.

The engagement began by communicating with the sibling who contacted the consultant. The initial contract was to conduct interviews and provide feedback to the siblings as to the challenges they faced as an ownership and leadership group and to provide some routes to addressing those challenges. A variety of information was collected from interviews with the siblings and their mother, reviewing several years of financial statements for the business, as well as shareholder agreements and any other documentation pertaining to the business that could help to determine the health of the business and the shareholders' rights.

It is important to note that the consultant repeatedly assured all family members that the client is the entire family business system. This is critical to building trust, because being viewed as any one actor's agent severely limits the ability to influence the system and to facilitate discussion.

The interviews were open-ended and meant to give each member a chance to tell his or her story. Each interview lasted approximately two hours, thus taking a full day for the initial interview stage. This format allows the consultant to gather information without having a set of questions that could be perceived as leading the family and company in a predetermined direction. The information gathering phase of the process also allows the consultant to determine which areas need to be focused on first by listening for the conflicts and issues that are raised again and again. Any statements made by family members are kept strictly confidential. Information is shared in a way that protects confidentiality and is communicated as coming from the consultant as issues that need work.

In this case, one reported area of contention that was consistent among three siblings was that one sibling had not reported ownership in a side business that could be in competition with the family business. There was a need for further investigation among the family members to determine if this was in fact a real threat, and if so, how they would go about resolving this issue. An additional source of conflict was that one sibling was occasionally rude, bordering on hostile, to family members, employees, and customers.

This growing list of issues begins to underscore the need for both business experience in family business consulting and an understanding of family dynamics. The business, as stated previously, was successful, but it was clear the conflict between two of the siblings was so deep that it had the potential to destroy the business. As is common in such situations, historical family issues were clearly interfering with the way business relationships were being carried out, and business issues added fuel to historical family rivalries and infighting.

The consultant reported back to the initial contact at the end of the interview phase in order to plan for a second visit to include a structured feedback session followed by facilitated dialogue. The two areas that were of most importance, in order to move forward and work on other issues, were the side business of one sibling and the conflict between two of the siblings. Until these two issues were resolved, it would be difficult to work on any other areas of the business without the risk of stirring up further conflict or false agreement on any policies set forth.

The family agreed to a meeting facilitated by the consultant. Prior to the meeting, the consultant met with each family member to discuss some of the issues and to get an initial indication on how each would behave in the meeting. This was done to further trust building with the consultant, uncover any new relevant information, and develop methods for dealing with tension that was likely to arise during the meeting. The meeting with the four siblings proceeded with the blessing of their mother, whose stated goal was for her children to be able to live and work in harmony. She was not included in the meeting so as to increase the willingness of the children to be open, which they often were not in the presence of their mother.

The facilitated meeting was highly contentious. One sibling had decided that he could no longer work with another sibling under any circumstance. Epithets and insults were plentiful. Two of the siblings felt they needed more time for a due diligence study in order to determine whether there was a true conflict of interest regarding the side business. Over the course of the meeting, the probability of maintaining family harmony while the two siblings in conflict remained in the business together became less likely. The consultant communicated to the family that two people in the system had differing goals, not only personally but also in terms of their views of the business. One saw the opportunity for growth, which would require risk, while one was satisfied with the status quo of the business. The consultant practiced many facilitation techniques during this meeting, including rephrasing, playing devil's advocate, reinterpretation of statements, and brainstorming options.

By the end of the meeting the consultant had concluded that as long as one sibling refused to even attempt reconciliation, the hopes for family harmony needed to become secondary to ensuring the business' longevity, which ultimately would allow the family to regain harmony. The consultant recommended that the two siblings willing to get along discuss whether they wanted to continue to encourage the family conflict by enabling the two feuding siblings to work together. The advice given was that if the two siblings would have a low consequence context in which to renegotiate their relationship, perhaps they could build enough trust to allow them to work together once again.

After several weeks, the conciliatory siblings decided they would ask the obstinate sibling to leave the business and gave him the option of selling his ownership and future interests. He was not *forced* to sell, in order to leave the option for his return open. Upon the consultant's advice, they clearly stated that he needed to work out his relationships and become a more collaborative partner. It is important to note that company dividends were substantial, so this move would not significantly financially harm the sibling being asked to leave. The sibling with the side business voluntarily, with much encouragement from the consultant, contributed shares of ownership in his side venture to his three siblings.

The following year saw the establishment of a Board of Directors. The sibling who left the business, after much distress and psychotherapy from local professionals, has calmed significantly and is enjoying new pursuits. The remaining siblings have continued to keep the door open for his return. Last, their mother, who required much counsel in order to not derail this chain of events, has become happy that her children once again willingly assemble for holidays.

As with all family businesses, ultimate success of a consultation cannot be easily measured. In this case, the family was stabilized and systems were put in place to facilitate further family communication and cohesion, as were mechanisms to promote thoughtful business decision making and financial success.

## THE FUTURE

The future is bright. It will also pose many significant challenges. Chief among these is the need to protect the credibility of the field as a whole. We strongly believe that this issue is larger than the competitive forces among consultants (and between individual consultants and small groups, and large law, accounting, and finance firms' family business divisions), and we urge family business consultants in leadership positions to investigate these concerns, lest they become a problem too great to overcome. We ought to practice what we advise our clients to do and discuss future problems before they are problems. In this case, if a credibility gap starts to grow, it is likely that blame slinging will become the order of the day, rather than solution seeking. We say this because the first challenges to credibility would come from a dissatisfied market that can identify individual sources of dissatisfaction, be they people or companies. Problems in credibility are not individual problems; they are the responsibility of the whole field.

There is also a need for sound research into which consulting interventions actually work, under what circumstances and with what success. While the models that people use to consult have developed well, such research will promote better development of techniques and interventions as well as the theories that undergird them. We vigorously disagree with consultants who claim that consulting is an art form and that family businesses are too complex to be studied in this manner.

The Internet is fast becoming a powerful tool for the development of consultants and for publicizing consulting itself. The amount of information available can easily enable consumers to become more aware of the consultative process and the variety of expertise available. People are taking great advantage of these resources. One consulting company we are familiar with reports several thousand visits per month by users of its family-business-oriented site. In many places on the Web examples of reports, agreements, and structures are increasingly available. This innovation is two-sided, as it can help the well situated or hurt those who need more than copying or adapting the agreements utilized by other family companies.

It is not clear at this point in the development of the field whether independent consultants, family-business-focused consulting companies, or more traditional consulting companies will end up dominating the field. Perhaps the answer will lie in the ability of those serving the field to act collaboratively and to make the future of the field, rather than immediate income, an urgent priority.

## SUMMARY AND CONCLUSION

Family business consultation in the United States has a young history and, in our opinion, a very bright future, with a large market, little competition, and great need for service. Adding to the positive situation is that many concepts from other disciplines are relevant to family business consultation, which means some models are already available for this work. In short, a systems approach seems necessary, and standard organizational development and action research models seem to apply well: a repeated cycle of contracting, information gathering, diagnosis, feedback, and action.

Family business consultation has some key differences from typical management consultation, in that the systems are often complex, family dynamics play a critical role, and the needs of the family often seem to be at odds with the needs of the business. Capitalizing on these differences requires a fair amount of training in a broad knowledge base of disciplines (including law, finance, business, psychology, and family systems) or working in consulting teams with a variety of professionals. It has also been shown, perhaps due to the complex and often sensitive nature of these systems, that professionals need a number of personality characteristics to be effective, such as being a good listener, empathetic, and patient.

While there is a good deal of clinical experience and many anecdotes from which to draw, and a variety of interesting theories about consultation available, one of the greatest weaknesses and biggest threats is that family business consulting today is at best loosely based in science. There is great cause for concern about the lack of research on the efficacy of consulting methods, approaches, and interventions. We still do not know what works, when, why, for whom, or for how long. Likewise, we do not know when we, as consultants, are inflicting unintended damage. We should all reflect on the fact that at one point in the recent past, as late as the 1950s and 1960s, many in the medical community continued to recommend the use of tobacco for a variety of ailments (Mahaney, 1994; Annals of Hopkins, 2004). This was in the face of the first published research suggesting a link between smoking and cancer as early as 1912 with very well-received studies being published as early as the 1940s. Clearly, as in medicine, we need more research, not just on what works, but what is harmful as well. Our sincere hope is that as bright as the future is now for family business consulting, that we practice self-monitoring behavior and exercise care and concern in order to help the future remain bright.

## REFERENCES

Annals of Hopkins. (2004). Puff daddies. *Hopkins Medicine,* Spring/Summer. Available online at http://www.hopkinsmedicine.org/hmn/S04/annals.cfm.

Aronoff, C.E., Astrachan, J.H., & Ward, J.L. (1998). *Family business policies: Your guide to the future.* Marietta, GA: Business Owner Resources.

Aronoff, C.E., & Ward, J.L. (2002). *Family meetings: How to build a stronger family and a stronger business.* Marietta, GA: Business Owner Resources.

Astrachan, J.H., Allen, I.E., Spinelli, S., & Wittmeyer, C.B. (2002). *2002 American family business survey.* Alfred, NY: George and Robin Raymond Family Business Institute.

Astrachan, J.H., Keyt, A., Lane. S., & McMillan, K.S. (2004). *The Loyola guidelines for family business boards.* Chicago: Loyola University Chicago.

Astrachan, J.H. & Kolenko, T.A. (1994). A neglected factor in family business success: Human resources practices. *Family Business Review, 7*(3), 251-262.

Astrachan, J., & McMillan, K.S. (2003). *Communication and conflict in family business.* Marietta, GA: Family Enterprise Publishers.

Astrachan, J.H., & Shanker, M.C. (2003). Family businesses' contribution to the US economy: A closer look. *Family Business Review, 16*(3), 211-219.

Babicky, J. (1987). Consulting to family business. *Journal of Management Consulting, 3*(4), 25-32.

Beckhard, R., & Dyer, W.G., Jr. (1983). Managing continuity in the family-owned business. *Organizational Dynamics, 12*(1), 5-12.

Bork, D., Jaffe, D.T., Lane, S.H., Dashew, L., & Heisler, Q.G. (1996). *Working with family businesses: A guide for professionals.* San Francisco, CA: Jossey-Bass.

Brown, F.H. (1998). The "softer side" of consulting to business-owning families: Understanding our clients and ourselves. *Family Business Review, 11*(3), 193-205.

Carlock, R.S., & Ward, J.L. (2001) *Strategic planning for the family business: Parallel planning to unite the family and business.* London: Palgrave MacMillan.

Cross, K. (2004). Family business consultation: A modified Delphi study. Unpublished doctoral dissertation, Purdue University, South Bend, IN.

Danco, K. (1981). *From the other side of the bed: A woman looks at life in the family business.* Cleveland, OH: University Press.

Danco, L. (1975). *Beyond survival: A business owner's guide for success.* Cleveland, OH: University Press.

Danco, L. (1980). *Inside the family business.* Cleveland, OH: University Press.

Danco, L., & Ward, J.L. (1990). Beyond success: The continuing contribution of the family foundation. *Family Business Review, 3*(4), 347-355.

Gallo, M.A., & Tomaselli, S. (2004). Family protocols in Spain: A survey on 10 years of experience. Family Business Network and International Family Enterprise Research Academy Annual Conference, September 8, Copenhagen, Denmark.

Hilburt-Davis, J., & Dyer, W.G. (2002). *Consulting to family businesses: A practical guide to contracting, assessment and implementation.* San Francisco, CA: Jossey-Bass/Pfeiffer.

Karofsky, P., Millen, R., Yilmaz, M.R., Smyrnios, K.X., Tanewski, G.A., & Romano, C.A. (2001). Work-family conflict and emotional well-being in American family business. *Family Business Review, 14*(4), 313-324.

Kaslow, F. (1993). The lore and lure of family business. *American Journal of Family Therapy, 21*(1), 3-16.

Kaye, K. (1991). Penetrating the cycle of sustained conflict. *Family Business Review, 4*(1), 21-44.

Levinson, H. (1971). Conflicts that plague family business. *Harvard Business Review, 49*(March-April), 2.

Mahaney, F.X., Jr. (1994). Oldtime ads tout health benefits of smoking: Tobacco industry had doctors' help. *Journal of the National Cancer Institute, 86*(14), 1048-1049.

Swartz, S. (1989). The challenges of multidisciplinary consulting to family-owned businesses. *Family Business Review, 2*(4), 329-339.

Upton, N., Vinton, K., Seaman, S., & Moore, C. (1993). Research note: Family business consultants—Who we are, what we do, and how we do it. *Family Business Review, 6*(3), 301-311.

Ward, J. (1987). *Keeping the family business healthy.* San Francisco, CA: Jossey-Bass.

# PART IV:
# A KALEIDOSCOPIC OVERVIEW

Chapter 19

# Economic Change Viewed Through the Family Office Window: The Multifamily Office in a Changing Global Economy

Dirk Jungé

When my first grandchild arrived earlier this year, my perspective on the future and the past shifted several degrees. I experienced the awe of grandfathers everywhere. Eight pounds feels like nothing, but holding your child's son is an event of great weight.

The uncertainty of today's world adds to the trepidation we naturally have when our families grow. I was fortunate that a few days before my grandson was born I had watched the coverage of the memorial for Ronald Reagan. On that day the world honored a former leader of the United States, a land where hopes and dreams are attainable. He was an example of the resilience of the human spirit even in adversity as threatening as an assassination attempt.

The cycle of life, beginnings and endings, makes me optimistic. It gives me hope for future generations and emerging leaders. The arrival of a new family member brought me to the intersection of my personal life and my professional life. I have devoted most of my career to helping families manage their wealth and achieve their dreams. Now, I have begun planning for my grandson's financial future.

Currently, I am the Chairman of the Pitcairn Financial Group, which began as a classic family office. Family offices and multifamily offices (MFO) are small, private companies designed to serve one or more wealthy families. A staff of accountants, lawyers, personal assistants, and wealth managers create investment strategies, handle family taxes, set up trusts, conduct family meetings, and perform many other tasks.

The knowledge of wealth management handed down by my predecessors and what I have learned over the course of my career combine to benefit the members of the Pitcairn family and the other families who make up

*Handbook of Family Business and Family Business Consultation*
Published by The Haworth Press, Inc., 2006. All rights reserved.
doi:10.1300/5491_19

our MFO, Pitcairn Financial Group. I am grateful for the heritage that is central to my life and the resulting opportunity it gives me: helping other families prosper.

Today, I think with added intensity about the many challenges faced by wealthy parents and grandparents. How do we protect our children and grandchildren from the lack of purpose and the overindulgence that so often affect wealthy young people? How do we instill the values, knowledge, and wisdom that our children need for fulfillment? How do we help them continue the legacy of wealth, family unity, productive work, achievement, and philanthropy for future generations?

Family offices and the expanded versions known as multifamily offices are described in detail in this chapter. The first few sections describe the role and contribution of such organizations. The final section is a case study of the Pitcairn Financial Group. It includes a list of dates that were key to its evolution.

## SEA OF CONFUSION

Change in the global economy and the growing number of individuals and families with significant wealth drove much of the evolution we have seen in family wealth services.

In the 1980s and 1990s, financial institutions expended much of their marketing and sales resources on institutional clients, which reflected the dramatic increase in pension, profit sharing, insurance, and endowment assets.

As the institutional market began to retrench in the mid-1990s, these same firms began to redirect their resources and strategies in hopes of capturing the emerging private client wealth that was being created from the exploding stock market, stock options, and generational wealth transfer.

In the past few years, banks, investment management companies, accountants, brokers, and financial planners began to market these as wealth management services. Their corporate quarterly reports in 2003 and 2004 cited the potential for significant profit from these services.[1]

Wealthy families that are evaluating potential providers ask consultants such as Kathryn McCarthy,[2] former managing director of Rockefeller & Co., Inc., to compare MFOs to other institutions that provide financial services. They are familiar with traditional service providers, such as bank trust departments, sophisticated tax and estate planning consultants, registered investment advisers, and accountants who file family taxes and pay bills for them.

Often clients have been working with, for example, six advisers from four different organizations. They are overwhelmed by the many brands, and they have a long list of unanswered questions. For example:

- What standards should they expect from service providers?
- How much interaction with the providers is appropriate?
- What do the fees cover?
- How can they reduce the stress of uncertainty when evaluating options?
- What do they need to do to safely preserve their wealth for future?

They are truly in a sea of confusion.

Consultants and other observers have witnessed a wave of naive and misleading advice, duplicated services, unanticipated costs, and contradictory recommendations. McCarthy says that much of the confusion is attributable to the nature of the changing industry. As more and more firms take on the mantle of "wealth management" and interpret that category differently, the term loses meaning. One firm may provide simple investment management; another may do only estate planning and tax consultation. Families fear that traditional service providers will recommend investment products likely to create the most income for their organization rather than those that might be more beneficial in a family's specific circumstances.

Tom Livergood,[3] who founded Family Office Management, LLC, points out that wealth management services provided by a traditional organization do not include all of the services provided by a family office or MFO. Another important factor in choosing between MFOs and other organizations is the latter's tendency to package services instead of customizing them to a family's specific interests or needs. Consultants caution families about the lack of expertise in traditional organizations, which are less familiar with the expense and challenges of serving the higher net worth market of families, typically defined as those with investible assets of $50 million or more.

## FEES FOR WEALTH MANAGEMENT SERVICES

A recently released study by Bloomberg (Beer, 2004) detailed a typical fee-structure of revenues for family offices and MFOs and reported the median revenues for the 64 companies they identified as family offices or MFOs.[4] In the following chart, the high dependence on asset-based fees, which are squeezed tighter and tighter by the competitive marketplace, highlights the importance of communicating the added value of expertise.

| Revenue Source | Percentage of Revenue |
|---|---|
| Asset-based (excluding trust) fees | 70 percent |
| Annual retainer fees | 25 percent |
| Trust administration | 13 percent |
| Hourly individual fees | 5 percent |
| Net-worth-based fees | 5 percent |

The varied approach to fees increases the confusion in the wealth management marketplace. Many traditional organizations do not publish all of their fees, and they do not disclose fee-sharing arrangements or commissions earned from third-party providers.

Most charges for financial services fall into three categories:

1. Asset-based fees
2. Hourly fees
3. Comprehensive annual retainers

Today, the cost of financial services typically reflects a combination of fee types. This industry trend is expected to continue, along with the confusion it creates in the marketplace. The ability of the MFO to clearly communicate the costs of a broad spectrum of services is one of its key benefits. There are many others.

## BENEFITS OF MULTIFAMILY OFFICES

Most people sit down several times a year to think about the big picture of their finances. That may be when their lives change significantly or when they prepare for a scheduled meeting with a financial consultant. The first step is creating a list of the areas to be reviewed and updated.

### Review Status for Financial Planning

1. Investments
2. Tax planning
3. Estate planning
4. Charitable giving
5. Insurance coverage

This innocent-looking list triggers a whirlwind of phone calls, meetings, fees, and sometimes difficult family discussions. The list grows longer as the level of wealth and complexity of the family situation increases. When we translate this brief list into locations on a map, we see the real picture (see Figure 19.1). The typical family visits their advisers at their offices on a schedule convenient for each.

Multifamily offices provide most services and invite other providers to meet with their clients in one location (see Figure 19.2). Wealthy families value the full-spectrum of services offered by a MFO, which includes the coordination of the roles and responsibilities of other trusted advisers. The decision makers responsible for significant wealth focus on the following priorities, in addition to tailoring services to the circumstances of each family member.

### Control

Families want and need to participate in decisions about investment vehicles, growing the family wealth, distributing it, educating family mem-

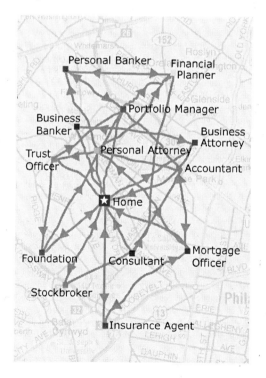

FIGURE 19.1. Families are faced with time-consuming challenges when meeting with multiple advisers.

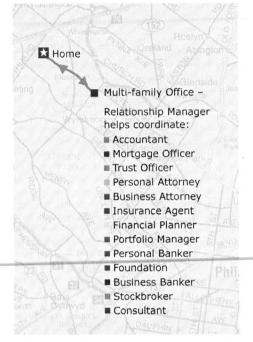

Multi-family Office –

Relationship Manager
helps coordinate:
- Accountant
- Mortgage Officer
- Trust Officer
- Personal Attorney
- Business Attorney
- Insurance Agent
- Financial Planner
- Portfolio Manager
- Personal Banker
- Foundation
- Business Banker
- Stockbroker
- Consultant

FIGURE 19.2. Multifamily offices help simplify the process by inviting advisers to meet in one location. (*Source:* Pitcairn Financial Group, 2004.)

bers about the responsibilities it carries, and taking advantage of tax benefits.

### Convenience

Running from adviser to adviser naturally motivates families to find an alternative. Families want to reduce the complexities of their finances, integrate their accounts and accounting, and implement holistic plans that take into account every aspect of their financial lives.

### Confidentiality

Concern about confidentiality is intense. Public interest in the wealthy has increased with ease of communication. Computer hackers continue to successfully attack the Web. Serious risks related to the physical security of family members are compounded by concerns about terrorism. Identity fraud via the Internet continues to make the headlines.

## Continuity

The strength of a family office is its continuity, which adds to its cumulative expertise and its understanding of family members and their goals. The financial industry changes along with other businesses. Long-term employment has virtually disappeared in our industry. The cost of expertise escalates when highly trained personnel are in demand. Mergers and acquisitions blur the roots of traditional institutions. Continuity creates the island of stability known as a family office or MFO in the sea of confusion seen elsewhere today.

It gives family offices and MFOs economies of scale and allows an organization such as Pitcairn to negotiate collectively for services that benefit its expanding client base. Each new business phase builds on the organization's history and experience, and this allows it to focus on growing wealth rather than simply maintaining it.

## Communication

Frequent communication with staff members, family members, and other clients is not the only key to success. Quality of communication is paramount. Does the newsletter, correspondence, or conversation tell clients what they want and need to know? Is each message relevant and timely? Is it accurate?

Communication is part of the way Pitcairn conducts its business. For example, we believe in transparency of fees, because it helps build trust and keeps family members and other clients informed. They are more comfortable with the services they receive if they have a better understanding of what they cost. Clients know that nothing is really free in the financial world.

Another of the principles important to the success of the family office or MFO is the following:

Disclosure = Trust = Satisfaction

Pitcairn symbolizes the importance of transparency through constant reference to our past as Pittsburgh Plate Glass Company (now PPG Industries), which provided the wealth of our family and the ability to offer other families the benefit of what we have learned over the past eighty-plus years.

Pitcairn client Arnold Zaslow, executive vice president and treasurer of ATD-American Co., recently explained that this expertise and long-term experience sets a family office or MFO apart.[5] He finds it easy to be enthusiastic about investing through a company that puts his money in the same place as their own family money. Add to that benefit the cultural compatibility of advisers who enjoy a similar lifestyle. Zaslow talks with a Pitcairn staff member almost once a week. And, one evening in 2004, he invited members of the Pitcairn family to join his family at a dinner meeting, where they talked about challenges they faced.

Zaslow likens MFOs to trusted automobile maintenance and repair shops:

> You do not keep your car in the finest running condition by taking it to one shop to check the distributor, another to tune the engine, and a third to repair the exhaust. You take your automobile to a shop that has expertise in all of these parts. They are best able to coordinate these activities in the most meaningful way. They are accountable, and you benefit immensely from their coordinated work.

## CHALLENGES OF FAMILY AND MULTIFAMILY OFFICES

Of the many challenges the family and multifamily office industry face, the most significant obstacles to be overcome are simply a reflection of changing times.

1. The Malthusian effect: Thomas Robert Malthus (1983) wrote in 1799 that poverty and distress are unavoidable because of population growth.
2. The redistribution of wealth due to taxes, especially estate taxes.
3. Acceptance of family dynamics that allow and expose conflicts related to wealth and power.
4. Low-cost competitors who identify themselves as the equivalent of family offices and MFOs.
5. Advances in technology, which have helped create a transaction mentality and give families online shopping cart financial services.

These five examples of obstacles, along with other challenges facing family offices and MFOs, might discourage wealthy families from establishing a family office of their own. On the other hand, the likely benefits compel others to consider the option seriously.

## OPTION: CREATING A FAMILY OFFICE

A family office or MFO serves as the primary source of financial advice, which means that a long list of questions must be answered when exploring this option. The starting place is understanding the end goal. What do the best family offices have in common?

Barbara R. Hauser, special counsel at Cadwalader, Wickersham and Taft,[6] identified these qualities in a *Journal of Wealth Management* article in 2001. She described the best family offices in the United States as those

> headed by someone who deeply understands the unspoken role of taking care of "everything" and "everyone" in a way that creates a very special home for the family. All of the services can be outsourced, but the primary staff must be the active, available conduit, always keeping the personal interests of the family in mind. . . . Filled with warmth and care, backed by capability and competence, these are the family offices that will endure. (p. 22)

With those qualities in mind, the research can begin. The first step is to determine whether the family office will be a for-profit business or strictly a service model that runs at cost. Choosing one model or the other is critical. Mixing the two structures creates conflicting priorities that end up frustrating everyone involved.

- When would the office need to be operational? How long would the various steps take? What is the capital required to fund it?
- The amount of liquid assets to be managed may present the need for a reality check. Are the expert resources available at an affordable cost?
- Should the family create the office, buy one, or join another organization? What resources are available? What should be outsourced? Consultant Tom Livergood reports that shrinking profits force MFOs to outsource highly specialized and labor-intensive services such as alternative investments and bill paying. What vendors are reliable?
- Can the family afford the high cost of the professional expertise needed?
- How would the office be organized? Who would govern it? What structure will reflect most appropriately the family's position on generational governance? Corporate governance defines how a company conducts its business, including the ethical standards and accountability applied to its leadership and employees. It provides for oversight of the company's management and leadership activities and assigns

specific authority and responsibilities to ensure that a business is well run and that all stakeholders—clients, owners, and employees—are treated fairly.
- Are the expectations of the family in line with what the organization can provide with the funds available?

### INDUSTRY TRENDS

Wealth management services once available only to the extremely wealthy are now accessible through MFOs. More options are available to baby boomers, who are expected to transfer trillions of dollars in assets to younger generations in the coming years.

Also, MFOs have overcome the conventional wisdom that blood and money do not mix. On the surface, sharing the management of shared money seems impossible. Yet families have only to implement and support a viable business structure. Three factors are essential.

1. Families must also keep in mind that inheritance is a process, not an event.
2. They must decide as a group to work through an organization or trustees so that no damage to the family fabric occurs. Adopting a business approach and a clearly defined governance structure prevents the negative impact of greed.
3. Good corporate governance enables family offices and MFOs to implement effective business processes and ultimately to prosper.

Generally, the economic health of family offices and MFOs is recovering, but they are highly vulnerable because of the confusion in the marketplace. To attract clients, MFO leaders have work to do.

Kathryn McCarthy and other industry consultants encourage MFOs to differentiate themselves in the marketplace. Otherwise, we risk losing potential clients to traditional financial organizations touting their less robust wealth management services. Differentiation from these organizations means building awareness to the point that the category of family offices and MFOs is widely recognized and has a clearly understood business model. Single-family offices can remain viable only if the family wealth is great enough to offset the cost of the necessary expertise.

Also, we must communicate the importance of the unique historical backdrop. For example, Arnold Zaslow compares working with Pitcairn to having a crystal ball: "The Pitcairn family has experienced the challenges we face and overcome them. They can advise us, because they know what works. We can follow their success."

Acquisitions of family offices and MFOs are growing, because their services are the building blocks of asset acquisition for other wealth management service organizations. Competitors interested in acquiring family offices or MFOs have a long list of attributes that they use to evaluate potential acquisitions. Advanced technology is high on the list. This interest in technology is primarily related to the expertise it represents: understanding what information, how much, and how it should be organized to build new wealth.

Pitcairn Financial Group Chief Information Officer Dain Kistner, also a Pitcairn family member, indicates that wealth management software is readily available. It is the in-depth understanding of wealthy clients and family members that makes it powerful. Connecting everything that we know about clients helps us define the strategy that fits them. It is a cornerstone of quality service.

Family Office Management executive Tom Livergood notes that today 50 to 60 percent of assets are invested through traditional institutions. About 20 to 30 percent of asset placement is managed by the asset owners. The remaining 10 to 30 percent of asset placement is up for grabs.

Another positive for family offices and MFOs is that journalists are now better informed about our organizations. They now do an improved job of explaining the differences. McCarthy believes that new competition makes MFOs more approachable and willing to talk to press to promote themselves and their unique services.

## CASE STUDY: PITCAIRN FINANCIAL GROUP

With our long-term heritage as a family office, we have an unwavering commitment to maintaining our proud record of honesty and integrity. We serve the needs of a diversified clientele, including individuals, families, family offices, foundations, and endowments. Pitcairn also partners with other trusted advisors and provides investment advisory services through other leading financial service firms. Because integrity, honesty, and communication are at the core of our company values, our clients profit from a close, engaged working relationship.

We have found that long-term wealth management is an integrated endeavor, well beyond the practical aspects of pure money management. We believe in tightly defined personal wealth strategies and clear lines of communication, in addition to exceptional performance and service.

Colleagues and potential clients often ask about the impact of economic change on the Pitcairn family over the past thirty years. What factors drove the decision to become a MFO? What role did family growth play in the decision? How did other factors changing the industry affect Pitcairn? Did the influx of new clients change the family's sense of ownership or act as a confirmation of their own pride and the company's resilience? Why did large numbers of Pitcairn family members continue their affiliation with the family office when the policy of free association was adopted?

Understanding the policy of *free association* is central to the future of our industry. Because family members can choose to obtain services elsewhere, they compare their opportunities with the family office with opportunities at other organizations. They become more aware of the benefits of their current affiliation. Or, they choose another.

For the Pitcairn family, our legacy plays a key role in maintaining the family financial bond. Today's generations feel pride and connection through their roots.

Second, the nature of our financial strength creates an interest in and benefit from affiliation. We extensively use long-term tax-advised multigenerational trusts, which have a built-in longevity. The 2004 MFO clients are income beneficiaries, but they respect and balance their needs with those of future generations—their remainder interests.

Third, the vast majority of Pitcairn family members share a common faith. Our faith encourages the investment of time and talent in work, family, and philanthropy.

One of the most important factors that has shaped the decisions made by the Pitcairn multifamily office in recent years is the increasing competition for professional talent in the financial industry. An understanding of the affluent family and the impact of change on their wealth is cultivated over a long period of time. Competing for clients means also competing for staff members who have that rare expertise. A growing business and the opportunity to share in the resulting profits not only invigorates and challenges these professionals, but also builds loyalty among professionals of this caliber.

Today, Pitcairn is well capitalized and poised for future growth. The breadth and depth of our resources demand patient, long-term capital. In addition to our full compliment of internal capabilities, we have many resources outside the company doors add to our stature in the minds of our clients and others in the financial industry (see Exhibit 19.1).

## *Corporate Governance*

The Pitcairn family office made corporate governance a top priority long before the issue became a hot topic in the industry. We regularly review our policies. We fully updated governance processes in the late 1990s.

As a private enterprise, Pitcairn Financial Group is not subject to the same corporate governance regulations as public companies. On the other hand, parts of our business are in the public domain. Pitcairn Financial Group, as a state-chartered trust company, is regulated and regularly examined by the Pennsylvania Department of Banking, and our mutual funds are regulated and examined by the SEC, governed by the Investment Company Act of 1940, and subject to the Sarbanes-Oxley Act of 2002. At Pitcairn, our goal is to meet the standard of corporate governance equal to the best private organizations and the standards applied to public companies.

We know that a financial service will prosper only if a clear and explicit corporate governance policy is in place at every level. When stakeholders know how the organization works and how decisions are made, their expectations

## EXHIBIT 19.1. Key Dates

The earliest examples of family offices developed in Europe, where powerful banking families, such as the Hamburgs and the Rothschilds, formed offices to manage their family wealth. The Pitcairns were among the prominent industrialists who established family offices in the United States.

1883    John Pitcairn co-founded Pittsburgh Plate Glass Company.

1913    The Pitcairn family broke ground for the Swedenborgian Cathedral.

1916    John Pitcairn's estate grew to almost $20 million.

1923    Three brothers formed the Pitcairn Company with their inherited assets of $32.6 million to consolidate their voting control of the PPG stock. The PPG stock made up 87 percent of the assets. The newly established family office took responsibility for management of family assets.

1960s   Long-term stewardship and commitment contributed to the success of PPG and benefited all shareholders, including the Pitcairn Family.

1970s   In the first fifty years, Pitcairn Company assets grew from $36 million to over $200 million, and the company paid out more than $750 million in dividends.

1980s   The company formed a Family Advisory Council and an Auxiliary Board made up of potential leaders. They took on the responsibility for identifying family and client concerns, recommending resources, and those with the expertise to educate family members on business issues, coordinating regular clan gatherings, and handling special Board projects.

The organization created a formal statement of mission and Pitcairn principles, along with a detailed succession plan.

The need for liquidity resulted in the sale of most Pitcairn Company assets, including the family's control block of PPG Industries stock.

The family instituted a free association policy to allow family members to seek alternative service providers.

In 1986, the firm moved to new headquarters at One Pitcairn Place in Jenkintown, Pennsylvania.

*(continued)*

*(continued)*

> Family members formed Pitcairn Trust Company in 1987 and a year later offered services to non-Pitcairn client families.

**1990s**  Three third-generation family members, seven fourth-generation family members, and one fifth-generation member served on the Board.

Pitcairn celebrated its seventy-fifth anniversary in 1998.

The company partnered with a key, objective consultant, Aspen Family Business Group,[7] to survey clients of Pitcairn Trust about their needs and concerns. The survey findings helped inspire

- a renewed entrepreneurial spirit,
- a reenergized focus on helping make Pitcairn Trust the new PPG Industries,
- a revitalized education program, and
- an overhaul of the governance structure.

By 1999, Pitcairn Trust Company managed $2.2 billion in assets for more than 300 clients in the 50 states, Europe, Canada, and Asia. Eighty Pitcairn family members held $1 billion in assets, and 220-plus non-Pitcairn clients held $1.2 billion in assets.

**2004**  Pitcairn continues to benefit from our long-term capital as we embark on our plan for growth. A new name reflects a new vision for the MFO: Pitcairn Financial Group.

Pitcairn opened its first regional office on the Main Line of Philadelphia in St. Davids, Pennsylvania, and began plans for a second regional office in Northern Virginia.

This branch of the Pitcairn family is now in its sixth generation of common and shared financial interests.

are realistic. Governance acts like glue to hold family and business relationships together. The Investment Policy Statement is just one example of a governance tool that we use to define client expectations and to guide our actions on behalf of the client.

Strong corporate governance helps us improve business processes and distinguish ourselves in the financial community. Not only is it the right thing to do, but it also creates a competitive advantage.

Poorly implemented governance structures and policies ruined the financial security of many Americans, cost corporations their financial success, shattered the credibility of numerous corporations, and sent their highly regarded leaders to prison. Examples appeared in news reports around the world.

- The status of charges against Janus Capital Group, Bank of America Corporation, FleetBoston Financial Corporation, Bank One Corporation, and Strong Capital Management Inc. were summarized in an April 2004 report on MSNBC.com.
- The painful impact of scandal on mutual fund companies was reported in September 2004 by *USA Today* (Waggoner & Dugas, 2004):

   The Securities and Exchange Commission and state regulators hit the miscreant funds with fines, but investors have administered brutal punishment by yanking billions from them. Lipper, the mutual fund tracker, says that scandal-tainted funds watched $155.6 billion flee from September 2003 through July, the latest figures. Untainted funds gained an estimated $128.6 billion.

- In October 2004, an article by Charles Gasparino in *Newsweek* questioned anew the ability of Wall Street to issue unbiased research. He reported that Fannie Mae's top five underwriters had continued their upbeat assessments despite growing signs that Fannie Mae was facing financial difficulties.

In some cases, an organization's integrity and ethics are severely compromised, but change can restore its reputation. The public corporation Tyco, for example, was a highly publicized case of corporate misconduct; since then Tyco has made the elements of governance relating to leadership and management accountability their top priority. It appears they are successfully rebuilding their business.

The goal of the Pitcairn Financial Group is to be the gold standard. We must demonstrate to all of our stakeholders that our commitment to integrity and accountability is among the strongest in the financial service industry. If the investment industry does not repair the breach of trust with investors, economic recovery could be short-lived.

Good governance begins at the top: the Board of Directors, Board Committees, and Management Committees. At Pitcairn, these groups are charged with ensuring that business is conducted in a thoughtful and prudent way. Committees regularly review our processes to ensure that we apply sound business practices to strategic planning, business planning, and all of the fiduciary relationships we assume on behalf of our clients. Following reviews, the committees present feedback to the Board.

Pitcairn has a Code of Ethics and a Code of Conduct that clearly set forth high standards for all constituents with respect to these two areas prone to conflict of interest issues. Reviews of governance and ethics go hand-in-hand. We set and maintain high standards for our clients, owners, and employees. Integrity has always been highly valued: in our advice, in our products as far back as Pittsburgh Plate Glass, and in our services.

## Pitcairn Financial Group Services

Based on our years of experience as a family office and later a MFO, Pitcairn Financial Group recently refined our list of services. These are some of our priorities:

1. Establish and monitor estate and financial plans.
2. Assess personal risk and identify risk tolerance level.
3. Determine investment objectives and establish an appropriate strategy.
4. Identify and implement appropriate steps to lower tax liability.
5. Evaluate and recommend appropriate changes to budgets and cash flow.

These services are broken down into a comprehensive matrix. Education is on the list because the continuation of each family's values depends on transmitting them to the children. Our clients do this through family meetings, retreats, conversations, employment in the office, and auxiliary boards. We encourage families to have fun as a group, through activities such as honoring elders and family talent shows. These events lessen the frustrations that are natural in families. As the number of family members grows, education increases in importance. Individuals need to feel included. The distribution of leadership typically becomes more democratic; family member participation broadens the power base, ultimately developing a democratic process.

## CONCLUSION

Multifamily offices have weathered economic storms. We have unique expertise that we can share with confidence and gain fulfillment through a job well done. We know what challenges we face, and we recognize the benefits offered to our clients.

We can meet the most significant challenges for family offices and MFOs today by adopting an important principle: Unity.

Potential clients are at sea because of the confusing marketplace. Leaders of family offices and MFOs must help them understand:

1. The differences between the services offered by our competitors and the full spectrum of services we provide
2. The effect of these differences on their family's financial security
3. The importance of a multigeneration financial strategy
4. The opportunity to grow family wealth for generations to come

We clearly define our space in the financial services industry. When I examine the financial services market today and see the number of firms positioning themselves as trusted financial advisors, I believe that family offices and MFOs should be able to legitimize their claim to this important role given their unique understanding of the human, social, intellectual, and financial capital of their multigenerational family clients. It is a beginning, like the arrival of my grandson, of a new generation. We can define and communicate our value and differentiate ourselves from others in this marketplace.

Family offices and MFOs are vital, viable organizational structures fashioned to help complex, affluent families manage their assets—financial and emotional—and to educate successor generations. The Pitcairn multifamily office has been chronicled to illustrate the nature of such an office.

## NOTES

1. Examples from quarterly report summaries, news summaries, and press releases were retrieved from *The Wall Street Journal Online* at http://online.wsj.com/home/us. They are as follows:
   — "S&P Affirms Sun Life Assurance Co. of Canada Ratings." Dow Jones Newswires; July 29, 2004.
   — "News Wrap: Merrill Lynch Net Rises 10 %; Revenue Nearly Flat." Dow Jones Newswires, July 13, 2004.
   — Edward Taylor, "UBS Posts 28 percent Earnings Gain, But Expects Slower Second Half." *The Wall Street Journal,* August 11, 2004, C5.
   — "First Republic Bank Acquires Interest in Cypress Wealth Advisors." Dow Jones Newswires, July 27, 2004.
2. Comments by Kathyrn McCarthy provided through personal communication, August 16, 2004. McCarthy is the former managing director of Rockefeller & Co., Inc., family office.
3. Comments by Tom Livergood provided through personal communication, August 16, 2004. Livergood is CEO and founder of Family Office Management, LLC, which promotes education and advocacy through conferences, publishing, consulting, and events. FOM is also the founding firm of Family Wealth Alliance, LLC (The Alliance).
4. This article reports the findings of a study completed with the cooperation of the Family Office Management, Oak Brook, Illinois. The firms reported an extensive menu of family-office services. The minimum average of assets in multigenerational client relationships was set at $4 million, and 25 percent of the firms' revenues were produced by these relationships.
5. Comments by Arnold Zaslow provided through personal communication October 26, 2004. Zaslow is executive vice president and treasurer of ATD-American Co. and a Pitcairn client.
6. Cadwalader, Wickersham & Taft LLP is a prominent global law firm with offices in New York, Charlotte, Washington, DC, and London. The firm traces its roots back 200 years and has long-standing relationships with many of the world's premier financial institutions.
7. The Aspen Family Business Group, headquartered in Fort Worth, Texas, is the premier international consulting resource for families in business. They have more than a century of experience helping families to maximize the potential of their business, promote family harmony, sustain positive family connections through the generations, and use their wealth and financial resources to serve their families.

# REFERENCES

Beer, K. (Ed.). (2004). Special report: Multifamily offices. *Bloomberg Wealth Manager, 6*(7), 75-86.

Gasparino, C. (2004, October 18). Wall Street covers its Fannie Mae [Electronic version]. *Newsweek.* Retrieved November 4, 2004, from http://www.msnbc.msn.com/id/ 6214018/site/newsweek/.

Hauser, B.R. (2001). The family office: Insights into their development in the U.S., a proposed prototype, and advice for adaptation in other countries. *The Journal of Wealth Management, 4*(3), 22.

Janus may pay $200 million in fines [Electronic version]. MSNBC. Retrieved August 12, 2004, from http://msn.com/id/4839052.

Malthus, Thomas Robert. (1983). In A. Greenhall & J.S. Levey (Eds.), *The concise Columbia encyclopedia* (p. 511). New York: Avon Books.

Waggoner, J. & Dugas, C. (2004, September 3). Painful year for funds in scandal [Electronic version]. *USA Today Online.* Retrieved August 12, 2004, from http://www.usatoday.com/money/perfi/funds/2004-09-03-funds_x.htm.

Chapter 20

# Managing Wealth, Liquidity, and Growth in the Global Family Business

François M. de Visscher

It is no mystery that the Western world is experiencing one of the most dramatic transitions of business leadership and family wealth in history.

The massive wealth created in the economic expansion years of the post–World War II era is now shifting to the most populous generation of all time—the baby boom generation. Many old family companies have already disappeared in that transition, victims of fierce forces of destruction from inside and outside. Yet many have survived. For those who have endured, a certain sense of relief and complacency tends to settle in once they get through their transition. However, the handing down of power and money is not an end point. *"Ces nouveaux heritiers qui doivent inventer l'avenir,"* as the French newspaper *Le Figaro* calls them—these new heirs who must invent the future—have a whole new set of challenges.

In Europe, expanding a family business entails facing unparalleled competition from well-capitalized nonfamily enterprises, which are taking advantage of the continuing opening of the European Economic Community (EEC). The new members of the EEC have become great safe-havens to relocate to and to compensate for the increasing social cost of businesses in "Old Europe." In Latin America, the opening of trade zones has forced many family businesses to transition from operating as monopolies in their own country to competing in much larger open markets. In the United States, the vast majority of family businesses are becoming "niche players" with high value added and a need to accelerate their growth to defend their position in the economy. So, it is no mystery that today's globalization requires vast amounts of capital for businesses to survive and to navigate the global waters.

*Handbook of Family Business and Family Business Consultation*
Published by The Haworth Press, Inc., 2006. All rights reserved.
doi:10.1300/5491_20

While family businesses have vast "capital needs" to global competition, family ownership and generation succession creates large "liquidity needs" among an expanded shareholder base. Companies that want to maintain family control and ensure survival of proper business and family governance must balance the capital needs of the business and liquidity needs of the shareholders. Balancing capital needs, liquidity needs and family control is essential to the survival of family companies and is depicted in the triangle in Figure 20.1.

These three issues—capital, liquidity, and control—often conflict as shareholders view their role as managers who want to grow the business, as owners who are looking for return and liquidity, and as family members who want to maintain the family heritage, tradition, and stewardship of the business beyond their current generation. The difficulty of balancing control, liquidity, and growth capital is further exacerbated by the many transitions that family businesses face when exposed to global economic and global family factors.

## *LIQUIDITY NEEDS OF THE FAMILY SHAREHOLDERS*

As a family company transitions from one generation to the next, it embraces more numerous and increasingly diverse shareholders, each with their own lifestyle, needs, and liquidity demands. At each generation, the business has its own challenges of balancing capital, liquidity, and control.

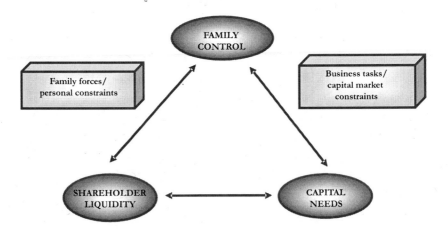

FIGURE 20.1. The Family Business Triangle. *Source:* Trademarked by de Visscher & Co. LLC.

## Founding Generation

The founding generation usually owns all the shares. Although they can certainly cash in on the value of the company at any point, most founders would never dream of doing so. They are, after all, in the mode of building a company and its value, not milking it. As an owner/operator, the founder(s) is more interested in supporting the growth plans of the business—for a potential exit down the road—rather than distributing liquidity. Achieving liquidity through dividends or capital realization is secondary to the desire for economic wealth and social status. This is not to say that founders do not have any liquidity aspirations, but these are part of an overall wealth and estate plan of the owner, which includes his or her legacy, philanthropy, and wealth diversification.

## Partnership Generation

The next generation—the "partnership generation"—may have several siblings and cousins owning shares. Some will work in the company, but others are not active in the management of business. Shareholders involved in the management of the family company are compensated as employees, collecting salaries and other incentive compensations. These "management shareholders" are instinctively more interested in reinvesting cash flow to continue to build the business, as their professional achievements will be a function of this growth. On the other hand, shareholders not active in management of the company see dividends and shareholder distributions as an important, if not essential, financial benefit of owning the inherited shares in the family company. The "nonmanagement shareholders" will inevitably have a bias toward a larger distribution of profits in the form of dividends or redemptions. Geographic distances may further exacerbate the dichotomy between active and passive, between management and nonmanagement shareholders because they further diminish the attachment to the roots of the business and the place of the family in the local community. Reconciling the liquidity objectives of the nonmanagement shareholder with the goals of management shareholders to conserve cash in the business for growth investment is the fundamental financial challenge of family businesses at the partnership generation.

## Coalition Generation

If the company is fortunate enough to transition to a third or fourth generation, a "coalition" of owners will now exercise control over the business.

During this "coalition generation," the number of shareholders will have grown, as will the proportion of shareholders not active in the business. Those who work in the business represent a small number compared to "nonactive" shareholders. The disparity among the owners group will increase along with the increased number of active and inactive shareholders, of different ages and even different generations, geographically disbursed throughout the world, and living in different social environments. In most cases, nonmanagement shareholders no longer depend on the revenues of the business to live and will seek outside professional income. Each member of this coalition generation owns relatively small interests in the company, and their need for liquidity from the family business will evolve. The few shareholders involved in the management of the business will be compensated as most executives are with salaries, perks, and incentive compensation packages. Their ownership in the family business is comparable to stock or stock options owned by management of large public companies. The large majority of nonmanagement shareholders, with relatively small ownership interests in the family business, evaluate their ownership in investment terms, bringing in the notion of risk and return, appreciation value, and liquidity flexibility. Hence it is no surprise that the liquidity challenges of coalition generation family businesses center around two fundamental issues: return on investment and liquidity flexibility.

In most successful coalition generation family businesses, we observe close collaboration between family members involved in management and those who are not. The management shareholders depend on stable "patient capital" of the entire shareholder group to support future business growth.

### Stewardship Generation

In Western economies the family business "stewardship generation" is beginning to evolve. When the management resources of the family have been exhausted and the family seeks outside management to take over the family business, the role of the family is to steward the patient capital for future generations. The family is now guided by investment principles and stewardship objectives of the patient capital for the generations to come.

Table 20.1 illustrates the unique financial and liquidity challenges of each generation in the development of a family business (Aronoff, Ward, & de Visscher, 1995).

The current generation transition underway adds complexity to the shareholder liquidity challenges of the family because of the generational conflicts they create between the senior generation and the younger baby-boom generation. Older members tend to approach growth and investment

TABLE 20.1. The stages of family business financial evolution and revolution.

| Stages | Conflicts/issues | Liquidity/capital sources |
|--------|------------------|---------------------------|
| 1. Founder Generation (Owner/operator) | Balancing personal cash flow with business capital needs<br><br>Ownership transfer | Business cash flow |
| 2. Partnership Generation (Sibling/partnership) | Increasing liquidity needs of shareholders, especially inactive shareholders<br><br>Providing financial incentives for active shareholders<br><br>Meeting strategic capital needs of the business | Business cash flow<br><br>External debt or equity financing<br><br>Internal recapitalization |
| 3. Coalition Generation (Cousins/collaborative) | Expanding capital needs of the family business<br><br>Liquidity flexibility needs of multiple minority shareholders<br><br>Transitioning from family ownership to family control | Ongoing liquidity programs<br>Internal recapitalization<br>Outside capital from<br>   Public and private equity sources<br>   Business alliances<br>   Joint ventures<br>   Disposing of assets |
| 4. Stewardship Generation | Corporate strategic development<br>Wealth diversification<br>Long-term family strategy<br>Philanthropy<br>Management of shareholder expectations<br>Professional asset management services | All of the above plus a family office for<br>   Internal liquidity<br>   Stewardship of patient capital<br>   Diversification of family wealth |

*Source:* de Visscher & Co. LLC.

initiatives with excessive prudence, being primarily concerned about liquidity and estate planning. The younger generation tends to be more interested in the growth of the family business.

This complex combination of constantly changing forces impacts the nature of ownership and control that the family is able to exercise. Because control is different at each stage of evolution, liquidity needs and business capital needs must be addressed differently from one stage to the next (Gersick, Davis, Hampton, & Lansberg, 1997).

## GROWTH CAPITAL NEEDS
## OF THE FAMILY BUSINESS

Just like any other business, family businesses need capital to grow. More than ever in today's global economic landscape, size and scale are critical components of shareholder value creation. Therefore, growth is no longer a choice for a business but a necessity for its survival. "Be number one, two, or three in your product or market or else," according to the global economic mode. Fortunately for family businesses, size in the global information age is defined by market reach and not just by physical assets. So a family business with strong brands, a loyal and dedicated employee base, and a long-term investment orientation can actually compete very effectively with the multinational giants. Globalization and the information age are windfalls for family businesses, not handicaps.

The global growth of a business is defined in its four components in Figure 20.2. The growth in existing markets with existing products (Organic growth on Figure 20.2) is often referred to as the "defensive growth strategy" against large, often well-capitalized, global competitors. Internal cash flow will most likely finance defense of one's markets or products, as it is difficult to raise outside capital on the premise of a defensive growth strategy.

Taking existing products into new markets (Product expansion on Figure 20.2) extends the family business core competencies into new territo-

|  | Existing products | New products |
|---|---|---|
| **New market** | **Product expansion**<br>Local financing<br>Mezzanine debt<br>Private equity | **Company reinvention**<br>Joint ventures<br>Spinoffs<br>Corporate reorganizations |
| **Existing market** | **Organic growth**<br>Internal cash | **Product innovation**<br>R&D financing<br>Venture capital |

FIGURE 20.2. Four components of global growth and financing. *Source:* de Visscher & Co. LLC.

ries, new countries, and new economic regions. This growth strategy will require two engines to succeed: communication technology and a strong local or regional distribution and marketing network to sell and bridge the cultural differences of entering new regions of the world. Capital sources are amply available in global capital markets to finance product expansion because the product has a track record or brand in its existing markets of origin. In some cases, new plants or acquiring physical assets in new markets can find successful financing by local sources, banks, or private investors/ partners.

New products in existing markets (Product innovation on Figure 20.2) require strong research and development efforts and commitment of the family company. Investing in technology is a critical component of growth in a global market. Development of new products and new technologies and protecting one's intellectual property require increasing outside investments. Venture capitalists and other technology investors would be the most likely financing sources for such projects.

Finally, family companies also can orient their growth toward new markets with new products (Company reinvention on Figure 20.2). This is often the riskiest of the four strategies because of the unproven status of the new products and the cultural novelty of the new markets. New products also require significant investments for either an acquisition, green-field marketing, or construction investments. Because of the risks involved in those investments, a family business would be well advised to share the risk of this strategy with an outside investor or new partner from the new market.

Growing a family business in global markets will inevitably invite two new types of owners outside of the family. Outside equity or quasi-equity investors, who have invested growth capital in the family business, have their own liquidity and control expectations. Competing in a global economy will also require the company to attract top-quality outside management, who will also expect to enjoy participating in ownership through stock options or other incentives programs. Suddenly the family business must embrace three types of owners with different expectations and liquidity horizons.

Capital needs are bound to start competing with liquidity needs of this diverse group of owners. Family owners, who represent patient capital, have the longest time horizon but still require some ongoing liquidity. Management equity, which increases based on performance, expects medium-term liquidity. Outside investor equity, which provides transitional capital, insists on relatively short-term liquidity.

## FAMILY CONTROL IN THE FAMILY BUSINESS

Family control and governance structures in this competing environment for capital and liquidity become increasingly important yet complex cornerstones of family business stability. The family must create a strong control structure that can unify the family yet ally it to outside sources of capital. The family control structure can also facilitate liquidity measures for family shareholders and reinforce the family heritage, an intangible but integral part of shareholder value.

The role played by these family control and governance structures evolves over time from a mostly financial and estate-planning tool to a family-management tool. Management shareholders should welcome the establishment of family structures that will take care of the business of the family and allow the management to focus on business growth. A family council is often a vehicle that can represent all factions of the family and handle issues such as family events, shareholder communication, and family liquidity issues. The family council is not a second Board of Directors. Delineation of responsibilities between the Family Council and the Board is a critical task. For instance, the Family Council may be in charge of studying and promoting liquidity programs for the shareholders, while the Board of Directors may take charge of aligning liquidity desires or recommendations with the capital needs of the business.

When the family reaches the coalition or stewardship generations, the objectives of the family governance structures expand from communication and liquidity planning to family wealth planning. This is often the time when a family will establish a family office to address the overall wealth-planning needs of the family. The family office becomes a helpful tool to reinforce the ownership of the family, plan for continuity of family wealth, including its liquidity needs, and serve as a catalyst for intra-family communications.

## PATIENT CAPITAL IN THE FAMILY BUSINESS

What becomes of family companies that fail to address the growth capital of the business, the liquidity needs of the shareholders, and family control objectives?

One example, XYZ Company, provided liquidity to one branch in the family by incurring excessive leverage to buy out some existing shareholders. As a result, the company's cash flow was largely dedicated to repayment of the debt, and hence not available for growth investments. The overly leveraged company became limited in its ability to compete globally.

This resulted in loss of value, a loss of confidence by the remaining shareholders, and the ultimate distress sale of the company.

On the other hand, the secret of those companies that have survived generations is simply that they managed their patient capital by properly balancing liquidity, capital, and control.

## *What Is Patient Capital?*

In accounting terms, patient capital is simply shareholders' equity and retained earnings. But in the family business context, patient capital has more than an accounting meaning. It incorporates all the capital that the family owners, generation after generation, have invested in the family business; it is more than the tangible value of the equity. It also includes the heritage, the association to the family business, the human capital, and the attachment to the business on the part of owners, generation after generation. This intangible value of patient capital is exactly what allows family shareholders to make long-term investment decisions, promote sound employee relations, and let go of short-term gains and short-term liquidity for long-term and sustainable rewards.

Successful family companies maintain this patient capital generation after generation by

- creating value for shareholders.
- providing liquidity programs for shareholders, allowing them adequate return, freedom of choice of their investment in the family company, and assessment of value. In other words, patient capital is not trapped capital.
- investing in the family effect, in order to reinforce the values, commitment, and family heritage.

## CREATING VALUE IN THE GLOBAL FAMILY BUSINESS

Creating value in a global family business requires four separate steps: the establishment of a family vision and a business vision; the development of a strategic plan for executing those visions and the implementation of liquidity plans for shareholders to access income and value gains. Once the family, management, and Board have agreed on strategic and liquidity plans, measurements have to be instituted to gauge progress relative to the plans. The strategic and liquidity plans will determine the outside capital requirements of the family business to achieve its growth objectives and provide the desired liquidity to the shareholders.

### Tools for Maximizing Growth Across the Globe

While family businesses in various cultures have their own sets of strategic issues, they have one aspect in common: the need to grow to survive. The pursuit of a sustainable profitable growth strategy is the only avenue toward long-term viability of any family company.

The strategic need for growth requires outside capital. What sources of outside capital are available to family-owned businesses? How are those sources unique for family businesses and from continent to continent? And how do the objectives of those outside capital sources compete with or complement the objectives of the family owners? A family company has three different sources for financing its growth: debt solutions, equity solutions, and strategic solutions.

Debt solutions available to the family company include lines of credit, term debt, leasing of assets, subordinated debt, and private placements. It is not in the scope of this chapter to outline all the forms of debt to the family company. However, I will point out that in a global economic environment there are three key elements in judging a debt solution: the overall interest rate cost (after fees), the covenants attached to the debt instrument, and the currency exposure. The latter consideration is often neglected by uninformed or overzealous bankers (see Table 20.2).

Take the example of a European family company that three years ago decided to finance an expansion in the United States by way of an unhedged borrowing in euro currency at its local bank. With the recent 30 percent depreciation of the dollar vis-à-vis the euro, this family company is faced with servicing a loan in high-value euros while receiving cash flow from its investment in the United States in a highly depreciated dollar. Many hedging techniques are available today to match the currency of the debt with the currency of the underlying asset, generating the cash flow to service that

TABLE 20.2. Investment criteria of three equity investors.

| Investment criterion | Venture capital | Institutional private equity | Family business investors |
|---|---|---|---|
| Family involvement | Family = negative | Neutral | Family = positive |
| Investors' control | Majority | Mostly majority | Minority |
| Target returns | >30 percent | 20-30 percent | <20 percent |
| Timing of exit | 1-2 years | 3-5 years | >5 years |

*Source:* de Visscher & Co. LLC.

debt. Natural hedging and currency swaps are just two examples of those techniques.

When it comes to equity solutions, private and public equity continue to be the most common sources of equity for family companies. Over the past several years, however, many family companies have shied away from the public-equity market. There are several reasons for this. First, in most major markets in the United States and in Europe, mutual funds and other large financial institutions have continuously increased their overall share of the volume of the stock markets. The interest of those institutions to treat large volumes has reduced liquidity in the market for smaller family company stock positions. The other reason is the trend in the markets worldwide toward greater regulation of corporate communications and corporate governance. Those regulations not only add to the cost of operating as a public family company, but also make it, in many cases, almost impossible to operate as a family-owned company in the public arena.

Because of the shortfalls of the public-equity markets for family-controlled families, many business-owning families have tapped into a growing private equity market to fund their business capital needs. Private equity is one of the fastest growing segments of the capital market. The amount of capital raised by private equity funds grew from $11 billion in 2002 to $42 billion in 2004. Over the same time period, private equity deal volume grew from $41 billion to $137 billion. The private equity market consists of many segments. The most common segments today are venture capital, institutional private equity, and individual or family offices, often called FBIs or family business investors.

- *Venture capital* has traditionally been used to fund high-growth investments or companies in the technology sector (broadly defined to include computers, information, and health care). Venture capitalists typically demand a high return on their investment with a rapid realization (exit) by way of an initial public offering or recapitalization or even sale of the company.
- *Institutional private equity funds* of corporate or financial institutions could take many forms (private equity, mezzanine investors, turnaround funds). These institutional private equity funds demand significantly less control and lower returns than venture capitalists. They tend to be more family friendly because they are not looking to make a quick exit: They are happy to stick with an investment for three to five years, compared with venture capitalists' one- to two-year horizons. Their biggest investors are insurance companies, pension funds, and other large institutions that must maintain broad asset allocations (including family companies) in their portfolios. They do not necessarily

target family businesses, but they do not rule them out or require family owners to step aside, as venture capital funds often do. Like venture capital, institutional private equity is becoming a worldwide market. Some of the largest U.S. funds have now raised significant money targeted for the European market to compete with the local European funds. Similarly in Latin America, funds specifically dedicated to make investments in Latin American companies have been growing exponentially.

- *Family business investors* are mainly private individuals or family offices who have pooled their money into funds to invest in family companies. Because FBIs have a family business background, they perceive the "family effect" not just as neutral but as a positive criterion they seek in all of their investments. FBIs are much more patient than venture capitalists or even institutional private equity funds, sometimes investing for ten years or more. They truly search for a financial and strategic partnership with the family to create long-term value for themselves and for the business-owning family. Obviously, at some point FBIs will want to exit their investment and return money to their own investors/families. Our experience tells us, however, that the form and nature of their exit is much more flexible than exits by venture capitalists or private funds. In one case of which I am aware, the family agreed to pay all excess cash flow over a certain threshold to the FBI and provide the FBI with an exit over seven years.

When searching for an investment partner, one needs to consider the partner's parameters for exit, control, return, and family friendliness. In addition, one needs to factor in the size of the investment fund, whether it is venture capital, private equity, or FBI. The size of the fund determines the amount of capital the fund is looking to invest in individual companies to maintain a diversified portfolio. A $20 million private equity fund might make five to seven investments of $3 million to $5 million. A $1 billion fund may make ten investments of $100 million or more.

The first step in a company's search is to clearly define *why* it needs a financial partner. Is it to provide growth capital to the business or to allow some shareholders to exit the business? Or both? Is it to provide long-term capital over the long haul or just for a one-time liquidity need?

The intended use of proceeds will often dictate the type of financial partner one needs. Is it a pure short-term financial partner, or one who can also provide some strategic input? Is a partner with international experience and know-how what is needed?

Good financial partners can provide not only financial capital but also strategic advice, human capital, and networking contacts. After all, they are creating value for themselves, too. In that sense, their interests are aligned with those of the borrowing company.

## Tools for Maximizing Liquidity to the Global Business-Owning Family

The second critical element of patient capital in the global family business is efficiently addressing the liquidity needs of the shareholders, which is just as important as developing a strategic plan for the business. Family shareholders generally have three types of liquidity needs: the need for income; for liquidity flexibility; and for exit or sudden liquidity.

The need for income in the form of dividends or other current income depends much on the generation of ownership and the tax jurisdiction of the business and/or shareholders. As family businesses evolve across generations, the structure of dividends should evolve from "pay what you can" to a formal dividend policy based on objective market criteria that are found in many coalition-generation family businesses.

Liquidity flexibility is a universal need of all family businesses and is often addressed by ongoing liquidity programs. When shareholders feel trapped in their investment in the family company with no way out, they are more likely to want to exit. By providing the opportunity for shareholders to sell stock on a periodic basis, the pressure is released. Our experience shows that in those cases, family shareholders do not sell stock at all or only very minimally. The other advantage of setting up ongoing liquidity programs is for shareholders to focus on the value of the stock and future value-creation opportunities, because ongoing liquidity programs are pegged to a consistent valuation of the stock year after year. That same valuation can also be used for management incentive programs, furthering the goal of allying the interest of management and shareholders.

Last, the need for exit or sudden liquidity is difficult to plan for family shareholders because it often results from unexpected family or personal exigencies such as death, disputes, divorce, or economic needs of shareholders. The one exit need that can be predicted is that of the outside investors, private equity, or others, and those in management reaching retirement age to the extent that they have been granted some stock ownership.

Family businesses would be wise to assess the liquidity needs of the various shareholder groups through interviews, questionnaires, or group meetings. Whatever the method, the company needs to collect information on the current income expectations of shareholders; whether and when those shareholders anticipate they will need or want to sell stock in the immediate future; and whether they want the flexibility to sell in the future and how often. This information is essential to formulating the appropriate liquidity program, including the dividend policy.

## Liquidity Programs

Most liquidity programs in family companies start with the payment of dividends to shareholders. Although some drawbacks do accompany dividends, they remain an important tool in the context of other liquidity programs. For many family firms, the lack of a dividend policy is a serious omission at best, and a recipe for a shareholder-relations disaster—or a family feud—at worst. At the same time, a dividend policy formulated without consideration of other liquidity options and outside the context of the company's overall capital needs is also a serious mistake.

In its duty to maximize value for all shareholders, the Board of Directors often faces the challenge of reconciling diverging liquidity needs and demands. Unfortunately, many companies rely solely on dividends to provide some liquidity to shareholders because dividends provide tangible proof of the value of a shareholder's investment, and thus can provide a safety valve for the pent-up frustration of inactive shareholders eager for a return that can be banked. The board and family leaders often see such payments as a kind of "peace money" to keep inactive shareholders happy.

There are, however, four downsides to dividends for family firms: First, the regular payment of dividends can lead to unrealistic shareholder expectations. Once shareholders begin to depend on a stream of dividend income to support themselves, any decrease in dividends can have serious repercussions for the family business and for healthy family functioning. Shareholders may bring pressure on the company to maintain a level of dividend payments long after such dividends can be justified by the company's financial performance.

Second, increasing demands for dividends can strain cash flow and prevent the company from reinvesting profits in future growth, as well as making badly needed capital improvements. In terms of allocation of financial resources, dividends may not be the most productive way of meeting shareholders' return-on-equity objectives. If one dollar of cash flow reinvested in the business will reap a higher return on investment than the same dollar paid out as a dividend and reinvested outside the family business, why not give the shareholders the benefit of this higher return?

Third, dividends are a blunt instrument for rewarding shareholders with diverse liquidity needs. Every share of the class of dividend-paying stock receives the same return, whether shareholders need or desire liquidity or not. For example, members who are drawing salaries will receive the same dividend per share as the inactive shareholders who may depend on dividends to meet their income needs. Although this nondiscriminatory policy honors the principle of equal rewards for equal ownership, it also makes dividends a less precise liquidity tool than other options.

Finally, in some jurisdictions such as the United States, dividends are a very tax-inefficient way of rewarding shareholders. Except in the case of S Corporations and other nontaxable entities, dividends are paid from after-tax earnings and then taxed again at the shareholder level.

Despite their limitations, dividends can and do play an important role in many family businesses. Companies find payments easy to implement, and shareholders find them easy to understand and appreciate—-provided the firm has a clearly articulated dividend policy. Increasingly, companies are therefore articulating dividend policies in the broader context of other liquidity options available to shareholders.

Today's most common methods of providing targeted income to the shareholders and at the same time providing liquidity flexibility include multiple classes of stock, company clearinghouses, redemption programs, company-sponsored loan programs, family opportunity funds, and internal recapitalization.

## Tools for Nourishing the Family Effect with Global Families

Companies that desire aggressive, global growth will need to expand shareholders' patient capital. A family CEO can manage shareholders by creating a written mission and values statement and performance goals that everyone can adhere to, and by veering away from chasing short-term gains and, instead, getting back on the track of long-term, sustainable growth (Hughes, 1997).

Family firms have a history of strong cultural values. They are close to the entrepreneurial mission of their founders. With a family company, the consultant does not have to create a whole "mission mind-set"; the message simply draws family and employees back to their roots.

The door to long-term, sustainable, profitable growth hinges on a strong family organizational structure, such as a family office, family council, or holding company, to be the steward of family values. This family organizational structure will be the focal point of discussions on family mission, family values, and wealth-related concerns, such as liquidity and diversification.

Depending on the jurisdiction and country of origin, the family office has taken many forms but is now recognized universally as the tool of choice that can help strengthen patient capital and reconcile the needs of the business and those of its various constituent shareholders. Unlike a family council, which mainly addresses governance and communication issues, a family office focuses on structural and financial responsibilities.

Much has been said about the role of the family office in financial families. (See Chapter 19 for another relevant discussion on this topic.)

Conventional wisdom seems to focus on the family office as an investment vehicle and hence a tool reserved for financial families, but we believe that a family office is an equally important tool for families who still operate an active business. In that context, the family office can take many forms, such as a family trust, a family holding company, or a family investment company, depending upon the family and its country of origin.

A family trust or holding company owns shares of the operating company, concentrates control, and regroups the family's ownership of the business to allow the entry of outside investors in the business capital structure. A family investment company is a structure that parallels the family business and manages assets outside the family company, such as real estate or liquid assets.

In either form, the family office, when combined with an operating business, will fulfill four important roles for the family:

1. *Family as owners.* The family office can provide stewardship of the family's patient capital, which may include setting investment guidelines for the operating company. My family office, for instance, works with management and the Board of Directors to clarify shareholders' return expectations—both return on equity and return on assets. The family office can also decide which family members will fill available seats on the Board of Directors.

2. *Family as employees.* The family office can determine rules of entry for family members seeking to join the business, as well as what kinds of training and development programs the business should provide for relatives who have management aspirations.

3. *Family as family.* How will the family perpetrate its heritage, maintain communication and resolve conflicts? How, if at all, will it financially support family members, and under what circumstances? Some family offices create a fund to invest in relatives' ventures.

One other critical role the family office can play is sponsoring educational programs on topics such as the family's business, new developments in the industry, personal finance, technology, or career planning. It also can help connect disparate family members and keep them informed about business, family wealth, and other issues.

4. *Family as part of community.* A family office can decide how and where the family wants to direct its philanthropic giving. It can also identify

leadership opportunities, such as open board seats, at charitable, community, industry, and other nonprofit organizations in which the family may want to maintain a presence.

Especially during times of family and business transition, a family office can help educate relatives about various options, help the family articulate and live by its values, and strengthen patient capital. Without a family office, the only glue holding together a growing, dispersed family may be the business. So shareholders may cling to the business—in its current form—to preserve its identity and closeness, even if that means passing up opportunities to expand, evolve, or sell the business. By providing another organizational structure around which the family can unite, a family office enables the family to base decisions on business and financial factors, not emotions.

5. *Family as consumers.* Family offices often provide many services and products beyond investment management. Today they may navigate different products for the family, such as insurance, personal lines of credit, and business and family travel and legal services. Family offices can also harness the family's purchasing power, enabling it to negotiate much better prices and terms on these products and services than individuals could negotiate on their own. The professional staff at some family offices even reviews business plans developed by family members attempting to launch new business ventures.

The size of one's business is not the most relevant factor; it is the size of the family, and how dispersed the relatives are. For example, take a second-generation business with one parent and three children active in the company, plus two other inactive children. This family may be able to learn and make decisions effectively among themselves. But what will happen ten or fifteen years hence, in the next generation? That same business family may have expanded from six members to twenty, with only a handful of shareholders involved in day-to-day management. The rest of the relatives may have spread throughout the country, or even overseas. The company may have grown, stagnated, or even downsized in this time frame. Whatever its circumstances, it likely will benefit now more than before from a family office.

## SUMMARY

So while family businesses in various cultures throughout the world have their own set of challenges and strategic issues, they also have one thing in common: the need to manage patient capital for their survival. The management of patient capital will require a sustainable profitable growth strategy of the business with the prospect of creating large value for the shareholders, efficient liquidity mechanisms to provide income and value realization for the shareholders, and, finally, strong family governance structures such as a family office to be the steward and the enhancer of the family effect.

## REFERENCES

Aronoff, C.E., Ward, J.L., & de Visscher, F. (1995). *Financing transitions: Managing capital and liquidity in the family business* (4th ed.). Marietta, GA: Family Enterprise.

Davis, A., Hampton, M.M.C., & Lansberg, I. (1997). *Generation to generation: Life cycles of the business.* Boston: Harvard Business School.

Hughes, J.E., Jr. (1997). *Family wealth: Keeping it in the family.* Princeton Junction, NJ: NetWRX, Inc.

Chapter 21

# Themes, Reflections, Comparisons, and Contrasts

Florence W. Kaslow

Clearly since early in the history of civilization, some form of family enterprise has often emerged to sustain families economically and emotionally, and to enable them to contribute to the society of which they were a part. These endeavors might be small or large, exist for a short time or over several decades or generations, and be modest or grand in scope.

But family businesses as a separate entity important enough to warrant major attention in the form of specific substantive courses at university graduate schools of business are a phenomenon that did not happen until the 1980s. Likewise, the field of family business consultation was founded in separate places in the United States by several pioneers, almost concurrently, in the early 1980s, and the several efforts coalesced in the formation of the Family Firm Institute (FFI) in 1985 (see Chapter 1 on FFI's history and Chapter 18 on the United States for an overview of these developments). After several years in existence, FFI ultimately decided to focus its efforts primarily to serving the needs and interests of family business consultants and advisors.

A parallel development centering on family businesses was occurring in Western Europe at the same time, and this culminated in the formation of the Family Business Network (FBN). (We regret that although several people who have been central to the evolution of FBN were invited to write a chapter on this topic for this book, none were able to do so.) The FBN is composed primarily of owners and senior members of family business firms, and their core mission is to serve the owners, not the consultants. According to reports received, the two organizations sometimes work collaboratively, as their goals and functions are supplementary.

Once the field evolved and came more into the foreground of its allied professions, it experienced rapid and substantial growth throughout the

*Handbook of Family Business and Family Business Consultation*
Published by The Haworth Press, Inc., 2006. All rights reserved.
doi:10.1300/5491_21

world. It has not been difficult for many in related fields to grasp the necessity and vitality of family businesses as a unique genre, and also to realize they can be complex, multifaceted systems in which handling the family dynamics and conflicts may demand more time and attention than the pressing family business decisions do. Thus it soon became obvious to those desirous of consulting to family businesses that they needed to be knowledgeable and skilled in many areas, and these became known as the core competencies. These consist of law, behavioral science, family dynamics and family systems theory (see Appendix explaining terminology), management science, finances, and accounting. A truly multidisciplinary, interdisciplinary specialty has been crafted over the years, and those entering the field now are expected to master as much as possible of this broad base of knowledge, as well as to be willing to work collaboratively with people possessing skills and knowledge that they do not have, first by attending workshops and being mentored, and later by using a team approach when the demands of the task exceed their individual competencies.

Over time, various teams and groups have been formed that work together on a rather continuous basis. Other individuals prefer to have arrangements with different colleagues with whom they link up when a specific need arises—and to keep their possibilities more flexible (see Chapter 1, Body of Knowledge section, and Family Firm Institute, 2005).

Almost from the beginning, as leaders in the field began to become known for providing valuable input in their consultative roles to companies in the United States, and for being inspiring and sagacious in their professional/teaching roles in academic settings and at family business centers, forums, and conferences, they began to be invited to consult and teach in other countries. Marta Vago was invited to chronicle her personal odyssey in Chapter 2. She does so with great sensitivity, highlighting the need for knowledge of multicultural variations, perspectives, differing expectations and modus operandi in several different countries—learning deftly by asking, observing, reading, and "sensing." In their descriptions of their travels to consult in Turkey and Saudi Arabia, respectively, David Bork (Chapter 16) and Joseph Paul (Chapter 13) display similar exquisite sensitivity to the influential cultural imperatives and more subtle nuances that influence their family clients. Bork has purposefully designed a way of having a family business member designated as his guide, while Paul acquired his tutelage from partners who were born and raised in Turkey and Saudi Arabia. No matter how one acquires their multicultural appreciation and competence, to attempt to consult to a family business in another country or one within one's own country in which the members have a markedly different ethnic, racial, sociocultural, religious, or educational background, or hold a divergent political philosophy, one should be mindful of the differences and what issues may therefore need to be dealt with in the consultation because of these, and treat the differences respectfully—even if he or she personally disagrees with a prescribed way of viewing a situation, such as according to very traditional gender role or birth order role patterns and definitions.

## VARIOUS SALIENT MODELS

As the field began to mature, leaders began to take time to reflect more on what they were doing and to analyze what worked well, with whom, and under what circumstances, as well as what did not. From these reflections, analyses, observations, and accompanying research to test the theoretical bases that were emerging and being articulated, various models of family business consulting/advising have come to the fore and have been promulgated widely. Three of these that have become well respected and are utilized by many other consultants are included in Part II of this volume. Each theory is described by its progenitors. The three theories are quite different, reflecting, among other variables, the different clientele each consulting team has focused on/appealed to, their own prior professional discipline of origin and theoretical predilections, where each team falls on what might be labeled a clinical versus an academic continuum of theorizing, as well as personal style dimension. Each also conceptualizes how they establish objectives for and with families and whether these are primarily substantive, primarily relational, or a combination of both. Taken together, I believe they represent the best of the depth and breadth of the field today.

To be more specific, the Aspen Consulting Process Model (Bork, Jaffe, Dashew, Lane, & Heisler, 2004) described in Chapter 3 is designed to bring about deep structural changes and relationship shifts in complex multigenerational enterprising family systems. The Aspen Group runs family group retreats, as well as retreats for executives of multiple families conjointly, where relational dynamics receive some attention. They also emphasize the importance of having relevant structures in place to enable more being accomplished and assist in getting various boundaries aligned as they should be. Facilitating effective communication, developing appropriate governance mechanisms, and writing essential documents are goals they believe need to be realized as part of the overall problem-solving process. Sometimes various members of their consulting group work with individual family businesses separately, and in different combinations, focusing on whatever sets of issues are determined to be most pressing.

The three circle model, elaborated by Hilburt-Davis and Dyer (2003) and discussed in Chapter 4, is the most frequently cited by other authors throughout the book, and perhaps throughout the literature of the field. (No content analysis has been done, so this can not be substantiated.) In brief, the model designates three intersecting circles representing three overlapping systems: the business system, the family system, and the ownership/governance system, with the family business consultants functioning in the areas in which the circles interface. They emphasize that consulting to family business enterprises differs from consulting to nonfamily business enterprises in four main areas: the adherence to a systems perspective; concern for process as well as content; collaboration in multidisciplinary teams; and concern for and with emotions. Overall, they measure achievement by assessing outcomes in two areas—heightened business success and improved family relationships. Here again we see attention paid to substantive governance issues, that is, how the process is conducted, as well as how the family members feel about one another and what is transpiring.

Comparing the three models, we find that Kadis and McClendon place the most emphasis on family dynamics in their exposition of their Interpersonal Model for Reconciling Relationships presented in Chapter 5. Their cornerstone thesis is that "good relationships are the foundation for the survival and ultimate success of all business enterprises undertaken by families," and that "when family members are unwilling or unable to reconcile or reestablish trust, their enterprise is highly vulnerable and may even fail—unless . . . changes are made to ameliorate relationship ruptures" (McClendon & Kadis, 2004, p. 1). Thus it follows that their Reconciliation Model keeps the emphasis on healing long-standing and recent hurts and breeches of trust so that family members can live and work together more harmoniously for the betterment and profit of all. They often work toward the formation of Family Councils, through which can come the reconciliations, as each person involved in the Council can retell their personal narratives here in a more positive way, to an attentive listening audience of relatives. From this, they can ultimately build more solid governance structures in the business which will receive more widespread support, based on the reconciliations that have occurred. The starting point for their interventions is an assessment of the relationship system—the ultimate target fans out into the larger family business enterprise.

Each of the three models shares similar, but not identical, objectives; however, they describe different methodologies and pathways for arriving there. This should provide the reader with several viable choices to which he or she can add his or her own ideas in fashioning the approach that will work best for him or her. We suggest it be kept flexible and adaptable to the people, situation, and challenges presented, and always be kept dynamic and responsive, while the consultant adheres to its core components.

## CONSULTATION TO FAMILY BUSINESSES
## IN DIFFERENT COUNTRIES

Each of the authors writing about family businesses and consultation in a specific country was asked to follow the same outline, in order to enhance consistency and comparability. They were instructed to comment briefly if a particular structure, such as Family Offices, does not exist in their country, as is true in Chile, Korea, Trinidad and Tobago. However, not everyone in this independent group of leaders in their fields in their respective countries, in their role as authors, followed the instructions rigorously—and so there are some variations and departures. Some of the nonconformity is attributable to the fact that English is not everyone's first language, and it is very difficult to write, particularly on a technical subject, in a language other than a person's primary one. And words have different meanings in different countries, and sometimes are nontranslatable; at times there is not an equivalent word in the other language. Some authors used translators to assist them. With it all, we believe that what has emerged is an informative medley.

To help the reader put everything in context, we are including the outline given to the authors of Chapters 6 through 18:

1. Family business landscape—percentage of companies that are family business owned, and what kind of companies.
2. History of FBC in your country:
   a. Early leaders—who were they, when?
   b. How they began—what gave impetus to their beginning?
3. Where are these consultants being trained; comment on philosophy.
4. What fields are they drawn from:
   a. Do they compete, or collaborate, across fields?
   b. What is their general status?
   c. Describe briefly what kind of firms/companies are likely to utilize their services.
5. What roles/functions do family business consultants perform? Discuss compensation, if you can. How important is it that consultants be fluent in the language of the country in which they are consulting?
6. Discuss important elements in the field today in your country and current state of the art. Differentiate ownership and management.
7. Comment on the following structures:
   a. Family Council
   b. Family philanthropies

    c. Family Offices

    d. Board of Directors—composition; balance of family and non-family members

8. Discuss the key conflicts you encounter between family business members when you are consulting; major issues surrounding succession and how you are likely to assist in this process.

9. Discuss emphasis (or lack thereof) on social and philanthropic responsibility.

10. Summarize major research findings on family business in your country.

11. Comment on use of the Internet by these businesses—particularly as they utilize consultants from another country or expand into overseas markets.

12. Give a case example drawn from your consulting practice that illustrates as many of the above points as possible (around six to eight pages). (For ethical reasons, be sure to get permission from the family if using a real case, or disguise it to be unrecognizable by combining several similar cases.)

13. Summary and Conclusion.

The individual country landscapes are each well etched against the prevailing political, economic, religious, and sociocultural ethos and climate extant in the past few decades in that particular country. Where the large, extended family network still reigns supreme and is tied into the government economically, as is true in Saudi Arabia, this is reflected in the patriarchal, hierarchical family business governance systems which are quite different from those found in more democratic societies that have stressed gender equality and more nuclear than kinship family systems, like those in the United Kingdom and the United States.

In some countries, a high value is placed on individualism; this includes Canada, Scotland, and perhaps Ireland, as well as the United States and the United Kingdom, while a much stronger emphasis is placed on the importance of loyalty to the family unit (familism) over the self in Brazil, Chile, Korea, Lebanon, Saudi Arabia, Trinidad and Tobago, and Turkey. These deeply ingrained values, whether at the individualism or familism end of the spectrum, have a huge impact on the dynamics and functioning of the family business—who is involved, where the power resides, and who can serve on the various governance structures, such as the Board of Directors, and even if there can be one, and the Family Council.

The history of family business consultation in each country proffered here reflects the reality and its interpretation from the author's knowledge base, vision, and perspective. So at best, it is a partial glimpse of the total picture of that country's evolution of family business consultation. But each one does provide enough information to convey an overall sense of how, when, and why the field began to evolve in their country. For example, consultation is still in its infancy in Trinidad and Tobago, and the rest of the Caribbean Islands, and one can infer this may be the case in Chile, as the author provided only research data and no actual case consultation data.

Training of consultants appears to be most organized and sophisticated in the United States, Scotland, and Canada. In each of these countries, some of the formal training takes place under the aegis of organizations such as FFI, and much has also been established in university graduate business schools and in family business forums and centers that are university affiliated. In the past few years, courses and/or conferences have also been established at the American University in Beirut, Lebanon; University College, Cork, Ireland; and in Mexico; a growing number are being conducted at university-based facilities in Canada, the United Kingdom, the United States, and Scotland. A good deal of training is reported to be occurring in Spain. Thus those seeking education and training in the future should be able to acquire it closer to, if not in, their home country. Not only will they be taught/trained by leaders from their own country who have trained at home and abroad formally at universities and/or through conference workshops, but quite probably they will also have some exposure to visiting consultants brought in from other countries to enhance their training and education. Hopefully, such events will contribute multidisciplinary and multicultural elements to the breadth of their training, thereby further enriching and diversifying it and challenging the trainees to think in new directions and to question their own beliefs and biases.

In the majority of the countries represented here, initially companies have relied on their lawyers, accountants, and financial advisors to help them solve all kinds of problems, so this is who they turn to when they need any kind of advice. However, in the last quarter of the twentieth century and the first decade of the new millennium, the ethnocentricity which characterized many countries has changed as travel has increased in all directions and people have been exposed to new ideas in their travels and met visitors to their country who may have come to work there; as more and more young people have been sent abroad for part of their education and come in contact with ideas and ways of thinking that are novel to them which they have brought home with them; and as the technological revolution has brought rapid dissemination of information by making everything known more easily accessible on television, the Internet, and in newspapers. As a result of these and other converging political and socioeconomic changes, xenophobia and doing things in traditional ways has often become less prevalent and acceptable. Still, lawyers and accountants may be the first professionals families turn to and may be among the first to seek training as family business consultants, when they learn of its availability, if it is reasonably accessible. Others from the various fields of business may be sought out about special issues in their areas of expertise as people in a given technical area, like construction or computer technology, may be in theirs. But it is in the realm of *delicate conflictual interpersonal family relationships* that families do not know who to turn to, and realize that their accountant or lawyer rarely has more skill in dealing with such dilemmas than they do. Also, personal family matters are often considered very private in many countries, and CEOs are decidedly uncomfortable at the thought of discussing their intimate family problems with outsiders, i.e., non-family members, no matter what their capacity or title may be.

Along with this goes a corollary problem. Except in the United States, and perhaps in Canada, mental health professionals are generally perceived as therapists or social welfare workers, or they are psychiatrists who are viewed as medical doctors. They are not known as providing consultation within the world of business, or as being sufficiently knowledgeable about this particular universe to know and to appreciate the impact of entangled family dynamics on a family business. By contrast, the evolution of the field has been quite different in the United States, where psychologists, family therapists, and other mental health professionals with a special interest in family theory, dynamics, structure, and function have also developed an additional specialization in family business consultation. They were among the original pioneers in the field in the United States, as indicated in Chapters 1 and 18; many have made an ongoing significant contribution to the expanding field and its body of knowledge as it has become more variegated, and continue to be held in high esteem as co-equal leaders with their colleagues who initially come from the professions on the "hard" side of the knowledge ledger. Thus one tends to find fewer family business consultants drawn from the mental health disciplines in other parts of the world, and when families in business in these countries face problems in their interfamilial relationship system, they may not receive the help they need for three reasons: (1) their deeply held value of family privacy and solving all problems within the extended family system on their own; (2) the tendency to rely on traditional advisors if counsel is finally sought—preferably their lawyer, accountant, or religious leader; and (3) unfamiliarity with, misperceptions about, or discomfort about utilizing the skills of a family business consultant with a mental health background capable of assisting them in resolving these unsettling, thorny issues.

The way that CEOs, CFOs, and COOs of corporations in Asia, Arabic nations, Eastern Europe, and other parts of the world are becoming aware of the use of people with mental health training as part of their background in consultative roles is through reading the literature, if they read English or if a book or article has been translated into their language, through attendance at workshops that introduce them to this idea, or if they happen to hire a team that includes a consultant who has such a background.

The roles and functions performed by consultants have been clearly described by most authors, and vary—depending on the business, their request for service, which may range from helping to write mission statements and company bylaws, to setting up governance structures, focusing on gender issues or succession planning concerns, transfer of wealth, ensuring continuity, expansion of the business, and helping resolve some longstanding generational and intergenerational conflicts, remaining competitive in rapidly changing markets, and many, many more. One appeal of being a family business advisor is the great diversity of the challenges presented to someone in this position.

Few of the consultants discussed the issue of financial compensation. Like the families they serve, this is a topic that they often prefer to keep private. From what we have been able to glean, fees may be based on an hourly, half-day, per diem, or a weekly basis. Sometimes there is an agreement on a fee for a total project or undertaking based on a projection of how much time and effort will be invested in preparation and on site. Expenses may be built into the total figure, or calculated separately.

Only a few authors addressed of the importance of consultants being fluent in the language of the particular family or of the country in which they are consulting. Those who did so believe that this is preferable, although not essential, as it certainly facilitates more direct communication and lends itself to easier mutual understanding. However, a skilled and attuned translator, particularly one who is also familiar with the subject matter, can help overcome communication barriers based upon language differences. My experience in consulting and teaching in more than thirty non-English-speaking countries concurs with what has been said in the foregoing.

## THE DIFFERENT COUNTRIES REPRESENTED

The current state of the art appears to be vastly different in the numerous countries discussed herein. In the chapter on Chile, Jorge Yunis draws upon no direct consultation cases. Instead he relies on research data comparing family and nonfamily firms, and the data sets are relatively small. Yet we decided to retain this chapter because it is thought to depict the extant reality in many South American countries. Conversely, Brazil is quite advanced and forward looking in terms of state of the art, several well-trained and sophisticated consultation firms are working in this vast country, where 78 percent of the labor force is employed by family businesses. There is a strong preference for hiring Brazilian consulting firms; a similar preference is given to indigenous firms in many of the other countries. Increasingly, women are achieving top-level positions in family firms but are still a rarity in the consultation world. An exception to this generalization is the chapter's author, Dorothy Nebel de Mello, who is a well-recognized consultant in her own country and who has served on the FFI Board. These two neighboring countries, Chile and Brazil, offer quite a contrast.

Trinidad and Tobago in the Caribbean are in the beginning stages of having family business consultation available with the chapter's author, Annette Rahael, collaborating to offer services with a local bank, and training through a local university. By contrast, Mexico, the only Central American country featured herein, has numerous consultants who sometimes meet together, are active in FFI, teach at different universities, and offer a wide spectrum of consultation services. Salo Grabinsky projects a consultation profile of great investment in the families he consults with, blending the professional with personal friendship in a way that has strong Latin overtones—warm, caring, intense, and deeply invested.

Canada has been at the cutting edge of the field almost from the beginning, and Denise Paré-Julian conveys the continuing excitement there as more and more of the new university-based family business centers collaborate with consultants to offer learning opportunities to clients and as their organizations, such as the Canadian Association for Family Enterprise (CAFE), continue to thrive. Productive research is being conducted and much collaborative work is being done with colleagues in the United States.

The forecast in Southern Ireland is optimistic, with Marcus Spillane, Bill O'Gorman, and Naomi Birdthistle describing a recently minted university family business center at University College, Cork, and much activity surrounding its launching in 2002. Their enthusiasm is contagious. Family businesses there date back to the eighteenth century and have a colorful history. Today's consultant combines helping put structures in place, running retreats and coaching, along with many other processes.

According to Ji-Hee Kim, South Korea has begun placing greater value on its family businesses since the downturn in the Asian economy in the late 1990s. The government realized that it was the family firms that had the greatest staying power and resilience because of their long-term commitment to one another and their own future progeny, and so it is now willing to invest more in this sector of the economy. As Kim is primarily an academic who conducts research, writes, and teaches about family businesses rather than consults directly, she selected two cases of large, well-known Korean family firms as her case examples (Samsung and Hyundai) and provides a performance picture spanning several generations for each—drawn from public records. One might ask at each critical juncture, "If I were the consultant, what might I have done, asked, or advised here?" These two histories of well-known firms provide much data that makes for exciting and instructive reading about local firms that became national in scope because of such variables as sheer determination, skillful planning, careful utilization of their human and capital resources, willingness to sell off segments of the operation that were least cost-effective and/or compatible with the overall corporate goals and operation, continual assessment of where global markets were heading and might be led, who comprised their competition and where their strengths lay, have been able to become major "players" and forces in the global marketplace. According to Kim's retrospective account, maintaining ethical behavior and placing a high value on the human capital of employees have proven to be among their major attributes.

Numerous commonalities emerge in the chapters on Saudi Arabia and Turkey. The large, extended, or kinship family form still predominates, and it is reflected in family businesses described by Joseph Paul, Zaher Al Munajjed, and Haluk Alacaklioglu. The independent, self-sufficient, and sometimes detached nuclear family unit, commonplace in the United States, is much less likely to exist there, and the dynamics are quite different. The patriarchal family system also prevails in the economic sphere in accordance with religious law of Sharia, and thus is influential in the concomitant political realm. The three systems of thought are reasonably consistent, and departures in ideology and behavior are not well tolerated. (That Sharia as the basis of civil law is alive and still respected was reinforced for all the world in July 2005 when the new Iranian constitution was promulgated.) Thus, disparate gender roles are defined and sanctioned, and power and control in business and in the handling of money are allocated to the men. Family councils, as known in the Western world, are less likely to exist, as a comparable extant structure may render them unnecessary. The senior and/or most important male family members meet frequently to discuss and decide on matters of consequence to the family and the business. Comparable but separate meetings may be held by the senior-ranking women to discuss items of concern to them. Channels for conveying what is of importance to both, back and forth, seem to be informal but to be known to all.

Wealthy families are expected to, and do, contribute to those less fortunate, as what they have ostensibly belongs to their society, according to their religious beliefs. So family philanthropies, set up specifically for this purpose, would be redundant.

We can glean from Bork's revealing treatise on Turkey that it differs from Saudi Arabia in that it appears to have two different visages—and one faces westward, expressing its desire to be part of the European Union. As such, principles of greater equality for all, regardless of gender, race, religion, and ethnicity, may have to find a way to co-exist with Muslim law, Sharia, and other long-held Turkish beliefs and traditions. As more non-Turkish businesses enter the Turkish market and as far-reaching Turkish firms expand to sell their products in other lands, this openness, and all that goes with the breaking down of ethnocentric barriers, is likely to ensue, but not without many pulls and counterpulls.

The portrait of Lebanon painted by Fahed-Sreih on yet a third Arabic country comes from more of an academician's view, like the chapter from Korea, than from the hands-on consultant's perspective which shapes the chapters on Saudi-Arabia and Turkey. In this country, family businesses comprise 85 percent of the private sector, which constitutes 90 percent of the total economy, and so offers the vast majority of job opportunities. It was only recently when the Lebanese American University (LAU) established the Institute of Family and Entrepreneurial Business in 1999 that the field of family business began to be recognized as a separate field. Most of the consulting has been performed by experts from financial companies and banks. Since the Institute at LAU was launched as the first academic center in Lebanon and the Middle East, and began offering programs in and on family business and conducting research, it has also housed a data bank on family firms in the Middle East. As in Saudi Arabia and Turkey, family businesses are passed on to the sons only; daughters may receive a share of the assets from other holdings such as real estate. Family firms here are incorporating all forms of modern technology in their operations.

Educational workshops for family business owners, training for family business consultants, and various kinds of services for all categories of people in the field of family business continue to be offered and thrive in Scotland. It has been, and remains, a hub of the Family Business Network and much of the activity that radiates out through Western Europe. Barbara Murray's inaugural study of 1,085 family firms conducted in 1994 in Scotland highlighted the significance of these companies and their qualitative and quantitative features, out of which she came up with a list of "The Challenges Facing Scotland Family Enterprises." This led to the launching of the United Kingdom's first Centre for Family Enterprise (CFE) in Glasgow, based on a stakeholder funding model. The CFE also became the Scottish Chapter of the FBN, and Scotland hosted the Annual World Conference in 1996, catapulting itself onto the global map. By 2000, a Scottish chapter of FFI was formed. Murray later served for a few years as director of the FBN.

Currently, authors Barbara Murray, Bill Gordon, and Kenneth Mc-Cracken work together collaboratively in a vibrant consultation group known as Family Business Solutions, to which they each bring different strengths, backgrounds, and foci. It provides a variety of services throughout Scotland and in several other countries also.

Family business advising as a discipline in its own right has only recently taken root in the United Kingdom. The chapter written by Tony Bogod, Juliette Johnson, Mark Jones, Peter Leach, and Francis Martin articulates their philosophy, the model that they use, and their grounds for optimism, yet they point out that the extent of future growth is unclear. The field was introduced and pioneered in the United Kingdom in the late 1980s by Leach, who had previously been working in family businesses and who had, during his travels to the United States, become interested in the way consultants and family business owners had begun to conceptualize family business concerns there. He studied with some of the leading figures in the United States before trying to adopt their work in the United Kingdom. In 1992, the Stoy Center for Family Business was founded; it publishes a regular newsletter, and organizes seminars. The consultants there usually "hail from a non-therapy professional background."

Universities and colleges in the United Kingdom have begun setting up courses for family members of family business firms in the past ten years. Some firms have internal systems to train staff, and research is being conducted by family business consultants who sometimes tender research reports to the families with whom they consult. Since 76 percent of United Kingdom's companies are family owned, as is the case in many other countries discussed in this volume, they represent a significant portion of the country's economy and should receive the best services possible.

The BDO Stoy Hayward Group, headquartered in London, has satellite offices in many other cities, and thus they can respond rapidly and more economically on the basis of geographic proximity when the need arises. They tend to use a very specific and structured format and to replicate this procedure in most consulting situations. Their contracts are all rather similar, and there seems to be less room for creativity and co-evolving solutions with the participant families than we see in Canada, Mexico, and the United States.

Joseph Astrachan and Kristi McMillan perhaps offer the largest, most colorful canvas, since the history of family business advising is the longest and the most diverse in the United States. There has been much experimentation, innovation, research, reflection, dialogue, interchange, reviewing, revising and updating of theories, assessing tools, models of consulting, and expansion in realms of intervention. Interest has been growing in what approaches work best, with whom, and in what circumstances. Activity continues focused on refining and updating the body of knowledge, mentoring people new to the field, and keeping family business advising an interdisciplinary and multidisciplinary endeavor, and these authors emphasize the urgency of establishing a sound research base to undergird our statements and activities. The funding and development of the Family Firm Institute and the initiation of the *Family Business Review,* FFI's journal, which has become the premier refereed journal in the family business field, both significant and continuous events, also receive ample attention here, as in Chapter 1, from different vantage points.

Concern is expressed periodically in this volume about the self of the consultant as he or she interacts with family businesses as systems and as organizations, and with the larger world of his or her own core discipline, whether law, accounting, finance, psychology, family therapy, or management science, and the field of family business consultation. As consultants, we believe in the importance of affiliation with key professional organizations such as FFI, and uphold our respective professional codes of ethics and conduct. There is an ongoing commitment to continuing education for ourselves and our colleagues through conferences, seminars, reading and authoring the literature, and becoming and attending FFI Fellows meetings. All of these standards and objectives have been reflected in the foregoing chapters.

## THE KALEIDOSCOPIC OVERVIEW

The final section was intentionally crafted to call attention to issues of accumulation of assets and wealth management. Dirk Jungé traces and highlights the evolution of the phenomena of the Family Office since the inception of this institution in Europe by powerful banking families such as the Hapsburgs and the Rothschilds, and in the United States with families such as the Pitcairns, who were then prominent industrialists. Family Offices here maintained a steady but not highly publicized existence until the last quarter of the twentieth century. Then, as more and more families and family businesses experienced greater prosperity, they became aware of a gap in their financial table of organization and realized they needed a more coordinated structure than the numerous financial professionals who handled different aspects of their financial life. The Family Office, with a well-trained director and possibly a few other staff members, depending on the size of the assets accumulated and scope of the investments, seemed to provide the consolidation they needed. It can also provide stability, continuity, and efficiency.

Often over many years, Family Offices have taken on additional functions, such as educating the younger family members about the meaning of wealth, how to manage it wisely, and the responsibility that goes along with the privileges it brings, and getting young people ready to take on positions in the family firm, family council, or family philanthropy. At times, a family philanthropy may be housed in the Family Office, which can lead to some cooperative ventures and economizing on rent, building ownership, and other cost sharing.

Jungé is now chairman of the Pitcairn Financial Group, and he uses the Pitcairn Family Office, one of the oldest, best known, and well respected in the United States as his case example. He is quite familiar with it as a member of the Pitcairn family who is very involved with the particular operation of this Family Office. He reports that one new trend is establishing multiple Family Offices. Instead of a family business that wants a family office beginning a new one in and of its own, it approaches an existing, well-respected one to determine if they can join together in some way. Pitcairn now has quite a few firms under its multifamily-office aegis.

One cannot help but wonder if something very similar to the Family Office structure and concept exists in Lebanon, Turkey, and Saudi Arabia but just is not given this formal title. Within the extended family kinship system there different important male members are allocated significant tasks in the hierarchy. I would assume, from all that I have read and heard, that one or several members are designated to handle the major financial affairs— tallying up what they have and how it should be divided and then spent, invested, or saved. Who should be educated and where they should be sent is also a matter for deliberation. If this assumption is correct, this individual or group of individuals function in much the same way as a family office does and may have more indisputable authority.

François de Visscher points out that concurrent with the pressing needs of family businesses for growth capital, ownership, and generation succession issues, the huge liquidity needs create an ever-widening family shareholder base. He depicts in triangular form how balancing capital needs, liquidity needs, and family control is mandatory for the survival of family companies. Further, in a lucid discussion of the stages of family business financial evolution and revolution, de Visscher recapitulates the four often acknowledged stages: (1) Founder Generation: Owner/Operator; (2) Partnership Generation: Sibling/Partnership; (3) Coalition Generation: Cousins/Collaborative; and (4) Stewardship Generation, and elucidates the conflicts and issues, as well as the liquidity/capital sources that are usually expected to be found at or accompanying each stage in the evolutionary process. His discussion is germane to all of the prior chapters and helps place them in their own evolutionary context; it also, perhaps inadvertently, highlights the importance of being attentive to cultural variations and determining if his model is equally applicable to businesses in authoritarian societies as it is for those in democratic societies. (He does not indicate if the data he provided is based on research drawn on a large cross-cultural sample.)

De Visscher captures and conveys both the risk and the excitement of growing a family business in the global marketplace and needing to include nonfamily and outside investors while still seeking to maintain family control, one of the essential cornerstones of family business stability. He also reinforces the multiplicity of functions the family office can provide as an investment vehicle, and as a family holding or investment company and/or a family trust—all of which can provide guidance and help solidify its leadership role in the communities of which it is a part.

Finally, Joseph Paul has provided a glossary of terms drawn from various family systems theories which are included here to help guide the reader who is not conversant with them.

I hope these reflections illuminate the reader's queries and responses further in the endless pursuit of knowledge and wisdom. We believe, based on all of the data provided in the foregoing chapters, that the field of family business consulting/advising will continue burgeoning within each country and among countries, and the need for astute, multiculturally informed, sensitive, competent, skilled consultants will also continue to escalate.

## REFERENCES

Bork, D., Jaffe, D., Dashew, L., Lane, S., & Heisler, G. (2004). *Working with family businesses.* Fort Worth, TX: Aspen Family Business Group.

Family Firm Institute. (2005). *Yellow pages: A resource guide for family business professionals.* Boston, MA: Family Firm Institute.

Hilburt-Davis, J. & Dyer, W. G., Jr. (2003). *Consulting to family businesses: A practical guide to contracting, assessment, and implementation.* San Francisco, CA: Jossey Bass/Wiley.

McClendon, R. & Kadis, L. R. (2004). *Reconciling relationships and preserving the family business: Tools for success.* Binghamton, NY: The Haworth Press.

Appendix

# Glossary of Family Systems Concepts Applied to Family Businesses

Joseph Paul

The following is a summary of some key concepts adapted to family businesses from family systems literature. The terms are presented in alphabetical order.

**boundaries:** Boundaries are the interface between systems and subsystems or different individuals (Minuchin & Fishman, 1981). The concept of boundaries in families is used to define alignments within the family business, for example, alignment of siblings as separate from the older generation, alignments of family who work in the family's business against those who do not, or alignments of divisions in the company. Boundaries are set by functions of the system, by the implicit rules defining who participates in the system, and by the rules that determine how they can participate and/or how they are included. Boundaries and the subsystems that they define in a family business may change over time or in response to a changing situation, such as the death of a family member or the opening of a new store. Systemic boundaries are characterized as being *diffuse, open,* or *closed.* Boundaries in a family business can also be categorized as either flexible or rigid. All of these terms describe how easily people (or ideas) come and go across the boundary, that is, whether the boundaries are permeable or impermeable (Minuchin, 1984). *Diffuse* boundaries are extremely open with no barriers to entry, while *closed* boundaries strictly define participation and access. *Open* boundaries are described as having the ability to define membership while extending temporary access to nonmembers. A family

---

This appendix was written in 1999, revised in March 2004 with input from Florence Kaslow.

*Handbook of Family Business and Family Business Consultation*
Published by The Haworth Press, Inc., 2006. All rights reserved.
doi:10.1300/5491_22

that makes exaggerated claims that all their employees are "like family" is defining a diffuse boundary, while a highly secretive Board of Directors that does not communicate with any non-Board members would be an example of a subsystem with a closed boundary. Rigid boundaries do not respond to changing situations whereas flexible boundaries do. For example, the willingness to use outsider advisors when a company enters a new market would be a sign of flexibility. The process of succession in a family business tests the capacity of the system to define, redefine, and maintain functional boundaries around the subsystems of family, owners, and management.

**closed systems:** These are systems which are self-contained as compared to open ones, which utilize free exchange with the external environment to alter internal functions, relationships, etc. A closed family business is organized to preserve the status quo and resist change. An example of this would be when new ideas can come only from the founder (Lewis, Beavers, Gossett, & Phillips, 1976).

**coalitions:** A coalition is two (or more) individuals working together to counteract or exclude the third party. Coalitions may not be stable and often shift to keep power somewhat distributed in the family business. An example of a coalition would be when the influence of an overbearing parent leads the other parent to join with a child to balance the power. This of course can be done at the psychological expense of the child.

**differentiation:** This is a Bowen Theory concept which addresses the development of individual maturity within the context of family relationships. It refers to the emerging ability of an individual to simultaneously balance the desire for family closeness with the desire to have emotional independence. Some families are good at raising children to achieve this balance in their adulthood, and some families struggle with facilitating individuation (Bowen, 1978). When a person works his or her entire adult life in the business parents founded or inherited, the struggle to differentiate takes on unique challenges. Bowen (1966) used the term *undifferentiated ego mass* to describe families that have failed at creating differentiated family members. Poorly differentiated families tend to be chronically anxious. This chronic anxiety can be shown in a wide range of behaviors, from dramatic emotional reactivity, in which the family goes from one crisis to another, to a very placid family atmosphere in which conflict is avoided at all costs. Generally in these families there is a tendency for emotions to dominate over intellectual functioning instead of balancing it. This is a particular problem for family businesses because they generally must function at an objective level more often than families who are not in business together.

Well-differentiated family business leaders will tend to have a calm and nonreactive presence, be able to enjoy close family relationships, and have a high degree of clarity about their responsibilities and purpose in the family and the organization. They tend to be seen as "their own person", as being fair, and, when necessary, they are decisive. They also tend to have a talent for remaining composed in the midst of other people's anxiety.

**entitlement:** Entitlement is a psychological attitude toward relationships that results from the balance or imbalance of fairness and trust with a parent early in life. Chronic states of feeling entitled are created in offspring by parents based on their capacity to care for their children. *Constructive entitlement* reflects a willingness to care about others based upon the experience of being cared about by one's parents. *Destructive entitlement* is based on the unwillingness to care about others and results from being mistreated, neglected, or exploited by parents. *Destructive entitlement* can also result from "overgiving" of things, or overindulgence in permissiveness by a parent while emotionally neglecting the child (Boszormenyi-Nagy & Krasner, 1986). "Having a chip on their shoulder" or "acting like the world owes them a living" are phrases that people use to describe *destructive entitlement* in others. Expression of entitlement is not limited to the relationship in which it was engendered. The positive effects of constructive entitlement and the negative effects of destructive entitlement can have long-lasting effects on all significant adult relationships. Some of the more powerful sources of destructive entitlement arise from emotional, physical, or sexual abuse of children by their parents and/or chronic addiction in parents. Long-standing destructive entitlement is typically the source of litigation between family members, although the focus of the litigation may be only a substitute issue for something more profound in the family's past (Kaslow, 2000).

**family systems theory:** Law, accounting/finance, management science, and behavioral science are the four disciplines that have contributed to the family business consulting body of knowledge. Family systems theory is a major division of the behavioral sciences and has a well-defined body of knowledge of its own that is distinct from individual psychology but draws upon developmental psychology and life cycle concepts. Systems theory, which postulates that all parts of the system are interrelated and interdependent, undergirds the multiple schools of family systems thinking. Within family systems theory there are many schools of thought that differ from one another in how they conceptualize key constructs in their theoretical base. Among these differences are the following:

1. History of conceptual precursors of the school of thought
2. The theoretical framework of what constitutes a healthy family and a dysfunctional family
3. The conceptualization of psychopathology
4. The assessment of function and dysfunction
5. How therapeutic goals are set
6. The structure of the intervention process
7. The appropriate role of the agent of change
8. Clinical techniques
9. The ideas about what leads to change in the client system (Gurman & Kniskern, 1991)

**ledger of merits:** This concept reflects the balance of fairness and trust in a relationship between two people. This balance has a strong influence on what is possible in that relationship. High trust relationships are more efficient than low trust ones in which the imbalances resulting from past transactions cause constant vigilance and suspicion of the other's motives. The basis of relational balance differs in *symmetrical* (brother-sister, husband-wife) and *asymmetrical* (parent-minor child, adult child-elderly parent) relationships. In the former, balance is reached through roughly equal give and take over time between the parties. In the latter, balance is based on what is equitable given the imbalance is power (Boszormenyi-Nagy & Spark, 1984).

**merit:** This refers to the basis for self-validation earned in the process showing due consideration of others. The desire to earn merit in relationship with one's parents motivates children to earn their parents' pride and respect. The virtues that parents recognize and support influence the paths that their children have in earning merit. Earning merit in a relationship leads to authority and influence in relationships. The outcome of succession is greatly influenced by the capacity the successor has to earn merit in both *symmetrical* and *asymmetrical* relationships in the business and family (Boszormenyi-Nagy & Krasner, 1986).

**multidirectional (or multilateral) partiality:** This is a relational posture assumed by a therapist, advisor, or consultant that is meant to prevent the outsider from being drawn into the dysfunctional dynamics of the client system. Methodologically, multidirectional partiality takes the form of sequential identification with each member of the family. This is typically done by trying to empathize with and credit each person for his or her contributions or attempts to contribute to the well-being of the family. This is done even if the actions were misguided or inept. Advisors earn merit and trust in the eyes of family members through successful execution of multi-directional partiality (Boszormenyi-Nagy & Krasner, 1986).

**narrative dissonance** (a term coined by the author): Members of a family carry stories in their head about other family members, about the history of the family, about events that have happened in the business, about what kind of person they are, etc. In some families the stories that reside in the minds of individual family members are similar. A high degree of similarity is a reflection of *narrative resonance*. Very different stories about the same events are a reflection of narrative dissonance. High degrees of narrative dissonance may be a reflection of long periods of chronic tension and anxiety in the family. Narrative dissonance interferes with the ability of two people or groups of people to deliberate, make decisions, and take effective actions. High dissonance also contributes to mistrust.

**parentification:** This refers to the process of turning a child (even an adult child) into a functional parent of their own parent. The parentified child is expected to take care of the parent and/or assume adult responsibility. In certain situations this is a normal adaptation to changes in the family, for instance, when a parent becomes incapacitated by illness or old age. Parentification becomes destructive when it is in service of the parent's manipulation of the offspring's natural inclination to be devoted to parents and a premature abdication of the real parental role. Creating a SPLIT LOYALTY is one way to engender a destructive form of parentification.

**presenting problem:** This is a term used to describe a condition for which a family seeks outside help, but which usually is a symptom of a more deep-seated problem that the family is ashamed of, or unconscious of. (*See* SCAPEGOATING.) A family business may engage a consultant with a "presenting problem" concerning compensation of key employees, when they actually have a problem with an incompetent successor but are afraid to mention it.

**scapegoating:** This refers to the process through which anxiety in the family is reduced by designating one member to be the chronic symptom bearer for the family. The classic example would be a pattern in which parents who are near divorce are drawn closer together whenever their child becomes depressed to the point of requiring hospitalization. All of the problems in the family are attributed to that child, who has become the scapegoat, i.e., the one they blame instead of facing the real dilemma. In this circumstance it is predictable that a fight between parents results in a hospitalization of the child. Thus the child's symptom actually becomes the glue that holds the parents' marriage together. The symptoms of the scapegoat in the family are often the PRESENTING PROBLEM of the family, behind which the deeper and more disturbing problems lurk (Satir, 1964, 1967)

**split loyalty:** This refers to a situation created by a parent or grandparent in which a child must choose between their loyalties to both parents, or between a parent and a grandparent. It typically takes place when a parent or grandparent tries to manipulate the offspring onto the elder's "side" in a controversial issue with another elder. To choose one is to be disloyal to the other, and this is a very distressing choice for anyone, especially a child. This is a deeply damaging experience to offspring, whether adults or minors, that can lead to serious personality problems, depression, or suicide (Boszormenyi-Nagy & Krasner, 1986)

**triangles:** Emotional Triangles are one of the four seminal constructs of Bowen Theory (Bowen, 1978). Triangulation occurs when a third party is drawn into the relationship between two others to balance something in that dyadic relationship. That which is balanced usually has to do with excessive intimacy or overconnectedness, negative reactivity between the two, or emotional distance that distresses other members of the family. Advisors and consultants can be easily triangulated into the emotional drama of two relatives, and often made a scapegoat as a result.

**trustworthiness:** This is a form of merit that accrues on the side of any predictable, responsible, competent, and considerate partner in a relationship. Trustworthiness is earned over time through the ability of two people to balance the process of give-and-take between reliable partners (Boszormenyi-Nagy & Krasner, 1986). Trustworthiness is seen as more important than love in family business relationships. A relationship with great love but without trustworthiness is usually a destructive relationship. In contrast, a trustworthy relationship between two people who do not necessarily love each other can still be very durable and a resource to both parties. High trust families, organizations, and cultures are far more efficient than low trust systems in that members do not need to expend energy to protect themselves from other parts of their own system. Low trust systems are typically more anxious, more prone to crisis, and less capable of planning, decision making, and implementation.

## REFERENCES

Boszormenyi-Nagy, I., & Krasner, B. (1986). *Between give and take: A clinical guide to contextual therapy.* New York: Harper and Row. (2nd ed., New York: Brunner/Mazel).

Boszormenyi-Nagy, I., & Spark, G. (1984). *Invisible loyalties.* New York: Brunner/Mazel.

Bowen, M. (1966). The use of family theory in clinical practice. *Comprehensive Psychiatry, 7,* 345-374.

Bowen, M. (1978). *Family therapy in clinical practice.* New York: Jason Aronson.

Gurman, A., & Kniskern, D. (1991). *Handbook of family therapy* (Volume II). New York: Brunner/Mazel.

Kaslow, F.W. (2000). Children who sue parents: A legal route for family destruction. In F.W. Kaslow (Ed.), *Handbook of couple and family forensics* (pp. 350-374). New York: Wiley.

Lewis, J., Beavers, W.R., Gossett, J.T., & Phillips, V.A. (1976). *No single thread: Psychological health and the family system.* New York: Brunner/Mazel.

Minuchin, S. (1984). *Family kaleidoscope.* Cambridge, MA: Harvard University Press.

Minuchin, S., & Fishman, H.C. (1981). *Family therapy techniques.* Cambridge, MA: Harvard University Press.

Satir, V. (1964; 1967) *Conjoint family therapy.* Palo Alto, CA: Science and Behavior Books.

# Index

Page numbers followed by the letter "f" indicate figures; those followed by "t" indicate tables.

*Handbook of Family Business and Family Business Consultation*
Published by The Haworth Press, Inc., 2006. All rights reserved.
doi:10.1300/5491_23